Speaking in Queer Tongues

Speaking in Queer Tongues

Globalization and Gay Language

EDITED BY WILLIAM L. LEAP
AND TOM BOELLSTORFF

University of Illinois Press
URBANA AND CHICAGO

Library of Congress Cataloging-in-Publication Data
Speaking in queer tongues : globalization and gay language /
edited by William L. Leap and Tom Boellstorff.
p.   cm.
Includes bibliographical references and index.
ISBN 0-252-02871-6 (cloth : alk. paper)
ISBN 0-252-07142-5 (paper : alk. paper)
1. Anthropological lingustics.
2. Gay men—Language.
3. Gay men—Cross-cultural studies.
4. Language and languages—Sex differences.
I. Leap, William L.
II. Boellstorff, Tom, 1969– .
P35.P57   2004
306.44'086'642—dc21   2003003715

Contents

Introduction: Globalization and "New" Articulations of
Same-Sex Desire   1
Tom Boellstorff and William L. Leap

1. Vague English Creole: (Gay English) Cooperative Discourse
   in the French Gay Press   23
   Denis M. Provencher

2. Qwir-English Code-Mixing in Germany: Constructing a Rainbow
   of Identities   46
   Heidi Minning

3. French, English, and the Idea of Gay Language in Montreal   72
   Ross Higgins

4. Dancing on the Needle's Edge: Gay Lingo in an Israeli Disco   105
   Liora Moriel

5. Language, Belonging, and (Homo)sexual Citizenship in
   Cape Town, South Africa   134
   William L. Leap

6. *Takatāpui*, Gay, or Just HO-MO-SEXUAL, Darling?
   Māori Language, Sexual Terminology, and Identity in
   Aotearoa/New Zealand   163
   David A. B. Murray

7. "Authentic, of Course!": *Gay* Language in Indonesia and
   Cultures of Belonging   181
   Tom Boellstorff

8. *Gay* Adaptation, *Tom-Dee* Resistance, and *Kathoey* Indifference: Thailand's Gender/Sex Minorities and the Episodic Allure of Queer English   202
     Peter A. Jackson

9. *Pájaration* and Transculturation: Language and Meaning in Miami's Cuban American Gay Worlds   231
   Susana Peña

10. Mother Knows Best: Black Gay Vernacular and Transgressive Domestic Space   251
    E. Patrick Johnson

   Contributors   279

   Index   283

Introduction:
Globalization and "New" Articulations
of Same-Sex Desire

TOM BOELLSTORFF AND

WILLIAM L. LEAP

> What do we mean when we say "gay" in a world where hybridity
> and syncretism provide the grist for cultural production,
> distribution and consumption?
>
> —Martin Manalansan

> The acquisition of new forms of language from the modern
> West—whether by forcible imposition, insidious insertion, or
> voluntary borrowing—is part of what makes for new possibilities
> of action in non-Western societies. Yet, although the outcome of
> these possibilities is never fully predictable, the language in which
> the possibilities are formulated is increasingly shared by Western
> and non-Western societies. And so, too, the specific forms of power
> and subjection.
>
> —Talal Asad

This collection of essays discusses new (and not so new) ways of talking about
same-sex desires, practices, and subjectivities that have emerged in various
regions of the world. One way to refer to these "ways of talking" is as languages, invoking an argument that has been developed in some detail elsewhere (Leap 1995, 2002). Other scholars prefer to use terms like *fashions of
speaking, codes, registers, varieties,* or *"genderlects."* Finding an appropriate
label is certainly important to this collection's discussion, and we return to
it elsewhere. Yet however one classifies text-making practices and the linguistic frameworks underlying them, the fact remains that ways of talking about
the everyday experiences of same-sex desire have been caught up in the transnational interchange of material and intellectual commodities associated

with the condition of late modernity (Harvey 1989; Ong 1999). How ways of talking about same-sex desires, practices, and subjectivities become incorporated into transnational interchanges, and how they become affected by these relationships, are two central concerns of this collection.

More Than Linguistic Description

Our interests, however, run deeper than these descriptive themes. Frequently, discussions of globalization assume a Western source, and a one-way movement of material and intellectual commodities from that source toward a recipient framed as "more distant," often through the term *third world*. As the essays in this collection indicate, speech communities located "over there" and "away from" assumed centers of political, economic, and cultural domination are not the only groups of speakers affected by the global circulation of same-sex-related linguistic practices. Same-sex-identified women and men in Western Europe, Canada, and the United States engage in such circulation as well—as both recipients and sources. How they talk about same-sex desire is affected by these patterns of circulation.

It is important to note that the linguistic commodity in question includes the conceptual frameworks, images, and textual products emerging from gay men's experiences (and often, white, privileged gay men's experiences) in the urban United States. Many ways of talking that figure prominently in these transnational interchanges are languages that several contributors to this volume identify as "gay men's English." That term—and the very existence of the linguistic material it claims to identify—have been criticized in several publications (Campbell-Kibbler et al. eds. 2002; Kulick 2000). Although mindful of those objections, we find it ethnographically and linguistically justified to refer to the global circulation of a gay men's English that originates in the United States. Doing so allows us to investigate what happens when this code interacts with already-existing ways of talking about same-sex desire outside of and within the North Atlantic domain.

Using the term, for example, invites consideration of how the so-called globalization of gay men's English coincides with the selective transformation of other components of North American, urban gay culture: the politics and symbolics of the Stonewall riots, the imperatives of the coming-out experience, and ideas of gay community and gay ghetto as well as rainbow flags, pink triangles, and other material markers of gay presence and gay pride. Using the term *gay men's English* draws attention to tensions between ways of speaking about same-sex desire that are closely tied to gay men's experiences on the one hand and ways of speaking that address the identities and experiences of same-sex-identified women on the other. It thereby raises questions about the adaptability of gay men's English to women's linguistic worlds. Finally, using—however flexibly and provisionally—a concept of gay men's English compels the determination of which men (and, in some settings, which women) provide the authoritative models for these globally circulating codes. Which individuals, that is, become fluent and proficient in the codes within settings construed as local and which individuals find themselves excluded from fluency and proficiency (and for what reasons).

Specific Sites, Broader Visions

Although the individual essays in this volume share the broad problematic just described, their theoretical perspectives are anything but uniform. Contributors come from a diverse set of academic backgrounds: anthropology, cultural studies, French studies, history, lesbian/gay studies, linguistics, literary studies, performance studies, and sociology. What they have to say about language, same-sex desire, "gay English," and other languages of same-sex desire reflects the interests of their respective academic disciplines in language, culture, and sexuality as well as each author's research agenda.

Many contributors share an association with the American University Conference on Lavender Languages and Linguistics, an annual meeting of researchers and activists interested in exploring the significance of language, broadly defined, in lesbian, gay, bisexual, transgender, and queer life. "Globalizations of Gay English" was the topic for the plenary session at the seventh Lavender Languages Conference in 1999, and chapters in this volume by Denis M. Provencher, Liora Moriel, and Ross Higgins are adapted from their presentations in that session. Audience discussion following these presentations indicated that the emergence of local alternatives to gay English was as important to panel interests as the transfigurations of gay English taking place in differing cultural contexts and indicated that gay language research had yet to pay attention to these alternatives.

Accordingly, we have worked to include, within the limits posed by any one volume, a diverse set of geographic, historical, and linguistic circumstances. In some cases the sites in question are part of the North Atlantic milieu and connected (albeit in varying ways) to the epicenters of urban gay culture that have emerged there: France, francophone Canada, urban and rural African America, and urban Hispanic America. Other settings (Indonesia, Israel, New Zealand, South Africa, and Thailand) are at an ostensibly greater distance from that milieu but remain connected to its authority because of travel and tourism, global media, trade agreements, political alliances, and other ties—

neocolonial, anticolonial, and postcolonial. In some of these cases, English is a well-established component of the local verbal repertoire although often regarded as a foreign tongue, a language of outsiders. Gay English mediates this uneven terrain in different ways in urban France than in urban Quebec or in black America rather than black South Africa. The tensions between gay English and locally or nationally identified ways of talking about same-sex desire take unique forms in each case.

Of course, there are other locations not included here where a globalizing gay English actively engages apparently local ways of talking about same-sex desire, subjectivity, and community—in Eastern Europe, for example, and in the Islamic Mideast, India, Central and Eastern Africa, and Latin America. Our intent in designing this collection was not to be exhaustive in our choice of sites; it is, after all, an edited volume not an encyclopedia. Our goal was to use a more modestly selected series of essays to show how persons who have same-sex desires, subjectivities, and/or communities mediate and renegotiate linguistic process and product under conditions of the ostensible "globalization of gay English." We hope the essays can thereby anticipate and push toward better understanding of what processes and products might be under construction elsewhere.

Treating "Gay" as Polyvalent and Contingent

The particular forms of same-sex desires, subjectivities, and communities under discussion in each chapter vary greatly. In some instances they are not named in local discourse. In others the desires, subjectivities, and communities might be more meaningfully described as bisexuality (or curiosity). There is no single term that completely embraces the wide range of sexual and gender diversities under discussion. For that reason, although we use the term *gay English* as a reminder of the apparent "source" language's linguistic and social location, we also use the word *gay* as a referential shorthand for a broad range of same-sex desires, practices, and subjectivities. We do so without presuming that this usage establishes a universal ethnographic referent and without implying that we only address the same-sex-related linguistic practices of male-bodied persons.

At the same time, although several chapters examine language use by same-sex-identified women, the linguistics of male-centered, same-sex desires and identities remain the dominant focus of the collection. In part, that reflects the enduring preference of researchers in language and sexuality studies to work with heterosexual women or homosexual men and for academic publications to be inventoried accordingly. The same-sex male focus of the collection also reflects Birch Moonwomon's (1995) argument that the differences between lesbian language and women's language, inclusively, are not drawn nearly as sharply as are those differences separating gay men's English from hetero-masculinist English codes. Recalling Blackwood's (1998) discussion of female masculinity (see also Halberstam 1998), it may be that the distinction between masculine and feminine women (e.g., "butch" versus "femme") will have more linguistic consequences than a generic contrast between lesbian versus straight women's speech, regardless of sexual orientation. Butch women can, after all, be homosexual, heterosexual, or bisexual and identify, or not, as transgendered in some respect. Peter Jackson's discussion this volume of gay adaptation, *tom-dee* resistance, and *kathoey* indifference in Thailand positions one such set of issues within a larger context of global/local linguistic change. It is our hope that the issues raised in this collection will encourage more researchers to examine women's experiences with gay English globalization and trace the linguistic consequences of those experiences in site-specific terms.

Understanding Globalization

Although a certain academic fatigue has set in around the topic of globalization, the need to understand the range of phenomena grouped under the term has not subsided. Like it or not, globalization is not going away, and social theorists—including language and sexuality scholars—must be prepared to explore its effects on everyday life in all their research settings.

We begin from the obvious point that there is no such thing as globalization in an abstract sense. Gathered under the rubric of globalization are a wide variety of economic, political, and cultural processes that not only cannot be reduced to each other but are also sometimes at cross purposes. We agree with Waters's view that globalization can be roughly defined as "a social process in which the constraints of geography on social and cultural arrangements recede and in which people become increasingly aware that they are receding" (1996, 3). Although circuits of migration, trade, and colonialism have linked the globe for millennia, we see globalization as more than a quantitative change, more than a simple ratcheting up or acceleration of these circuits. It is predicated on qualitative changes in technology and social relations that fundamentally transform the relationship between space and subjectivity. Contemporary globalizing processes open new "homoscapes"—to cite Parker's clever extension of Appadurai (1999, 218–21)—that rework the relationship between same-sex desire and constitutions of the local.

Three elements of globalization debates are pertinent to the essays in this

volume. The first concerns the tendency to equate globalization with Westernization, that is, to see it in unilinear and teleological terms such that if X
is impacted by globalization then X must be becoming more like the West.
A large body of work on alternate modernities illustrates the utter falsity of
that assumption (Appadurai 1996; Brenner 1996, 1998; Gaonkar ed. 1999; Hall
1991; Hannerz 1996, Miller 1995; Morris 2000; Rofel 1999). As the essays in this
volume indicate, it is not only that many globalizing processes result in greater
difference but also that the calculus of similitude and difference is always
culturally constituted and thus caught up in the globalizing processes it seeks
to describe. In other words, how we determine what counts as "the same"
or "different," what counts as "change" or "continuity," is a product of globalizing processes. A second element of globalization debates, linked to the
first, concerns the view that globalization is inevitably bad. As Tom Boellstorff
notes in his chapter, "The possibility of a nonthreatening or nonantagonistic relationship to processes of cultural globalization is almost completely
absent in the LGBT literature on globalization." Although there are indeed
many negative effects of globalization, many of them predate contemporary
globalizing processes or are due to parallel but distinct factors such as neo-
colonialism (which need not be globalizing).

Of particular relevance to this volume, Gibson-Graham (1996) has shown
how understandings of globalization on the contemporary Left draw from a
Western "rape script" in which capitalism is gendered male, capitalism's other
is gendered female, and globalization is metaphorically construed as rape itself. This normalizes a view of globalization as inevitable and of the local as
doomed to penetration and violation by capitalism. Drawing from Sharon
Marcus's critique of rape scripts (1992), Gibson-Graham asks how we might
enable globalization to "lose its erection" by portraying it as vulnerable to re-
appropriation and co-optation. Furthermore, Gibson-Graham considers it
critical to question the heteronormative principles on which the globalization-
as-rape script is based: "The global economy may have been opened up by
international financial markets, but nothing 'other' comes into or out of this
opening. It would seem that the homophobia that pervades economic theorizing places a taboo on such thinking" (1996, 137). Accordingly, Gibson-Graham concludes, "A queer perspective can help to unsettle the consonances and
coherences of the narrative of global commodification" (144).

The essays in this collection demonstrate how the translocation (not globalization) of gay linguistic practices challenges not only received understandings of sexuality and language but also of globalization itself. The essays take issue not only with dystopic visions of globalization but also with
triumphalist visions that assume that adopting gay linguistic practice in some

form moves speakers toward a unified global, gay-centered political movement (Adam, Duyvendak, and Krouwel eds. 1999). Although there can certainly be affinities, coalitions, and linkages among non-normative sexual
subjectivities worldwide, that does not mean all these subjectivities are on a
single trajectory or that the trajectory automatically ends in an Americanist
vision of sexual life, sexual politics, or linguistic performance. Indeed, we
argue (and the essays in this volume show) that discarding the modernist
fantasy of convergence may prove helpful in forging a more inclusive, respect-
ful, and decentered sexual politics.

A final element of globalization debates important to this volume is that
of authenticity. Globalizing processes often bring about crises of authenticity because in the dominant Western cultural logic (and in some, but by no
means all, other cultural logics) authenticity is founded in locality and im-
mobility. Tradition is not supposed to come from somewhere else. When
cultural logics move, then, a concern with authenticity can result, especially
if part of what has moved is the Western obsession with authenticity. That is
particularly true in many postcolonial states, where globalizing processes lend
a new and troubling dimension to the paradox of nation-states that claim
autochthonous cultural logics (in other words, traditions unique to that
nation) even while citizens are keenly aware that the concept of nation has a
Western provenance (Chatterjee 1986).

Gay linguistic practices that seem to originate in the West can compound
the dilemma of authenticity, a problem that several contributors to this volume explore in terms of sexual citizenship, transculturation, and belonging.
What is needed is a processual approach that avoids defining ahead of time
what will count as authentic in favor of investigating the cultural logics
through which authenticity is shaped in particular settings—in the way that,
for instance, gay men in Indonesia claim authenticity in urban parks (Boellstorff, this volume) or that French gay men attribute "gay French" authenticity to gay English discursive practices (Provencher, this volume).

Gay Language, Speaker Subjectivity, and Desire

The interests in language, subjectivity, and same-sex desire addressed in these
essays are also part of an ongoing debate over the existence of gay English
and other varieties of gay language. We use two elements of Kulick's (2000)
analysis of the debate as a touchstone for discussion in this section: his critique of circularity and his call for a shift from the study of language and
sexuality to language and desire.

A central aspect of Kulick's critique of much contemporary work on gay language is that a "circular argument emerges. If we ask 'What is Gay English,' the answer is 'English spoken by gay men.' What makes it gay? The fact that gay men speak it. Why do gay men speak it? Because they are gay men. And so on, round and round" (2000, 264). We agree with Kulick that where gay languages exist they are frequently neither necessary nor sufficient conditions for the subject positions with which they are believed to be connected. Yet in many cases such linguistic practices are indeed part of the speaker's sense of selfhood, can effect the broader social context, and thereby have impact on the subjectivities of other individuals—gay, straight, or otherwise—who are not competent in such linguistic practices. Furthermore, unless gay language is completely secreted within the speech community in question (a rare circumstance indeed), these linguistic practices can assume a critical role in interlocutors' reactions to a speaker as a gay person. They can also affect interlocutors' sexual and gendered assessments of persons not competent in these practices. Thus "an aspect of linguistic practice may legitimately be considered gay if gay people use it and perceive it as a 'gay marker,' even though it is used by others for the same or different purposes" (Wong, Roberts, and Campbell-Kibler 2002, 2). Moreover, "Certain linguistic features may become markers of different social groups, even if they are not used by all and only members of the groups which they symbolize" (Wong, Roberts, and Campbell-Kibler 2002, 3).

What is necessary at this stage of research, we believe, is openness to gay languages with unique linguistic features (as in the case of *gay* language in Indonesia) and to the gay linguistic practices characteristic of a community of practice wherein what is at issue is not a difference in language considered as a formal object but in contexts and details of use.[1] In the first case, Kulick's concerns about circularity are irrelevant because the presence of unique structural features provides an objective basis for identifying the code, for tracing which members of the local speech community speak it, and for assessing how use of the code coincides with sexual subjectivity. In the second case, we avoid Kulick's concerns about circularity by approaching the relationships between language and subjectivity as forms of reciprocity. As addressed in discussions in E. Patrick Johnson, David A. B. Murray, Susana Peña, and other essays in this collection, we see the subject positions in question as constituted in part through linguistic practices and the linguistic practices as constituted in part through assertions of speaker subjectivity.

Our concern in this regard is the relationship between identity categories and social analysis hinted at by Eckert (2002, 101). All emic analyses are circular in that they take people's categories as a starting point without imposing external criteria of validity. That kind of reciprocal constitution of subjectivity appears in many other contexts as well, for example, confessional religions. An external evaluation of who counts as Christian could possibly ask whether they believe in the Trinity or whether they drink real wine at communion. An analysis aiming to understand the experience of being Christian in a particular community, however, is more likely to use an emic definition that, by virtue of its emic character, appears circular to an outsider. Who are Christians? People who say they are Christians. What makes them Christian? That they say they are Christian. And so on, round and round.

A key point in this regard is that linguistic analysis, while recognizing the emic character of cultural domains, argues strongly against accepting any culture's claim that those domains—like those of identity and language—are self-contained. Because subject positions are not simply schema held in the minds of individuals but processual logics emergent in social relationalities, over time gay language/linguistic practices can have impact on even individuals who do not know of them. Such attention to the diachronic effects of language on subjectivity is often deemphasized in the dominant linguistic paradigm. Gay men and lesbians in the United States can construe kinship in unique ways that have impact on gay/lesbian subjectivities although there are no distinguishing features of that kinship (for the most part it does not invent new kinship terms but transforms those at hand) and not all gay men and lesbians in the United States use or even know of these kinship forms (Weston 1991). Gay language can also have powerful effects on gay subjectivities, even in the absence of distinct linguistic forms or universal competence.

The question of the impact of gay language/linguistic practices on gay subject positions leads us to Kulick's appeal for a conceptual retooling that would shift inquiry from language and sexuality to "language and desire" (2000, 272–77). Kulick defines this quite inclusively as "everything that arguably makes sexuality sexuality—namely, fantasy, desire, repression, pleasure, fear, and the unconscious" (270) and bases his appeal for a focus on desire on dissatisfaction with the superficial treatment of sexuality in much of the gay and lesbian language literature, particularly assumptions concerning community and identity.

We share Kulick's frustration but take issue with his claim that the missing theoretical agenda is "desire" (see also Eckert 2002). Kulick's psychoanalytic treatment of desire allows him to steer away from the essentialized focus on identity that dominates work on gay language. He does not make the link explicitly, but we see this position as a gesture toward the massive uncertainty about questions of agency and volition that has dominated sociolinguistics and anthropological linguistics for many years. It is addressed, for instance, in more recent scholarship on language ideology (Kroskrity ed. 2000; Schiffelin, Woolard, and Kroskrity eds. 1998). Like so much work outside structuralist linguistics, this work on language ideology shows that language is at once fundamentally volitional (we choose when to speak, what to talk about, and even how to say it in many respects) but at the same time foundationally preconscious (we do not consciously engage in the process of grammar, for example, conjugating verbs, assigning cases to nouns, and syntactically arranging lexical items in an utterance, unless learning a language). Nor do we typically exercise conscious control over paragrammatical dimensions of language such as intonation. Hence, as Denis M. Provencher, Liora Moriel, William L. Leap, Peter A. Jackson, and E. Patrick Johnson show in this volume, it is possible for linguistic practices to indicate gay presence within a conversational moment yet remain within the constraints of local languages and speech traditions. Moriel, for example, suggests that the absence of grammaticalized means for indexing female versus male object reference in Israeli Hebrew has made globalizing forms of gay English linguistic practices into resources for Israeli Hebrew-based gay linguistic practices even though the details of the resulting linguistic code are anything but English-based.

Questions of volition are important because Kulick, in calling for a move from the study of sexuality to that of desire in gay language, shifts the debate over volition from language to gayness itself, suggesting that sexuality is (arguably) conscious but often repressed. In doing so, however, Kulick sidesteps Foucault's insight about such a suggestion invoking the "repressive hypothesis" that prevents understanding the dominant Western construction of homosexuality. It was in response to this position that Foucault proposed that the "rallying point for the counterattack against the deployment of sexuality ought not to be sex-desire, but bodies and pleasures" (1978, 157).

In raising Foucault's point we do not argue for the abolition of "desire" as a conceptual term; indeed, many contributors to this volume use it to great effect. We do, however, agree that understanding the relationship between language and subjectivity in terms of desire or sexuality cannot be predicated on assumptions that the psyche is a self-contained cultural domain that can then desire. Just as we argue that language cannot be effectively regarded as a self-contained domain, so we argue that desire cannot be understood as a self-contained domain. One of the most enduring contributions of anthropological work on sexuality is its demonstration of the intersectional character of sexuality. It does not originate in one domain (such as the psyche) and then come out to other aspects of life. Rather, sexuality comes into being at the conflicted conjunctures of cultural domains—and language frequently marks the domain within which these constructions of desire emerge (Herdt and Stoller 1990).

It is here that the particular focus on globalization addressed in this collection—specifically, the apparently global circulation of gay language/linguistic practices and the limits imposed on this apparent circulation by locally emerging linguistic practices—is of the greatest import. Cultural domains are not only intersectionally constituted within a single culture (despite claims they are self-contained) but also constituted at the articulation between cultures. That has been true throughout human history, but the character of this articulation is currently undergoing a sea change via globalizing processes, and the essays in this volume are concerned with the implications of that sea change. Yanagisako and Delaney remind us of the need "to ask how culturally-specific domains have been dialectically formed and transformed in relation with other cultural domains, how meanings migrate across domain boundaries, and how specific actions are multiply constituted" (1995, 11). In the context of the present volume, we extend this "productive question" to ask how culturally specific domains of homosexual subjectivity are created and transformed in relation with domains from other cultures—and what contributions gay language/linguistic practices make to these ends.

We proffer articulation as a concept for approaching the question of the dialectical relationship among gay subjectivities, globalizing cultural logics, and language. The term *articulation* has two meanings, roughly, "to utter" and "movement around a joint." Although the first meaning might appear more relevant to a discussion of language, it is the second that has been emphasized in social theory, given the association of the term with the work of Marx (and later Marxist theorists such as Balibar and Althusser) regarding the articulations between different aspects of a mode of production and the articulation of different modes of production in a society or on the world stage. In fact, the German *Gliederung* has only the second meaning, of motion around a joint. In developing that meaning of articulation, Stuart Hall summarizes, "The unity which [the articulated elements] form is thus not that of an identity, where one structure perfectly recapitulates or reproduces or even 'expresses' another; or where each is reducible to the other; or where each is defined by the same determinations. . . . The unity formed by this combination or articulation is always, necessarily, a 'complex structure:' a structure in which things are related, as much through their differences as through their similarities" (1980, 325).

This notion of articulation can be used to capture the idea that cultural domains are not self-coherent realms of experience but articulate with other cultural domains both within and among cultures (and in the process play no small role in demarcating where one culture ends and another begins).

To this notion of articulation inflected by political economy we can then juxtapose the sense of articulation as utterance to underscore how gay languages/linguistic practices articulate (in both senses) gay subjectivities. Gay subjectivities are not isomorphic with gay languages/linguistic practices; some gay people do not engage in gay languages/linguistic practices and vice versa. In Hall's terms, they are not reducible to each other but articulate in a complex structure where difference can serve as a mode of connection. At the same time, through the utterance of gay languages/linguistic practices (not always or solely by gay individuals), gay subject positions are simultaneously reconstituted and transformed. The essays in this volume help articulate that complex, emerging convergence of language, sexuality, and globalizing processes.

Sexual Cultures, Sexual Languages

The starting point for the explorations of language, globalization, and same-sex sexuality presented in this volume is the idea of sexual culture, which, building on work by Gilbert Herdt, we define as culturally based ideologies and practices related to sexual behavior: "[A] sexual culture is a consensual model of cultural ideal about sexual behavior in a group. [It] suggests a world view based on specific sexual and gender norms, emotions, beliefs, and symbolic meanings regarding the proper nature and purpose of sexual encounters. Sexual cultures thus function as power systems of moral and emotional control" (Herdt 1997, 17).

As Herdt suggests, sexual cultures are closely grounded in the everyday experience of particular groups of people and thus situated socially and historically. Their details are learned and shared, albeit unevenly, not only across divisions and boundaries within those domains but also among them through processes of intercultural articulation that include those of globalization. Sexual cultures are not seamless, organic, unified constructions but are closely tied to broader structures of power and inequality and to other components of political economy. Accordingly, participants in a sexual culture often show some level of agreement regarding the ideologies and practices of which that culture is composed, although disagreements are also common. Far from being static constructions, sexual cultures are as much products of ongoing debate as they are guardians of seemingly timeless values and mores.

If there are sexual cultures then there must be sexual languages, that is, modes of describing, expressing, and interrogating the ideologies and practices relevant to the sexual culture(s) to which speakers of that language belong and modes of communication through which they constitute agreement and disagreement. Gay English is one example of sexual language under this argument. So are the women's ways of talking examined by Tannen (1990) and Coates (1996), the hyper-masculinist conversational styles explored by Cameron (1997), and the culturally "impossible talk" about women who "share the blanket with" (have sex with) other women in Lesotho (Kendall 1999).

To foreground sexual languages in the study of sexual cultures, we need a theory of language that investigates text-making and broader constructions of intersubjective meaning while it attends to the linguistic and cultural knowledge that underlies and enables those textual and discursive practices (Leap 1996). Grammar, discourse, and text-making are not speaker-specific activities but shared—albeit unevenly—across divisions and boundaries within the social domain. These uneven circulations of linguistic knowledge and practice ensure that different ways of talking about sexuality will command different degrees of authority. Similarly, studying sexual languages in terms of grammar, discourse, and text-making—not just words and phrases —draws attention to the tensions between sexual politics (that is, the social contestation of sexual ideologies and practices) and sexual desires and to the effects these tensions have on a speaker's understandings of his or her own sexual subjectivity. Structuralist psychoanalytical theorists such as Jacques Lacan and Julia Kristeva have hinted at such connections when they suggest that desire is structured like language, but the point of view developed here situates such lines of analysis in culturally, historically, politically, and materially specific contexts.

A framework of sexual languages can therefore help in approaching the imbrication of sexual politics and sexual desire. Johnson's exploration of the undercurrents of race, masculinity, and "deviant" sexuality in African American men's gay language suggests some of the forms such articulation can take. Provencher's reflections on efforts to construct a homosexuality that affirms national identity as well as same-sex desire suggests other dynamics, as does Higgins's discussion of cultural identity and sexuality in francophone Montreal. The efforts to build sexual citizenship (i.e., a socially acknowledged status for nonheterosexual subjectivities and relationships within the body politic) from personal expressions of sexual belonging (i.e., efforts to lay claim to association as a sexual person) addressed by Provencher are also found in Leap's discussion of language and township homosexuality in South Africa and in Boellstorff's analysis of *gay* language in Indonesia.

Sexual languages show how speakers' linguistic resources (Fairclough 1989, 34–35) incorporate a wide range of cultural and linguistic practices, some closely associated with the cultural logics construed as local, others seen to be aligned to outside sources. Which cultural and linguistic practices become incorporated into the grammar, discourse, and textual practices of a particular sexual language is an important issue to pursue in any setting. Evidence of linguistic materials from sources construed as outside may point to areas of reference that speakers have trouble representing through sexual languages construed as indigenous. Such evidence may also indicate that linguistic practices seen as indigenous have been superseded by linguistic practices seen to have come from outside—in recognition of the outside code's prestige and authority or in response to missionization, colonial rule, or transnational political economy.

Studies of sexual languages can provide ethnographically detailed and conceptually nuanced analysis concerning the reterritorialization of what are often seen as globalizing cultural practices and logics. Although such phenomena can unfold on a worldwide scale, the processes by which they circulate and localize are in no sense uniform or even inevitable. It may surprise readers to learn that many persons and communities of same-sex desire within the North Atlantic (Euro-American) domain resist and challenge the authority of dominant North Atlantic gay cultures. Although some sites outside the North Atlantic have been able to incorporate aspects of its dominant gay cultural norms without disrupting sexual cultures construed as local, the indeterminacy of globalizing forces means that in some cases North Atlantic sexual cultures are experienced as distant or even irrelevant.

What is true for the globalization of sexual cultures is equally true where the globalization of sexual languages is concerned. Recalling the title of this collection, Are persons outside Euro-America who use gay languages—in particular, languages that draw from gay English—speaking in another's tongue? To what extent has the emergence of languages of same-sex desire across the globe been dependent on the transnational circulation of North Atlantic–based gay English? To what extent has the transnational circulation of gay English preempted the authority of locally based gay languages? To what extent has the transnational circulation of gay English enhanced local gay language authority?

Previewing the Chapters

Although we make no claim to global coverage, the places under discussion in this book were chosen with the idea that the particular analyses would raise comparative questions of more general interest. As a result, we focus on the encounter between various gay languages and gay English in France, francophone Canada, urban African America, Cuban American Miami, Germany, Israel, South Africa, Thailand, Indonesia, and New Zealand. Research interviews, ethnographic fieldwork, life-story narratives, articles in newspapers and magazines, popular music, poetry, and informal everyday conversations provide the substantive grounds for the discussions. In some cases (Boellstorff, Higgins, Jackson, Johnson, Minning, Moriel) the authors have participated in the struggles they describe as members of the communities in question or been allies of the communities, and those chapters draw on the insights gained through these direct engagements. In all cases the analyses are guided by extended periods of residence and engaged social interaction. In that sense each chapter can be read as an ethnographic statement as well as a commentary on the articulations of language and same-sex desire in a globalizing world.

Provencher, Minning, and Higgins examine cases where Continental French, German, and Canadian French linguistic codes seen as locally gay come into unequal dialogue with gay English. This is a simultaneous process of text-making by speakers and speaker-making by texts. Senses of selfhood are shaped by the reterritorialization of gay English, even as subjects themselves participate in reconfiguring these linguistic codes. That is why the chapters consider whether the textual products should be described as English-, French-, or German-based or inclusive of those linguistic regimes. Provencher shows how gay English, which often appears to dominate messages in gay French magazines, cannot be understood in isolation from the gay French that accompanies it. Minning shows how gay English usage has become so widely embedded in German linguistic discourse that talking in gay English in such contexts may be better described as speaking gay German. And because Canadian French, not English, was the language of choice from the beginnings of the gay rights movement in Quebec, Higgins describes how English-speaking gay men in that province had to shift language loyalties (gay English to gay French) in order to participate fully in the public work of gay liberation—and how gay English thereby became a private rather than public language of same-sex desire.

Moriel discusses the formation of lesbian/gay languages in Israel and explores other ways in which conceptions of locality and globality affect the emergence of public gay cultures. Reference in Hebrew, animate or inanimate, must be grammatically marked for masculine or feminine sex/gender. That tends to make sex/gender salient in conversational contexts, frustrating efforts to conceal sexual identities in Hebrew public discourse. Moriel (who was part of a politicized struggle to develop gay Hebrew) notes that the absence of obligatory gender-marking in English (third-person, singular pronouns excepted) gave it utility in certain cultural contexts. But while an Israel-centered gay English began to upstage efforts to build gay Hebrew, Israeli gay English is itself now being upstaged by the creation of a "disco scene lingo" that incorporates linguistic material from multiple language sources to create new forms of discourse that reflect a broad range of marginalized sexualities.

Moriel's essay is the first of several that examine the convergence of social, cultural, and historical conditions in the emergence of linguistic practices seen as both locally based and concerned with same-sex desires, experiences, and subjectivities. Leap addresses this theme by exploring why same-sex oriented residents of Cape Town's black townships use Xhosa-English code-switching rather than monolingual text-making (Xhosa or English exclusively) as their language for claiming citizenship as (homo)-sexual persons in post-Apartheid Cape Town. The code-switching in question is anything but arbitrary, and the "language" that emerges through these practices marks a sharp distinction between township-based and City Centre–based (homo)sexualities. In this and other ways, Xhosa-English code-switching is much more relevant to everyday experiences of township-resident same-sex subjectivities and desires than is any form of gay linguistic practice based in English.

In contrast, Murray shows how a different set of linguistic practices have emerged among same-sex-identified Māori men in New Zealand. As in Cape Town, English has been a helpful resource for discussions of same-sex desire. As Murray explains, however, several factors have favored the use of Māori-based language resources and a preferential use of Māori linguistic/sexual discourse in those discussions. First, same-sex-oriented indigenous people have affiliated themselves with the emergence of lesbian/gay activism in New Zealand. Second, the mobilization against HIV/AIDS in New Zealand has brought male same-sex desires and practices into the foreground. A third factor is the resurgence of Māori-based political activism, which legitimized Māori-based efforts toward social change in other arenas such as that of sexuality. Working against such efforts are government resettlement and education policies that have led to a state of affairs in which many Māori no longer speak their ancestral language. Although language loss makes conversations on any topic in Māori difficult, the ongoing resurgence of Māori self-determination strongly supports efforts toward language relearning and creating a discourse of same-sex desire as part of the relearning process.

Boellstorff describes a rather different articulation of inside and outside in Indonesia, a region of great linguistic diversity. There, *gay* language is closely aligned with the national language, Indonesian. The distinctiveness of Indonesian in Indonesia's complex linguistic landscape appears in the way the language is seen as national; it is singled out and contrasted with other languages that are thereby framed as local and indigenous. Indonesian is thus marked as appropriate for purposes of political unity and for subjectivities not based in tradition. *Gay* language's close connection to national language foregrounds nationalism in *gay* language text-making. Moreover, the pragmatics of *gay* language's use—not primarily as a secret language but as a language of interaction—show how *gay* Indonesian men find themselves both linked to and ignored by dominant conceptions of national authenticity.

Jackson discusses how discourses of homosexuality in Thailand reflect yet another type of engagement between linguistic traditions and conceptions of spatial scale (local, national, and transnational). In Thailand, *gai* has become an accepted and popular term for same-sex-identified men, and although "lesbian" has not become an accepted reference among same-sex-identified women, Thai women do employ the English-based *tom* and *dee* (the *tom* of *tom*boy and the *dee* of la*dy*) to refer to masculine and feminine women in same-sex relationships respectively. The resistance (and indifference) to gay English reference centers around male-to-female transgendered persons and transsexuals, who find cultural resonance in such Thai-language concepts as kathoey and *phu-ying praphet sorng.* (This also reflects the fact that North Atlantic terminologies of transgender language have to date been globalized to a far lesser degree than language associated with gay men and lesbians outside of medical and sexological circles.) The variable presence of English distinguishes these nationalized sex/gender constructions from constructions like gai and tom-dee, whose linkages to sexual cultures beyond Thailand are quite clear. In this sense, as in other settings examined this collection, the variable status of gay English text-making reflects broader themes in social history and cannot be described effectively in terms of an acceptance versus resistance dichotomy.

Gay English fluencies do not unify male-identified men of Hispanic/Latino backgrounds in cities like Miami, Florida. They can, however, provide a way to articulate experiences of same-sex desire in the United States with the sexual cultures linked to their countries of recent origin—hence the oppositional references to transculturation and *pája*ration in the title of Peña's chapter. Peña reports that a recurring theme in these articulations is speaker dissatisfaction with conditions of gay culture and society in both the United States and elsewhere. Fluency in (gay) English thus provides a linguistic framework through which Hispanic gay men articulate multiple components of this dissatisfaction, even while such linguistic practices interpellate them into marginal subject positions. Talking gay English in these settings allows Hispanic/Latino men to voice anger, express same-sex identities and desires, and become caught up in cultural logics that shape their subjectivities as Hispanic/Latino in a white-dominated society.

Johnson also examines how forms of gay English, so influential elsewhere around the globe, intersect with ways of "talking gay" that have already taken root in English-speaking gay contexts. Johnson analyzes how something not completely alien to the multilingual alternatives Peña describes for Hispanic/Latino settings is also present within urban African American settings. Mainstream-based gay English is certainly present, but it is not fully accepted. Instead, as Johnson shows, African American gay men are impacted by and draw upon heterosexual tropes of domesticity—in particular, references to mother, family, and home—to articulate varieties of gay English that speak more directly to the conditions of racism, normative whiteness, and homophobia with which they contend.

Conclusions

Taken as a whole, these essays indicate the value that attention to language offers the study of the interface between globalizing processes and sexual subjectivities. In particular, they demonstrate the danger of assuming that what will count as local, traditional, or indigenous before the globalizing encounter—an orientalist fantasy of the pure native culture that not only assumes ahead of time that people outside the North American core who call themselves lesbian or gay are inauthentic but also has little in common with the long histories of transcultural communication we find in every chapter of this volume. At the same time, these essays show how globalizing processes do not result in homogenization but can, as Daniel Miller notes, result in a posteriori differences (Miller 1995, 2–3). In other words, globalization appears to be making the world more different just as much as it is making the world more the same. It all depends on the culturally contextual rubrics used to decide what constitutes difference and similarity. Difference is not an acultural, ahistorical attribute but the forging of cultural distinctions in particular contexts and power relations. Finally, by challenging us to rethink definitions of "the political" through gay language/linguistic practices, we come to understand how groups articulate claims to recognition and belonging that may not be recognizable as political from a post-Stonewall, U.S. perspective yet are deeply engaged with conceptions of the public and visions of social justice.

Note

1. In all text that discusses Tom Boellstorff's work the term *gay* will be italicized not only because it is part of the contemporary Indonesian language but also to underscore how

gay subjectivity in Indonesia transforms what was once an ostensibly Western term into something "authentically" Indonesian. In other words, *gay* is more than just "gay" with an Indonesian accent.

Works Cited

Adam, Barry D., Jan Willem Duyvendak, and Andre Krouwel, eds. 1999. *The Global Emergence of Gay and Lesbian Politics: National Imprints of a Worldwide Movement.* Philadelphia: Temple University Press.

Appadurai, Arjun. 1996. *Modernity at Large: Cultural Dimensions of Globalization.* Minneapolis: University of Minnesota Press.

Asad, Talal. 1995. *Genealogies of Religion: Discipline and Reasons of Power in Christianity and Islam.* Baltimore: Johns Hopkins University Press.

Blackwood, Evelyn. 1998. "Tombois in West Sumatra: Constructing Masculinity and Erotic Desire." *Cultural Anthropology* 13(4): 491–521.

Brenner, Suzanne A. 1996. "Reconstructing Self and Society: Javanese Muslim Women and 'the Veil.'" *American Ethnologist* 23(4): 673–97.

———. 1998. *The Domestication of Desire: Women, Wealth, and Modernity in Java.* Princeton: Princeton University Press.

Campbell-Kibler, Kathryn et al., eds. 2002. *Language and Sexuality: Contesting Meaning in Theory and Practice.* Stanford: Center for the Study of Language and Information Publications.

Cameron, Deborah. 1997. "Performing Gender Identity: Young Men's Talk and the Construction of Heterosexual Masculinity." In *Language and Masculinity,* ed. Sally Johnson and Ulrike Hanna Meinhof, 47–64. London: Basil Blackwell.

Chatterjee, Partha. 1986. *Nationalist Thought and the Colonial World: A Derivative Discourse.* Minneapolis: University of Minnesota Press.

Coates, Jennifer. 1996. *Women Talk: Conversations between Women Friends.* London: Oxford University Press.

Eckert, Penelope. 2002. "Demystifying Sexuality and Desire." In *Language and Sexuality: Contesting Meaning in Theory and Practice,* ed. Kathryn Campbell-Kibler et al., 99–110. Stanford: Center for the Study of Language and Information Publications.

Fairclough, Norman. 1989. *Language and Power.* London: Longmans.

Foucault, Michel. 1978. *The History of Sexuality,* vol. 1: *An Introduction.* New York: Vintage Books.

Gaonkar, Dilip Parameshwar, ed. 1999. *Alternative Modernities.* Durham: Duke University Press.

Gibson-Graham, J. K. 1996. *The End of Capitalism (as We Knew It): A Feminist Critique of Political Economy.* Cambridge: Basil Blackwell.

Halberstam, Judith. 1998. *Female Masculinity.* Durham: Duke University Press.

Hall, Stuart. 1980. "Race, Articulation, and Societies Structured in Dominance." In *Sociological Theories of Racism and Colonialism,* ed. Stuart Hall, 305–45. Paris: UNESCO.

———. 1991. "The Local and the Global: Globalization and Ethnicity." In *Culture, Globalization, and the World-System,* ed. Anthony D. King, 19–40. London: Macmillan.

Hannerz, Ulf. 1996. *Transnational Connections: Culture, People, Places.* London: Routledge.

Harvey, David. 1989. *The Condition of Postmodernity.* London: Basil Blackwell.

Herdt, Gilbert. 1997. *Same Sex Different Cultures: Exploring Gay and Lesbian Lives.* Boulder: Westview Press.

Herdt, Gilbert, and Robert J. Stoller. 1990. *Intimate Communications: Erotics and the Study of Culture.* New York: Columbia University Press.

Kendall. 1999. "Women in Lesotho and the (Western) Construction of Homophobia." In *Female Desires: Same-Sex Relations and Transgender Practices across Cultures,* ed. Evelyn Blackwood and Saskia E. Wieringa, 157–80. New York: Columbia University Press.

Kroskrity, Paul V., ed. 2000. *Regimes of Language: Ideologies, Polities and Identities.* Santa Fe: School of American Research Press.

Kulick, Don. 2000. "Lesbian and Gay Language." *Annual Review of Anthropology* 29: 243–85.

Leap, William L. 1995. "Introduction." In *Beyond the Lavender Lexicon: Authenticity, Imagination, and Appropriation in Lesbian and Gay Languages,* ed. William L. Leap, vii–xx. Newark: Gordon and Breach.

———. 1996. *Word's Out: Gay Men's English.* Minneapolis: University of Minnesota Press.

———. 2002. "Studying Lesbian and Gay Languages: Vocabulary, Text-making and Beyond." In *Out in Theory: The Emergence of Lesbian and Gay Anthropology,* ed. Ellen Lewin and William L. Leap, 128–54. Urbana: University of Illinois Press.

Manalansan, Martin. 1995. "In the Shadow of Stonewall: Examining Gay Transnational Politics and the Diasporic Dilemma." *GLQ: A Journal of Gay and Lesbian Studies* 2(4): 425–38.

Marcus, Sharon. 1992. "Fighting Bodies, Fighting Words: A Theory and Politics of Rape Prevention." In *Feminists Theorize the Political,* eds. Judith Butler and Joan Scott, 385–403. New York: Routledge.

Miller, Daniel. 1995. "Introduction: Anthropology, Modernity and Consumption." In *Worlds Apart: Modernity through the Prism of the Local,* ed. Daniel Miller, 1–22. London: Routledge.

Moonwomon, Birch. 1995. "Lesbian Discourse, Lesbian Knowledge." In *Beyond the Lavender Lexicon,* ed. William L. Leap, 45–64. Newark: Gordon and Breach.

Morris, Rosalind C. 2000. In *The Place of Origins: Modernity and Its Mediums in Northern Thailand.* Durham: Duke University Press.

Ong, Aihwa. 1999. *Flexible Citizenship: The Cultural Logics of Transnationality.* Durham: Duke University Press.

Parker, Richard. 1999. *Beneath the Equator: Cultures of Desire, Male Homosexuality, and Emerging Gay Communities in Brazil.* New York: Routledge.

Rofel, Lisa. 1999. *Other Modernities: Gendered Yearnings in China after Socialism.* Berkeley: University of California Press.

Schieffelin, Bambi B., Kathryn A. Woolard, and Paul V. Kroskrity, eds. 1998. *Language Ideologies: Practice and Theory.* New York: Oxford University Press.

Tannen, Deborah. 1990. *You Just Don't Understand: Women and Men in Conversation.* New York: Ballantine Books.

Waters, Malcolm. 1995. *Globalization.* London: Routledge.

Weston, Kath. 1991. *Families We Choose: Lesbians, Gays, Kinship.* NewYork: Columbia University Press.

Wong, Andrew, Sarah J. Roberts, and Kathryn Campbell-Kibler. 2002. "Speaking of Sex." In *Language and Sexuality: Contesting Meaning in Theory and Practice,* ed. Kathryn Campbell-Kibler et al., 1–12. Stanford: Center for the Study of Language and Information Publications.

Yanagisako, Sylvia, and Carol Delaney. 1995. "Introduction." In *Naturalizing Power: Essays in Feminist Cultural Analysis,* ed. Sylvia Yanagisako and Carol Delaney, 1–19. New York: Routledge.

1. Vague English Creole: (Gay English) Cooperative Discourse in the French Gay Press

DENIS M. PROVENCHER

The emergence of North Atlantic constructions of gay culture has resulted in the circulation of a "universal gay identity" across various national boundaries. Both print and electronic media have helped transmit this identity in such diverse places as Germany, France, Holland, South Africa, Australia, and Japan. The commercial gay and lesbian press, for example, aided by advertising from multinational corporations, informs homosexuals about where to travel as well as how to talk, dress, shop, define relationships, have (safer) sex, exercise, and sculpt their bodies.[1] In particular, the rise of the gay and lesbian press in the United States and Western Europe has contributed significantly to the invention of a transnational gay culture, a gay "way of being" determined by Western-style consumerism.

In contemporary France, gays and lesbians regularly turn to the print media for a large portion of information about their "inside" world. Frank Arnal, a longtime journalist and contributor to the French gay magazine *Gai-Pied*, describes French gays and lesbians as a by and large "learned community" that greatly relies on print journalism.[2] "[It] is the transmitter of ideology which is of prime importance for anyone who wants to understand the specific Frenchness of the French gay movement" (Arnal 1993, 38). At the same time, many French gays now subscribe to a way of being reminiscent of a community-based gay identity in the United States. Frédéric Martel reminds us of the influence of the American model on French gay identity when he states, "Coming out of the closet and homosexual visibility, imported from the American movements, appeared in the 1970s as the alpha and the omega of gay French militancy" (1996, 399).[3]

This visibility was most evident with the establishment of gay political organizations in France during the 1970s—for example, Front Homosexuel d'Action Révolutionnaire (FHAR) and Comité d'Urgence Anti-Répression Homosexuelle (CUARH)—and the establishment of AIDS organizations during the 1980s, particularly ACT UP PARIS, which is based on the U.S. model of the same name. Similarly, glossy gay and lesbian news magazines, in the genre of such identity-based publications as *The Advocate* in the United States, have gained significant popularity in France since the 1980s. That was most evident with the commercial success of the long-running *Gai-Pied* (1979–92) and remains true for *Têtu* magazine.

Têtu (Stubborn-headed), which appeared on French newsstands in July 1995, represents France's attempt to establish a national gay magazine geared specifically toward a gay male readership.[4] Didier Lestrade, the former president of ACT UP PARIS and a regular contributor to *Gai-Pied,* introduced *Têtu* with the help and financial support of Yves Saint-Laurent and his work associate Pierre Bergé, the current director of *Têtu*. Under Lestrade's direction (the former adjunct editor-in-chief and current editorial advisor), the editorial staff decided to create a French gay magazine inspired by its American counterparts. In taking on that project, Lestrade wanted to create a sense of sociopolitical and cultural community for French gays and lesbians similar to that which has existed in the press for several years in other countries, including the United States and Great Britain.[5] As Lestrade described his project, "We want to create a real gay lobby, although it has remained embryonic until now. . . . Like in the United States, this magazine should be owned, operated and represented by gays" (Zemouri 1995, 22).

In fact, U.S. national gay news magazines such as *The Advocate, Genre,* and *Out* have inspired Lestrade's magazine. Pascal Loubet (*Têtu*'s first editor-in-chief from 1995 to 1997) has acknowledged the influence of the American gay press, indicating, for example, how the sarcastic, tongue-in-cheek tone and presentation in *Out* helped shape *Têtu* (Loubet 1997). Indeed, the U.S. media have long influenced French media and not only within a gay context. Raymond Kuhn has pointed out that American television shows such as *The Wheel of Fortune* and *The Muppet Show* have been produced in France as the popular *La roue de la fortune* and *Le Bébête Show* (1995, 238–39). In addition, Kuhn argues that weekly news magazines such as *Newsweek* and *Time* were the models for *L'Express* and *Le Point.* It is not surprising, then, with such U.S. media influences that *Têtu* at times resembles American counterparts in both form and content.

Does that mean, however, that the French and American gay presses use a similar rhetoric to discuss cultural and political phenomena? Does the circulation of similar media images and messages in the United States and France contribute to the breakdown of both cultural and linguistic differences across national boundaries? Do French gays adopt a sort of gay English, but one tinged with a French accent, when they speak of their experiences in the French gay press? Or does a certain authentic French element, as described by Arnal, still persist despite the hegemonic presence of both U.S. language and culture?

In this chapter, I examine the presence of "gay English" in France's national gay magazine, *Têtu*. Gay English uses both lexical elements (Chesebro ed. 1981; Lumby 1976; Ringer ed. 1994) and principles of gay-related cooperative discourse (Leap 1996) that call upon shared knowledge and gay-centered cultural themes within a specific cultural context. *Têtu* magazine includes several English lexical elements related to a consumer and mass-media culture situated within a larger, transnational (Anglo-American) context. Moreover, the magazine calls upon several elements of cooperative discourse through many references to prominent U.S. and British figures and events in gay history. The magazine includes, for example, articles about such figures as Greg Louganis, Ellen De Generes, George Michael, Jimmy Somerville, Rupert Everett, Catherine Deneuve, Etienne Daho, and Boy George; references to the Stonewall riots and Vermont's same-sex civil union bill; and debates surrounding the French domestic-partner bill (PaCS). *Têtu* reveals signs of a transnational gay culture as it borrows, but not too heavily, lexical and cooperative elements from anglophone cultures.

Being Gay in French Culture

The interplay of global and local forces at work on gay and lesbian cultures in various locales has been examined. Adam, Duyvendak, and Krouwel maintain that gay and lesbian movements around the world "demonstrate a Foucauldian point . . . [they] are both *a part of* and *apart from* the societies around them, both resisting and participating in—even reproducing—dominant public discourses" (1999, 9, emphasis added). With specific reference to France, Fillieule and Duyvendak argue that the French gay movement must operate through the French state system. As they view this process, "In contrast to the United States, which provides a rich substrate for group differentiation . . . the French state often approaches specific groups with a view to privatizing them, repressing them, dispersing them, or subjecting them to centralized, hierarchical control" (1999, 205).

Indeed, centralization and hierarchical control have long played a role in the French system. That is evident in several historical and cultural contexts, including absolute monarchy established in the seventeenth century under Louis XIV; the French national educational system, which was instituted by Napoléon and still remains strongly centralized through a national curriculum and examinations; and the general bureaucratic nature of countless French organizations and offices, ranging from the local *préfectures* (city hall/municipal offices) to the national PTT (telephone and postal service). The French gay and lesbian movement and culture are like other national cultural institutions in that they must operate within the bounds of a larger dominant national framework.

Frédéric Martel dispels the notion of an autonomous gay community or identity that exists independently of a larger, more encompassing, universal identity within France such that gay and lesbian identities (a "particularity") work in relation to a larger social organization/state system ("universality") (1996, 404). Therefore, Martel argues that French gay identity must be considered in relation to a national identity, and he calls for an intermediary position that would fuse multiculturalism with the republican ideal of the state.

This contention supports the powerful French myth that has long argued for the nation's unity and homogeneity. During the Third Republic, for example, Ernest Lavisse's well-known *Histoire de France* educated both French and French colonial schoolchildren through a similar republican ideal. In the introduction to his elementary text Lavisse reminds all "French citizens" of their common descent and adds a universal message to love "our ancestors, the Gauls" ([1916] 1919, 1–11). More recently, Mona Ozouf has examined the role of women in France since the revolution and argues for that same sense of universality. She contends that French women—compared to their American counterparts, for example—have long participated in equal fashion alongside men to contribute to the collective whole (1995, 323–97). She attributes such equal participation to a spirit of universalism that has long existed in the French republican state. Such reasoning then is like that found in other instances of French discourse about individual and group rights.

Consequently, French gays may reach to the larger transnational gay culture wherein they can participate as "sexual citizens," yet they are still firmly planted in an egalitarian ideology.[6] Unlike U.S. gays and lesbians who at times identify so closely with their sexual identity that it is seen as a kind of ethnic separateness, gays and lesbians in France must view themselves, first and foremost, as citizens of the French republican state. First, they must locate themselves politically and culturally in the motherland of *l'Hexagone*. Furthermore, they must speak the French "language of egalitarianism" (Fillieule and Duyvendak 1999, 190), a mother tongue that emphasizes sameness and inclusion instead of difference. Thus, to a certain extent, discussions of French gay experience, as in examples from *Têtu,* must operate through the regulatory discourse of the nation's cultural and political system, even if it draws heavily on English references.

Vague English Creole: Lexical Evidence of an English Presence

Due to the influence of U.S. media, and to a lesser extent British media, within a French context, the linguistic messages in *Têtu* at times resemble a variation of French that has come in contact with a form of (gay) English and thus in a sense resembles a "vague English Creole," a socially useful linguistic compromise between an indigenous and external language traditions (Morgan ed. 1994). I draw this term from an article on gay vacations that appeared in *Têtu* ("Gay Destinations" 1996). In it, French gays are instructed to take to hot spots of gay male interest during the late summer. The supposed linguistic convergence that occurs at sites such as Ibiza, Sitgès, Mykonos, Key West, and Fire Island is described: "Of course, the indigenous do not speak exactly the same language, but the frenzied community that swoops down on these places from the first hints of sunshine, like a cloud of locusts on a day of scourge in Egypt and bustles about feverishly, speaks the same lingua franca, *vague English Creole* tinged with Italian, French, German, Scandinavian and Spanish accents in more or less equal proportions" ("Gay Destinations" 1996, 67, emphasis added).

The author describes an imagined community of European and Scandinavian travelers who have acquired sufficient linguistic competence to communicate in English, the language of the dominant gay culture. The implication is that French gays speak a "broken (gay) English" or pidgin English with a slight French accent. Like other European and Scandinavian travelers, these gay interlocutors adopt a certain linguistic identity in order to be conversant and participate in a global gay culture of desire and leisure.[7] The assumptions of a Western-style capitalist affluence are evident. Both the author and editorial staff assume an imagined community of gay readers financially able to afford vacation time and frequent prime vacation spots both in Europe and the United States.

English lexical items appear throughout *Têtu* in both advertisements and articles that help illustrate an English presence or the existence of a "vague English creole." The advertising *Têtu* regularly includes for leisure activities

uses slogans containing English terminology. Among the English lexical items
that have appeared regularly from 1995 to 2000 are "Queen: gay tea dance,"
"Mousse: The Ultra Hot Gay Foam Party," and "Miss Cuir" (pronounced
"Miss Queer"). All refer to nightclub culture (dance parties and leather com-
petitions) that take place at French gay clubs such as Queen on the Champs
Elysées. The magazine also includes regular references to "House and Techno" music played in such spaces. Moreover, it prints advertising for saunas
("Pink Beach: Le Sauna Number One"), sex shops ("enter the sex universe"
and "sex shop and cruising area"), travel agencies ("Eurogays"), on-line
meeting places ("gay liberty" and <www.twogayther.com>), and specialized
lesbian material ("DykeGuide 2000–2001").

English-speaking visitors who happen to pick up a copy of *Têtu* could
easily decipher the intent of such advertising or participate in those cultural
events in order to meet non-English–speaking counterparts (perhaps a goal
of the editorial staff). Moreover, many slogans or names for commercial
products and services could just as easily have appeared in the U.S. or British gay press or in poster advertisements in gay sections of any large international city, for example, New York, Montreal, Cape Town, Bali, Bangkok,
or Tokyo.

Saskia Sassen has observed that "major cities have emerged as a strategic
site not only for global capital but also for . . . the formation of transnational identities" (1998, xxx). In a sense, major publications such as *Têtu* function as similar sites. These publications provide the "global capital" of English language–based commercial advertising that promotes a global
consumer culture based on a North Atlantic way of life like that shown in
gay (and straight) magazines throughout the world. The English lexical items
found in *Têtu* thus reinforce the presence of a postmodern and transnational
gay culture based primarily on commercial aspects of leisure, including bars,
clubs, saunas, dance music, travel excursions, and on-line chat rooms.

Many of the previous examples illustrate an English influence in a gay
consumer culture of leisure and desire. Of course, I could argue that this type
of presence in *Têtu* occurs only on a surface level because the English language appears in print format (advertising) rather than in everyday individual
speech or behavior. Altman notes the need to "disentangle commercial media from changes in consciousness" (1996, 85). Other English lexical items,
however, appear that seem to suggest a more deep-seated Anglo-American
presence in the French gay press and in the collective consciousness of its
readers. These include English lexical terms that French gays use to identify
themselves as part of a homosexual community as well as the language used
to discuss gay pride, coming out, and HIV/AIDS education.

First, *Têtu* and its journalists consciously and regularly use the English term *gay* (both the noun and the invariant adjective) instead of the French term *gai* when writing about male homosexuality. That is most evident in the magazine's subtitle—"le magazine des gays et lesbiennes" (the magazine of gays and lesbians)—that appears on the cover. It also marks an important divergence from *Gai-Pied,* a magazine that used the French equivalent "gai" in its title for approximately thirteen years. Alain-Gilles Minella and Philippe Angelotti (1996) have examined the emergence of an American identity–based collective consciousness in France and entitle their volume *Générations Gay* for the same reason. The word choice in *Têtu* and other, more recent, publications suggests a certain intentionality of recognition (or outright acceptance) of an American-style way of being homosexual.

In the discussion of gay pride, *Têtu* regularly uses the English expressions *Lesbian and Gay Pride* or *La Gay Pride.* An advertisement for Paris's gay pride celebration, for example, announces "Lesbian and Gay Pride 2000, 24 juin, Rendez-vous à Paris!" The slogan is easily decipherable to both Francophones and non-Francophones. It is also very important to note that the magazine seldom uses the feminine French *la fierté* (pride) in articles on gay pride, nor does it use that term in advertising such events.

With regard to the expressions associated with coming out, *Têtu* occasionally uses the French expression *sortir du placard* (to come out of the closet) but most often uses the terms *faire son come-out, coming out,* and *outing.* That is best exemplified in "Outing," the April 1999 special issue on that topic. Traditionally, the French have remained quite reluctant to discuss private (sexual) issues in the public realm (Rosario 1993). Michel Foucault, for example, refused to discuss his homosexuality and HIV status in the public sphere despite the fact that his scholarly writings have had strong impact on late-twentieth-century thought about the social constructions of homosexuality (Macey 1993). Similarly, relatively few openly gay or lesbian French celebrities have appeared in *Têtu*'s feature-length articles or on the magazine's front cover. Nonetheless, the intentional choice by gay French authors to use English lexical items such as "outing" suggests an embryonic shift in the collective gay French consciousness with regard to sexual identity and self-disclosure.

English items also appear with regard to HIV and AIDS education and prevention. Lestrade decided to devote a substantial section in every issue to that topic (a section of the magazine is entitled "Cahier Sida / *Têtu*+"). The articles published there and throughout the magazine include such English terms as *safe(r) sex* and *HIV* as well as the equivalent French acronym, "VIH."

Considering the influence of U.S. models on both ACT UP PARIS and the

French gay press as well as the U.S. role in AIDS research since the 1980s, it is unsurprising that English terms that refer to HIV and AIDS education find their way into the magazine. Moreover, the discourse on HIV/AIDS control and safer sex is part of global language related to gay culture: "It is clear that the language of HIV/AIDS control, surveillance, and education has been a major factor in spreading the notion of 'gay identity' and in facilitating the development of gay consciousness" (Altman 1997, 425). In that sense *Têtu*, with the use of select English terminology, helps instruct French gays about the transmission of HIV and correct (safe) collective sexual practices. Its regular use of English lexical items suggests the emergence of a common way of thinking, a global collective consciousness and means of conceptualizing and talking about certain homosexual experiences.

Cooperative Discourse in *Têtu*

Evidence of a "vague English creole" is not limited, however, to a disjointed repertoire of English lexical terms; scholarship in gay studies reminds us that gay language moves beyond the "lavender lexicon" (Leap ed. 1995). Leap draws out the notion of gay language by referring to "cooperative discourse" and other elements that contribute to what he considers distinctively gay text-making. Central to cooperative discourse is the process of "co-construction," which involves "speaker comments [that] appeal directly to shared knowledge and experience, particularly knowledge and experience building on gay-centered cultural themes" (1996, 19). Elements of co-construction include exaggeration, persistent sexual and erotic messages, gay-oriented metaphor and innuendo, insults or verbal dueling and teasing, (self-)parody, misogynistic remarks, comic relief, and references to gay characters and events in history. Text-making in these terms appeals to collective notions of authentic gay experience and ensures that speakers become co-participants in the speech event.

   Many elements of an English-based cooperative discourse occur in the text-making found in *Têtu*. First, that publication draws much of its visual imagery with reference to gay people and history, or people of gay interest, from an American or British context. The special July–August 1999 issue, for example, was dedicated to the thirtieth anniversary of Stonewall and entitled *L'Amérique*.[8] Moreover, many of *Têtu*'s covers and articles during a five-year period featured such prominent U.S. and British figures as Armistead Maupin, Tom Cruise, Matt Damon, Keanu Reeves, Liza Minnelli, Edmund White, Ellen De Generes, Marky Mark, K.D. Lang, Madonna, Rupert Everett, Boy George, George Michael, and Jeff Stryker. The cast of characters in-

cluded celebrities who either draw a queer audience or have become identified as gay or lesbian. Only two French celebrities—Catherine Deneuve and
Etienne Daho—appeared on the front cover, however, and neither self-identifies as homosexual.

The linguistic manifestation of English-based cooperative discourse proves
just as interesting as its visual markers. Many elements of cooperative discourse, including tongue-in-cheek humor, self-mocking, persistent sexual or
erotic messages, and gay-oriented metaphor, appear in *Têtu*. In the inaugu-
ral issue of July–August 1995 the magazine constructed its own notion of gay
readership through a subscription solicitation:

> Voici 12 choses que vous ne pourrez plus acheter une fois dépensé l'argent de
> votre abonnement à *Têtu*. . . .
>
> 200 F—un an 11 numéros. 200 F =
> ½ Levi's, 1 Caterpillar (pied gauche ou droit),
> 2 entrées dans un sauna, 4 places de cinéma,
> 4 gin-tonics dans un club, 2 entrées dans un club +
> 2 vestiaires + 1 Chupa [lollipop], 13 paquets de cigarettes,
> ¼ d'aller-retour Paris-Londres en charter,
> ¹⁄₁₀ d'aller-retour Paris-New York en charter,
> 28 quotidiens, 2 heures de 36.15 [an on-line message board], 1 fois le tour du
> périph' en tarif de nuit.
>
> En revanche, si vous préférez acheter 200 capotes à 1 franc, on vous comprendra.
> [Photo of *Têtu*'s inaugural issue.]
> Mensuel homosexuel vraiment nouveau et plutôt intéressant . . . 200 F un an
> 11 numéros. (11)
>
> (Here are 12 things you can no longer buy once you have spent your money on
> a subscription to *Têtu*. . . .
>
> 200 francs—1 year 11 issues. 200 francs =
> ½ pair of Levi's, 1 Caterpillar boot (left or right foot),
> 2 passes for a sauna, 4 movie tickets,
> 4 gin and tonics in a club, 2 passes for a club +
> 2 coat checks + 1 Chupa, 13 packs of cigarettes,
> ¼ round-trip charter ticket, Paris-London,
> ¹⁄₁₀ round-trip charter ticket, Paris–New York, 28 daily newspapers, 2 hours
> on-line, one nighttime taxi ride around Paris.
>
> However, if you prefer buying 200 condoms at 1 franc a piece, we'll understand.
> A really new and quite interesting gay monthly news magazine . . . 200 francs—
> 1 year 11 issues.)

The implication is that readers who do not spend money on *Têtu* would be spending it on other items of affluence, many of which are associated with an international gay culture, whether Levi's jeans, Caterpillar boots (worn by gay men in order to appear butch), movies, nightclubs, and coat checks (spaces that offer the potential for sexual encounters), cigarettes, alcohol (gin and tonics), objects on which to suck (the word *chupa* is derived from the Spanish verb *chupar,* to suck), trips to exotic places (anglophone cities known for gay nightlife and where gay "relatives" can be visited and gay English learned), other newspapers, two hours on the Minitel (on-line chat rooms), or a taxi ride around the Bois de Boulogne on Paris's periphery (a gay meeting and cruising spot). Of course, none of those items is exclusive to gay people. What this text does, however, is negotiate a gay cooperative discourse through a series of references known to gay men (and potentially others) familiar with a culture of leisure and desire.

The advertisement constructs what Mary Talbot (1995) refers to as the implied reader of mass-media publications.[9] Despite *Têtu*'s editorial, which describes the magazine as offering a little for everyone, including women, such an advertisement constructs an implied gay male reader who is socially and sexually active and perhaps of a certain age group. Like mainstream advertising aimed at straight people, commercial gay advertising constructs a middle-class, consumer-oriented, gay-male culture whose participants enjoy a set range of pastimes. The example also makes frequent use of tongue-in-cheek humor and persistent sexual message. Thus *Têtu* actively forges the identity of its readership with the help of elements of cooperative discourse that draws from larger cultural contexts (both gay and non-gay) and invites readers to place themselves within a larger cultural context.

A second article of particular interest in the discussion of cooperative discourse compares heterosexual and homosexual identities in a humorous and self-mocking way. Consider an entry from the July–August 1996 issue:

Les différences entre . . .

Hétéros:
- Reviennent de vacances bronzés et reposés
- Voudraient coucher avec Madonna
- Regardent dans les vitrines
- Sont obsédés par leur bite
- Donnent leur âge quand on leur pose la question

Homos:
- Partent en vacances bronzés et reviennent épuisés
- Voudraient être Madonna

- Se regardent dans les vitrines
- Sont obsédés par la bite
- Répondent: Tu me donnes quel âge?

• Adorent les blondes en lycra moulant	• Adorent être blonds en lycra moulant
• Aiment parler des femmes	• Aiment parler au feminin
• Veulent entrer au Queen	• Veulent entrer au Queen
• Passent leurs vacances à la mer	• Passent leurs vacances chez leur mère
• Regardent le foot à la télévision	• Regardent seulement les interviews dans les vestiaires
• Veulent tous avoir une BM	• Disent qu'ils sont BM
• Regardent *Alerte à Malibu* pour Pamela Anderson	• Regardent *Alerte à Malibu* pour David Charvet
• Se coiffent mal	• Se coiffent trop. (8)

(Differences between . . .

Heteros:
- Come back from vacation tan and rested
- Would like to sleep with Madonna
- Look in store windows
- Are obsessed with their own dick
- Give their age when asked
- Adore blonds in tight lycra
- Love talking to women
- Want to get into Queen
- Spend their vacations at the ocean
- Watch soccer on television
- All want to have a BM [*bien montée*]
- Watch *Baywatch* for Pamela Anderson
- Do their hair poorly)

Homos:
- Leave on vacation tanned and come back exhausted
- Would like to be Madonna
- Look at themselves in store windows
- Are obsessed with dick
- Respond: How old do you think I look?
- Adore being blonds in tight lycra
- Love speaking in the "feminine"
- Want to get into Queen
- Spend vacation at their mother's
- Watch the locker-room interviews
- Say they are BM [*bien monté*]
- Watch *Baywatch* for David Charvet
- Do their hair too much)

In comparing straight and gay identities, *Têtu* defines a hetero as a straight man who spends vacations at the shore and comes back tan and rested. In addition, he gives little time to personal care or fashion (he is poorly coiffed), desires Madonna and other women in tight lycra, and longs to have a well-built significant other, someone *bien monté(e)* (BM) or "well built" or "well hung." He also obsesses over his penis and talks about women while watching televised soccer matches and Pamela Anderson on the series *Baywatch*. Nonetheless, the straight man is hip enough to frequent Queen.

The gay man vacations as well, but he leaves already tan and returns exhausted, especially if he spends it at a gay hot spot (culture of desire) or at his mother's house because he is spoiled and unable to cut the umbilical link to his maternal figure. This is an excellent example of cooperative discourse; many popular culture texts define relationships between gay men and their mothers as traditionally close.[10] Like a straight man, a gay man is also obsessed by physical appearance, especially genitalia (he is still a man, after all). Yet he obsesses over his physical attributes, an action linguistically reinforced by such reflexive French verbs in the original text as *se regarder* (to look at one's self) and *se coiffer* (to do one's own hair). In addition, the gay man looks at himself in store windows, styles his hair too much, skirts questions about age, and claims to be well hung. Gay men are also said to spend time contemplating being Madonna (a bold female icon often associated with androgyny or flamboyant bisexuality) or some other desirable blond in lycra pants. Moreover, they identify with other feminine figures, frequent Paris's gay nightclub, and use feminine speech.

Leap argues that gay cooperative discourse functions "in relation to" and not "at distance from" a socially dominant discourse—assumed to be a straight discourse (1996, 11). It is notable in this excerpt from *Têtu* that only one reference from the list derives directly from gay culture: Queen. All other references derive from popular culture at large (either U.S. or European) through the examples of Madonna, vacations, shopping, sports cars, personal care, and gender stereotypes. These references are appropriated in gay cooperative discourse to construct both heterosexual and homosexual identities associated with certain characteristics, such as machismo and sexual drive for straight men and narcissism and effeminacy for gay men. Consequently, and as in the previous example, cooperative discourse in *Têtu* relies on references from larger (often anglophone) cultural contexts to construct its discussion of gay culture. In addition, the editorial baseline reads "cette année, tentez une variante: partez bronzés ET épuisés" (This year, try something different: leave tan AND exhausted).[11] That bit of humor and self-parody demonstrates that the magazine's editorial staff does not take itself too seriously. Indeed, gay cooperative discourse in *Têtu* employs humor and self-parody to illustrate the permeability of gender and sexual identities and construct a variety of gay identities that attract a gay male readership.

Locating French (Gay) Identity: Global and Local Forces at Work

English language and cultures play a role in French gay text-making. But if gay English permeates the cooperative discourse in the French gay press, then how and where do we locate an authentic French (gay) identity linguistically? Where does the use of English cooperative discourse end and a French cooperative discourse begin in *Têtu*'s text-making?

I believe the answer lies somewhere between a global gay culture propagated by U.S. civilization and Western-style capitalism and the local French (national) cultural context. Altman reminds us that most people and cultures live in an "intermediate position between tradition and (post) modernity" (1996, 77). French gays, for example, may sport Levi's 501s and Tommy Hilfiger pullovers; they continue, however, to eat *pain au chocolat,* sip *express* in local cafés, and speak a seemingly homogenous French language monitored by the Académie Française. To take another example, consider the "McDonaldization" of French culture. McDonald's restaurants, along with Big Macs and strawberry shakes, have found their way into virtually every French city. Nonetheless, elements of an "authentically French experience" persist. A modified McDonald's menu caters to a typically French palate with items that do not appear on a McDonald's menu in the United States, for example, mineral water (Evian) and French beer (Kronenberg) as well as ketchup made from a more moderately sweetened formula.

The same type of cultural appropriation takes place within the French gay press and its use of elements of gay cooperative discourse. French gay men may incorporate select English terms in discussing their homosexual experiences. Moreover, the way of writing they may adopt about a French homosexual experience includes elements of English-like camp humor, misogynist remarks, persistent sexual innuendo, and references to prominent gay people and events. Nonetheless, the French gay press continues in many ways—for example, in the lack of openly gay or lesbian French celebrities it discusses—to rely on traditional narratives and ways of being that are part and parcel of a national cultural landscape. In many other instances, English language presence aside, *Têtu* resembles the local French culture as much (if not more so) than it represents American and British cultural phenomena.

Cooperative French Discourse in *Têtu*

There is sufficient lexical evidence of a French presence in the French gay press; *Têtu*, after all, is published in French. More interesting however are the many "French" elements of cooperative discourse that occur in *Têtu* and suggest a French mentality at work within the nation's gay culture. Such discourse may contain specific references to gay people, and events that involve them, in France. These include mention of the country's long literary tradition and those who have written on homosexuality, such as Marcel Proust, Colette, André Gide, and Jean Genet; contemporary events such as Gay Pride Paris; the prohibition against gay pride rainbow flags in the Marais (a Paris district inhabited largely by gays and lesbians); the domestic-partner benefits bill; and the role of French political figures who support equal rights for all citizens. Among the politicians are Jack Lang (former French minister of culture, Socialist Party), Jacques Chirac (president of France, Gaullist Party), Elisabeth Hubert (minister of health, Socialist Party), and Roselyne Bachelot (a Republican Party deputy). Also in the French tradition, *Têtu* journalists have decided to embark on a gay "Tour de France" by interviewing and featuring everyday gays and lesbians from such regions as Languedoc, Alsace, Brittany, and Normandy.[12]

Visually, *Têtu* also features many French and Francophone celebrities who may interest both gay and straight readers. Among them are Renaud Camus, Guillaume Dustan, and Rachid O. (novelists who have written about French gay culture); Jean-Paul Gaultier (a French clothing designer of queer interest); Etienne Daho (a French musician of queer interest); Catherine Deneuve, Brigitte Bardot, Edith Piaf, Mylène Farmer, Dalida, and Céline Dion (actresses or singers who are strong female figures and of queer interest as are Madonna or Barbra Streisand for American gay men); and Gaël Morel and Stéphane Rideau (actors of gay male interest and the stars of *Les roseaux sauvages,* a 1995 French film that deals with male homosexuality). Many of these people do not self-identify as gay or lesbian, thus reinforcing the fact that few French celebrities are openly out.

Other examples of cooperative discourse reinforce the French hesitancy to discuss private sexual matters in a public space. Baselines in *Têtu* make reference to the trend: "Vous êtes français et célèbre et vous voulez faire votre *come-out?* Appelez-nous" (You're French and famous and would like to come out? Call us! [July–Aug. 1995, 45]) and "Curieux que la seule célébrité *out* en France soit un Anglais, non?" (It's curious that the only *out* celebrity in France is an Englishman, no? [June 1996, 23]). The first phrase invites French celebrities to come out of the closet, whereas the second makes reference to an out

British celebrity (Alex Taylor) living in France and featured in *Têtu*. It would likely take a reader who is French to understand the sarcasm in such phrases. The baselines offer commentary on a current situation in France, requiring a common base of local knowledge.

Other humorous baselines also require some French cooperation on the part of readers. In a July–August 1996 article on drag queens, for example, the baseline promises a follow-up story: "Le mois prochain: Les vaches folles à Mykonos" (Next month: The mad cows of Mykonos). In this case, a gay reader must know of other events in Europe (namely, the mad cow virus in England) and recognize "Mykonos" as a reference to a gay Greek resort where many French and other European gay men go on summer holiday. Gay men living in North America may not necessarily understand that reference because many of them supposedly flock to domestic spots such as Provincetown, Fire Island, and San Francisco. Moreover, within a French context, the word *vache* (cow) often connotes a negative feminine image. Therefore, the French gay press weaves together a European reference (mad cow disease) with a French reference related to negative female imagery to establish a cooperative discourse. There are some elements of French cooperation in gay text-making, or at least a cooperation that requires knowledge of a French or European context.

With such a large portion of the publication devoted to HIV and AIDS education ("Cahier Sida" / *Têtu+*), *Têtu* also informs readers about the current HIV situation as well as sexual practices in Paris and around France. Some excerpts present French sexual practices in a self-mocking manner, perhaps to cover up the high rate of HIV transmission that has existed in France since the 1990s. For an article on Europe's Summer Gay Games, the baseline in the July–August 1996 issue reads "si la séroconversion était une discipline olympique, la France raflerait toutes les médailles" (If seroconversion was an olympic event, France would run off with all the medals [104]). Cooperative French discourse uses self-parody and comic relief in this context to alleviate the difficulty readers may have in facing specific facts about the AIDS situation in France. Moreover, such discourse recognizes long-standing sexual stereotypes and presents French gay sexual identity in relation to French sexual practices.

Similarly, *Têtu* notes the sexual appetite of the French in a July–August 1996 article entitled "Destinations Gay . . ." (Gay destinations . . . not always so new or exciting) with reference to gay men who convene in vacation spots that adopt a "vague English creole." The article offers information to help gay French travelers recognize other French men as well as international travelers. As French men are described (75), "Français: Reconnaissable de (très)

loin, les Français ont une mauvaise réputation qu'ils semblent cultiver à plai-
sir. . . . Pratiques sexuelles odieuses" (The French: Recognizable from [very]
far away, the French have a bad reputation which they seem to cultivate with
pleasure. . . . Odious sexual habits).

That stereotypical representation evokes a negative reputation of the
French on many levels not limited to gay men. The representation of a
Frenchman as possessing obnoxious and excessive sexual habits has a long
history. In *Disease and Representation,* for example, Sander Gilman discusses late-nineteenth-century German culture's construction of a Frenchman
as someone who represents sexual excess: "This is the German's caricature
of the sufferer as a fop, as a Frenchman, as the outsider already associated in
German myth with sexual excesses and deviancy" (1988, 250). The French gay
press, therefore, represents gay male identities in relation to—not at distance
from—mainstream social conventions, as Leap has shown in the American
context. Gay French text-making calls upon mainstream references and stereotypes about characteristics of French national culture and reappropriates
some in its representations of gay male identities.

The article on gay vacationers also distinguishes French identity from other
nationalities and their sexual identities. Again, these identities are defined in
relation to, and not at a distance from, national stereotypes. The British, for
example, are described on pages 72 through 75 as slightly "gras et humides"
(fat and sweaty) and with a taste for clothes made by obscure designers.
Moreover, they always seem to be distracted by a cricket game, drink luke-
warm beer, and participate in sexual habits that are "compulsives, frénétiques,
entachées de culpabilité" (compulsive, frenetic, marred by guilt). In addition,
Belgians and the Swiss are depicted as innocent and naive, easily confused
with "des Français de province" (provincial French). Like their unrefined,
naive cultural habits, their sexual habits are "traditionnelles et antiseptisées"
(traditional and antiseptic).

The allusions to such national identities within the French gay press resemble the stereotypes held by French society at large. The French joke regularly, for example, about Belgians as being naive and ignorant, even in regard to naïve sexual practices. A French comedian, Coluche, regularly made
fun of prostitutes, Belgians, and gays. For example, "A Belgian whore killed
herself. She had worked as a prostitute for a year in Paris when she discov-
ered that her sidewalk colleagues were getting paid" (July, Lanzmann, and
Joffrin 1986, 45).

The *Têtu* article also depicts the United States unfavorably through representations of Americans from gay urban areas. In New York City, for example, the diet for gay men includes doughnuts, pepperoni pizza, chili con

carne, Quarter-Pounders, Dr. Pepper, vitamins, and drugs of all kind. They use phrases like "Juan is horny" and "Special K, por favor," both references to sex and healthy food that suggest the important Latino influence in the city—specifically, the gay Latino community. A visitor to New York, however, would most certainly leave the city feeling "vidé, lessivé, amaigri, déprimé, ruiné" (drained, washed out, emaciated, depressed, ruined).

Since the age of industrialization the French have often regarded the United States—especially large cities such as New York and Chicago—as unfriendly, inhuman urban spaces. In his classic diatribe against the United States, *Scènes de la vie future,* Georges Duhamel describes Chicago as "La ville tumeur! La ville cancer! . . . Cette ville monstrueuse" (The tumerous city! The cancerous city! . . . That monstrous city) (1932, 102–3). Gay French cooperative discourse, therefore, uses long-standing national stereotypes and recontextualizes them for gay identity constructions.

Similar French cooperative discourse is also at work in other French cultural productions. Two twentieth-century titles of gay interest, for example, demonstrate cooperative French discourse that contains references to a larger French context. First, the title of Jean Genet's *Notre-Dame des fleurs* (1948), which chronicles the lives of several drag queens and the thieves and pimps they serve and adore, draws its name from Notre-Dame de Paris. Genet's choice of title is also reminiscent of Victor Hugo's nineteenth-century novel of the same name. In a sense, the choice of title delivers some cultural legitimacy and French authenticity to Genet that may have helped neutralize the criticism sparked by the sexually explicit nature of his novel.[13] The titles of Frédéric Martel's volume on the history of homosexuality in France, *Le rose et le noir* (The Pink and the Black), and Erik Rémès's gay popular novel *Je bande donc je suis* (I Get Hard, Therefore I Am) function in a similar manner. Martel freely adopted the title for his work from Stendahl's nineteenth-century novel *Le rouge et le noir* (The Red and the Black), whereas Rémès exploited a maxim of Descartes: "Je pense, donc je suis" (I think, therefore I am). The expression of gay experience in France, therefore, is often born out of the specifics of the nation's history, culture, or literature.

French cooperative discourse is also at work in a discussion of the domestic-partner bill, a draft of which appeared in *Têtu*'s January–February 1999 issue (49). Article 1 (515–1) of the bill classifies the types of individuals eligible for these rights. The document reads: "Un pacte civil de solidarité peut être conclu par deux personnes physiques de *sexe différent* ou *de même sexe* pour organiser leur vie commune" (A civil pact of solidarity may be determined by two people of *different sexes* or of *the same sex* in order to establish a common household) (emphasis added).

At first glance, the document may appear to offer the same types of equal rights set forth in such U.S. contexts as the Vermont legislation that offers civil-union partnerships to same-sex couples. This "discourse of inclusion," however, which takes into account couples of the same sex and different sexes remains quite French in that it closely resembles other discursive moments concerning civil rights legislation in France.[14] During the 1970s, for example, FHAR launched an antidiscrimination campaign that emphasized "le droit à la différence" (the right of difference) (Fillieule and Duyvendak 1999, 189). The French political culture demanded that FHAR posit its argument in the vague voice of universalism by generalizing the demand for difference to include other minorities. Consequently, FHAR's slogan evolved to include those who had fallen victim to a discriminatory society, which necessitated a second slogan: "Their struggle is our struggle." Thus any possible distinction was erased between FHAR's own struggle and those of other groups (Fillieule and Willem Duyvendak, 190).

SOS-Racisme, another French organization, launched a similar campaign during the 1980s to combat racism and anti-Arab sentiment by adopting a slogan identical to FHAR's: "droit à la différence" (Fillieule and Duyvendak 1999, 203). Thus, French cooperative discourse as seen in the example of the PaCS bill works "in relation to and not at a distance from a socially dominant discourse." I do not believe it coincidental that the PaCS bill was written in this manner, and, I would argue, its adoption is partially due to the document's use of the universal French language of sameness and inclusion. That is best summarized by Fillieule and Duyvendak: "The new movements not only formulate their demands in terms of the republican rhetoric of universalism and egalitarianism but also forge alliances with the dominant discourse of the older movements. In concrete terms, this prompted many new movements to seek the shelter of traditional leftist parties and movements in order to learn to speak the language of the left-wing political family" (1999, 187).

Conclusion

English lexical items are most present in the French gay press with regard to the discussion of consumer and mass-media culture. In particular, English appears in advertisements that deal with the leisure activities associated with a culture of sex and desire (bars, nightclubs, and saunas, for example). Moreover, gay English cooperative discourse appears in the discussions of HIV/AIDS education and safer sex as well as the discussion of gay and lesbian pride.

Nonetheless, gay French cooperative discourse is not merely a "vague

English creole." It may call upon a select English lexicon and other elements of gay English cooperative discourse, yet there are underlying and authentic French ways of articulating this French gay way of being. Indeed, U.S. models may help shape the politicization of the French gay movement, but French cooperative discourse is most useful in the expression of those equal rights, especially as seen in the discussion of the PaCS bill. The rhetoric found in the French gay press is based on a language that shows signs of an English influence rather than a creole of English tinged with a French accent. In other words, French gays may reach toward the global by adopting elements of English cooperative discourse in their discussion of individuality and sexual citizenship. They most often express this, however, through local cultural and political specificities: "The [French] gay and lesbian movement is not only dependent on the solidarity of social movements and other allies; it also has to 'fit' into the emancipation model used by other groups in [a specific] society recognized by authorities as valid and justified" (Adam, Duyvendak, and Krouwel eds. 1999, 349).

Certainly, France represents a nation of amalgamations of "diverse and contradictory" identities forged together over many centuries.[15] A multitude of migrations have occurred over several centuries that have left France a land of refuge and a melting pot of diverse cultures constituted by—but not limited to—North African and Asian immigrants as well as those from other European countries and Jews. Moreover, because of the European community, both external and internal factors help define the national identity as an ever-changing, dynamic space. Gay French identity and gay French cooperative discourse remain complex issues due to such cultural fluxes.

Future research will need to take into account the various identities and multiple discourses that persist on the French cultural landscape. Many factors related to the diversity of French cultural identities merit some attention. These include a cooperative expression of, first, difference due to race and ethnicity, especially for *maghrébins* and *beurs* (people of North African origins); second, regional differences and how local provincial issues interact with a hegemonic Parisian cultural presence; third, European influences, especially with regard to a European identity and the discussion of pride celebrations such as Europride that unite gay, lesbian, bisexual, and transgendered folk throughout Europe; fourth, French territorial differences, especially with regard to how French (gay) cooperative discourse interacts with the cultural and linguistic specificities of Martinique, Guadeloupe, and French Polynesia; fifth, differences related specifically to women (lesbians), bisexuals, and transsexuals within French GLBT communities; sixth, generational differences for French queer citizens; and, seventh, class differences, especially with regard to discrepancies in access to gay and lesbian cultural events and cultural productions. These seven elements are listed in order to initiate continued (and needed) research to help shed better light on the uniqueness of French gay cooperative discourse and experience and their relationship to gay English and other language-specific ways of being.

Notes

A version of this chapter was presented in September 1999 as part of the plenary session on "The Globalization of Gay English" at the seventh annual Conference on Lavender Languages and Linguistics held at American University in Washington, D.C. Several colleagues have read various drafts and offered helpful suggestions during both the conceptualization and rewriting of this chapter. In particular, I would like to thank Bill Leap, Vera Mark, Rudi Gaudio, and Jeff Maskovsky. I would also like to thank Luke Eilderts for his timely bibliographic work. A version of this essay has appeared under the same title in *Contemporary French Civilization* (Provencher 2002).

1. In the U.S. context, see Streitmatter (1995).

2. Indeed, the truth of this statement is tempered by issues such as class, ethnicity, and regional affinity. I return to this in the final section.

3. All translations are my own unless otherwise noted. For more on this issue, see also Minella and Angelotti (1996).

4. The editorial note in each issue of *Têtu* addresses both male and female readers. Nonetheless, the majority of articles and advertisements deal primarily with issues of gay male interest.

5. Lestrade also mentions the success of the gay press in Germany, Holland and Australia (Minella and Angelotti 1996, 114–15).

6. For more on the topic of sexual citizenship, see Brown (1997) and Stychin (1998).

7. Browning (1994) argues that gay male culture is based on elements of erotic desire.

8. The editorial staff selected three myths associated with gay American culture and published these images on three separate magazine covers for this special issue. These include sexually charged representations of a Native American chief, a football player, and a cowboy (reminiscent of the Marlboro Man), all of which help perpetuate stereotypes of U.S. gay culture as a culture of desire.

9. Talbot argues that a lack of face-to-face interaction between the producers of mass-media publications and their readers causes the producers to construct "an implied reader . . . as members of communities . . . represented . . . as a single 'community.'" Talbot examines the American publication, *Jackie,* which attempts to build a female teenage readership. *Jackie,* like all publications, makes use of strategies such as "synthetic personalization" and "simulation of friendship." These two techniques help create a sense of false sisterhood with a female reader and attract her to such publications. Their articles informally and directly address the reader in an inviting tone and friendly style (synthetic personalization). In turn, the magazine creates a false sense of belonging on the part of the reader (simulation of friendship). Talbot argues that women's publications such as

Jackie, which attempt to create sisterhood and community through a mass-media format, in fact forge synthetic and false sisterhood grounded in patriarchal and capitalistic consumer beliefs. Talbot recognizes the fact, however, that readers are not passive during reception of such information and are able to scan printed material critically. Nonetheless, Talbot contends that such media-constructed "consumer femininity intrudes into the subjectivities of women" and thus, on some level, influences individual self-image.

10. Lelait (1998, 37–43) discusses this mother-gay son attachment in his book chapter entitled "J'habite seul avec maman . . . Papa est en voyage d'affaires." He evokes a Freudian analysis to explain this close bond as a strong "feminine" identification with the mother, which, in turn, creates a sense of distance from and attraction to the father.

11. For approximately its first eighteen issues, *Têtu* provided an editorial baseline at the foot of each page. The editorial staff used the device to either summarize the content of a news article or react to the polemic content of that article in a humorous way. Pascal Loubet (1997) maintains that the baselines render the various ideological points of view presented in *Têtu* less polemic and help editors, writers, interviewees, and readers take themselves less seriously.

12. See, for example, volumes 6, 11, 13, and 19.

13. For more on the publication of *Notre-Dame des fleurs,* see White (1993) and Bullock and Provencher (2001).

14. Fillieule and Duyvendak (1999, 188) also note how *Arcadie,* the first publication that openly addressed the interests of French homosexuals during the 1950s, instructed them to behave as "normally" as possible.

15. See, for example, LeBras and Todd (1981), who question contemporary French identity in relation to its anthropological and political structure. See also Todd (1988) and Braudel (1986).

Works Cited

Adam, Barry D., Jan Willem Duyvendak, and André Krouwel, eds. 1999. *The Global Emergence of Gay and Lesbian Politics: National Imprints of a Worldwide Movement.* Philadelphia: Temple University Press.

Altman, Dennis. 1996. "Rupture or Continuity? The Internationalization of Gay Identities." *Social Text* 48 (Fall): 77–94.

———. 1997. "Global Gays/Global Gaze." *GLQ: A Journal of Gay and Lesbian Studies* 3: 417–36.

Arnal, Frank. 1993. "The Gay Press and Movement in France." In *The Third Pink Book,* ed. Aart Hendriks, Rob Tielman, and Evert van der Veen, 38–45. Buffalo: Prometheus Books.

Braudel, Fernand. 1986. *L'identité de la France.* Paris: Arthaud-Flammarion.

Brown, Michael P. 1997. *RePlacing Citizenship: AIDS Activism and Radical Democracy.* New York: Guilford Press.

Browning, Frank. 1994. *The Culture of Desire.* New York: Vintage.

Bullock, Barbara E., and Denis M. Provencher. 2001. "The Linguistic Representation of Masculinity and Femininity in Jean Genet's *Notre-Dame des fleurs.*" *French Cultural Studies* 12(1): 43–58.

Chesebro, James W., ed. 1981. *Gayspeak: Gay Male and Lesbian Communication.* New York: Pilgrim Press.

Duhamel, Georges. 1932. *Scènes de la vie future.* Paris: Mercure de France.

Fillieule, Olivier, and Jan Willem Duyvendak. 1999. "Gay and Lesbian Activism in France: Between Integration and Community-Oriented Movements." In *The Global Emergence of Gay and Lesbian Politics: National Imprints of a Worldwide Movement,* ed. Barry D. Adam, Jan Willem Duyvendak, and André Krouweled, 184–213. Philadelphia: Temple University Press.

"Gay Destinations . . . Not Always So New or Exciting." 1996. *Têtu* (July–Aug.): 66–75.

Gilman, Sander. 1988. *Disease and Representation: Images of Illness from Madness to AIDS.* Ithaca: Cornell University Press.

July, Serge, Jacques Lanzmann, and Laurent Joffrin. 1986. *Coluche: C'est l'histoire d'un mec.* 1919. Reprint. Paris: Éditions Solar.

Kuhn, Raymond. 1995. *The Media in France.* London: Routledge.

Lavisse, Ernest. [1916] 1919. *Histoire de France: Cours élémentaire,* ed. Marguerite Clément and Teresa Macirone. Boston: D. C. Heath.

Leap, William L., ed. 1995. *Beyond the Lavender Lexicon: Authenticity, Imagination, and Appropriation in Lesbian and Gay Languages.* Newark: Gordon and Breach.

———. 1996. *Word's Out: Gay Men's English.* Minneapolis: University of Minnesota Press.

Lelait, David. 1998. *Gayculture.* Paris: Anne Carrière.

Le Bras, Hervé, and Emmanuel Todd. 1981. *L'Invention de la France: Atlas anthropologique et politique.* Paris: Librairie Générale Française.

Loubet, Pascal. 1997. Interview by author. Paris, France, 8 May.

Lumby, Malcolm E. 1976. "Code Switching and Sexual Orientation: A Test of Bernstein's Sociolinguistic Theory." *Journal of Homosexuality* 1(4): 383–99.

Macey, David. 1993. *The Lives of Michel Foucault.* London: Hutchinson.

Martel, Frédéric. 1996. *Le rose et le noir: Les homosexuels en France depuis 1968.* Paris: Éditions du Seuil.

Minella, Alain-Gilles, and Philippe Angelotti. 1996. *Générations Gay.* Paris: Éditions Durocher.

Morgan, Maryllena, ed. 1994. *Language and the Social Construction of Identity in Creole Situations.* Los Angeles: Center for AfroAmerican Studies, UCLA.

Ozouf, Mona. 1995. *Les mots des femmes.* Paris: Librairie Arthème Fayard.

Provencher, Denis M. 2002. "Vague English Creole: (Gay English) Cooperative Discourse in the French Gay Press." *Contemporary French Civilization* 26(1): 86–110.

Ringer, R. Jeffrey, ed. 1994. *Queer Words, Queer Images.* New York: New York University Press.

Rosario, Vernon. 1993. "Sexual Liberalism and Compulsory Heterosexuality." *Contemporary French Civilization* 16: 262–79.

Sassen, Saskia. 1998. *Globalization and Its Discontent.* New York: New Press.

Streitmatter, Rodger. 1995. *Unspeakable: The Rise of the Gay and Lesbian Press in America.* Boston: Faber and Faber.

Stychin, Carl F. 1998. *A Nation by Rights: National Cultures, Sexual Identity, and the Discourse of Rights.* Philadelphia: Temple University Press.

Talbot, Mary. 1995. "A Synthetic Sisterhood: False Friends in a Teenage Magazine." In *Gender Articulated: Language and the Socially Constructed Self,* ed. Kira Hall and Mary Bucholtz, 146–61. New York: Routledge.

Todd, Emmanuel. 1988. *La nouvelle France.* Paris: Seuil.

White, Edmund. 1993. *Genet: A Biography.* New York: Alfred A. Knopf.

Zemouri, Aziz. 1995. *"Têtu* et fier de l'être." *Le Nouvel Observateur,* 22 June, 22.

2. Qwir-English Code-Mixing in Germany: Constructing a Rainbow of Identities

HEIDI MINNING

Sind wir homosexuell
Oder schon schwul?
Oder bereits gay?
Haben manche schon den Olymp erreicht und sind queer?
Oder qwir?

(Are we homosexual?
Or already 'schwul'?
Or even gay?
Have some of us reached Olympus and are queer?
Or qwir?)

—Markus Hagel

The questions in the epigraph are taken from the heading of a short news item in *Sergej,* one of Berlin's free monthly gay magazines. The author teasingly poses them by way of leading into an announcement for a twelve-week "Qwir-Culture" course conducted by the locally well-known *Dampfbadtunte* (steambath queen) Ovo Maltine. Attendance at various theme evenings on such topics as exhibitionism, flagellation, transsexuality, and perversion leads to a "Queer-Sex-Diplom" (queer sex diploma). The tone is unmistakably camp and ironic, not the serious growl of someone debating the relative merits of a local *schwul* (gay) identity movement, globalization of Anglo-American gay culture, or queer power.

But the use of terms such as *homosexuell, schwul, gay,* and *queer* carries the weight of ideological tensions few readers would miss. Why does the author use this particular mixture and sequence of words, some of which are English and others German? I will discuss linguistic strategies involving the use of English among German-speakers in various queer communities of practice in Berlin, Germany. To do so, I will consider text from spoken and printed sources and its pragmatic significance for speakers within discourse contexts and then apply the analytic framework of code-switching/mixing versus borrowing to consider the broader sociopsychological implications such language use may have for those who employ it.

Gay and Lesbian Identity Marking and German to English Code-Mixing

People with social contacts in schwul and *lesbisch* (lesbian) "communities of practice" in the sense of Eckert and McConnell-Ginet (1992, 1995) are exposed to, and frequently adopt, a wide set of linguistic and symbolic resources, many of which are clearly traceable to Anglo-American sources. Such resources contribute to a style German-speakers use to identify themselves as gay, lesbian, or one of an array of nonheterosexual identities. I refer to this style of speech as "lavender German" and use "lavender-German code-mixing" to refer to any use of English or German to convey gay, lesbian, queer, trans, or bisexual meaning that takes place in contexts where German is the primary (host or matrix) language. That includes words, concepts, and practices borrowed from English-speaking sources as well as related symbolic resources that contribute to that meaning. Such queer text-makers in Germany rely heavily upon "queered" language from international sources (especially English, French, and Latin) as they create and express local meanings. The result is a richly expressive language that contributes to a sense of transnational identity at the same time it strengthens local, community-based identities. I use the expression *lavender English* (or *lavender language*) to refer to expressions nonheterosexual individuals use in English-speaking settings to create gay, lesbian, or queered text—in this case, ones appropriated and/or adapted for use in German contexts.

In addition to printed sources, I will discuss examples of English use I encountered during participant observation and while conducting conversational interviews with a hundred people in Berlin who are members of long-term, committed, same-sex relationships.[1] All of them self-identify as schwul or lesbisch in at least some contexts, and some also as *bisexuell* (bisexual) or queer. The topic of the interviews was how partners are integrated into family relationships, but many other issues flowed into the conversations. Stories about coming out and developing partner relationships were nearly always shared as necessary background information for stories about meetings between partners and family members.

It is from this context that I will report on several roles that English plays in the language strategies of people in this group. The frequency and variety of English use seems related to how involved people were in gay and lesbian communities of practice and followed a similar pattern for lesbians and gay men, despite some differences in specific expressions and topics. In using the term *lavender* to discuss features that apply to both, I do not intended to downplay or discount differences between lesbian and gay men's language with regard to other features.

Identity Politics: Out and Proud

During the interviews, which lasted between one and five hours and averaged about ninety minutes, I purposely avoided using code-mixed or identity-specific terminology as much as possible in order to hear what categories were important to the people being interviewed and to find how local people described them. Probably no single word, phrase, or topic from English is used as often in German gay and lesbian communities as "coming out." Virtually every interviewee mentioned this topic, using the English loanword *coming out* as a compound substantive or with morphologically assimilated forms of the reflexive verb *sich outen* (to out oneself). Even those who said they had no coming out experiences considered it significant to supply information about the topic.[2]

The level of English-borrowing is related to discourse topics and is very common when people are talking or writing about aspects of gay and lesbian life related to public image and rights. The expression *coming out,* for example, features prominently in a cover story about the public visibility of gays and lesbians in Germany that appeared in 1998 in Berlin's leading gay and lesbian monthly magazine, *Siegessäule.* Here "coming out" is used to refer to the multilayered sense of acknowledgment of homosexuality, both toward oneself and in public. Code-mixing, in the form of lexical insertions borrowed from English, is unusually frequent, with eight instances on the first page alone. Specific examples are the terms *Happy-Homo-Welle* (happy homo wave), *Lifestyle-Schwule* (lifestyle gays), *Trend-Lesbe* (trend lesbian), *Talkshows, Pink Power,* "out and proud," *Out-Sein* (being out), and *das Outing.* Such frequency indicates how prominent borrowing is in framing topics of this type.

Another topic of almost universal interest to interviewees was the annual Christopher Street Day (CSD), the pride celebrations and parades held in most cities. In Berlin, it drew three hundred thousand people to the streets in 1998. It is a local event that draws attention to being part of a movement which extends beyond city and national boundaries, even if not all participants are fully aware of the Stonewall riots or the origin of the name.[3] Several couples I interviewed had met at the CSD, and it formed an important part in the social lives of many others. Herbert, for example, a twenty-five-year-old architecture student, had been the youth group coordinator for Christopher Street Day events in his home city before he moved to Berlin. He described how he and his partner had decided to hold a commitment ceremony as part of their participation in preparations for that year's CSD.

Es war, es war einfach so, daß wir generell, ich glaub, es war auch CSD, der CSD der Anlaß, und, es wurden natürlich immer wieder viel über die Homoehe diskutiert, und, wir hatten halt so auch überlegt, wie sieht das denn aus, möchten wir eigentlich mal heiraten, irgendwann, weil wir merkten so, wir sind sehr, sehr eng verbunden. Und, ich glaub das war sogar bevor noch zusammengezogen sind. Und, dann dachten wir uns, Hochzeit funktioniert halt nicht in Deutschland, das geht nicht, und, ja, jetzt nach Schweden oder sonstwohin, nach Dänemark zu fahren, das ist halt ja sinnlos, weil es hier eh nicht anerkannt wird und wegen der Zeremonie, hatten wir uns dann halt diese Verlobung ausgedacht. Wir wollten schon irgendwo nach außen auch ganz deutlich machen, wir beide gehören zusammen, wir stehen zu, zueinander und wir möchten gerne alle unsere Freunde so und Bekannten an unserem Glück teilhaben lassen.

It was, it was simply the case that we, generally, I think, it was also the CSD, the CSD was the occasion, and naturally there was a lot of discussion, again and again, about "gay marriage" and we started considering what it would look like, do we actually want to get married, sometime. Because we noticed, ah, that we are very, very closely connected. And, I think that was even before we moved in together. And then we thought, marriage won't work here in Germany, that's not possible. And well now, going to Sweden or anywhere else, say, to Denmark, that is senseless, because it isn't recognized here, and because of the ceremony, we thought up this betrothal idea. We wanted to make it perfectly clear to the outside world that we belong together, that we stand by each other, and we would like to share our joy with our friends and acquaintances.

The Christopher Street Day committees to which Herbert and his partner belonged served as communities of practice in which a discourse of *Homoehe* (gay marriage) had come to challenge heterosexual hegemony in this area of social life and therefore encouraged the formulation of plans to become *Verlobt* (betrothed). The committees serve a cultural entity in which new conventions are established and where conditions are forged for the felicitous performance of same-sex unions.[4]

The lack of English code-switch with regard to the commitment ceremony shows a preference for appropriating, or queering, terminology from heterosexual German. It is *Verlobung* (engagement, betrothal), for example, rather than "commitment ceremony," a political stance also reflected in the use of the word *Homoehe*. The point of the ceremony, as Herbert says, is to make a clear public statement that he and his partner "belong together," so it would be self-defeating to use an imported word that many of the two hundred guests would not have understood, especially the heterosexual ones.

Where a strategy of appropriation and queering of heterosexual meaning is being carried out, borrowing is avoided; speakers do not necessarily choose to code-switch from straight German terminology to an unambiguously queer language use that English would signal. This is not to deny that such borrowing is sometimes used in mixed contexts where queer and non-queer people interact but that it may serve a different pragmatic function in many such instances.

Indirectness

After group identity-marking, the second pragmatic function involving code-mixing is that it also participates in a strategy of indirectness. Rudy Gaudio observes in connection with the Hausa-speaking *yan daudu* (men who talk and act like women) that the use of *habaici* (innuendo) and *karin magana* (proverbs) are instances of indirect speech used to breach "socially and/or personally sensitive subjects that most other Hausa speakers would rather not discuss" (1998, 416). Code-mixed expressions appear to lend themselves to this use because people may not perceive them as being as transparent or direct as words that have the same meaning in their first language. That is particularly the case if these words are associated with negative evaluation or have been used as slurs and insults, as have schwul and lesbisch in Germany.

An example of one type of indirectness was described by Betty, a twenty-nine-year-old professional musician from East Berlin who, after many years of non-lesbian-identified, same-sex relationships, has joined with a partner, Jeanette, who is very involved in queer and lesbian activism. Now Betty is finding her way toward adopting a lesbian identity, both for herself and in ways that affect her relationship with her daughter and parents. She has told me that the topic of being lesbian was never discussed explicitly with her family of origin, despite the fact that she had a live-in lover for several years in their house. Her parents have never used the word *lesbian*. When I asked whether she had used it with them, she hedged and replied that she was able to convince her father to make a donation to the CSD.

B: Na ja und da gibt es Berührungsän-ste zu sagen "meine Tochter lebt so und so." Ich glaube auch nicht dass sie das Wort *lesbisch* schon mal im Mund genommen hat. Kann ich mich eigentlich nicht daran erri-nern.

H: Und du? Bei ihr?

B: Ich bei ihr, ja, ja, na ja, ich habe meinem Vater sogar dazu gekriegt dass er für den CSD hundert Mark spendet . . . [laughs] das fand ich ziemlich gut.

B: So of course there are the fears to say "My daughter lives so and so." I don't believe that she has ever tak-en the word *lesbian* into her mouth. Or at least I can't remember it.

H: And you, in her presence?

B: And I in her presence, hm, hm, well, I even got my father so far that he donated 100 DM [$75] for the CSD [Christopher Street Day parade] . . . [laughs] that was good.

Here, like euphemism, ellipsis, and frequent use of modal auxiliaries, En-glish code-mixing with the expression *CSD* has become part of Betty's prag-matic strategy of indirectness to mitigate the presentation of a lesbian self to her parents. Lesbianism is a taboo subject in this family, as Betty empha-sized repeatedly in our interview and during other conversations. Therefore, to mention it to her (powerful) parents would represent a potentially "face threatening act" (FTA) (Brown and Levinson [1978] 1987). This indirectness is an example of what Brown and Levinson call "negative politeness" in that it is a behavior aimed not at interfering with a hearer's face wants. In more general terms, one could say that it allows people in powerful positions to save face. In contrast, the practice of employing in-group codes with inter-action partners uses a "positive politeness" in which positive face needs of people are recognized and a sense of belonging is strengthened. Thus it is not surprising to find gays and lesbians using strategies of indirectness toward unsympathetic individuals or in potentially threatening public contexts.

Betty's eight-year-old daughter, Isabelle, however, has no problem using these words, code-mixed or otherwise. Betty was clearly very proud when she told me how her daughter had raised her hand during an exercise in school that involved drawing a family tree. She asked the teacher if she could include her mother's girlfriend (and son) because "wir sind eine lesbische Familie" (we are a lesbian family).

B: Ja sie hat ja Überhaupt kein Problem damit. Es ist für sie normal und sie nimmt die Wörter in den Mund und sie war im CSD und hat erzählt darüber hier und da, ah,

B: Yes. For her, it is just no problem at all. It is normal for her, and she takes the words in her mouth and she was at the CSD and told about it all over, ah,

H: [Laughs.]

B: da habe ich gedacht, da hat die MUT die Kleine! Daß hätte ich ihr nicht zugetraut, daß sie so offensiv damit umgeht, aber ist halt so ihre Familie, mit Jeanette und Igor . . .

H: [Laughs.]

B: and I thought, boy, she's got COURAGE, that little one! I wouldn't have put it past her, that she deals with it so offensively. But it is her family, after all, with Jeanette and Igor . . .

Betty explained how courageous she found her daughter. "For her," she said, "it is just no problem at all. It is normal for her, and she takes the words in her mouth and she was at the CSD and told everyone about it all over." She emphasized her concern that Isabelle might not be able to assess the possible negative consequences of telling people that her mother is lesbian. Such awareness also reflects her cautious course of identity development.

In considering instances of how the phrase *Christopher Street Day* lends itself to different pragmatic strategies, it becomes clear that much more in the way of shared knowledge, attitudes, and experience is involved in creating gay or lesbian meaning with lavender language. Knowing when and how to use a set of borrowed words and expressions is only one small part of achieving communicative competence. Herbert and Betty participate in gay and lesbian communities in very different ways, and they also present their sexual identities differently. That is evident in their use of lavender languages. Betty's daughter, in turn, a "founding member" of a new generation of lavender-language-speakers, has begun to "creolize" its use by extending it beyond the original community of users. The topic for lavender-language research will be promising as the queer baby boom provides more and more sources of data.

Mixed Pragmatic Function

In the program for the month of November 1998 at the Berliner Sonntags-Club, the oldest organization for gays and lesbians to have originated in the former German Democratic Republic, indirectness and group identity strategies are used simultaneously. Specialty evenings are advertised for various groups. One for transsexuals, for example, includes the viewing of a film entitled *Picket Fences,* a gay and lesbian youth disco evening is entitled "Westend Girls and Boys," erotic massage for men is labeled "erotic touch," and an evening of card playing is referred to as being for "playing girls." There is also a "Französische Nacht" (French night) for women only and with a *chambre noir* (darkroom), and a "body night" is held for men, with a "safer-sex party" presented by the "Gaywatch-Team." Here English and French are used to construct a "tasteful" yet explicit account of the activities offered at the club (which is in large part funded by the state). Such usage illustrates that strategies of group membership and indirectness are not mutually exclusive and that use of various lavender-language codes may serve more than one social goal simultaneously. This calls to mind the "simultaneity" Kathryn Woolard (1999) has discussed regarding bilingual Catalan/Castilian radio broadcasts.

One example where a borrowed lexical item simultaneously serves diverse pragmatic strategies is the use of the word *queer*. As an identity marker, its content signifies a challenge to traditional sexual norms, yet as a somehow technical-sounding foreign word its form also signals an indirectness far removed from the shock effect the word may have for some English-speakers. Perhaps this versatility has encouraged the use of the word in printed texts, such as in a booklet—*Absolut Queer*—the Sonntags-Club published to commemorate its twenty-five years of activism. As such, the group claims as "queer" a movement that began in the former G.D.R. during the 1970s, when the club began meeting covertly. Perhaps no single institution in Berlin can lay as solid a claim to being a staunch proponent of queer activism as this group. It is one of very few places in the city—if not the only place—where people of all gender and sexual configurations are actively encouraged to gather.

Direct references to queerness were rare during interviews, which may be related to the specific people I was able to contact. One very involved lesbian activist, Lila, made reference to a "queer party" and said she explains to colleagues at the pharmaceutical firm where she works that the rainbow flag on her desk stands for "queer nation." The disclosure process she reports using is reminiscent of "scaffolding," a language practice described in acquisition literature as a strategy that fluent speakers of a given language variety use to introduce new terminology to those unfamiliar with it. Those who are fluent move from simple, familiar concepts to more complex new ones. In effect, scaffolding moves from implicit ways of disclosing potentially threatening information toward more explicit ones. As Lila says:

Und dann dachte ich, na ja die Heteros machen das ja eigentlich auch so. Die stellen sich auf den Schreibtisch ein Bild von . . . wenn es ein Mann ist, ihrer Ehefrau, wenn es eine Frau ist ihrem Mann oder ihr Kind oder was auch immer. Also sie, tragen ja auch praktisch Zeichen mit sich rum, daß sie heterosexuell sind. Also mache ich	And then I thought, yeah, well, the heteros do it like that, too. They put photos on their desks . . . if it's a man, then of their wives, if it's a woman, then of her husband or her child or whatever. That is, they carry signs around with them, that they are heterosexual. So I do it with signs, too. Why should I tell everyone, what's go-

das auch über Zeichen. Weswegen soll
ich allen Leuten erzählen, wie es gerade
in meinem Privatleben aussieht. Und
deswegen habe ich halt Regenbogen-
fähnchen gehängt. Und das ging gut.
Die Leute haben zum Teil gefragt, wo-
für das steht. Dann habe ich gesagt,
"Das ist für Queer (?) Nation" und habe
dann noch erklärt was Queer ist. Ein
Arzt wurde zum Beispiel rot und sagte,
"Da sind Sie also 'lesbisch'[?]" Da sagte ich: "Ja!"

ing on in my private life. And that's
why I have hung up a rainbow flag [in
her office] and that went well. Some
people asked what it stands for. Then
I said, "That is for queer (?) nation"
and then explained what queer is. One
doctor got red, for example, and said,
"So then you [formal] are 'lesbian'[?]"
And I said: "Yes!"

The scaffold begins with the nonthreatening symbol, the rainbow flag,
moves forward with the use of a loanword *queer* (after which the transcriber placed a question mark because he did not understand quite what was
meant), and finally moves to a more explicit discourse regarding her sexual
orientation when the colleague asks, "So then you [formal] are 'lesbian'?"
One advantage of this strategy is that it allows the interlocutor to participate
in regulating how explicit the discourse will become. This segment of the
conversation shows just how different the effect of the term *queer* is in a
German-language context compared to the provocative force it carries for
many English-speakers.

In contrast, when used in primarily gay or lesbian contexts the word *queer*
is an unambiguous marker of nonstraight identities. In most German uses I
encountered, "queer" is used as a shorthand form of "gay, lesbian, bisexual,
and transgendered" and is less often intended to be a challenge to the essentialized binary underpinnings of homo/hetero sexual categorization. *Queer,*
for example, is published in Cologne and has four regional editions. With a
circulation of about seventy thousand, it may be Germany's largest nonhet-
ero publication. It calls itself "Die Monatszeitung für Schwule und Lesben"
(the monthly newspaper for gays and lesbians).

Homosexual? Gay? Lesbian? Queer?

It would appear that some sort of reassessment of gay and lesbian identity
politics is underway, because the word *queer* is borrowed and used in prominent positions in the press and for political organizing. In academic circles,
queer theory is making the rounds, as the title of a symposium that took place
in Berlin in 1998 would indicate: "Queering Demokratie." The word *queer*
is used productively not only as a substantive and adjective but also, in some

contexts, as an unassimilated gerund. In some instances the local construct of queer seems to coexist with notions of schwul and lesbisch, and with less tension than often found in the United States. Many people I interviewed in Berlin, both men and women, assumed that sexuality and gender are traits with which they were born. Few appeared to assume the meanings attributed to physical traits are social in origin rather than naturally predetermined. For them, "queer" signifies a cool new term for ways they may feel different from social norms. That "coolness" is the butt of the irony used in the passage from Markus Hagel in this essay's epigraph.

Hagel is playfully bantering with identity labels as he asks, Are we homosexual, "schwul," gay, or queer? He uses an inclusive first-person plural *wir* (we) meant to refer to himself and his readers as a collective. As Mühlhäusler and Harré (1990, 178) have pointed out, "One of the most prominent features of *we* has been its use to signal group indexicality. By selecting *we* rather than another pronominal form a speaker introduces a bond with his/her interlocutors." Hagel is not only referring to the bonds of an existing community but also using language that is part of the practice that creates a sense of community.

Hagel defines the collective and the fact that three of five adjectives used to focus the indexical reference of "we" stem from English: queer, gay, and qwir. It is no coincidence that he begins with the term *homosexuell*, which most contemporary gay men in Germany reject as being old-fashioned and somehow associated with pathologizing same-sex erotic behaviors—or at least putting them in a scientific, analytic category. Schwul (generally glossed as "gay"), however, is likely to be the term of choice for young male readers now and can be considered the "unmarked" label for them.[5] It is ubiquitous in the gay press and in general use, and some standard reference works point out that the term *schwul* is used by gays to refer to themselves (Skinner 1997). Yet Hagel offers three more categories, implying with repeated use of "already" that readers who have not yet moved on to one of them risk being thought less than cool. Referring to the epitome of coolness as Mount Olympus, however, Hagel uses irony to play along with the imported notions of gay and queer and also defang them, making a further joke by irreverently positioning the nonsense queered form, "qwir," at the end of the sequence.

Other people sympathetic to the life-style and political agendas of gay men adopt the word *schwul*, whereas more critical or distanced speakers prefer the term *homosexuell*. Gay men appear aware that adopting such usage of schwul, which has been and continues to be used as a slur and insult, may help carve out a social niche and be a useful tool in fighting discrimination. Germany's strongest gay rights organization calls itself the Schwulenverband, for exam-

ple, and the usage may be related to a pattern initiated by U.S. gay and lesbian pride movements (D'Emilio 1983). German-speakers may use "gay" and
"queer" as part of this confrontational strategy, but they do not, as "foreign"
words, have the same power to shock as does "queer" for some speakers of
English or "schwul" for some German-speakers.

Selling Goods and Services to Queers

Advertisements for sexual and erotic products and services represent the
heaviest concentration of English use in German advertising. The pages of
telephone sex advertisements in *Siegessäule* consist of nearly equal tokens of
English and German language, with attention-getting running headlines in
English dominating the format. Not a single advertisement on a representative page fails to make prominent use of English. One full-page notice for a
cruising bar in Hamburg reads "MALE, men, action, fun, cruising, blue movie,
bar, enjoyment" in large, bold print. The address and Web-site are given in
small print at the bottom, and a tiny notice in the top border of the adver-
tisment reads "Neu: täglich geöffnet von 20.00 bis 04.00 uhr" (new: open
daily from 8 P.M. to 4 A.M.). Once again, only the essential information in the
advertisement is in German. The prominent, attention-getting parts are in
English, borrowings that are part of the basic repertoire of loanwords commonly used by lavender-German text-makers.

German lesbian language of the erotic is no less enriched by borrowings
from English as well as French and Latin, as analysis of two (not entirely randomly selected) pages from *Lauras Animösitäten und Sexkapaden: Das Lesbische Sexwörterbuch* (The Lesbian Sex Dictionary) show (Mérrit 1994). A
wide range of expressions humorously defined appear on those pages. Mérrit, a Berlin author who is also a linguist and an activist for sex workers, includes English borrowings, from "community" to "cunt." Not a single key
word defined on the two pages is of German origin, and nearly half the words
throughout the book are of non-German origin. Alignment with an international lesbian sexual emancipation movement is intentional and highlighted symbolically; photographs on the first and last pages depict "Laura"
draped in an EU flag and posed like the Statue of Liberty.

The global nature of the AIDS epidemic is also expressed by code-mixed
warnings in every gay periodical to practice safer sex (which has become the
official term used in anti-AIDS campaigns aimed at German gays). Very likely
this social field also encourages English-language use in its guise as an international medium for scientific exchange.

Products and services related to the sexual and erotic activities of queer people (e.g., gay bars, lesbian escorts) are easily recognizable to their target population whereas more neutral products and services such as automobiles, cigarettes, insurance, or beer, must establish an image for themselves as gay- or lesbian-friendly by means of advertising. The strategies of code-mixing in this field, therefore, can be expected to function differently.

The use of English loanwords and mixings during conversation and in the press is shaped by (and shapes) the discourse content and how individuals display their alignment with identities based on sexual orientation. In advertising, however, these same expressions function as signifiers of queerness along with symbols such as pink triangles and rainbows or photographs of same-sex couples or famous gay or lesbian people. These signifiers participate in the semiotic construction of queer-friendly product images. As in the United States, the goods and service sections of guidebooks and magazines are sometimes labeled to the effect of "keep it in the family," and much effort is made to encourage same-sex-identified people to patronize gay or lesbian businesses by calling them family businesses. The connection is also overtly made in the German media by referring to *Familie* (family) in newspaper and magazine headings dealing with services and products or by referring to "community," using code-mixed English (which is unambiguously queer and therefore an item I would classify as lavender German). The (straight) German term for community, *Gemeinde,* is not used in these contexts.

In describing developments of gay and lesbian activism in France, Olivier Fillieule and Jan Willem Duyvendak have observed, "As subcultures become increasingly *commercialized,* many gay organizations can survive only by becoming more pleasure oriented and less political. Gay journals in particular will show a tendency toward commercialization, by publishing more erotic material and less political information" (1999, 185). Language participates in this tendency, which can also be recognized in the patterns surrounding code-mixing. Terms such as *community* and *identity,* culled from the North American and British gay and lesbian political identity movements (Adam, Duyvendak, and Krouwel eds. 1999; D'Emilio 1983), are enlisted for commercial purposes and fill advertising for automobiles, beer, insurance, clothes, and a wide array of consumer goods and services. In turn, the use of these items becomes a new vehicle for creating and maintaining gay and lesbian identity. Using an advertising strategy analogous to that of drawing potential consumers' interest by means of riddles and puzzles, gay and lesbian consumers are encouraged to position themselves as gay or lesbian subjects if they are to appreciate the full meaning of an advertisement that uses lavender-German code-mixing or other indexes of queerness.

There is nothing inherently gay or lesbian about an automobile or an insurance policy, but drawing on Judith Williamson's analysis of ideology and meaning in advertising, an intuitive volume entitled *Decoding Advertising* (1978; cf. Bignell 1997), I would suggest that such indexing through gay-language code-mixing shows that advertisers are drawing on a familiar referent system by using lavender language as a sign. An example of this is a lavender-English–English code-mixed advertisement that appeared in *The Advocate,* one of the most widely circulated national gay and lesbian magazines in the United States. The following descriptions were prominently displayed around pictures of a vehicle: "comfortable with its orientation," "very secure with its identity," and "universally appealing." The text invited readers to substitute their personal needs for characteristics ostensibly attributed to the product, with words such as *orientation* and *identity* indexing a specifically gay or lesbian meaning.

The same technique, and even the same words, are used in lavender German as well. The all-gay German corporation Pride Company, for example, is located in Cologne and uses English expressions in German-language advertising and in the names of the company's divisions. The text of an advertisement for their insurance services reads:

LIFE IS IDENTITY. Für die Sicherheit der COMMUNITY (for the security of the community).

Jan Bommer, in charge of Pride Consulting, studied economics in New York before joining with Michael Adamcziak and Jutta Lau to found Pride Telecom. Among their enterprises are Pride Collection (fashions), Pride Finance, Pride Entertainment, Pride Images (advertising), Pride Internet Services, Pride Online, and Pride Travel. In each case, the businesses are named by English terms. This marketing device works not only to sell products that have meaning but also to encourage potential consumers to adopt self-images as being members of a unified and proud gay, lesbian, or queer global community.

It is impossible to assess exactly how much influence such language use might have on the formation of a sense of community and identity. Given the prioritized role of consumption and accumulation of goods in capitalist societies, however, it is safe to say that the prominent market positioning of lavender German offers significant validation of gay and lesbian lifestyles, not only for those involved in subversive movements but also for people who consider themselves part of traditionally powerful mainstream social groups. Whatever the social implications, there is no doubt that lavender German is a salient feature of marketing strategies aimed at queer members of the population, which I take as evidence of its increased value (capital) on the linguistic market (Bourdieu 1991).

Code-Mixing or Borrowing?

In describing how lavender English is used by German-speakers who participate in queer communities of practice, I have referred to borrowing English terms and code-mixing from German to lavender German. The distinction may not be clear to many, nor may it be immediately apparent why I think it is relevant. Some observations are necessary about whether to call the phenomenon in question borrowing, code-mixing (CM), or code-switching (CS).[6]

Bhatia and Ritchie (1996) provide four criteria for distinguishing between borrowing and CM or CS. According to this schema, borrowing has the following characteristics:

1. It has the linguistic function of filling a gap in the lexicon of a matrix language or as prompted by nonlinguistic features such as modernization or both;
2. It is restricted to specific lexical items of the matrix language;
3. It is assimilated into the matrix language by regular phonological and morphological processes of either the matrix or embedded language, and;
4. It is part of the lexicon of monolingual speakers as well as bilingual members of the community.

CM and CS in contrast:

1. Are motivated by sociopsychological factors such as social identity;
2. Do not restrict mixed items, which are chosen freely from both matrix and embedded languages;
3. Generally unassimilate the items to the phonological and morphological processes of the matrix language, and;
4. Are limited to bilinguals in the speech community.

The Linguistic Function of Borrowing

Most of the instances of English mixing/borrowing found in the body of some 150 hours of taped interviews, political and educational meetings, and family or couple interactions as well as from a selection of print materials from a four-month period in 1998 do not fill lexical gaps in the usual sense. Common lexical items such as "gay," "lesbian," "pride," "pink," or "orientation" are used alongside the existing expressions *schwul, lesbisch, stoltz, rosa,* or *Orientierung.* When an English expression is selected, it tends to index queer identity in a less ambiguous manner than when either expression is used in a monolingual matrix. That is, the use of "pink" for monolingual English-speakers exhibits bivalency in the sense of Woolard (1999) and multivocality in the Baktinian sense. A straight person may think of it as a just another color. As used in gay or lesbian text-making, however, it can index gay or lesbian identity. The same is true for the use of "rosa" in a monolingual German context. Yet the selection of "pink" in a German context is a robust index for queer meaning. A list of additional items and parallel German expressions can be found in the appendix.

A number of English expressions found in my research might be considered to fill lexical gaps: "queer," "hate crime," "commitment ceremony," "significant other," "straight," "crusing," and "safer sex." The use of these items, however, is fairly restricted to members of the gay and lesbian communities. For them, they may indeed represent instances of borrowing. A number of the terms are included as entries in German lexicons and dictionaries that focus on gay and lesbian words. In her lexicon of German expressions for lesbians, gays, homosexuality, Jody Skinner (1997) includes nine English words: "pink," "queer," "coming out," "call boy," "camp," "gay," "queen," "butch," and "boy." Ulf Meyer and Axel Schock (1996), in their travel aid that translates German gay-talk into English, Italian, French, Spanish, and Dutch, include other words and terms of gay-English origin: "safer sex," "skinheads," "cruising," "callboy," "coming out," "outing," "poppers," "darkroom," "jack-off party," and several dozen more specifically referring to sexual acts and objects. Only a few have crossed over into use among the general population: "party," "safer sex," "sich outen," and "coming out." All are nevertheless markers of identity for this group.

The questions arise of what constitutes a lexical gap and how (and when) such a category manifests in people's experience. Those who experience same-sex desire may perceive many such lexical gaps where straight people do not experience them. Moreover, these occur where lexical items exist but homosexuals are excluded from participating in their meaning, as in, for example, Herbert and his partner's use of "Verlobung." This is, of course, the lexical field where appropriation or queering takes place—itself a process of borrowing or mixing—but here "straight" words are borrowed to create "queer" meaning.

In this scheme, a gay and lesbian culture exists, with art, music, rituals, literature, ideologies, claims to physical and symbolic space, and people whose identities are intertwined with each other's. Some lexical gaps are jointly perceived by the members of this culture but not by straight or "normal" Germans. Unlike the problem of naming an imported item such as a non-native fruit or a new product of technology, the gaps are the result of developing awareness and ideology. The language that grows out of this need participates in the production of new need. Lavender-German borrowed English fills a lexical gap and is an identity marker.

A Restricted Set of Items

Although a core set of items is taken from Anglo-American sources, there are no limits on the items that serve as resources. In advertising and announcements aimed at gay and lesbian populations, for example, any number of English expressions and words participate in text-making. The announcement for the 1998 Gay Games in Amsterdam, for example, contained the English terms *opening* and *closing*. Moreover, nearly every telephone sex advertisement looked at in this study includes some item of English, not only drawing upon the closed set of commonly borrowed (identity-specific) sex terms but also on an open set of expressions used to index the advertisement as exotic, modern, youthful, and/or sophisticated.

Individual speakers and writers use this resource in different ways. Many who use it in creative ways that extend beyond individual lexical items have gained communicative competence in the use of lavender English in native settings. Several people I interviewed, for example, had lived in English-speaking countries or were active in international gay and lesbian or human rights organizations that use English as a lingua franca (e.g., the International Lesbian and Gay Association [ILGA] and Amnesty International). One company-owner who makes widespread use of English code-switching in his advertising studied economics in the United States. Several others were currently or had been in relationships with speakers of English. They mixed English in their language production in ways more prototypically considered code-mixing. They employed creative mixing, which, in turn, is likely a catalyst for introducing new terms (as borrowed elements or loanwords) into general queer community usage. Such words, however, remain foreign to those who do not participate in gay and lesbian communities of practice.

Economic factors limit the availability of translations of books and dubbed films that have gay and lesbian themes, forcing individuals who may not be fluent in English into contact with the language. Popular songs have long exerted a similar effect on young people, particularly gays and lesbians. This is another source for language contact and accounts for some elements of potential cultural diffusion.

Thus, for many gays and lesbians who do not speak English or participate in English-speaking communities of practice, the use of English may be limited to a finite set of words that have unambiguous queer meaning. For others, especially more active members of community and international groups, any aspect of English may be used as a resource for creating specifically gay or lesbian meaning in otherwise German-language contexts. Advertising and personal announcements are two contexts where this often occurs.

Phonological and Morphological Assimilation

Very few items have undergone assimilation in the matrix language, the most notable exception being outen, sich outen, *geoutet sein* (to out, to out one-self, to be outed), and the related expression *coming out*, which is borrowed only as a substantive and does not undergo morphological transformations. A number of expressions lend themselves to playful and creative construction of new lexemes, the most productive being "gay" and "queer." Queer is phonologically and semantically similar enough to the German word *quer* (across, going against) to be interchanged in order to produce creative new compounds—and it is well known that German-speakers enjoy making compounds. Some examples culled from the press are *Queer-schnitt* (queer/cross section) and *Queer-schläge* (queer/cross sections). "Gay" has proven an even more productive feature of lavender German as a phonological equivalent of the morphological marker -ge, used to construct participles and gerunds as in *gay-laufen* (gay-walk) instead of *ge-laufen* (walked).

Several expressions of English origin are also found as loan-shifters or calques (e.g., *Zwangsheterosexualität* [compulsory heterosexuality] and *tanz-tee* [tea dance]). In these cases a German translation is used instead of the imported word being retained. The meaning of such expressions may be more transparent to speakers as well as easier for them to pronounce. The tendency to integrate new terminology has traditionally been very strong and extends to much contemporary language. English and German words in particular seem to be competing in fields that deal with science and technology, where loan-shifters such as *Datenautobahn* and *Rechner* may be preferred over their English counterparts "information highway" and "computer."

By this measure, although there is some evidence of borrowing in the examples I have cited, by far most of the terms I encountered retain the phonological and morphological properties of their source language, which is evidence of mixing.

Monolingual Lexicon or Limited to Bilingual Use

Four populations have varying sets of linguistic varieties of interest in determining whether a term is in their lexicon: speakers of English, lavender English, German, and lavender German. Although German-speakers borrow and mix freely from English sources, they do not tend to have access to items stemming from lavender-English sources. Speakers of lavender German, however, have access to (and make active use of) both English and lavender English. Evidence can be found in margin notes made by non-gay German transcribers. Having asked them to mark text passages they did not understand, I found question marks on such expressions as *'n' Hete* (referring to heterosexuals); the word *straight,* as in *ganz streight* [*sic*] *Heterosexuell* (very straight heterosexual); and *queer, butch,* and *femme* when they appear in narratives. One transcriber wrote "ELGA" instead of "ILGA" (the International Lesbian and Gay Association) and "CFD" instead of "CSD," the abbreviation generally used in place of the cumbersome "Christopher Street Day."

For the monolingual transcribers (speakers of Standard German who have never participated in nonheterosexual communities of practice), such expressions are not accessible. For the gays and lesbians who use them regularly, however, they are part of active repertoires. Thus, members of German gay and lesbian culture who use terms from lavender English can be considered bilingual in the sense that they are fluent in both German and lavender German, even if they do not have direct access to lavender English or English. Lavender English is "borrowed" into lavender German. When speakers in the community employ it, that use constitutes a code-switch, not from German into English but from straight German into lavender German.

Why does it matter if this phenomenon is borrowing or code-switching? A strong case can be made that fundamental difference exists in the psychological reality underlying these two types of language use. Borrowing occurs when a large number of speakers finds a use for an expression, and it becomes incorporated in what may be perceived as "mono-lingual" lexica. Code-mixing or code-switching occurs when speakers make fluid use of two or more variants perceived to be different. For some populations, mixing and borrowing may not always be mutually exclusive categories. The analytic framework provided by borrowing and CM/CS alone may not be sensitive to the practices of specific cultural groups who share a matrix language but differ in terms of core issues of identity. When considered against the backdrop of communities of practice as described by Eckert and McConnell-Ginet (1992), however, these categories may offer insight into the relationship between how speakers convey messages and the various identity positions they occupy—who, that is, they are.

Ideologies Pertaining to English versus Lavender English as Resources for Speakers of Other Languages

Code selection has been shown to be sensitive to the context in which it is used, such as domain, activity type, networks, social roles, and discursive objectives. Examples from a variety of contexts experienced by the gay and lesbian population confirm this. Terminology is not borrowed indiscriminately from English but occurs systematically and involves the use of what some researchers have come to refer to as lavender English. It is important, however, to point out that it also intersects with language ideologies associated with the more general use of English arising from the social, political, economic, and cultural position of Germany relative to English-speaking countries. Most speakers from the former western part of Germany will have been involved in the use of English code-switching based on borrowing from British and North American pop culture, whether as a resource learned in school or a lingua franca while traveling abroad during business or academic exchange or perhaps from contacts with foreign visitors and occupation troops in Germany. English code-switching has come to be associated with *Jugendsprache* (youth language) and modernity, academic or erudite speech, and usage arising from professional activity such as international trade, or technical fields (e.g., information processing and telecommunications) (Clyne 1995; Stevenson 1995). Thus, age, educational level, and profession are the indicators of code-switching in Germany, most frequently consisting of lexical insertion such as "Wir hatten ein 'Agreement'" (we had an agreement) or formulaic borrowing (e.g., "as soon as possible").

In addition, several factors have spurred the proliferation of lavender English. The success of the gay and lesbian rights movement in the Anglo-American countries is an impressive model for continental communities. Germans were ready for such models, with the thriving sexuality rights movement of the 1920s under Magnus Hirschfeld destroyed and the entire queer population murdered or forced into hiding by Hitler and his supporters. Local activists also participate in international political and cultural activities for which English is the lingua franca, even among groups who do not speak it as a mother tongue. Now more than ever queer Europeans are willing to look beyond local borders for political and social recognition. German political leaders such as Volker Beck, the openly gay Green Party member of the Bundestag, call upon local and national legislative bodies to act on the European Parliament's mandate for equality based on sexual orientation.

Conclusion

From the ubiquitous use of the term *coming out* to "Christopher Street Day" as the name for gay pride celebrations, people who participate in various queer communities of practice make widespread but selective use of code-mixing, loanwords, and loan-shifters to create gay, lesbian, queer, trans- , and bisexual meaning. The resulting sociopsychological function is one of constructing group membership and a sense of the self as a participant in larger gay and lesbian local and transnational cultures. It is a use that does not supplant local traditions but draws upon transnational resources to create a sense of "we" that is distinct from straight and "normal" Germans. Seen not as a phenomenon where speakers of German as a matrix language use English-borrowing but as a case of German-matrix language-speakers drawing on lavender German, it is a case of identity-linked code-switching. Thus it signals a shift from what I have referred to as "straight" German to "lavender" German. In some cases the children of code-switching speakers acquire lavender German as their first language and "creolize" it, taking its use for granted in contexts outside queer communities of practice. That will most likely become more pervasive since enactment of the Eingetragene Lebenspartner Gesetz (Registered Life Partners Law) in August 2001, legislation that grants same-sex partners a marriagelike option for the legal recognition of their relationships. Follow-up research is needed to trace future developments.

In an attempt to formulate an more complete account of how English, as a component of lavender German, is used by this community, I have also examined instances where it is used in contexts where communication is not limited to members thought to belong to the community. In uncomfortable or uncertain situations, for example, self-identified gays and lesbians use lavender language as part of a pragmatic strategy of indirectness. In addition, advertisers use these words and expressions to index products and services as "community-friendly" and contribute to a commodification of queer identities.

English is also influenced by discourse content, with sex and the gay and lesbian social and political movements as the most common areas of social experience for mixing and borrowing. "Queer" and "queering" have become increasingly visible in language use and social assessment. That, too, is related to the two pragmatic strategies of identity-marking and indirectness.

The heteroglossic features of language use I have discussed constitute an example of systematic variation within a matrix language. They highlight the advantage of using a relatively detailed analysis of language as practiced in order to understand how social identities and language interact. Traditional, monolithic approaches to language, which deal with entities such as "German" and "English," are not sensitive to this type of variation. As an entity, lavender German may be an ideologically motivated construct, but then so is Standard German. Both are useful for pointing out social realities for the group of speakers for whom they serve as resources.

Appendix: Some Lexical Items Used during Lavender-German Text-Making

This is a list of some of the expressions involved in lavender-German code-mixing. I am much more interested in how these words are used than in compiling lists but have found it useful to focus on locating them in various contexts, whether in the queer press, at political debates or educational seminars, or during taped conversational interviews ranging from one to five hours. Asterisks indicate the expressions people used during interviews; brackets enclose German expressions I have not heard used in lavender German. There is also a repertoire of exclusively lavender-German words and expressions, such as *Klappe* (gay men's language for public toilets used for male/male sex) or *fummel* (drag). These words are italicized.

I. G/L/B/T Political and Identity Movement(s)

gay*	*Schwul**	Productive varient of *ge-* , which signifies the past participle (for example, instead of writing gay + *laufen,* gay + *sehen* an author writes *gaysehen*). Rendered by the letter *g* (*G Punkt*), which sounds like *gay* and is sometimes playfully substituted, as in *Ge* + *lüste* (desire, craving).
lesbian*	*Lesbe**, *lesbisch**	
queer*	[?]	Also apears as variant of *quer* (across) in compounds: *Queerschläge, Verqueere Welt.*
pride*	[Stolz]	
coming out*	*Sich outen**	also productive in compound formation; *out-sein** (to be out), *Outing-Hürde, Outing-Geschicten, Outing-gegner, Outing-Beratung*
hate crime*	[?]	
going public*	Used as a substantive: *"Ich hatte mein 'going public'"* (I had my going public)	
closet*	[Kloset]	As substantive and to form compounds
diversity	[Diversität]	
orientation	*sexuelle Orientierung**	
community*	*Szene**	
family*	*Familie**	

life-style	[Lebensstil]
	*gleichgeschlechtliche Lebensweisen**
	(same-sex lifestyles)
rainbow	*Regenbogen**
pink	*Rosa**
triangle	*Dreieck**,
	*Lila** (lavender),
	Bund für das Leben (life-long union)
commitment	[Verpflichtung]
ceremony	*Verlobung** (betrothal or engagement to be married)
domestic	
partner	(*LebenspartnerIn*)*, *Lebensgefährt(e)In**
domestic	
partnership	*Eingetragene Partnerschaft**, *Homoehe**
gender*	[?] *Geschlecht* (sex) There is no German word to distinguish between "gender" and "sex," both being translated as "Geschlecht"
significant	
other	[?]
identity	*Identität*
artificial	
insemination	*kunstliche Befruchtung**
drag	*Fummel**
transgender	[?]
transexual*	*Transe**
travestieshow*	
bi*	
hetero*	(*Hete**)
straight*	"*Normal*"*
family of	
choice*	(*Wahlfamilie**), *Wahlverwandtschaft* (Antiquated term for "kindred of choice," also title of a novel by Goethe [1809])
family of	
origin*	(*Herkunftsfamilie**), *Blutsfamilie**
family/	
femili*	*Familie*
patchwork	
family*	[?]
piercing*	[?]
butch*	*Kesse Vater*

femme*
outsider-
  *Gefühl**   [outsider-feeling] *Gestylt**
compulsory
  heterosexuality   *Zwangsheterosexualität**
Suzi Sexpert*

II. Geographic Locations/Spaces

Christopher Street (*CSD*)
Castro Street
San Francisco
Fire Island
                    Motz Dreieck (Motz Triangle), Schwules Dreieck* (gay
                    triangle), Berliner Zoo, Nollendorferplatz
Stonewall*
                    Names of commercial spaces: local bars,
                    discos, parties, cafes, etc.

III. Sex and relationships

	*baggern**, *anbaggern** (lesbian)
hot	*heiß*
men	*Männer*
boys*	*Jungen*
action	
cruising*	[?]
dark room*	[Dunkelkammer—photo.]
toys*	*Spielzeuge*
safer sex*	[sicherer Sex]
party*	[Fete, Fest]
bodies	[Körper]
pick up	[abholen]
steam	[Dampf]
bad	[schlecht]
hard	[fest, hart]
soft	[weich], *gleichgesinnt*
teahouse	*Klappe**
tea dance	*Tanztee*
blind date*	[?]
lover*	[Liebhaber/in], *Sexclusivitäten*

Notes

1. I use "conversational" instead of "ethnographic" or "in-depth" to refer to these interviews because of the concerted effort I made for them to resemble a naturally occurring conversation between two people getting to know each other. To this end, I encouraged interviewees to choose their homes as the site for interviews (although leaving it up to them to choose a place where they felt most comfortable) and brought food to meetings. I did not use a catalog of questions but instead, after telling them about my research and sharing some of my experiences, more or less let them tell me whatever they considered relevant. This is not a claim that we had conversations, because we did not. Our interviews were recorded on audio tape, and my agenda was entirely clear. The term *conversational interview* best describes this hybrid form of talk. It was productive for collecting the kind of data I sought and well suited to the kind of relationship I feel that I have to this community, having lived more than twenty years in Germany and having spent most of that time in lesbian relationships. This was conducive to establishing a collaborative relationship with the interviewees. All methodological decisions were strongly influenced by feminist principles (Cameron et al. eds., 1991; Reinharz 1992; Seidman ed. 1996; Weedon 1987).

2. I deal with the social implications of this issue in a separate essay (Minning 2000), because there are significant differences in the coming out experiences of individuals from the former eastern and western parts of Germany that extend far beyond the topic of code-mixing.

3. Despite the large numbers of people who attend this event in cities in all parts of Germany and the media coverage it receives, it is surprisingly unknown outside the queer population.

4. As Austin (1962) has outlined, performative speech consists of doing something, as opposed to constative speech, which involves stating a fact. As Livia and Hall (1998) point out, however, he goes on to question this dichotomy, concluding that all speech acts do something but in different ways. He then looks at how various verbs act on the social world rather than focusing on whether they act or describe. That places the burden of explaining the construction of linguistic meaning on understanding the process whereby meaning is created rather than linking meaning to facts supposedly located in the natural world. This motivates a detailed study of language in the social context in which it occurs and invites linguists to discover how conventions underlying performativity are established and used.

5. Same-sex erotic attraction has a long tradition in Germany, particularly in Berlin, which by the 1920s was the site of dozens of gay and lesbian clubs and public spaces and home to the Magnus Hirschfeld Institute for Sexual Research. At the height of Hirschfeld's nearly successful push to abolish legislation against sodomy, his Committee for Human Rights had thousands of supporters (Plant 1986). The era provides a rich legacy of linguistic and symbolic resources for gays and lesbians now in Germany and may help account for areas where borrowing has been resisted. It is also worth noting that the disruption of gender binaries has a long history in German cabaret and carnival performances, although not necessarily as a subversion of hegemonic categories advocated by Butler (1990).

6. I will not consider CM/CS (intrasentential/intersentential code use) as separate entities for the purposes of this discussion.

Works Cited

Adam, Barry D., Jan Willem Duyvendak, and Andre Krouwel, eds. 1999. *The Global Emergence of Gay and Lesbian Politics: National Imprints of a Worldwide Movement.* Philadelphia: Temple University Press.

Austin, John L. 1962. *How to Do Things with Words.* Cambridge: Harvard University Press.

Bhatia, Tej, and William Ritchie. 1996. "Bilingual Language Mixing, Universal Grammar, and Second Language Acquisition." In *Handbook of Second Language Acquisition,* ed. William Ritchie and Tej Bhatia, 627–88. San Diego: Academic Press.

Bignell, Jonathan. 1997. *Media Semiotics: An Introduction.* Manchester: Manchester University Press.

Bourdieu, Pierre. 1991. *Language and Symbolic Power.* Trans. Gino Raymond and Matthew Adamson. Cambridge: Harvard University Press.

Brown, Penelope, and Stephen Levinson. [1978] 1987. *Politeness: Some Universals in Language Use.* New York: Cambridge Unviersity Press.

Butler, Judith. 1990. *Gender Trouble: Feminism and the Subversion of Identity.* New York: Routledge.

Cameron, D., E. Frazer, P. Harvey, M. B. H. Rampton, and K. Richardson, eds. 1991. *Researching Language: Issues of Power and Method.* London: Routledge.

Clyne, Michael. 1995. *The German Language in a Changing Europe.* New York: Cambridge University Press.

D'Emilio, John. 1983. *Sexual Politics, Sexual Communities: The Making of a Homosexual Minority in the United States, 1940–1970.* Chicago: University of Chicago Press.

Eckert, Penelope, and Sally McConnell-Ginet. 1992. "Think Practically and Look Locally: Language and Gender as Community-based Practice." *Annual Review of Anthropology* 21: 461–90.

———. 1995. "Constructing Meaning, Constructing Selves." In *Gender Articulated: Language and the Socially Constructed Self,* ed. Kira Hall and Mary Buchholz, 469–507. New York: Routledge.

Fillieule, Olivier, and Jan Willem Duyvendak. 1999. "Gay and Lesbian Activism in France: Between Integration and Community-Oriented Movements." In *The Global Emergence of Gay and Lesbian Politics: National Imprints of a Worldwide Movement,* ed. Barry D. Adam, Jan Willem Duyvendak, and André Krouwel. Philadelphia: Temple University Press.

Gaudio, Rudolf. 1998. "Not Talking Straight in Hausa." In *Queerly Phrased: Language, Gender, and Sexuality,* ed. Anna Livia and Kira Hall, 416–29. New York: Routledge.

Hagel, Markus. 1998. "Sind Wir Homosexuell?" *Sergej* 17(11): 9.

Leap, William L. 1996. *Word's Out: Gay Men's English.* Minneapolis: University of Minnesota Press.

Livia, Anna, and Kira Hall. 1998. "'It's a Girl!': Bringing Performativity Back to Linguistics." In *Queerly Phrased: Language, Gender, and Sexuality,* ed. Anna Livia and Kira Hall, 3–18. New York: Routledge.

Mérrit, Laura. 1994. *Lauras Animösitäten und Sexkapaden: Das QueerLesbische Sex Wörter-buch.* Berlin: Verlag Claudia Gehrke.

Meyer, Ulf, and Axel Schock. 1996. *Der Schwule Sprachführer.* Frankfurt: Eichborn.

Minning, Heidi. 2000. "Who Is the 'I' in 'I Love You'? The Negotiation of Gay and Lesbian Identities in Former East Berlin, Germany." *Anthropology of East Europe Review: Central Europe, Eastern Europe, and Eurasia* 18(2): 103–15.

Morgan, Robin, and Kathleen Wood. 1995. "Lesbians in the Living Room: Collusion, Co-Construction and Co-narration in Conversation." In *Beyond the Lavender Lexicon: Authenticity, Imagination, and Appropriation in Lesbian and Gay Languages,* ed. William L. Leap, 235–66. Newark: Gordon and Breech.

Mühlhäusler, Peter, and Rom Harré. 1990. *Pronouns and People: The Linguistic Construction of Social and Personal Identity.* Oxford: Basil Blackwell.

Plant, Richard. 1986. *The Pink Triangle: The Nazi War against Homosexuals.* New York: Henry Holt.

Reinharz, Shulamit. 1992. *Feminist Methods in Social Research.* New York: Oxford University Press.

Seidman, Steven, ed. 1996. *Queer Theory/Sociology.* Malden, Mass.: Basil Blackwell.

Skinner, Jody. 1997. *Warem Brüder, Kesse Väter: Lexikon mit Ausdrücken für Lesben, Schwule und Homosexualität.* Essen: Die Blaue Eule.

Stevenson, Patrick. 1995. *The German Language and the Real World: Sociolinguistic, Cultural, and Pragmatic Perspectives on Contemporary German.* New York: Oxford University Press.

Weedon, Chris. 1987. *Feminist Practice and Poststructuralist Theory.* Oxford: Basil Blackwell.

Williamson, Judith. 1978. *Decoding Advertisements: Ideology and Meaning in Advertising.* London: Maron Boyars.

Woolard, Kathryn. 1999. "Simultaneity and Bivalency as Strategies in Bilingualism." *Journal of Linguistic Anthropology* 8(1): 3–29.

3. French, English, and the Idea of Gay Language in Montreal

ROSS HIGGINS

In the spring of 1971, nearly two years after the Stonewall riots in New York, gay liberation came to Montreal. The city's gay movement was born at one of the most intense moments of struggle between Montreal's two major cultural and linguistic groups. During the "October Crisis" of 1970, a British diplomat and a minister in the provincial government of Quebec were kidnapped. The minister was later murdered by members of the Front de libération du Québec. That resulted in the suspension of civil liberties, occupation of the city by the Canadian army, and interning of more than four hundred *indépendantistes* and leftists by the federal government of Canada.

By ironic coincidence that October also saw the beginning of a new magazine, *Mainmise,* whose main role over the next few years would be to transmit the ideas of the American counterculture to French-speaking Quebec. Drugs, Eastern mysticism, free love, and the virtues of returning to the land in rural communes filled its pages. Right from the start, the editors included articles on gay themes. In March 1971, in the offices of *Mainmise,* the first meeting leading to the creation of the city's first gay liberation group was held in response to a call published in the magazine (de Maujincourt 1971; see also Garneau 1980).

Pierre, one of the group's leaders during the first year, described the chaotic scene at that meeting.[1] Although joints passed from hand to hand, the charged political atmosphere of the day led to a major confrontation between the nearly equal numbers of Anglophones and Francophones who attended.[2] For the first few meetings the debate raged over the choice of name and the language to be used by the group. Galvanized by events of October 1970, the Francophones were adamant that French be the only language used and that the name should certainly not be bilingual. Supported by a small number of bilingual Anglophones, that position eventually won out. Most of the other Anglophones withdrew in horror at what they saw as the honoring of indépendantiste terrorists when the group chose the name "Front de Libération Homosexuel" (FLH).[3] But, as Pierre pointed out, that name was nothing but a direct translation of "Gay Liberation Front," a name chosen by similar groups all over the world in the sudden explosion of gay organizations at the beginning of the 1970s.

That historic moment brings to the fore many themes I will address in examining the interplay between French and English in gay life in Montreal. Language practices lie at the heart of the symbolic processes by which individual gay men signal gay community affiliation to themselves and others. In learning and using the linguistic and discursive conventions of the group, an individual proclaims attachment to it publicly. But what constitutes a gay language practice? How does the presence of two "dominant" cultural groups in one city intersect with the affirmation of individual and collective identity?

Although French now dominates public life and the private lives of Francophones in the world's second-largest French-speaking city, English remains dominant as the language of the encircling anglophone majority of North America and as the most widely used world language. The early call of gay liberation was heard most plainly by English Montrealers. How was the new ideological discourse reproduced and accepted on the other side of the duality of language practices and cultures? How necessary or important was the influence of gay English in the development of a sense of gay community for Quebec Francophones? What is the specifically linguistic component in the cultural influence of anglophone notions of collective self-hood for French-speakers who have access to the works of Gide, Colette, Proust, and Genet in the original? How different is the influence of English today, when large-scale gay movements and celebrations occur in many other cultural settings, especially Paris?

Under a dual linguistic/cultural hegemony, two sets of institutions and cultural norms coexist, collaborate, and come into conflict. They vie with each other as well as with the social forces present in a culturally homogeneous setting. Daily interaction and historic moments both provide countless arenas of interaction that merit study. In studying gay language practices—isolating conversations and documents with this thematic focus or perspective that took place within a rather circumscribed social context spanning the linguistic/cultural boundary—a manageable subject for observation serves as a model for similar studies in other social groups.

I draw on the interviews I have conducted with men who participated in

Montreal gay life in the period before gay liberation, the extensive historical documentation collected by the Archives Gaies du Québec, and personal experience in the city's gay community and movement since 1975. My examination of the social relations between Francophones and Anglophones focuses on three general themes: the pragmatics of individual gay identity in relation to language, language practices and problems on the social level in a bilingual city, and the relationship of language to the history of the local gay community. I will first survey some of the theoretical issues raised in studying these three themes and then will sketch the outlines of an approach to modeling the patterns of coalescence and divergence, overlap and separation, in discourse patterns and cultural knowledge between Montreal's two major groups. Three types of data will be presented: individual life trajectories in relation to language and cultural affiliation, formal aspects of language and discourse, and knowledge-sharing in the gay world. My views necessarily reflect my position as a member of the first generation of gay liberation and a native English Canadian from outside Quebec who is fluent in both languages. As the events of 1970–71 indicate, tensions can run high between English- and French-speakers in Montreal. Those with differently situated viewpoints due to age, ethnic origin, and linguistic ability may see things differently.[4]

Studying Montreal's Language Patterns

Despite Montrealers' obsession with language, scholars have made relatively few attempts to investigate the lived experience of language as it plays out in the daily round of our lives. Perhaps the emotional, frequently acrimonious nature of the question so easily aroused political passions and agendas that are seldom deeply hidden that it keeps researchers from venturing into the field to record how Montrealers really talk to each other. Notable among the studies is Heller's (1982) examination of how telephone operators at a major hospital decide which language to use with callers. Genesee and Bourhis (1988) looked at cross-language exchanges and code-switching in customer-salesperson interactions as well as workplace usage and street encounters between strangers. Daveluy (1994) and others have framed questions about language use in a way that breaks down the arbitrary assignment to speech in one's native speech community. Her survey concerns forms such as the negative that are used by Anglophones who speak French rather than just Francophones. In my view, however excellent the work dealing with public aspects of this complex reality, it provides only part of the necessary foundation for an inquiry into relations among language, identity, and community. I fully support Heller's (1996) call to further develop the anthropology of language in Quebec. Her overview of research on the social aspects of language, as well as the survey by Thibault (2001), underscores the almost complete dominance of sociolinguistic studies of formal variation, whereas very few investigations exist on language in social interaction. The ethnography of communication in Quebec largely remains to be built.

In interaction, language continually shapes notions of group identification. It forces, promotes, or discourages various forms of inter-group accommodation and provides many occasions for the verbal fun and games (as well as headaches) of living in a bilingual metropolis. The linguistic geography of Montreal is complex, and its language etiquette takes some time to learn, as I found out when I moved to the city in the mid-1970s. When cultural competence is paired with purely linguistic competence, a more realistic framework for studying interactions is provided than using a model based on language alone. Individuals can occupy a much wider range of positions, defined by degree of linguistic and cultural competence, than is recognized by the conventional wisdom that people are either unilingual or bilingual or by the Quebec government's classification of Francophone, Anglophone, and Allophone. In attempting to come to grips with that complexity, I have devised a typology (Table 3.1) that combines linguistic with cultural abilities. Mere fluency does not predict how language will intersect with issues of identity and community.

Some people, generally those who have one parent from each group, acquire native ability in both languages as well as native or near-native familiarity with the jokes, sayings, literature, and other cultural dimensions that come with membership in a speech community. At the other extreme are many unilingual people who have little language ability and only incidental cultural knowledge of the non-native group. Only new arrivals from France or the United States, residents of isolated rural areas, or members of the oldest generation (especially Anglophones) can be counted as truly unilingual.[5] The largest part of the population would likely fall into the category of "function-

Table 3.1. Typology of Linguistic/Cultural Competence

Dual:	raised with two native languages, actively maintained as an adult (may have varied writing ability and reading habits)
Usual:	assimilated to/living permanently in the other language
Cultural:	fluent enough to be fully engaged with the second language culture
Bilingual:	speaking the other with no problems but not engaged with the culture
Functional:	able to speak the other in instrumental settings
Minimal:	some ability to deal with exchanges in the second language
Unilingual:	only a smattering of the other language; cultural knowledge only to the extent it is available in translation

al" or the other categories in the middle of the table, bilingual or cultural. Many Montrealers can deal effectively enough in the other language for practical exchanges at work or in the marketplace, even as neighbors, without investing in the culture of the other in any significant way.

The set of somewhat fuzzy categories provided in the table is offered in order to break away from the usual narrow focus on linguistic competence and gain a perspective on pairing pragmatic linguistic/cultural competence, including familiarity with the cultural knowledge underlying discourse in the second language. An anthropological understanding of the issue requires more than the simple set of three categories used in official and media discourse, often unproblematically reproduced in interpersonal interaction. If the social sphere is modeled as consisting only of Francophones, Anglophones, and Allophones, the entire gradation and multiplicity of competences that characterize the social world is neglected. We fail to represent the full range of variation among participants in the complex interplay of daily life. Although I have only begun to apply the seven categories in Table 3.1 to the concrete analysis of Montreal gay language patterns, they are an essential component of a fine-grained ethnographic approach to issues of identity, community, and language.[6]

Speech Genres and Discourse Communities

Language involvement is a profoundly powerful symbol of community attachment that signifies an emotional commitment to the group. During the 1970s, sharing gay language led many gay men to participate in the struggle for gay rights; during the 1980s, community attachment was a key element in access to AIDS care and prevention information and thus saved lives (Kippax et al. 1993). The importance of community, the sense of identification with a collectivity extending beyond an intimate circle of friends, merits intense study using all means available. The framework that I propose for this undertaking draws on the conception of sexuality as the ongoing product of a process of social construction. I incorporate elements of Gramsci's (1971) notion of hegemony with Foucault's (1976) insistence on the diffuse nature of power and the exercise of disciplines in authoritative and popular discourse. In addition, to get at the diversity of social discourse I rely on Bakhtin's (1981) model of language practices as dialogic and heteroglossic. Through social discourse, a range of social voices (official or resistant, defined by geography, age, ethnicity and race, class, religion, gender, or lifestyle) participates in an ongoing struggle to define social reality, creating, maintaining, and enforcing a set of speech genres through which to do so. The most important element in the model is Bakhtin's "speech genre," which has been extended and refined by Swales's (1990) notion of the discourse community, a label for any group that manages its own set of discourse genres.

What is a speech genre? It need not be oral. Speech genres can be songs, novels, or Web-sites as well as different sorts of conversation. Throughout his life Bakhtin sought to point out the defects of the excessive formalism of the discipline of linguistics in its concentration on "langue" (the system of language) and its neglect of "parole" (actual speech or language production, whether oral or written). Rather than study only abstract forms like words and sentences, as linguists do, Bakhtin suggests analyzing utterances (units of parole) in order to trace the links between individuals and the language collectivity. Forged in the crucible of real social interactions, utterances exhibit forms of a different sort from sentence forms. Their structure is defined by turn-taking, switches between speakers, rather than grammar. These forms ("speech genres") thus are characterized by linear organization (externally by turn-taking and internally by subcomponents, as in literary genres), thematic and semantic content, the social settings where they may occur, and the social roles with which they are associated.

Although Swales (1990) does not acknowledge a link to the earlier speech genre theory, "genre" is one of his central concepts. To it, however, he adds both a psychological and a sociological level, extending aspects left implicit in Bakhtin's model. He defines genre using the schema theory that psychologists and cognitive anthropologists have developed to model knowledge structures. "Schemas" provide Swales with a convenient unitary concept that links analysis of genres as linear forms with their compositional rules with the analysis of the thematic contents of particular utterances. Both consist of knowledge structures or schemas (or "schemata"). On the sociological level, Swales uses the term *discourse community* for any group that decides the norms of genres. Thus the existence of genre practices is a symptom or index for the existence of a community. The fact that generic practices are in constant shifting movement, and in speech they are especially difficult to study, does not lessen their value as indicators of patterns of belonging. Communities rely on genre conformity of various sorts to police members and detect intruders. In an urban society where millions of potential interactants live in close proximity, the study of genre-sharing, overlap, and separation provides a key tool for mapping the often-ineffable structures and processes that construct identity and community.

The role of the discourse community in creating and maintaining speech genres provides a way to address a paramount question in lesbian and gay studies, How is the sense of community generated and maintained? Many categories of persons have the opportunity to become communities, but only some do. How does this happen? We know that a major historical shift occurred in Western countries after World War II when homosexuals gradually, and then more or less abruptly, redefined their collective identity, shifting from outcast nobodies to self-confident members of a political, economic, social, and cultural community claiming its place among other groups in society. Language behavior plays a critical role at the intersection of these four levels of analysis. Speech genres, Bakhtin maintained in a pivotal essay, "are the drive belts from the history of society to the history of language" (1986, 65). Turning this around, I will argue, does no violence to that analysis. Bakhtin's theory of heteroglossic discourse fits well with notions of hegemony and agency, with the possibility of resistance, and with the exercise of power diffused through all social levels. He would, I believe, have no trouble accepting the use of new speech genres by oppressed groups struggling to overturn the conditions of their existence. It seems to me that it was this active role that drove, facilitated, and enabled the shift in the social organization of homosexuality that occurred during the twentieth century.

Language in Social Interaction

In earlier research on how men who had participated in the gay world of Montreal before 1970 developed a sense of community, I investigated the roles of language, ethnicity, and other factors such as social class (Higgins 1997). Gays from both linguistic/cultural groups participated in interactions through which individual linguistic practices construct collective identity. I concluded that awareness of language items or styles and the attitudes, shared knowledge, and emotional attachment they encode was critical to the growth of a sense of belonging to a social whole that transcended the French/English boundary. Some additional background is needed to understand language and culture in social interactions in Montreal.

Private and Public Language Practices

Language use in private life outside the world of work derives importance in the definition of self from the dominant Euro-American cultural separation of public and private spheres, the sharp separation of the world of institutions and strangers versus the home. The home is the setting in which the personal self is most itself (so to speak). Motivation for language use in leisure, as opposed to workplace, interactions comes closer to who people actually are. Private linguistic practices have thus played a central role in constructing a public gay world.

Gay language comes from the kitchen, the living room, and the dining room as well as from the bedroom. The private sphere was the first site where collective goals were formulated and the ideal of community was conceived for gay men. In these private settings, "gay language" developed in ways that united people across the linguistic/cultural divide that has characterized Montreal since 1760. Although not everyone felt a need or call to join in, at least enough gay men did to allow a community to be established that had intercultural norms for language behavior.

Speakers live in the world of utterance; utterances heard and utterances made coexist against the backdrop of all surrounding overheard speech production and the constant stimulus of media. Each person follows a trajectory through the social world, which in any metropolitan city in North America or elsewhere will inevitably cross the lines imagined to divide one "natural" group from another. These boundaries in a city with a two-to-one French-English split, as was the situation in Montreal after the war, are highly conventionalized. The supposedly rigid but in fact quite porous division of the island into francophone east and anglophone west did not prevent extensive interaction across the language boundary.[7] Very large numbers of people speaking the "wrong" language have always lived on both sides of the line. Montrealers have readily available practical knowledge that shows this to be a fiction but speak of it as a fact when it suits them. As a functioning municipality, the city and its suburbs, along with provincial and federal administrations and miscellaneous boards and commissions, need to have a pattern of language use that will keep the system going. So do speakers engaging in neighborhood and street encounters, workplace and service interactions, and, for gays, in romantic moments in dark corners of bars. In some senses the discourse of two distinct groups is very real, but it also arises from cultural knowledge or appreciation and thus is far from a simple result of linguistic difference.

Cultural Baggage

Members of the two dominant linguistic/cultural groups bring different sets of cultural knowledge and thus different values to living in the gay world. The degree of bilingualism, or rather the linguistic and cultural competence that may be called for in gay world interactions, varies considerably among individuals. The number of people who fit into the extremes of the categories outlined in Table 3.1, dual or unilingual speakers, is relatively small; most Montrealers have some ability in the non-native language. Varied ability creates potential social impasses in bar encounters, political meetings, dinner parties, or street pick ups. Gays, however, may well be more likely to meet people of other origins socially than other population groups whose inter-group contacts are more likely to be instrumental than recreational.

Linguistically mixed social networks (whose frequency has never been measured) ensure the diffusion of gay language practices and their underlying cultural knowledge/interests across the French-English divide. Although some language practices, ranging from intonation to such genre conventions as the "coming out story," transfer easily, other culture-specific references (e.g., "friend of Dorothy" or *"le onze août"*) do not. The result is an inter-locking set of language practices that constitutes a twofold gay language system in the city, one shared to very different extents by differently situated individual participants. Not everyone is part of linguistically mixed networks. Many Montrealers harbor resentments or fear appearing incompetent before native speakers, but all have easy access to a more diverse range of media and cultural inputs than most North Americans (at least before the Internet). That pattern of linguistic/cultural overlap and separation will be found in other aspects of Montreal gay language practices as well.

It is important, in order to understand the overall cultural/linguistic web, to keep in mind that generations mix in the social world, maintaining distinct sets of language practices (notably, vocabulary), but that generational differences are also reflected in shifting areas of knowledge and interest. As in language, there will certainly be a large terrain of overlap, but there will also be different singers whose lives are discussed, different jokes, and different hassles with an evolving bureaucratic/corporate world to sort out, depending on when you were born. Generational speech variation is a wild card among other sources of variation; identity components may remain in steady balance or shift over the life course. First Nations people and members of ethnic minorities have further complex inter-relations among identity viewpoints and values, as expressed in or about the gay world. I do not mean to underestimate the importance of non-French and non-English cultural groups, but my discussion will concentrate on the two dominant cultures in order to understand the broad framework in which everyone interacts. Such analysis can help clarify in more general terms the relationships among gay language practices, social diversity, and the idea of community.

Cafe Pragmatics: Language Choice and Code-Switching

During the late 1960s Pierre understood English but seldom spoke it. He came of age just as the renewed Quebec nationalism was emerging in the "Quiet Revolution" of that decade. Sometimes, he said, standing up for the rights of French-speakers made him reject an approach in English. At other times, however, given that the prevailing norms did not require Anglophones to speak French, he would overlook it in the interests of sex. The gay community emerged at the same time as the political shifts that resulted from the October Crisis that would lead to the election of the indépendantiste Parti Québécois government in 1976. The anglophone world has changed dramatically, and now it is common to hear two Anglophones engaging in a preliminary exchange in French, as the new conventions for public interaction require, until they realize that the other is a native English-speaker (which, in short encounters, may be never).[8]

In our daily lives, gays, like other Montrealers, make language choices under a sometimes contradictory diversity of influences and impulses reflecting the situational and the historical context. Just how should you go about picking someone up in a bar or some other gay location when you cannot guess what language the other person speaks? Serious consequences can result from starting in the wrong language, although interest on another level (i.e., sex) may lead even the most militant defenders of French language rights to overlook a faux-pas that would otherwise cause them to cut off communication.

Language issues in Montreal society constantly impinge on daily life, whether in the gay world or among any other group in the city. Choices are made that have meaning within shared and fought-over codes for public language behavior. I'll start with my view (or rather a small sketch) of some aspects of life in a city where I have lived for more than twenty-five years. Sitting at a table in a café in the Gay Village with three or four other men, some of whom I do not know, language becomes an immediate issue. In general, and subject to many intervening factors, Montreal *politesse* (my term and point of view) requires the use of French as the primary vehicle of public communication. The interpretation of "intervening factors," of course, opens a universe of possibilities and intentions. In Village cafes, many people may well be tourists, especially if it is the height of the summer tourist season or the Black and Blue circuit party weekend in the fall. For Montrealers, tourists cannot be expected to play by local rules in the eternal back and forth between French and English. In order to have a conversation, therefore, you have to find out who your interlocutors are.

In always concrete, socially defined circumstances with specific interlocutors, successful conversation requires mapping semantic domains and knowledge universes that can be jointly mobilized to allow communication. Being in a mainly gay place is the first clue, and we rely easily on shared knowledge of the gay world to bridge, if possible, to other areas of sharing. Maybe we can talk about Provincetown or Amsterdam, gyms or operas, gay marriage, AIDS, or suicide among young gays. Anglophones rely on such things as sitcoms with gay characters or the latest episode of *Queer as Folk* on television (in 2001) to get talking. Francophones may plunge into discussion of local references, for example, the gay aspects of the television series *La petite vie* or the current state of gay affairs in Paris or elsewhere in the French-speaking world. If one or more of the men at that cafe table is a Francophone with Anglophones or an Anglophone with Francophones but belongs in one of most bilingual categories of linguistic/cultural competence and knows about what is being discussed, he may (or may not) wish to communicate this at some point in the conversation.

There is ongoing response by active speakers of the two languages to the complex array of prescriptive and playful possibilities of widely shared access to two major world cultures and to two overlapping, deeply embedded, local cultural traditions. We live in the intense language arena of Quebec politics, in the most bilingual, most multilingual region of the province. The Village lies in a multilingual district near the urban core. Respect or disrespect for the rights of French-speakers are central to intercommunity interactions. But that consideration is counterbalanced by the knowledge dimension in gay (as in other) interaction and by observing or breaching politesse. Of course, if I make an English joke that someone doesn't get, it's a matter of politesse that I explain. But maybe the man has annoyed me in some way and I decide to get back at him by ignoring his incomprehension. My companions, seeing my bad behavior, may then intervene to explain and profit from an opportunity to show me up in the ongoing game of gay insulting shared across this linguistic/cultural boundary.[9]

Initial language choice and code-switching within conversation are fundamental signifiers in a bilingual community. Each time I address a stranger I rely on factors of geography (where we are in the city), personal appearance, occupational role, and psychology (my social intention toward the other), as well as my judgment of the other's appearance or role, to guide my choice between French and English. Within a conversation I may switch languages, registers, or voices, all forms of code-switching. I can do funny voices in French almost as easily as in English and gossip or talk office jargon in both with few problems.

The choice of language and language-switching during an interaction often signals some kind of struggle between discourse participants.[10] For shoppers, including those interacting with gay salespeople, some service encounters can take the form of a sparring match in which both participants vie for control of the language to be used. On the whole, this game no doubt helps pass the hours spent waiting on customers at the sock counter or snack bar.

Determinedly speaking the language of the other, both participants manifest a desire to assert total fluency and implicitly question the other's status as an *interlocuteur valable en français* (someone who really speaks French) or someone who *really* speaks English. Generations of visiting Ontario school children have had their linguistic comeuppance at the hands of mature clerks in downtown stores when they tried to show off painfully acquired high school French.

Increasingly, Francophones from Montreal as well as visitors and immigrants from Quebec's regional hinterlands reacted to the challenge to their identity when confronted by the English-only norms of the downtown core in the 1950s and 1960s. They became increasingly dissatisfied with the fictive dominance of English and developed a strong sense of national Québécois identity that has characterized public life in Quebec and in Canada ever since. The former dominance of English, which obliged predominantly bilingual Francophones to cater to the needs of unilingual Anglophones, has changed since the 1970s. Two-thirds of Anglophones can now interact more or less effectively in French although the proportion of Francophones mastering English has declined. The decade of their births greatly affects how native Montrealers navigate the linguistic minefield throughout their lives.

For immigrant children, education in French schools became obligatory in 1974 if the child did not have at least one parent who was educated in English (Brazeau 1992). The measure reversed what had been an overwhelming preference for English on the part of immigrant parents. At the same time, immigrants arrived from Portugal, Haiti, Vietnam, and Latin America who were French-speaking or French-oriented in some sense. As with all other aspects of associational life in Montreal, the policy change and preexisting patterns of language knowledge or orientation have led to divisions that crisscross groups that exhibit, in other large cities, more social cohesion. The black community is divided into English-speaking immigrants from the United States and the Caribbean on one hand and Haitians (and smaller communities of French-speaking Africans) on the other. The longtime English-speaking Ashkenazi Jewish community closely linked to larger Canadian and American communities has been joined since the 1970s by larger and larger numbers of Sephardic Francophones.

Interlingual and intercultural interactions are thus not at all unique to the gay world among Montreal's identity groups. Older immigrant communities such as Montreal's Italians have developed widespread trilingualism among the young. At present Montreal's gay Italian group functions largely in English (the Italian spoken by members varies widely by dialect) and attracts Francophones, many Hispanophones, and anglophone Italophiles.[11]

Now that there are large numbers of Spanish-speakers, who began to arrive as refugees following the overthrow of Allende in Chile and the war in El Salvador, there is a Latin gay bar called Exotica where announcements during drag shows are made in all three languages but with an emphasis on Spanish. In the new ethnic and linguistic diversity of Montreal, such observations must be tempered by recognition that degrees of identification, ideas about the ethics of language choice, and the pragmatic consequences of choices vary continually. Even more than their counterparts in the past, Montrealers now wend their way through a complex world of utterance to traverse language boundaries that did not exist in the 1960s.

Language Practice: Personal Trajectories in History

In my research on the emergence of a sense of community across the language and culture barrier in Montreal (Higgins 1995, 1997, 1999a), I interviewed thirty older gay men. Two-thirds were Francophones, and nearly one-third were Anglophones; several were highly bilingual or had dual competence. This non-representative sample was constructed on a quota basis in order to obtain information from a range of viewpoints in terms of age, ethnicity, class background, and mode of involvement in gay life. In what follows I will discuss the lives of these men in three historical periods and trace (as far as possible) the ways their varied personal trajectories reflect or contradict the general linguistic and cultural trends of the period. Although they are merely examples, the men afford a selection of situated points of view in the language and culture dynamics of mid-twentieth-century Montreal and the complex web of interaction among language and the domains of family, work, leisure interests, and gay identity. The following sections are chronologically arranged, but all the men were active speakers and maintained distinctive combinations of language, knowledge, and interests during the period of interviewing from 1989 to 1992.

The 1930s and 1940s

A contrasting pair of long-term gay couples illustrates the old pattern of language politics before the rise of modern Québécois nationalism and legislation on language use in the 1970s. The oldest Anglophones in the interview group were unilingual Anglophones, immigrants from Toronto. In 1933 Percy and Walter moved to Montreal because Percy was transferred by his company after they had been together for only about a year and a half. With contacts from Toronto, they moved swiftly into a very English gay circle at the elegant Piccadilly Club in the Mount Royal Hotel on Peel Street, the major thoroughfare of the anglophone downtown. Their circle included a minority of Francophones fluent in English. The only time they went to bars in the lower-class, French-speaking eastern part of the city was after Canada entered the war in 1939.[12] For the duration, the flood of military people passing through on the way to Europe temporarily transformed the traditional mapping of the east-west linguistic-cultural divide onto the bar world and made every bar a gay bar. Things returned to normal after the war, and Walter and Percy returned to the Piccadilly Club, venturing occasionally east to one tavern they liked from time to time. By the 1970s Percy still could claim only newspaper-reading ability in French. Walter acknowledged total lack of ability in the language because he worked as a designer in the garment industry, where bosses imposed English on all workers, most of whom were Francophones and immigrants. The couple's friends and numerous lovers during periods when Percy's work took him back to Ontario included many bilingual Francophones. They reflected the dominant pattern of bilingual Francophones and mostly unilingual Anglophones of the period, as did the second couple in my interview group.

Slightly younger than the Anglophones, Normand and Jean were both from lower-middle-class francophone Montreal families. Both were so fluent in English and accustomed to its social position in their working past that they preferred to be interviewed in that language. They were typical businesspeople of the mid-twentieth century and eventually ran their own trade magazine for Canadian food products. English was essential to their success because their market extended into the Maritime Provinces and Ontario. After meeting in a bar in the early 1950s they preferred to frequent the more distinguished Anglophone clubs downtown, expressing strong dislike of the "low-life" world of the Main. Their leisure pursuits included frequent travel to the United States, both to Provincetown and New York. Nevertheless, their lives at home were almost entirely shared with other Francophones because they did not tend to form many ongoing relationships with Anglophones.[13]

The 1950s' Generation

One Francophone from the next generation maintained a preference for the downtown scene while socializing almost entirely in French. Émile was from a working-class family in the Estrie (Eastern Townships) region and had little experience of English until he moved to Montreal at twenty to get a job. Most of his working life was spent in a municipal office; the city provided one of the few institutional bastions of French in the Montreal work world before

the 1970s. Émile's habitual outings during his bar days to the downtown Tropical Room with large groups of francophone friends illustrate how the image
of the divided city's cultural geography is belied by personal reports of social
practice. Later, perhaps as a result of contacts made downtown, he became
fluent in English and nearly moved to San Francisco when he fell in love during a trip there during the 1970s. His mother prevented it, however.

A more intellectual contemporary of Émile's, Charles was a Francophone
from northern Ontario who grew up in a French-speaking suburb of an anglophone mining town. He left to study in Ottawa and then Paris and finally
did graduate work in Chicago before settling in Montreal. His early life in
French defined his long-term linguistic identity, and, despite the fact he had
an excellent knowledge of English, his social circle was largely Francophone.

Anglophones of the same generation continued to have very little ability
in French, although perhaps slightly more than that of their older peers.
Knowing some French was important for Len, who had very few long-term
lovers and whose social world centered on bars and the friendship groups
based in them. The language-mixing of the war had worked in both directions, although there are few firm reports on how many Francophones had
been regulars at downtown bars before 1939. Len spoke just enough French
in the 1950s to manage social or sexual encounters, but the increased presence of Francophones downtown did not cause him to develop a real interest in francophone culture. He said he did not really care for the Gay Village
in the east, where the new bilingualism of the young holds sway.

1960 to Stonewall

After 1960 language politics began to shift at the same time as did the politics
of homosexuality. One man with nearly dual language and cultural skills, Armand Monroe, was a focal point for the development of a public bilingual
gay culture. As a pioneering entertainer and club manager, Monroe's stun-
ningly bilingual and bitingly camp humor and charm captivated patrons of
the Tropical Room. Beginning in 1957, he was instrumental in introducing Anglophone gays to French culture and Francophones to Broadway and English
gay slang. He hosted gay clubs on and off for more than three decades and is
remembered by virtually all men who were in the gay world before 1980. Now
in the midst of a diversified media career, he sometimes guest hosts events in
the Gay Village, where a thriving neo-drag culture has found a home.

Patrick, the only man interviewed who was a fully dual speaker of the two
languages, was also one of the youngest. He had entered the gay world pre-
cociously as a B-boy at the Tropical, where he was something of a protégé of

Armand Monroe. Born in 1943 to an upper-middle-class family in Montreal, Patrick's teenage rebellion, linked to his sexual identity, led to his leaving secondary school without graduating. He entered the gay world in 1956 at thirteen and has been a regular there, with long periods of employment as a bartender in several downtown establishments. With easy fluency in both languages and an eclectic knowledge of both cultures (especially show business), he was involved in gay radio shows in both English and French during the early 1980s and has served as master of ceremonies at large public events in the gay community.

Of the four francophone men interviewed who had participated in the early Front de Libération Homosexuel, all but one were already highly competent in English before 1971. Étienne came from a francophone middle-class family in Montreal. Born in the late 1930s, he studied at university in French but learned English through an American graduate student who introduced him to gay life. One of his later mentors was Alfred, a French immigrant who spoke fluent English and encouraged him to read homosexual fiction and social analysis in both languages. A frequent visitor to New York and Provincetown with his friend Eugène, Étienne began reading *The Advocate* (then a much more radical magazine than it is now) as soon as it began publication in the late 1960s. He and his friends were keenly interested in the developing gay liberation rhetoric that culminated in the Stonewall riots.

One anglophone narrator illustrates the opposite type of move. Ralph went from the bar scene to an ongoing involvement with a mainly francophone social group that met every week for Sunday brunch. His former "factory French" (he, too, worked in the garment business) became "factory plus gay French," the latter calling on a much wider range of language resources.

The backdrop against which a range of shared language practices (and the shared knowledge providing the topics of discourse) has emerged over the course of social contacts and casual associations thus has many aspects. Differently situated individuals hold various attitudes toward learning the other language and culture. On a social level, in terms of both specific linguistic items and knowledge structures, the linguistic/cultural boundary between English and French results in two partly separate, partly overlapping, universes within Montreal gay language practices.

Gay Language Features and the Question of Gay Language

Is there a gay language? Can an examination of language features in a city where two natural languages mingle in a gay community help clarify what is meant by that question? My tour of the prosodic, lexical, and discursive features of Québécois gay French in relation to North American gay English practices is intended to extend the debate beyond the usual focus on English. It is necessary to overcome a certain inertia of self-focus among English-speaking scholars. With an unexamined assumption that other traditions only merit interest in reflecting English-speaking patterns, many fail to recognize the autonomy of even neighboring European languages let alone those further afield. It is easy to exaggerate the influence of English with a survey of features reported from outside. An insider's view from language-borrowers reflects a little more humor than a bare description indicates.

In Montreal's Gay Village, people mix in a territorial center of language practices that has been well-defined since the early 1980s. There is intense interaction among local and global ways of speaking, topics of which to speak, and points of view as visitors, locals, newcomers, and straight tourists sip latté, cruise, dance, shop, and do whatever they are there for. Gay language practices are not confined to that space, however. They occur wherever gay men go, wherever there is talk. In a city of the "first world" it is, in practice, impossible to separate local and global, only to point out tendency. An important addition to the following overview would be a consideration of how the French gay language practices in Quebec intermesh with those of other societies where French is widely spoken, including the Arab world.

Individual degrees of participation vary widely, but in some circumstances there is enough overlap, despite tensions and confusions, to permit the community to function as a social unit. Prosodic and lexical patterns are just as much learned and community-managed as genres. Straight men rarely shriek, for example, and they say "fabulous" much less. Shrieks translate easily in Montreal, and the word *fabulous,* used in both languages, is highly integrated among gay Francophones. Thus a sketch of features is also a linguistic geography but always a fuzzy, multilayered one.

Prosody

Although shrieks are an extreme extension of what prosody normally includes, the variations in pitch, rhythm, and intonation in gay language are commonly thought to have specific prosodic characteristics. Over-enunciation and intonation mark gays, or so generations of humorists in both French and English would have us believe. Effeminate aspects of gay pronunciation and intonation in French, for example, were targeted by a "yellow newspaper" item in the 1950s:

> Trois homos, Gary, Raymonde et Claudette, ont bien amusé la foule, dimanche soir, à Thetford, pendant l'intermission, à la joute de baseball entre Plessisville

et Thetford. Les "ma chère," "toua," "moua," "voiiiyons" revolaient de tout bord et de tout côté.

(Three queers, Gary, Raymonde and Claudette, really entertained the crowd last Sunday night in Thetford Mines at the intermission in the baseball game between Plessisville and Thetford. Calls of "thweetie darling," "you-all," and "gracious me" darted from side to side above the heads of the throng.)[14]

The diphthongization of personal pronouns and the expression *Voiiiyons!* (literally, "let's see," but in context the word could be translated as anything from "Gracious me!" to "Really!" to "Oh come on!") is exaggerated. The general style of these language features seems similar in the two languages. Enunciating too well can be a sign of effeminacy. Cory (1951, 32) mentions over-enunciation as a characteristic of gay talk and thus a way of signifying gay identity to those with the discursive skills to recognize it.

In recounting his work experience, Émile presented a highly significant example of the pragmatics of prosody and gay identity. Speech style gave him away when he started a new job in a municipal office, a problem he blamed on his studies at a theater school: "Alors, pendant un an et demi, ça a été l'enfer parce que moi, je sortais d'une école de théâtre. Je faisais attention à ma diction—'ici et là' Pis en 1957, 'ici et là,' tu passais pour une belle tapette" (So for a year and a half, it was hell because I had just come out of a theater school. I paid attention to my diction—'ici et là [here and there]. And in 1957, if you said 'ici et là' you really got taken for a faggot).[15] Émile solved his problem with co-workers in a municipal office job by the simple and courageous decision to come out to them in the late 1950s. After that the harassment ceased, and he worked there until retirement.

English Gay Vocabulary in Quebec

There are no extensive studies of gay lexicography in Quebec. That is less important for English usage because it is relatively undifferentiated from that in other parts of North America, for which major sources such as Rodgers's *The Queens' Vernacular* (1972) and Dynes's *Homolexis* (1985) are available. Locally, Leznoff's (1954, 1956) pioneering sociological study of the Montreal gay community contains a great deal of information on gay slang in the early 1950s. Lenzoff makes it clear, for example, that the word *gay* was widely used at the time among working-class Anglophones, who were the focus of his research.

In my own interviews, I added a few intriguing English lexical items, such as the way two narrators interviewed jointly described places using the term *kicky* (not to be confused with *kiki*) in speaking of a sauna and a third described a restaurant as having "very working toilets" (a term that had nothing to do with plumbing). The oldest men interviewed, Percy and Walter, used several expressions I have heard nowhere else, whether in regular or in gay English. One occurred when Percy spoke of a man who liked to have many "affairs" with him in one night. With only one source, I am unsure if the use of "affair" to mean "individual sex act" is now unfamiliar because of a generational change or whether the idiom was particular to this couple or their group.

Some systematic study of Quebec English has been undertaken (e.g., McArthur 1989). Borrowings of French words into English result from the need to describe the circumstances of daily life for Montreal Anglophones. Although no detailed studies document local gay English, *dépanneur* (corner store) is now an English word that has a shortened form (*dep*). Anglophone gay Montrealers differ from gays in most other cities in calling bathhouses "saunas."

French Gay Vocabulary in Quebec

For French, the lack of systematic lexicographic study is more regrettable because Québécois usage is radically different from that in France or other francophone countries.[16] The major sources on gay French in Quebec are Lapointe's short word list (1974, 58–59), which has a brief section on homosexuality that includes about twenty-five words and expressions, and Garneau's (1980) examination of labeling practices among adolescents and among adult gay men in Quebec City. An excellent and nonscholarly source for francophone gay language that reflects its playful use of borrowings from English is the theater and the fiction of Michel Tremblay and other writers.

Québécois Identity Labels

Identity labels are of special interest. One interesting but unexplored avenue of research is the past use of the French word *berdache* (or "bardache," a more common pronunciation). With the other organizers of a colloquium on the gay movement and its history in Montreal to celebrate the twentieth anniversary of a movement magazine called *Le Berdache* (1979–82), I recalled how the title was chosen at a time when the third-gender or transgender roles among native people in North America were simplistically seen as equivalents to homosexual identity. Francophone members of the group also pointed out a historic Québécois usage as they learned over the period of publication.[17] Especially in rural Quebec, the men recalled, popular speech had retained the early modern usage of *bardache* in France (Courouve 1985) either in the sense of homosexual or to indicate a broader meaning of gender deviance.[18] Ironically, the magazine's name had better justification and deeper resonance with tra-ditional Quebec language practices than had been initially realized by those who chose it. At a meeting in 1979 when the name was decided, I voted for "berdache" because the other option was *le péril rose* (pink peril).

In spoken Québécois, the most common word now for homosexuals is undoubtedly *fifi* (Lapointe 1974). Too vulgar for the mainstream media, the word appeared often in the yellow press. On February 16, 1957, a reader ob-jected to a story in *Ici Montréal* that asserted that all male nurses in the Chi-coutimi region of northern Quebec were fifis. Five years later, on June 30, 1962, the same publication again used the word in a derogatory sense as part of the large front-page headline: "Fifis versus Homos." The article set up a dis-tinction between the effeminate fifis and the masculine *homos* that ran counter to a widely held popular conception of gays as necessarily effemi-nate, an exceedingly rare opinion to find voiced in the print of that period.

In her study of the folk taxonomy adolescents use to describe homosexu-als Garneau demonstrates just how severe judgment by teenage peer groups can be. One informant assured her that being the only boy in a group to take piano lessons immediately led to the label *tapette*. The adolescents' five cat-egories—*fifi, tapette, menette, Miss,* and *fif*—are based on both feminine ap-pearance and relationship to areas of activity associated with women rather than any notion of sexual activity. English equivalents are impossible to as-sign, but all these words have the general implication of "pansy."[19]

Garneau maintains that the exclusionary practices of teenagers were par-alleled by the exclusionary use of terms for effeminate men in the adult gay world of Quebec City. She describes an elaborate ranking system, with labels ranging in increasing order of queeniness from *petite folle* to *petite grande* to *grande folle* to *géante* and, finally, to the ultimate, *mur à mur*. The translations are all variants on "queen," for which English has only an augmented form: "screaming/flaming queen." Perhaps English should consider borrowing *mur à mur* (wall-to-wall queen). The first three terms were explained to me dur-ing a bar visit with my language tutor, whose demonstration of the vocabu-lary (shouting "grande folle" at a man across the room) resulted in a beer glass smashing against the wall between our heads. Many gay men do not care for effeminizing labels.

Despite such anti-effeminate feeling, speakers of English and French gay language share a strong tendency to feminize personal names and references. Among Anglophones, Alvin told a story in which the punchline was "she's one of us" (Higgins 1997). The choice of the feminine pronoun indicates adherence to group norms, and the use of "us" in this 1951 anecdote points to the taken-for-granted existence of the gay community itself. Two men recalled labels for gay men that referred to their stereotypically feminine preoccupation with fashion. An Anglophone could discreetly identify someone as gay by talking about how "smart" he was, whereas a Francophone could say, "Il est à la mode."

An indication of the gap between French and Québécois usage comes from an *Ici Montréal* item of October 13, 1956, that presumed Québécois readers would not understand the term *pédé:* "Un des plus grands chansonniers de Paris, un pédé (faites-vous expliquer), viendra à Montréal après les fêtes. On dit qu'il est sensationnel" (One of Paris's greatest singers, a pédé [find someone to explain it to you], will be coming to Montreal after the holidays [11]). Short for *pédéraste,* the term is the most common French slang name for "gays" and has no connotation of child molestation in that context. Here it is used to target a popular singer coming to Montreal "after the holidays" (undoubtedly a reference to Charles Trenet). To emphasize its exotic nature, the writer follows the word *pédé* with bracketed instructions to "get somebody to explain it" to emphasize its exotic nature. Québécois usage has never accepted pédé as other than an exotic linguistic item, understood but not used except to mimic the voice of a *Français de France.* It is a word never applied to self except among the large community of gay immigrants from France.

There are a number of specifically Québécois identity labels (Table 3.2). The consensus around the word *gai* is quite broad, especially because the untranslatable "queer" is difficult to comprehend because its multiple associations in English are not known. Also popular are the terms *tapette* and the rarer *moumoune,* both comfortable as joke labels for "self."[20] In general use, the word *folle* is more frequent than *grande* or any of the variant labels for effeminate men reported by Garneau. These words have been "reclaimed" by younger gays honoring the pioneers of the past.

Borrowings

Encircling and interpenetrating Quebec society, English is a social reality in Montreal as it is in many parts of the world for colonial, postcolonial, commercial, or geographic reasons. Montreal's English dates to the early stages of the European expansion and an event referred to in both Quebec and Canada in general as "The Conquest." English became the "command lan-

Table 3.2. Québécois Identity Labels

• en être, être à la mode (to be gay)
• Il marche (he is gay.)
	• faire la planche (act/make like a plank)
	  i.e., to be sexually serviced without
	  reciprocating, similar to English "trade"

guage" in 1760, and borrowing English terms became prevalent in the spoken language of urban industrial Quebec and, through the spread of automobile and other technical terms, to much of the province (Orkin 1971, 44).

Both European and Québécois gay usage in French is thus heavily influenced by English. As in Paris, the prestige of Americanisms is evident in the names of bars and public events.[21] "Native" vocabulary for identity categories ("bear") and acts ranging from "cruising" to "golden showers" or "fisting" consists largely of English words. Borrowings may be adopted without modification (as in the invariant adjective *gay* in France) or may adopt the endings and other characteristics of French word classes (*tu cruises/vous cruisez*).[22]

Quebec's selection from the pool of available terms in English (Table 3.3) is different from that made by the French. Many words used in France are not common in Canada and vice versa. There is a specifically Québécois gay French vocabulary that is unknown in France. Examples include the expression "il marche" (to say someone is gay) and "il a fait son coming out," the half-borrowed way of saying someone has accepted/announced his sexual orientation. His life will go more easily if he has "un beau basket" because people will say, "O! Regarde le beau lunch."

One especially striking example of linguistic borrowing from English into Québécois French is the multipurpose word *chum*. Soon after my arrival in Montreal, a neighbor referred to his roommate as "mon chum." Although I understood the word (as an English word), I had no idea what it really meant coming from him. My language tutor provided a rich explanation. In North American English, "chum" is archaic, suggesting a long-past world of British schoolboys. The word presumably entered Québécois French a long time ago through interaction with the English-speakers who used it. Its meanings cover a delightfully ambiguous semantic range that transcends its sense in English. In the context of the two heterosexual roommates it meant "my friend/companion," but it is also one of the primary words to designate a romantic partner, boyfriend, girlfriend (*ma tchomme*), or lover. That usage is also extremely widespread in the gay world. Among gay men, however,

Table 3.3. Québécois Borrowings from English

• gay/gai (English borrowing from French in the seventeenth century, acquired current meaning by the 1920s, re-borrowed into French in the 1970s)	• faire son ("coming out," possibly losing ground to "sortir du placard," come out of the closet)
• straight	• score, roommate, chum
	• golden showers, rimming, backroom, . . .

probably more than among heterosexuals, "chum" has been borrowed back into Montreal English in the sense of "lover."

The adoption of borrowed words into popular usage is not just a knee-jerk response to a powerful stimulus.[23] People take up language items if they like them. Francophones say they find English wonderfully, often hilariously, direct. Quebec gays, like hippies, appreciated the monosyllabic force of "straight" instead of "heterosexual," for example. Francophone gays in Montreal and in France have adopted a large (and variable) part of the terminology of sex. To say "rimming" in French, one has to use a quite vulgar locution like *léchage de cul* (ass-licking) rather than a single allusive word. The attraction of such usage is a combination of linguistic playfulness, efficient expression of meaning, demonstration of cultural sophistication, and recognition of the influence of English on gay life internationally.

Gay Discourse Forms

Beyond the level of words and expressions, the overlap between the two poles of language practice becomes more marked, although I would not be surprised if more detailed research also revealed patterns of separation. Scholars have already paid great attention to the discourse genre of the "coming-out story," which, as Biddy Martin ([1988] 1993) has pointed out, is a conventionalized recasting of personal experience that makes the move into the lesbian or gay lifestyle the outcome of a long process of self-acceptance. Francophones share this genre to the full, and Martin's critique of the monolithic way the genre constructs gay community in the image of the white middle class is equally intelligible in French. Discourse processes that construct the speaker's "us" are critical (Elias [1987] 1991; Plummer 1995), and areas of overlap such as the coming-out genre play a central role in constructing the dual gay community of Montreal as a unified collectivity.

In addition to the coming-out story, several other candidates should be considered as gay speech genres. The first is from Leznoff's (1954) analysis of the gay friendship group he studied in the early 1950s. Among this relatively stable group there was constant interaction. The retelling of personal sexual adventures served, Leznoff asserts, to establish a hierarchy of prestige among members. I am not convinced, however, that prestige is the only objective in such tellings. The oldest narrators in my group, Percy and Walter, whose gay language practices had been acquired in Toronto during the late 1920s, were separated by Walter's military service. Remaining in Montreal, Percy bragged that he had served the war effort on his knees. In the anecdote featuring the word *affair,* he recalled a merchant seaman whom he saw every time the man's ship came into port:

> He only got to Canada about once in six months, then he'd be on furlough or whatever for quite a while. And he'd been so long at sea, that when you went to bed with him, he wanted five affairs during the night. He was really a sexy person. Periodically, he'd come and stay with me. So one night, I had a friend from New York staying with me—in just the one bed. He was sleeping with me. He was gay, too. . . . I had to get up in the morning and go to work, of course. So, after we'd gone to bed, the doorbell rang. . . . This was my sailor. I didn't say anything to my friend from New York, but after I let him in, I went to bed with the sailor on the chesterfield in the living room, and he had to have five affairs during the night. So in the morning, I said to this sailor, "Now, after I leave, you go in and get in bed with the chap in the bedroom," which he did, and nearly killed the chap from New York with the amount of affairs he had— another five. That was quite—he was really sexy. Anyway you wanted it as long as he could have it. He was just a small chap, too, but he knew sex from one end to the other.

In the joint interview Walter reacted to this anecdote by relating that the man had turned up the night he was discharged from the army. When Percy introduced him, however, the sailor fled, never to return (much to Walter's regret).

The story typifies the interested and amused way Percy and Walter talked, when interviewed in their eighties, about their own (and each other's) sexual adventures over the course of their long relationship. The proud repetition of the story decades later, bearing the hallmarks of many intervening retellings, may involve mild bragging about past exploits, but it also celebrates sex itself and the kinds of social contacts to which sex led over the course of the two men's long life together.

This kind of storytelling is an integral part of gay sexual culture. Because, in the gay world, sexual adventures were not taken as necessarily having deep emotional and symbolic significance they were often the source of hilarious, overtly embroidered, anecdotes. Anticipating a fuller discussion of gay narrative and other discursive genres, I believe Leznoff is right in assigning them a central place in the construction of a collective sense of self. Leznoff errs, however, in thinking that sexual conquest is the main or only theme because stories superficially readable as narratives of sexual conquest may have a far more complex thematic structure in the hands of expert language-users.

Conversational chaining, a different speech genre in gay language, is discussed in Leap's study (1993, 1996) of the structure of banter at a gay brunch as a form of cooperative discourse. He analyzes patterns of one-upmanship and topical chaining among a gay friendship group, a discourse practice common to some kinds of gay gathering. Participants in such conversations try to come up with witty comebacks to what has just been said that may, in practical terms, constitute a change of topic, but they must pick up on a word or theme presented by the previous turn-taker. In a Montreal example of humorous comebacks as a cooperative discursive device for reaffirming friendship, Donald accused John of being a slave to Slavs (generalizing from the word *Polish* in the preceding utterance), an example of the kind of funny non sequitur Leap describes (Higgins 1999a).

Gay discourse practice, on some social occasions, is characterized by humorous interference with the narrator's attempt to get through a story. Listeners heckle, picking up on cues in what is said to accuse the narrator of some heinous crime, or divulge personal information to which other listeners may not be privy, to the pseudo-embarrassment of the speaker, or they make catty comments on his sexual success (or lack thereof) and general tastelessness. Storytelling with hecklers is a favorite discourse form in some circles, and personal experience shows how readily it traverses the French-English boundary.

Other formal categories of stories could be added to the list of gay speech genres, and other forms of conversational chaining could be identified. Many stories would be variants on the general theme of disaster and misfortune or relate to other aspects of gay identity. Homophobic parental mistreatment or the revelation of meeting someone not known to be gay in a bar or sauna may have particular forms. They are also types of stories that rely on a final characteristic of gay language: the shared knowledge that underpins discourse. Again the pattern between Francophone and Anglophone is one of separation and overlap.

Discourse Content: Gay Knowledge

Linguistic and cultural differences are relatively unimportant for understanding stories of misfortune and tragedy. The underlying knowledge of what it is like to lead a gay life in a homophobic society draws discourse participants together across the linguistic cultural divide between Francophone and Anglophone. It is even stronger than shared vocabulary items and particular forms of stories or sayings common among gay life knowledge of the gay world (or gay lore that supplies a great deal of the topical content for gay conversation).

Active regulation of discourse forms by communities is implicit in Bakhtin's speech genres. The concept of genre in Swales's (1990) discourse community model integrates the study of discourse forms or genres (formal schemata) with the underlying knowledge structures (content schemata). The form, the sequential ordering of discourse elements, and the content of specific instantiations of a genre are under control of a social group, the discourse community. This may be something like an academic discipline with all its institutions and practitioners or a less structured but still quite powerful social grouping such as the gay community. The discourse community model stresses the way social groups create and maintain genres and use them to reward or sanction particular speakers or writers for success or failure in producing successful instantiations of genre patterns the communities regulate.

From the perspective of functional linguistics, Lemke (1985, 1988) adds that such forms govern content in terms of the combination of topics and situated points of view in the interests of the varying participants in heteroglossic discourse. Proper ideas about parent-child relations, for example, constitute a topic on which gay men share a point of view based on understanding what it is like to be thrown out of the family because of sexual orientation.

There are many other forms of shared knowledge that are pragmatically salient in gay life. The entire spectrum of bar knowledge, which involves knowing where to go, when to go, and what to wear, is one such schema or set of schemata (cultural model) (D'Andrade 1995). As well as holding memory for bar names, locations, and many other pertinent facts, gay men's bar schemata in the age of clandestiness also held a full set of bar nicknames to cloak identifiably gay references to places in conversations outsiders might hear.

A pair of examples illustrates the complex intertwining of knowledge, vocabulary, pronunciation, and ethnicity in Montreal gay language. The pair at first appears to be lexical but on deeper analysis reveals patterns of acquaintance with gay lore that strongly express community membership. Some Québécois French-speakers regard August 11 as a gay holiday, although it is not much celebrated as such. The date is chosen because of a supposedly stereotypic gay pronunciation of "le 11 août" and the words *on joue* (one plays) although no one can explain why that should be significant. It just sounds funny.[24] The effeminate pronunciation was even satirized in a *Jour et Nuit* item on "la fête des tapettes" on January 20, 1962: "Le '400' fermera ses portes, le 11 août prochain. Nombre de clients de Radio-Canada sont passablement ravis qu'on ait choisi cette date du on z'oue . . . fête par excellence des tapettes" (The '400' [a club] will close its doors next August 11. Many customers from Radio-Canada [the French side of the Canadian Broadcasting Corporation] are quite thrilled that they chose the date when [one plays, untranslatable pun], the queers' biggest holiday [2]).

Knowledge of the obscure expression *11 août* is not widespread among younger gays; I learned it from a young man in the 1970s. Perhaps better

known is the English expression "he's a friend of Dorothy," a code for saying someone is gay that is derived from gay men's fondness for Judy Garland,
whose character in *The Wizard of Oz* bore the name. If the explanation seems
labored to an English-speaking audience, it must be stressed that very few
Francophones would be able to decode it because, for the most part, they have
never heard of Garland or her cult. Similarly, Anglophones who have not been
exposed to French gay culture will not likely recognize the equivalent Parisian stars Barbara or Mistinguett. There is also a whole other set of gay icons
in Quebec (e.g., Alys Robi and Diane Dufresne), and many are as little known
to people from France as to English-speakers.

There are two separate worlds of show business knowledge. These furnish
incommensurate sets of referents that can only be learned by outsiders
through considerable effort. The examples of "11 août" and "Dorothy" point
to the complex variability of shared language practices and the knowledge
that supplies the content of conversation. Not only ethnicity but also generation, class, and varying interests or inclinations differentiate groupings within the gay world, as they do in any other urban collectivity in which membership overlaps the many other affiliations that make up the fragmented
identities of the postmodern person.

Conclusion: Language and Patterns of Belonging

Many elements combine in the web of cultural and language interaction in
Montreal, and it is not easy to bring them smoothly within the span of understanding through simple models. Such things as language choice and
code-switching, multiple personal positions, and strategies are deployed by
individuals and reflect constantly evolving historical contexts, communicative conventions, and technologies. We act out a daily sequence of largely
undocumented interactions, sometimes conforming to and sometimes flouting the rules of our discourse community as we understand them. Each act
requires or allows some choice among the nuanced community affiliations
we claim.

Montrealers use language choice in many ways to reinforce identification
with separate, bounded identities and simultaneously affirm a shared identity as gay. The Montreal experience is particular but may be compared to
some extent with the situation of Latino gays in American cities. There, too,
two world languages cohabit the urban landscape and the gay world is both
separate from and joined to the dominant culture. Outnumbered by Anglo-
Americans in a way that did not happen in Quebec, Latinos struggle with
similar issues of language and identity. American Hispanics straddle the

immigrant/non-immigrant line, and their cultural referents in Latin American society provide a less forthright defense of homosexuality than the great writers of France did in the early twentieth century.

How does the Montreal experience illustrate the role of gay English in spreading the ideas of gay liberation, projecting the existence of an authentic gay self derived from Anglo-Saxon experience into cultures where it is absent or less developed? Purely linguistic factors do not suffice in rendering the full richness and complexity of language usage or the cross-currents of influence in the pragmatics of social interaction. Vocabulary items are adopted from English but then fit into the semantic sets of the adopting language. Shared vocabulary is less meaningful as a sign of influence than the knowledge underlying it. Participation in club life, gym culture, and musical interests shapes willingness to learn about the ways the prestigious culture of English views such things.

There are limits, however, in the extent to which Francophones learn the lore of Hollywood and Broadway or the language of American identity politics. There are also generational differences in which terms or knowledge sets are adopted. In Montreal, a potentially unified gay language/culture system is fully developed only among those who have the highest cultural competence in their non-native language. They follow the discourse on homosexuality in both languages. Moreover, they act as transmitters of linguistic and cultural knowledge, as when English Montrealers tell visiting Americans about the meanings of chum or the writings of the new generation of gay scholars in Quebec and France. Gay English is a factor, but the knowledge it encodes is not a full description of homosexuality in the Euro-American world. Unilingual Anglophones do not see the full picture and should not assume they know the meaning of a word without fluency in the local cultural context of its use.

In this preliminary investigation of the complexities of interaction among people with varied points of view I have tried to point out some promising avenues of research that will stimulate further work. In the relatively small and particular gay segment of the population, the historical development of a discourse community can be studied through utterances analyzed as speech genres produced by and for discourse communities. Through documents and retrospective interviews we can observe the ongoing process through which a community in the making has directed language forms and contents.

The proposed model offers a start toward getting at more interesting aspects of gay men's real lives in language and provides what I hope is a useful contribution to the anthropology of language in Quebec by going beyond technical, policy-driven issues that have so far dominated sociolinguistic research on Quebec. With an emphasis on change and the highly flexible central concepts of genre, schema, and discourse community at its core, I believe this theory satisfies important goals in documenting the process of change in the way homosexuality was experienced during the twentieth century and the resulting emergence of the public gay community.

Further elaboration of the analysis can provide valuable insights into the ways that patterns of shared discourse operate in the choices and actions that constitute gay language or other kinds of discourse. In Montreal as elsewhere, a manifold, complex way of speaking what is conveniently called "gay language" has entered an intersecting array of heteroglossic voices engaged in contesting the specific social issues (including language itself) that channel power struggles over who gets to define social reality. The most definite things these data suggest are that gay language is a process not an entity and that the local has many resources for resisting the global.

Notes

The work presented here would not have been possible without the generous support of many people. The men who told their life stories to me in my research on the period before 1970 are joined by many others who not only explained Montreal gay life to me but also showed the inner workings of its language patterns. I must also thank the many patient people who have, over the years, enriched my knowledge of Québécois gay French and its counterparts in France and elsewhere. This project would scarcely have been conceived had it not been for Bill Leap's work on gay English and his hard work to create an annual forum for scholarly investigation of lesbian, gay, bisexual, transgender, and queer language. Tom Waugh and Line Chamberland have both provided invaluable moral and material support for many years. Thanks also to Denis Boullé, Bernard Lavertu, Robert Beauchamp, Denis Dumas, Jérôme Rousseau, and the francophone members of the Archives Gaies du Québec team, all of whom have put up with my ignorance, taught me how to make jokes, and then groaned at my bilingual puns over the years.

1. Author interview with Pierre, Aug. 1990. Men identified by first names only have been given pseudonyms.

2. In this text I have followed a minority convention in capitalizing these linguistic group designations.

3. The word *gai* did not gain widespread acceptance among Quebec Francophone gays until the latter half of the 1970s. For an overview of early movement history in Montreal, see Higgins (1999b).

4. The relation of social diversity in terms of generations and gender are discussed at greater length in Higgins (1998).

5. As I learned early in my career as a teacher of English as a second language, there are few "real beginners" in Quebec. That means, for example, that the use of such English words as "joke" and "job" has meant the addition of their initial phoneme to the repertoires of all speakers of Québécois French, distinguishing them from French-speakers in France.

6. I make no attempt here to include trilingualism, a common capability among members of Montreal immigrant communities.

7. The social geography of Montreal is conventionally divided into east and west by Boulevard St. Laurent, known to English-speakers as Saint Lawrence Boulevard. To the east of this street, the English press traditionally saw a vast, lower-class, French-speaking area referred to as the "East End." The equivalent "West End" was not used. Rather, the word *downtown* was applied to the city's English-dominated commercial center located there. The term *West Island* is used in both languages to refer to the western, traditionally wealthy, English-speaking suburbs on Montreal Island. This version of social geography has always been a gross oversimplification of real demographic patterns but still has currency in the popular imagination. Thus Montrealers use "the East" (l'Est) and "the West" (l'Ouest) to imply both bicultural and class associations of urban geography.

8. Linguistic duality can also have its uses. When we want to elude unwanted pursuers, we can always try pretending not to speak whichever language he has used, although doing so might lead him to try the other.

9. There are many varieties of "gay insulting" beyond the very formal types described by Murray (1979) and Read (1980).

10. Jerome Rousseau, personal communication, May 1995.

11. Gaspare Borsalino, personal communication.

12. This meant the world of the "Main" as Boulevard Saint-Laurent was known, and the whole surrounding area, which was called "le Red Light" in French and vividly revealed in Michel Tremblay's plays and novels.

13. They disagreed with one another on this point when it was raised in the interview but did not name many close Anglophone friends.

14. *Ici Montréal,* Aug. 9, 1958, 7. A "yellow newspaper" was a type of small, sensationalist weekly popular in Quebec from about 1950 to 1970 (Higgins and Chamberland 1992). "Moua," an elongated pronunciation of *moi* (me), has no obvious equivalent in English.

15. Émile's articulation contrasted with popular preference for *icitte* and *là* pronounced with a longer, darker vowel.

16. Thus Courouve's (1985) excellent reference work on French homosexual vocabulary is only of limited and historical value for Quebec.

17. Ménard (1985) considers the term *berdache* as a reflection of traditional Québécois culture in light of this experience.

18. The variation from "berdache" to "bardache" follows a regular pattern, as in "vierge/viarge" (also a marker of lower social status). Québécois French resulted from a pooling of resources by early colonists who spoke various local dialects and adopted the French of Paris as a common vehicle of communication. Since the nineteenth century observers have noted the retention of older forms in Québécois French due to separation from France after the Conquest (Beaudet 1991).

19. This was confirmed by Gérard, who recounted that one in the Lower North Shore village where he lived with his grandparents was publicly labeled a "menette à queue" because he helped the women with their work rather than doing masculine tasks. The word *menette* is a diminutive of *main* (hand).

20. "Moumoune" has an expanded meaning close to *mémére* (the feminine form meaning "old gossip" or "busybody"). Denis Dumas, personal communication, September 2001.

21. Montreal's Bad Boy Club organizes one of the biggest circuit parties, the "Black and Blue."

22. French has borrowed the twentieth-century English *gay,* whether invariant with a *y* or, as in Quebec, following normal French adjective patterns based on "gai." "Cruiser" competes with a real French word, *draguer,* which seems to have gained popularity over the period I have observed.

23. Francophones now need explanation of the historical meaning of the word *dude* because it was redefined in late-twentieth-century English.

24. The expression *11 août* is likely a Québécois one, because in Québécois French the final *t* of *août* is silent. The joke does not work in Parisian French, although it would in other French dialects in Europe. This insight was pointed out by Denis Boullé and further refined with the help of Denis Dumas.

Works Cited

Bakhtin, M. M. 1981. "Discourse in the Novel." In *The Dialogic Imagination: Four Essays,* 259–422. Austin: University of Texas Press.

———. 1986. "The Problem of Speech Genres." In *Speech Genres and Other Late Essays,* ed. Caryl Emerson and Michael Holquist, trans. Vern W. McGee, 60–102. Austin: University of Texas Press.

Beaudet, Marie-Andrée. 1991. *Langue et littérature au Québec, 1895–1914.* Montréal: L'Hexagone.

Brazeau, Jacques. 1992. "Évolution du statut de l'anglais et du français au Canada." *Sociologie et Sociétés* 14(2): 103–16.

Cory, Donald Webster. 1951. *The Homosexual in America.* New York: Greenberg.

Courouve, Claude. 1985. *Vocabulaire de l'homosexualité masculine.* Paris: Payot.

D'Andrade, Roy. 1995. *The Development of Cognitive Anthropology.* New York: Cambridge University Press.

Daveluy, Michelle. 1994. "Le français parlé par des francophones et des anglophones de Montréal." *Culture* 14(2): 85–93.

De Maujincourt, Gilles Hugues Yvonne (pseud.). 1971. "Pour un front gay à Montréal." *Mainmise* 3 (Feb.): 186–91.

Dynes, Wayne. 1985. *Homolexis: A Historical and Cultural Lexicon of Homosexuality.* New York: Gay Academic Union, Scholarship Committee.

Elias, Norbert. [1987] 1991. "Changes in the I-We Balance." In *The Society of Individuals,* ed. Michael Schröter, trans. Edmund Jephcott, 153–237. Oxford: Basil Blackwell.

Foucault, Michel. 1976. *Histoire de la sexualité,* vol. 1: *La volonté de savoir.* Paris: Gallimard.

Garneau, Brigitte. 1980. "L'homosexualité masculine au Québec." Master's thesis, Laval University.

Genesee, Fred, and Richard Y. Bourhis. 1988. "Evaluative Reactions to Language Choice Strategies: The Role of Sociostructural Factors." *Language and Communication* 8(3–4): 229–50.

Gramsci, Antonio. 1971. *Selections from the Prison Notebooks.* Ed. and trans. by Quentin Hoare and Geoffrey Nowell Smith. New York: International Publishers.

Heller, Monica S. 1982. "Negotiations of Language Choice in Montreal." In *Language and Social Identity,* ed. John J. Gumperz, 108–18. New York: Cambridge University Press.

———. 1996. "Langue et identité: l'analyse anthropologique du français canadien." In *De la polyphonie à la symphonie: méthodes, théories et faits de recherche pluridisciplinaire sur le français au Canada,* ed. Jürgen Erfurt, 19–36. Leipzig: Leipzig University Press.

Higgins, Ross. 1995. "Murder Will Out: Gay Identity and Media Discourse in Montreal." In *Beyond the Lavender Lexicon: Authenticity, Imagination, and Appropriation in Lesbian and Gay Languages,* ed. William L. Leap, 107–32. Newark: Gordon and Breach.

———. 1997. "Sense of Belonging: Pre-liberation Space, Symbolics and Leadership in Gay Montreal." Ph.D. diss., McGill University.

———. 1998. "Identités construites, communautés essentielles: De la libération gaie à la théorie queer." In *Les limites de l'identité sexuelle,* ed. Diane Lamoureux, 109–33. Montreal: Éditions du remue-ménage.

———. 1999a. "Baths, Bushes and Belonging: Public Sex and Gay Community in Pre-Stonewall Montreal." In *Public Sex/Gay Space,* ed. William L. Leap, 187–202. New York: Columbia University Press.

———. 1999b. *De la clandestinité à l'affirmation: Pour une histoire de la communauté gaie montréalaise.* Montreal: Comeau et Nadeau.

———, and Line Chamberland. 1992. "Mixed Messages: Gays and Lesbians in Montreal Yellow Papers in the 1950s." In *The Challenge of Modernity: A Reader on Post-Confederation Canada,* ed. Ian McKay, 422–31. Toronto: McGraw-Hill Ryerson.

Kippax, Susan, R. W. Connell, G. W. Dowsett, and June Crawford. 1993. *Sustaining Safe Sex: Gay Communities Respond to AIDS.* London: Falmer Press.

Lapointe, Ghislain. 1974. *Les mamelles de ma grand-mère, les mamelles de mon grand-frère: Petit lexique québécois incomplet.* Montreal: Éditions Québécoises.

Leap, William L. 1993. "Gay Men's English: Cooperative Discourse in a Language of Risk." *New York Folklore* 19(1–2): 45–70.

———. 1996. *Word's Out: Gay Men's English.* Minneapolis: University of Minnesota Press.

Lemke, J. L. 1985. "Ideology, Intertextuality, and the Notion of Register." In *Systemic Perspectives on Discourse,* ed. J. D. Benson and W. S. Greaves, 1:275–94. Norwood: Ablex.

———. 1988. "Discourses in Conflict: Heteroglossia and Text Semantics." In *Systemic Functional Approaches to Discourse,* ed. James D. Benson and William S. Greaves, 29–50. Norwood: Ablex.

Leznoff, Maurice. 1954. "The Homosexual in Urban Society." Master's thesis, McGill University.

———. 1956. "Interviewing Homosexuals." *American Journal of Sociology* 62: 202–4.

Martin, Biddy. [1988] 1993. "Lesbian Identity and Autobiographical Difference(s)." In *The Lesbian and Gay Studies Reader,* ed. Henry Abelove et al., 274–93. New York: Routledge.

McArthur, Tom. 1989. *The English Language as Used in Quebec.* Kingston: Strathy Language Unit, Queen's University.

Ménard, Guy. 1985. "Du berdache au Berdache: lectures de l'homosexualité dans la culture québécoise." *Anthropologie et Sociétés* 9(3): 115–38.

Murray, Stephen O. 1979. "The Art of Gay Insulting." *Anthropological Linguistics* 21(5): 211–23.

Orkin, Mark M. 1971. *Speaking Canadian French.* Toronto: General Publishing.

Plummer, Kenneth. 1995. *Telling Sexual Stories: Power, Change and Social Worlds.* New York: Routledge.

Read, Kenneth E. 1980. *Other Voices: The Style of a Male Homosexual Tavern.* Novato: Chandler and Sharp.

Rodgers, Bruce. 1972. *The Queens' Vernacular: A Gay Lexicon.* San Francisco: Straight Arrow Press.

Swales, John M. 1990. *Genre Analysis: English in Academic and Research Settings.* New York: Cambridge University Press.

Thibault, Pierrette. 2001. "Regard rétrospectif sur la sociolinguistique québécoise et canadienne." *Revue Québécoise de Linguistique* 30(1): 19–42.

4. Dancing on the Needle's Edge: Gay Lingo in an Israeli Disco

LIORA MORIEL

While almost all contemporary nation-states justify their existence by claiming links to the past, such a sense of birthright is of particular importance in Israel, to which Jews have flocked from more than a hundred countries to revive not only what they perceive as a divine deed to the land but also the biblical language, Hebrew. Although Jews have lived in Israel continuously, they were a poor, remote, and struggling community under foreign rule before Zionism (defined by the on-line Jewish Virtual Library as "the national movement for the return of the Jewish people to their homeland and the resumption of Jewish sovereignty in the Land of Israel") inspired Jews to immigrate in great numbers over the past century. Since then, Israel has become a thriving Jewish state with a substantial non-Jewish Arab minority that has also lived there for centuries, a minority linked linguistically to the multitudinous Arabs in surrounding countries.

For Israeli Arabs, Israel reifies both a religion and a language that are foreign to them. True, under the Declaration of Independence signed in 1948 Israel is a democratic country that values all its citizens equally—indeed, the state funds all religious institutions and gives them sole power to marry, divorce, and bury. Because of the century-old armed conflict between non-Israeli Arabs and Israeli Jews, however, Israeli Arabs have been treated like second-class citizens. Moreover, because of the never-ending armed conflict, Israeli laws have established a difference in the services provided to those who have served in the army (most Jews and Druze men, as well as Bedouin trackers) and to those who have not (mostly Arabs). This difference has created a widening wealth gap between the Jewish and non-Jewish population, as well as between secular and ultra-Orthodox Jews, because the latter do not serve in the army.

Some Israelis have been advocating a more secular approach to governance that would allow the non-Jewish populace to feel truly equal to Jews, and they are beginning to advocate for civil marriage, divorce, and burial but with very little success. The introduction of more liberal streams of Judaism into Israel since the 1980s—the Reform and Conservative movements have set up schools and synagogues—also augurs well for slow but incremental social change. In addition, the peace agreements between Israel and two of its immediate neighbors, Egypt and Jordan, as well as the more recent U.N.-sanctioned unilateral Israeli withdrawal from Southern Lebanon, have helped reduce some of the regional tensions. But the part of the Arab-Israeli conflict that concerns the West Bank and Gaza, formerly parts of Jordan and Egypt but since 1967 administered by Israel, is the site of an ongoing violent confrontation. The inhabitants of these territories, who form a separate entity from Arabs and call themselves Palestinians, as do many Israeli Arabs today, seek a country of their own, Palestine, which would incorporate the West Bank and Gaza, with Jerusalem as its capital and a land bridge in between. This vision is shared by many in the world community, as well as by most Israelis but has yet to be implemented, its inevitability delayed by more myopic forces on both sides.

Language has played a central role in this conflict. For example, 1948 is for Jews the date of the creation of the State of Israel through the War of Independence, whereas for Palestinians it signifies *naqba,* the catastrophe that led to exile from their land and made them homeless refugees in squalid camps. Moreover, language plays an almost insurmountable role in the on-again-off-again negotiations between Israel and the Palestine Authority as each side parses the other's words for hidden meanings and advantages. Finally, language is explicitly emphasized as a key element of building Israeli society. New immigrants are urged to immerse themselves in the language in *ulpanim,* special schools for teaching the basics of Hebrew quickly. The use of biblical Hebrew in everyday life by both women and men, both secular and observant and, indeed, by both Jews and non-Jews, is a remarkable achievement. The resurgence of Hebrew from the ancient language of holy texts to a language of everyday life—a mother tongue again for the first time in centuries—stands as both symbol and leading edge of a broader assumption that posits Israel as the embodiment of an ancient kingdom, a modern country in which a storied past comes to life in the bustling present.

Israel has two official languages—Hebrew and Arabic—but for all intents and purposes everyday life almost exclusively revolves around Hebrew. Hebrew, like Arabic, is a gendered language that favors the male grammatically. Only recently has the Academy of Language decreed that if the majority of those addressed are women, an audience can be addressed in the female (a moot point because by now most Israelis have little grammatical idea of how to do so). It is thus understandable that for both Hebrew- and Arab-speaking Israelis English, which they learn in school and perceive to be gender-free, offers what Adrienne Rich called the "dream of a common language" that is universal and unbiased.

Of course, English is genderless only in dreams. In reality, as Itamar Even-Zohar, Porter Chair of Semiotics at Tel Aviv University, has pointed out, English is gendered, although not as fully as Hebrew, because it "has distinct words for female and male creatures (such as distinguishing between 'a dog' and 'a bitch'), as well as clear classification of various objects, even though in the later standard they are referred to as neutral: for example, a ship is 'she,' and so is nature." Better candidates for genderless language, Even-Zohar suggests, would be Turkish and other Turkic languages: "In these languages, there is no gender whatsoever in any part of the language (so, for example, there is no distinction between 'she' and 'he')" (personal communication, Feb. 24, 2001).

Although this critique is useful and valid for Israel's emerging lesbian, gay, bisexual, and transgendered communities (LGBTs), gay English seems to provide not only (the perception of) a gender-neutral language but also access and connection to the (imagined) worldwide LGBT community. Israel's position in the hub of the Near East, flanked by Arab states and a Palestinian Authority poised to become a state, dictates both insularity from and openness to differences. Israeli LGBT culture, specifically the gay male subculture of public sex situated in the busy intersections of the Israeli and Palestinian people, offers a rich playing field of encounters that is in itself multicultural, multilayered, and multinational (Fink and Press 1999). For lesbians, emotional rather than sexual satisfaction seems to be paramount (Moore ed. 1995).

According to Amit Kama (2000), since the 1990s gay Jewish men have mainstreamed fully by seamlessly blending into Israeli society. This is a sweeping claim that is not yet borne out by the lived experiences of all Israeli LGBTs. True, LGBT acceptance has increased markedly since 1988 when Israel's sodomy laws were repealed. That is especially true in the army, where since 1993 there are no restrictions on the enlistment and promotion of LGBTs (some transgendered soldiers have even been helped to transition on army time). As Lee Walzer (2000) cautions, however, the army is not doing as much as it can by not confronting soldiers' homophobia head-on in a sweeping educational campaign, as it does on other social issues as the country's premier institution of socialization. Similarly, Adital Tirosh Ben-Ari's (2001) research shows the power of the army for gays by noting that young men raised on generally egalitarian but specifically homophobic kibbutzim find the army, that otherwise "total institution," liberating: "They reflected on their military service as an opportunity to come to terms with their sexual orientation—an opportunity that has not existed while living on the kibbutz" (115).

In addition, in 2000 Luz and Avni's original book about coming out by Jewish Israeli gays and their parents (in Hebrew) was published by Shufra, a press dedicated to work by LGBTs. Meanwhile in Jerusalem, a unique book-store-cafe-restaurant, Tmol Shilshom, co-owned by gay writer David Erlich and his life-partner and situated on the cusp of Jewish and Palestinian Jerusa-lem, is trying to stay alive despite the *intifada* (uprising). Similarly, Laila, a gay nightclub catering to Israelis and Palestinians, is finding it difficult to survive the violence and the political and economic uncertainty it has spawned: "After almost two years of bitter fighting, trust between Israelis and Palestinians has never been lower. But in a packed, smoky nightclub on the edge of Jerusalem's ultra-Orthodox Mea Shearim district, the gay commu-nities from both sides still bridge the growing divide, breaking down racial and political barriers as Jews and Arabs defy traditional stereotypes and threats of suicide bombers" (Halpern 2000). Sadly, the friendly hugs and kisses inside belie the escalation of violence and retribution outside, which may well unravel any hope for a peaceful resolution to the conflict.

This unraveling is profoundly disquieting for moderates in Israel, includ-ing LGBTs. In 2001 I was one of the signers of a full-page advertisement in the *Pink Times* to include a resolution about an end to the occupation of Palestinian territory by Israel as part of any discussion of LGBT rights. It was dismissed by most LGBT readers as extreme. Nevertheless, there is growing understanding that civil rights are basic human rights and that LGBTs must get involved as part of their own struggle for liberation. Also in 2001, a new group, K'visa Sh'chora (Black Laundry), composed mostly of lesbians, be-gan in-your-face demonstrations within pride parades and other LGBT events to underscore this approach. Members often carry signs that read, for example, "Transgender Not Transfer" and hand out flyers in lavender and black that educate the public about the dire economic situation and the need to come out of the closet for social justice.

Such public militancy, although rare in Israel, is part and parcel of a new examination of national identity and of Zionism itself by Benny Morris and other "new historians" since the 1990s. The pioneering ideal of fighting men and strong (but beautiful) women returning to the Promised Land has been eroded by years of war, mass immigration from Ethiopia and the former Soviet Union, and the pull of the global (bubble) economy. As Ruti Kadish notes, "Moreover, even despite the breakdown in Israel's national consensus and changes in Israeli culture, the binary paradigm of just warriors [men] and beautiful souls [women] continues to carry purchase. . . . The fact that these models are still those with which to identify, or against which to react, is evident in much of the gay and lesbian Israeli discourse. It is striking that even the harshest critiques begin at this point" (2002, 228).

The phenomenon of refusing to serve as a soldier in the Occupied Territories of the West Bank and Gaza has garnered new steam now that an increased number of officers are joining these ranks, including some gay soldiers. What was once seen as outright treason is now an almost-legitimate subject for discussion. LGBTs have entered every arena of national debate and national consensus and are now part of the linguistic (r)evolution as well, having moved decisively *me ha-aron la-salon* (from the closet to the living room).

Although there have been a number of recent studies about various aspects of LGBT life in Israel, little attention has been paid to the role of language in LGBT life. Addressing language is important because language, in contemporary Israel, is more than a medium of communication. For Israeli Jews, the Hebrew language is a key element of the "Promised Land" that the nation-state of Israel represents. One issue I will address in this chapter is what happens when certain persons, namely, LGBT Israeli Jews, appear to be abandoning Hebrew, at least partially, in favor of what is construed to be global gay English. To the degree they do this, do such LGBTs still belong, or are they seen to abandon the Promised Land?

Linguists have shown that lesbians, gay men, bisexuals, and transgendered people sometimes use language differently from their heterosexual counterparts (Leap 1996; Livia and Hall eds. 1997) and that gender differences exist within the LGBT community. Solomon (2001) has shown that HIV/AIDS educational material targets gays and lesbians differently; moreover, gender-non-specific material in diacriticless printed Hebrew further dilutes the message for men.

There is diversity in language use and meaning in Israel. But because the nation is isolated politically and landlocked geographically, for some Hebrew- and Arabic-speakers, as informants tell me, the English language has taken on the allure of international inclusion, sophistication, and style. Thus, in the Israeli LGBT community the use of English has the added attraction of making them harmonize with what they perceive to be an international "family" of like-minded, like-speaking LGBTs who may also include non-native-speakers who use only a more limited subset of the English lexicon that they believe to be a worldly gay English.

Although it is important to note that even the most abridged version of a language can be nuanced and thus variant among users, it is nevertheless equally important to remember that a basic, agreed-upon common usage is understood by most handlers of the abridged version of the English language described here. Jacob Aronson (1999), for example, recalls his 1990 sojourn in Hanoi, when friends would point out "people like you" and strangers would deduce his sexuality. And yet, as he came to understand:

> If it is a sociolinguistic truism that Southeast Asians tend to speak indirectly about things, it is even more true that Vietnamese and their foreign friends have developed exquisite skills of circumlocution, of elaborate paralipsis, in which the topic of conversation never gets spoken but is nonetheless certainly understood for being unsaid. Indeed, "don't ask, don't tell" could well serve as the national motto, whether it is sex or politics we are not talking about. . . . [W]e never use the words that would explicitly define ourselves or our shared interests, nor do we have to. (210)

On the whole, although it is sparsely spoken, gay English is a kind of universal language for Israel's Jewish, Muslim, and Christian gay LGBTs. For the most part, gay English has become, like the rainbow flag, the pink triangle, and the band Queen, a definitional part of belonging to this particular subculture in Israel.

Because I am trained in comparative literature, my investigation of the way LGBTs use gay English in Israel is based on close readings of poems by bisexual poet Yona Wallach, gay poet Zvi Mermelstein, and lesbian poet Shez as well as a song by Dana International, a transgender diva. In addition, I focus on how gay English is used not only in terms of actual words chosen from the gay English lexicon but also in terms of the idealized nature of a supposedly "gender-free" language, English, against the background of a strongly sex/gendered language, Hebrew—the international flavor of gay English versus the Bible-based locale and history of modern-yet-ancient Hebrew. By "gender-free," I mean that for Hebrew- and Arabic-speakers in Israel, who are bound by the grammatical conventions of a language that lets no word out of the male-female binary (each word must be grammatically sexed and gendered), English seems to provide a language unfettered by such conventions and thus seemingly gender-free, although linguistically that is not the case.

It is this use of gay English in Israel that I wish to explore. Although it may be true that same-sex dance floors everywhere vibrate to the sounds of "It's Raining Men" and "YMCA," same-sex potlucks everywhere screen *Desert Hearts* and *Priscilla, Queen of the Desert,* and same-sex youths everywhere sprinkle conversations with words like "queer" and "gay," it is probably equally true that gay English is as much a commodity as a language in places where English is not the vernacular. By "the vernacular," I mean the lived and spoken language of a place—in this case of a perceived, imagined, self-described, or advertised gay space.

The use of a vernacular as a subversive and powerful tool for the newly included is not limited to gay usage of English. In the case of Hebrew, for example, Jewish women were for centuries barred from learning the sacred language in much the same way that most Christian women were barred from learning Latin. As Donovan explains, "Only when the Latin influence had weakened, when serious prose was being written in the vernaculars, in a nontraditional form, and only after the rhetoric of the home and of the forum had once again merged could women hope to have equal access to the means of literary creation" (1980, 216).

Although it is in the vernacular, the nonstandard version of a language, that slang and creative play best flourish, Labov cautions nevertheless that "differences between Standard and non-Standard English are not as sharp as our first impressions would lead us to think" (1994, 559). Where English is not the everyday language, at least some gay English is the lingo of choice for local LGBTs. Its use is at once limited (because it is usually considered to be the language of the educated) and liberating (because it is considered to be the language of the stylish and sophisticated).

Gendering Language, Gendering People

Hebrew, unlike English, is a fully gendered language in which humans, animals, and even inanimate objects are grammatically sex/gendered. Hebrew has no genderless "it" or "you" and no third sex; someone or something must always be referred to as either female or male. Without exception, each noun and adjective in Hebrew is assigned a male or a female gender, often arbitrarily. Only one word has no gender assignation, the word *I* when used without referent. Because such usage is not grammatically satisfactory ("I" alone is at best a fragment), the "I" must attach to a verb or being that gives it sex or gender, for example, "I am" and the verb/being immediately sex/genders the otherwise genderless "I." The arbitrary nature of sex/gender assignation to inanimate objects is underscored by the fact that synonyms can have different sex/genders. For example, both *yare'x*$_m$ and *levana*$_f$ mean "moon" in English (I am using here the convention of presenting the Semitic guttural *kh* or *ch* as an *x*). Roca (1989) shows that in Spanish, too, synonyms can vary by sex/gender. For example, both *ciudad*$_f$ and *pueblo*$_m$ mean "city" in English.

Roca concludes that "strictly semantic or phonological criteria fail to yield adequate description of the data, and thus that gender must be construed as an abstract morphological property which is syntactically transmitted from the head noun to its modifiers" (10). Not too abstract, of course, because the default sex/gender in the case of such abstraction is nevertheless male, as is the case in Hebrew.

Such inconsistencies pertaining to the role of sex and gender in the use of language have occupied some linguists (e.g., Robin Lakoff, Dale Spender, and Deborah Tannen) for decades. Do women and men understand different things by usage, for example, and do they mean different things even when using the same words just because they are of different sexes? Such questions—and those about possible sex differences as well—are important. As John A. Lucy has shown about "the hypothesis that differences among languages in the grammatical structuring of meaning influence habitual thought," "It seems safe to conclude that there is good preliminary evidence that diverse language forms bear some relationship to characteristic cognitive responses in speakers" (1992, 148). By extrapolation, sex and sexuality differences may also play a role. As Deborah Cameron notes, "Although 'language and gender' might in some cases be more accurate, since we are dealing with a social rather than a biological category, the term gender has a technical meaning for linguists which has caused many writers to prefer the term sex" (1988, vii).

In the case of Hebrew, until very recently there was no separate word for "sex" and "gender." Both were covered by the same word, *min,* which is also the word for "sort" or "type" and thus itself a categorizing tool. Now the newly minted word *mig'dar* specifically denotes gender, whereas "min" denotes sex only.[1] Whether the introduction of mig'dar is a positive step in bringing an ancient language up to date or whether it is an acultural worldly catch-up is unclear. Certainly, it did not develop organically but rather grew out of a need to join a global epistemological trend.

When a language is fully gendered it provides a sociolinguistic opportunity to examine the way gendering people and objects impacts quotidian life, with the caveat that sociolinguistics has come under attack by feminist linguists who argue, as do Cameron and Coates, that "sociolinguists have often been insufficiently aware of the specific condition of women's lives" when attempting to show sex differences in the use of language (1988, 24). Women were formerly assumed to lack the full and proper use of language, but now the emphasis must shift to the "different" usage by the sexes rather than on any presumed "deficit" on the part of women users (21). In Israel, the use of gay English appeals to gay men and to lesbians equally, just as Standard English appeals to marginalized Israeli and Arab women.[2]

I have elsewhere defined "sex" as hardware and "gender" as software.[3] I agree with Judith Butler (1990) that gender is performative:

> [A]cts, gestures, and desire produce the effect of an internal core or substance, but produce this on the surface of the body, through the play of signifying absences that suggest, but never reveal, the organizing principle of identity as a cause. Such acts, gestures, enactments, generally construed, are performative in the sense that the essence or identity that they otherwise purport to express are fabrications manufactured and sustained through corporeal signs and other discursive means. That the gendered body is performative suggests that it has no ontological status apart from the various acts which constitute its reality. (136)

If "the gendered body is performative," as Butler argues—and if, as I maintain, a body's gendering is arbitrary—then what you see is what you get. But what you get is not necessarily what it seems; language choice can be as arbitrary as gender choice. The gendering of a language is imperative to understanding the limitations of gay English, even as it sweeps the globe, making moneyed LGBTs happy consumers of LGBT paraphernalia to the delight of capitalists of every orientation. No pride parade is complete without rainbow flags, rainbow stickers, rainbow caps, rainbow jewelry and logos, and rainbow music by rainbow artists who have either come out of the closet or are known by everyone to be LGBT although still closeted or by celebrities who are LGBT-friendly, having begun their career by performing for LGBT audiences and/or by being aware of and responsive to LGBT fans, who are tenaciously loyal. In Israel, this adulation explains the rise of several local divas, especially Dana International, who in 1998 won the Eurovision Song Contest as the official Israeli contender.

Hebrew is not an easy language for the transgendered, because it forces the user to choose a sex for referring to oneself and to one's partner as well. For example, in Hebrew and other fully gendered languages, the statement "my lover and I" is not, as it is in English, a gender-neutral statement. In English, gay or otherwise, when I say the word *lover* it is not immediately obvious whether that person is of the opposite sex or the same sex. But if I wish not to draw attention to my non-heterosexuality in fully gendered Hebrew, then the word *lover* must be gendered as someone of the opposite sex, thus "inning" me (in other words, I would have to lie). To avoid outing my partner or myself, I would have to choose what is heteronormative in a lover's gender assignation for my culture and vernacular. But if I say $ahuvatee_f$ (a male would say $ahuvee_m$) $va'anee$, although $va'anee$ (and I) is not sex/gendered, I am seen and thus perceived as either male or female (usually but not always unambiguously). Thus, by making the public oral statement "my $lover_f$ and I_f" in a setting where the audience is not aware of my sexuality I am subvert-

ing that heteronormative gender paradigm of speech. I am drawing attention to the fact that my lover and I are not of the opposite but of the same
sex. So the statement becomes, potentially, a courageous, perhaps even a rev-
olutionary, act.

It is against this backdrop that gay English is being played out in Israel,
with LGBTs articulating a diverse way of thinking, speaking, and being that
is reshaping the language in terms of both style and substance. As Leap notes,
"Certainly, displacement of expectations and disruption of the ordinary are
recurring themes in Gay English text making. Whether the speech setting is
private or public, whether the participants are all gay or mixed-gender, and
whether the text content is cordial or combative, restrained or outrageous,
gay text design packages gay meanings within an impression of 'familiar'
language, and retrieving gay message involves a rejection of self-evident assumptions about text and a disruption of the familiar" (1996, 163).

Why has gay English been embraced, albeit not fully, in Israel? Perhaps one
reason is status-seeking, a way of signaling erudition and savvy, and in this
it is not unique to urban elites. Another reason gay English has been embraced
may be that it is perceived to be gender-neutral. In fully gendered Hebrew,
to be gay in English is to be neither sexed nor gendered, which is why gay
English has a unisex allure for same-sex discourse. LGBTs interviewed during the 2002 Pride Parade in Tel Aviv gave another reason for using gay English: doing so implies sophistication and belonging to an international co-
hort that can be oblivious to binary categories of sex/gender that the user
would rather imagine as fluid.

But that sense of belonging, argues Kulick (2000), can also skew the research
into gay English because knowing that a speaker is LGBT tends to make LGBT
linguists parse speech as "gay" even if there is no "gay" there: "Discussion of
the tendency in post-1980s work on gay and lesbian language to proclaim com-
monplace interactional features to be characteristic of queer language leads
us to the extensive work of Leap" (263), which Kulick critiques as a "circular
argument" (264). Although I agree that much of the early work on the gay
components of language, whether English or others, seems circular, I do not
agree that it was a dead end in the road. Rather, such early research helped
shape the pathways of more recent research, some of which has at its theoretical basis approaches, such as psychoanalysis, that I find equally tautolog-
ical despite Kulick's affection for "the language of desire" (276).

The battle over ideology is the battle for power over naming, defining, and
inscribing. To talk about language and the gendering of its parts is not an es-
oteric academic discussion but a basic political one. To ignore language and
its power to help shape norms of speaking and acting is to succumb to the

power of those who manipulate language to entrench ideology. As Kulick remarks, "Language ideologies seem never to be about language—they are always about entangled clusters of phenomena, and they encompass and are bound up with aspects of culture like gender, and expression, and being 'civilized'" (1998, 100).

Gay English in Bible Land

Many vernaculars do not have a neutral word for homosexuals. Hebrew, a modern language that is still overwhelmingly biblical, is no exception. This is why, in 1991, as editor of *Nativ Nosaf,* the only regular publication catering to the LGBT community, I asked readers to suggest a way to refer to us in Hebrew. The Bible, after all, has no language for LGBTs beyond one specific act of sodomy. Until then, the words used for lesbians, gays, bisexuals, and transsexuals were the clinical foreign ones used with local accents and twists, like *homosexu'al* and *les'beet* or the French *koksi'nel* (transgender), along with more colloquial versions like *mitro'mem* (floater) and *aliz/aliz'a,* a direct translation of "gay."[4] All these words have negative connotations in Israel, as they do elsewhere, so I thought it time to do some linguistic consciousness-raising by encouraging a search for a more benign term.

The winning entry came from Richard Isaacs, a non-native Hebrew-speaker in the United States. Isaacs urged the use of a Hebrew word based on the concept of pride that actually sounds like the gay English term and therefore suggested *geh/geh'ah,* which sound like "gay" but in Hebrew means "proud" (more precisely, "proud male"/"proud female"). Because I was also, at the time, chair and spokeswoman of the Society for the Protection of Personal Rights (SPPR), as the advocacy, service, and resource group for LGBTs in Israel was called at the time, I immediately started using the terms in press releases and interviews. Other community members soon embraced them, and activists emerged who used the terms instead of those previously in play to create a more engaged LGBT sub-subculture. In fact, the new words had such currency that when dozens of LGBTs flocked to the Israeli Knesset (parliament) in February 1993, the radio announced that *geh'eem ve geh'ot* (gay men and gay women) had just completed a historic meeting there.

The "languaculture" activists thereafter consolidated public opinion and galvanized lawmakers to introduce legislation championing equal rights for all, regardless of sexual orientation—rights, unfortunately, not yet extended to other minorities, including Arab Jews and Palestinian Arabs and, to some extent, to Israel's Arabic-speaking Mizrahi Jews (and women) as well.[5] As for gay and lesbian Israeli Arabs, they are trying to fashion a position that is both included in the general LGBT community and differentiated from it. That endeavor has only just begun, however, and support groups are springing up in Jerusalem and Tel Aviv. The Jerusalem Open House, for example, is a fiercely independent place where all LGBT Jerusalemites, whether Israeli, Palestinian, male, female, activist, partyist, observant, or secular, feel at home. On the day I visited, a gay Israeli Jew, in military garb and clutching an M-16 rifle, was surfing the Internet while two gay Arabic-speaking youths —perhaps Israeli, perhaps Palestinian—were laughing at a nearby table in surreal oblivion of the political drama playing out just outside.

Meanwhile, as is the case in many other parts of the world, gay English has become the rage in Israel. Ironically, with its steady rise comes a decline in use of the newly minted words for *gay* in Hebrew. "Geh" and "geh'ah" fell into disuse as the LGBT community reembraced the international words *homosexual, les'beet* (the female Hebrew form of the gay English "lesbian"), *bi* (bisexual), and *trans* (transgender/trans-sexual), albeit with a Hebrew accent. By 1996, when Michael Gluzman and Gil Nader published their alternative Hebrew-language gay dictionary, they noted that despite efforts to introduce it widely, the word *geh* had not entered the Israeli gay vernacular but was only used in "written literature" (32).

The final coup de grace came in 1999, when Israel's umbrella LGBT organization officially renamed itself the association for homosexuals, lesbians, bisexuals, and transsexuals (the Agudah), and its monthly publication, the *Pink Times,* inked those internationalized words under its masthead. Gay Hebrew was out, and gay English was in—not American but British English, as befit a former colony. Like everything else in Israel today, the trend is global not local, universal not particular, and English not vernacular. If cafes are called "Sweet and Low," clubs are called "Rainbow," and cyberspace is called "Netvision," why not call a homosexual a "homo" and an Internet portal "Gay Way"?

It is cool—"koolie" as it is called in "Hebrish," the Hebrew-English hybrid—to be with it on the international plane where LGBTs walk the same walk (pride parades) and wave the same rainbow flags as (it is presumed) everyone else. Of late, cool, too, is coming out of the closet and is fashionable, photogenic, and freely commodified (judging by the newspapers, advertising, and products sold). In Israel, for example, a singer who comes out officially guarantees a sell-out next album and series of performances, and a celebrity who performs at a pride event is guaranteed undying adulation and, of course, sales. Both are sure to grace the covers of many magazines and appear on trendy television and radio shows, garnering even more publicity and sales.

In fact, judged by the media alone, Israel is gay heaven. Since February 1992, when my partner Susan Kirshner and I came out publicly on prime-time television in Israel, supported by my mother, Ruth, the media has embraced queers to an almost embarrassing degree. With the help of that positive exposure we activists were able, in one short decade, to acquire many legal protections, from the workplace to the army, thereby positioning Israel among the most progressive countries in the world for gays and lesbians. In everyday life, unfortunately, more traditional forces prevail and make some individual lives miserable. But as a young man from a socioeconomically deprived development town told me, "My mother would rather I was a homo than a drug addict."

Ordinary LGBTs in Israel are drawn to gay English as a means of self-expression and inclusion, for they see themselves more as part of a global gay space than of any local gay place. This attitude received a boost during World Pride 2000 in Rome, when a multinational alliance of LGBTs from all over the globe converged on the Italian capital to advocate for international LGBT rights, and it will be enhanced again when Israel hosts World Pride 2004. Making a concerted effort to include Arab and Palestinian gays and lesbians each year, Israel has joined the premier league of places where gay pride celebrations attract large crowds and international attention. In 2001, even after nine months of the intifada or uprising (constant fighting between Israel and the Palestinian Authority), the local pride parade drew Israeli, Arab, and Palestinian participants as it wound along Tel Aviv avenues officially decorated with rainbow flags. The postparade show starred Dana International, just returned from an unprecedented Foreign Ministry–sponsored U.S. tour in time for the festivities. In 2002 Jerusalem celebrated its own pride parade for the first time, as did the southern port city of Eilat. The more established Tel Aviv parade drew forty-five thousand marchers and onlookers despite security concerns that kept most Arab and Palestinian LGBTs away. The music was international disco—in English, of course—blaring from floats featuring high-heeled drag queens and bare-chested, muscular young men surrounded by crowds of aficionados.

Urban young Israelis are eager to gender-bend and blend, whatever their sexual orientation. Unisex clothing is the height of teenage fashion, and gay dance venues are the rage with everyone who loves to dance, whatever their sexual orientation; young heterosexual women often "hang out" with young gay men. True, bands of restless youths sometimes converge on public parks looking for gays to harass, but there are also a growing number of active groups around the country where gay, lesbian, bisexual, transgendered, and questioning youths gather for support and strength. Whatever their age and "out" status, many lesbians, gay men, bisexuals, and transgendered people in Israel absorb gay English as a way to feel connected to the gay world at large. Moreover, unisex names are now common for the newborn, so much so that names formerly designated male or female exclusively are now refashioned as equally trendy for both. Thus, Gal (wave), Tal (dew), and Sha'har (dawn) are as unisex as No'am, which formerly was strictly male. My own name used to be the female equivalent of the male Lior but is now a unisex name, as is Or (light).

The fact that mainstream Hebrew baby-naming is defying the gendered nature of the holy language is of monumental importance in a traditional society. It signals a fundamental change in the approach to the established usage of the Hebrew language as always gender-based. This opening to modification allows for other subversions as well, such as sprinkling gay English into the language along with interspersed words and syllables from other languages. But in Israel's LGBT subculture, where words like *gay, queer, dyke,* and *straight* predominate, there is a gendered Hebrew touch. Thus, because "dyke" is a term for lesbian, it is treated like a feminine adjective and given a feminine ending, becoming *dyke-eet*. Similarly, "straight" is the term for a male heterosexual, whereas *straight-eet* is the equivalent term for a female heterosexual. "Queer" and "gay" remain gender-neutral and thus the preferred term by some. In lesbian circles one is either "butch-eet" or "femme-eet." The transgendered in Israel are as well versed in Riki Anne Wilchins and Kate Bornstein as anyone in the United States. Academic courses in queer studies proliferate while other programs are depleted due to the regional economic slump. Informants maintain that using gay English terms, style, and ideology makes them feel universally connected and stylishly sophisticated, "in."

Meanwhile, however, Israeli gay men and lesbians have taken up the challenge of deconstructing and restructuring the ancient grammar, delighting in inventing a local lingo that is a blend of gay English and vernacular and, more specifically vulgar, Hebrew and Arabic. The dance scene of gay male cruising is the location for the creation and dissemination of gay English as well as gay Hebrew and Arabic. As soon as clubs close, the new words float about and are absorbed by others, including through a compilation work of Ron Fairy in the *Pink Times:* the ongoing, not-yet-published "Even-Shoshana Dictionary," a feminized reference to the definitive Hebrew language dictionary first compiled by Avraham Even-Shoshan.[6]

In the August 1998 issue of *Pink Times* Fairy published a story in his version of the current multilingual slang he was archiving. The beginning paragraph is given in Roman not Hebrew script, including interspersed English words: "Kalat Fifi ha-feyah lil Sindismel: Come back lil beit until xatzot ve im lo—tahafxi mi diva le Sindisemel again. Kalat Sindismel: No problema ve raxti lil party" (Fifi the fairy said to Cinderella: Come back home until midnight or you will turn from diva to Cinderella again. Said Cinderella: No problem, and went to the party (8, Fairy's translation into Hebrew and mine into English).

Because Israel is situated between East and West, the Arab and the European world, its slang, including gay slang, borrows not only from English but also from Arabic and non-English European languages. Words on the page do little justice to the flavor of the language that Fairy documents, which is female although used by gay men. Earlier in the column, Fairy told readers that he had just returned from London with the latest slang terms—not one of which was in English. In fact, he returned with a Hebrew alternative to the English word *passive: noshexet kariot* (pillow-biter$_f$). The example given for this usage, in translation, was, "She goes and tells everyone that she is the active one but in fact she is a pillow biter." The word *active* is given in the English-to-female-Hebrew mode, *active-eet*. On the same page, Dana G. began an article on "The Woman's World" with Dalit Baum's assertion that she is a butch who does not believe in femininity. "Femininity," Baum stresses, "is a male characteristic, created by men for men." The extreme form of this femininity is the "drag queen," a term for which there is no Hebrew equivalent so the English is used, along with "drag king."

Against the Grain: Poets on the Language Frontier

The Hebrew language of today is based on the Torah and other ancient writings; some believe it is thus unique, a modern vernacular based on an ancient written, not oral, tradition. Like Arabic, Hebrew is written from right to left and includes diacritics (dots and dashes) for vowels. As Harris Solomon (2001) reminds us, "Such markings are orthographically placed around consonantal letters to delineate the sounds of the word itself, which can signal a variety of grammatical morphemes, including gender morphemes" (231). Diacritics have been removed from most secular texts being published, making it possible for written texts to gender-bend, at least in theory. Words like *itax* (with you$_f$) and *it'xa* (with you$_m$), for example, are written the same way in the basic root form *LX*.

In advertising, ambivalent teasers are popular, but in song lyrics they are infrequent. In published poetry, however, diacritics are always used, and sex/gender is thus always unambiguously indicated, making the work of poets most interesting linguistically. That is why I have chosen to focus on three LGB poets in this section: Zvi Mermelstein, Shez, and Yona Wallach. It should be noted that in Hebrew there are no capital letters, and poetry is generally distinguished from prose only by diction and shorter lines.

Mermelstein and Shez disrupt gender by feminizing masculine words and masculinizing feminine words, challenging their audiences to rethink Hebrew and, by extension, Zionism as gender-bound systems of language and policy. Mermelstein and Shez are well versed both in gay English and in global gay trends. Nevertheless, they prefer to work exclusively in Hebrew and redefine the war-torn terrain of power to suit their own agendas. For Mermelstein, whose mother tongue is English, the use of Hebrew is an always-conscious choice, and his diction, rich in literary and biblical imagery and vocabulary, is impeccable. His poetic power comes from an approach that seeks to reclaim the orgasmic male erotic life force that energizes his creativity. For Shez, an Israeli-born punk rocker turned poet, it is to reclaim her body from the silence of incest and proclaim herself a sane survivor of that private holocaust (a loaded term she uses with full cognizance). The late, openly bisexual, bohemian poet Yona Wallach relished wordplay and subversive word usage to deconstruct the binding binary of sex/gendered Hebrew. Misunderstood in her too-short lifetime, Wallach has gained a large following, both in the mainstream and among gender minorities such as feminists and queers. In 1997 musician Eran Tzur produced ata_m $xavera_f$ $sheli$ (you$_m$ are my girlfriend), an event (and CD) devoted to musical renditions of her poems.

Mermelstein often uses the form of the Sapphic ode, favored by the well-known Greek lesbian poet of old, to address both God and a lover, thus creating poetry that is like a veritable set of Russian dolls, one enclosed in the other, layered, nuanced, and rich in symbolism and subversion. In "Apology for My Tendencies: A Sapphic Ode" (37), the first line would be:

> s'lax$_m$ li adonai$_m$
> (forgive to me My Lord/God)
> im be-rov regog nafshee$_f$ z'nuteet$_f$
> (if with most longing my soul [is] harloty)

Translations of poetry cannot be literal precisely because each language has its own grammatical and literary conventions, many of which are not directly transferable. In Hebrew, for example, the verb *to be* is implied, it is virtual not real. Like French, in Hebrew the genitive is in the form of "to me/ you/him/her" (and so on) rather than "mine/yours/his/hers." As I have translated the first stanze of Mermelstein's ode:

> Forgive me, Lord, / If my soul prostitutes itself for excessive longing,
> And if it endlessly / Pursues conversationalists in [public] gardens.

> Forgive me, truly, for this / I will kiss You/you there, I am searching
> for You/you in them.

"Soul" is gendered female in Hebrew, and God is male. Sappho may have
delighted in young women, but Mermelstein clearly prefers men. He is careful not to use gay English in his poetry, but his culture is more universal than
particular, and his longing for God à la John Donne is given a double-edged
signifier. Is the poet longing here for God or for a conversationalist/young
man to worship? The ambiguity of referents and signifiers is especially striking and subversive amid the traditional use of "Sabbath," that is to say high,
language in his poetry.

Shez began her career in the punk era as an angry young woman performer
in smoke-filled discotheques in Tel Aviv. Because of a prolonged family feud,
she wanted to change her given name and chose "Shez" as the acronym for
"temporary name." The temporary became permanent. Shez was the first
celebrity to come out of the closet but did so too early and spent years bat-
tling for recognition on her own terms. Since the late 1990s she has finally
gained critical acclaim (and equal opprobrium) after publication of poems,
short stories, and even a play. Her themes are often harsh and assaulting.
Whether the poems deal with her private hell or with an idealized relationship, Shez tends to be bold and unsparing. She has allowed me to translate a
short poem, "Elohim" (God) (1996) that is powerful from its confrontational
first line despite its lyricism as a whole. The line in Hebrew reads, "ve-elo-
him$_m$ ohevet$_f$ otee," the literal translation of which is "And God$_m$ loves$_f$ me"
(literally, to "I," the one sex/gender–neutral word in the Hebrew language).

In Bereshit Aleph:26–27 (Genesis 1:26–27) *elohim*, which I (and others)
translate to mean a plural "gods," having created heaven and earth, oceans
and sky and land, animals and all living and inanimate things, determine to
create adam, which I (and others) translate as "an earthling/a being from the
earth." Thus "adam," like elohim, is not sex/gendered male at this early stage
in the cosmic narrative. In Hebrew the verses clearly indicate the plurality
and male-female sex/gendered nature of God and the male-female sex/gen-
dered nature of Adam, especially verse 27, which in Hebrew reads, "va-ivra
elohim et-ha'adam be-tzalmo be-tzelem elohim bara oto zaxar u-n'keva bara
otam," which I translate as "and God(s) [he] created the earthling in [his/
its] image in the image of God(s) created it male and female [he] created
them." An authoritative English translation "sanctioned by the [Chief] Rab-
binate" in Israel reads, "So God created man in his own image, in the image
of God created he him; male and female created he them" (Friedlander ed.
1953, 3).

This is the first and most often overlooked rendition of the human creation story, and its relevance to gender minorities cannot be overstated. The idea that the first human being was created in the image of God as both male and female is comforting and confounding at once. It opens the door to variant interpretations and translations and thus to the feminist and queer need for the fluid over the binary. Shez exploits this ambiguity to strike at the convention of addressing the plural and male-female-sex/gendered God(s) as singular and male in the first line of the poem. To dramatize the possibilities that arise from the multi-sex/gendering of elohim—Is it not ironic that for English readers this wonderfully fluid word for God(s) should include a decided male component?—Shez imagines God not only as female but also as her same-sex, tender, and loving lover. The sacrilege and subversion of the poem thus go beyond the grammatical flouting of sex/gender convention to strike at the hierarchal, patriarchal nature of institutional religion and social institutions. The entire poem reads:

> and god loves me
> right now she is kissing me softly with the dew
> she is caressing me gently through wind
> her words do not ever end but increase and are soft
> and you are here again
> again
> here

For centuries some Jewish women have grappled with the maleness of the monotheistic God of the Bible and the erasure of so many women in its narratives, as did Elizabeth Cady Stanton in *The Woman's Bible.* Jewish feminists in the last half of the twentieth century moved from berating the status quo to changing it. One of the ways to do so has been to challenge biblical language itself. With the advent of female rabbis this trend has intensified. For Shez, however, the ability to gender God in the female is not the result of a feminist approach to Judaism but of a personal confrontation with a gender-enforcing tradition that puts her in a place she has no desire to inhabit. Moreover, for Shez everything is personal and love is the goal of every interaction, sexual or otherwise; God becomes a partner not only in caring but also in a caress. God is not the masculine master here but the soft, feminine presence Shez has shied away from showing in herself, publicly.

To promote such talented young poets, Ilan Sheinfeld, himself a poet, established a new publishing company, Shufra (the best), dedicated to publishing works primarily by Israeli LGBTs, although "sometimes we also publish straight literature" its promotional material (re)assures. Shufra has published books by young Israeli writers and poets, as well as *Figs, My Love* (2000) by the bisexual journalist Dana Peleg and *Mom, I've Got Something to Tell You* (Luz and Avni 2000), an anthology of coming-out stories. In addition, Sheinfeld has opened a cafe as part of his bookstore, named Theo for Israel's oldest living activist, Theo Meintz. The cafe and poetry may help Israeli LGBTs invent a gay Hebrew to complement their gay English, but, sadly, the poets Mermelstein, Sheinfeld, and Shez may be the last living writers for whom Hebrew in its biblical glory is still important. Some younger writers tend to reject high-culture Hebrew for street Hebrew to command larger audiences. It is anyone's guess if the three poets are a dying breed or harbingers of a backlash to the erosion of Standard Hebrew.

This tradition-bucking tendency to mold Hebrew as if it were less gender-specific is not new. Yona Wallach knowingly trampled over its gendered aspects to create powerfully moving poetry during the 1980s. In her poem "Ivreet" (1985, 17), the title can be translated as "Hebrew" in the context of the work and is sex/gendered female. But the word has wider cultural ripples that go back to the biblical Jonah, the first man identified as *ivree* (Jewish, Israeli), a Hebrew man who is part of the Hebrew people. Wallach summed up the sex (and gender) differences between the English and Hebrew languages. It is almost impossible to translate this long and rich poem into English because Wallach uses her understanding of gender-free English to manipulate the too-gendered Hebrew, including the use of the word *min* to denote both "sex" and "gender" by subsuming the latter in the former. Its first line reads:

> bi-shmot min yesh le-Anglit kol ha-efsharuyot
> (in names [of] sex/gender there is for English all the possibilities)

Wallach is playing with the sexiness of the foreign allure of English as the language of, say, cinematic romance, with the star system of desirable actors of every sex and style, celebrities of every gender and genre. Although entitled "Ivreet," the poem is more an encomium for English and its endless possibilities for sex/gender performativity. The first part of the poem and the last couplet follow:

> In sex/gender names English is full of possibilities
> Every "I"—in actuality
> Embraces every possibility of sex/gender
> And every you$_f$ is you$_m$
> And every "I" has no sex/gender
> And there is no difference between you$_f$ and you$_m$
> And all things are this—not man not woman

It is not necessary to think before relating to sex/gender
Hebrew is [a] sex-maniac$_f$
Hebrew discriminates for bad or for good
Puts in a good word, provides privileges
. . .
Look what a body the language has and size
Love her now without cover of tongue.

Obsessed with textures, sex, power, gender inequality, and wordplay and breathlessly overlapping in stream-of-consciousness style, Wallach is the consummate poet of difference, of challenge to the unquestioning status quo. She makes her point about the sexual nature of life and language: Sexed language has the power to dominate and to colonize. For her, English offered the possibility of a pastoral utopia of genderless equality and power-sharing. In a like vein, Dana International is an instructive case study of what happens when a fully gendered language (Hebrew) meets non-gendered (gay) English.

Bananas, Potatoes, Pleasure: The Video Clip

For the past few years I have been fascinated by Dana International's sassy approach to gendered language. Her mix of music and machismo, a transitioning of the power principle of gender privilege from male to female (and, should the balance tip too far in the other direction, from female to male), may propel gay English in the Middle East into a linguistic gumbo spiced with her unique blend of words and syllables culled from disparate dance dictionaries. Although a book has been published in Egypt denouncing her as the devil, Dana International is nevertheless hugely popular in the Middle East, with thousands of bootleg cassettes sold. Past performances have included imaginative double entendres based on the Arabic word for "crazy" and using it sex/gendered as both male and female. From her debut in Israeli gay clubs in 1993 Dana International has been political, punchy, and fabulous, using her talent to preach for inclusion as well as to entertain.

Dana International, an openly transgendered singer who is Israel's preeminent dance diva, and her musical manager Ofer Nissim produced a video clip in 1997 specifically for MTV, which chose not to air it. The clip provides insight into the use of gay English alongside the local gay Hebrew lingo that is, as I have indicated previously, a "disco Esperanto" made up of "sampled syllables" from an array of Middle Eastern and European languages. Entitled "Cinquemilla," the song became mainstream Israel's premier dance video that year and won the composers' union prize. The song is a strange brew of words culled from a variety of clichés and scripts and thus a tempting object for linguistic analysis.

Nominally, it is Dana International who is credited with writing the lyrics and Ofer Nissim who is credited with composing the music, but in fact they collaborate on both. In any case, they sample at least as much as they create, forming a techno hybrid common in the global music scene. English— gay, abbreviated, ebonic, or standard—has become the international dance vernacular, as if the genre has become a series of ABBA clones.[7] The ditty "Cinquemilla," which can be translated as "Number 5000," is not about numbers per se but can with a bit of a stretch be considered a song about scoring, that is, finding a willing sex partner. Because the song is space-specific, detailing a space that is at once queer, rhythmic, and polyglot, it seems to be self-referential to Dana International's own dance-space turf, which is mainly, but far from exclusively, gay, male, and sexed. For Dana International, judging from a multitude of interviews she gave the media in 1998, it is presumed that a listener/dancer's sex partner will be chosen for pleasure alone and in complete oblivion of social norms and expectations, although those do not necessarily have to be thwarted for desire to be fulfilled. Thus, "Cinquemilla" and indeed all her songs are meant for those who choose freely from the full array of human possibilities, whatever the gender and sexual orientation of the participant. Unlike Hebrew, which has no capital letters, Dana International's lyrics in internationalese are written only in capitals.

"Cinquemilla" begins with the statement "THIS IS MY HOUSE," which seems to be a pun on the dance music she performs, often called "house" as well as "techno" or "dance" music (at one point in its more melodic larval stage it was called "disco"). She immediately announces as much by singing "TO THE RHYTHM" with no linguistic bridge, leaving the meaning hanging in the silence. Dana International's language thus seems to contain words but has no syntax. For good measure, the phrase "to the rhythm" is repeated before she riffs into a syllabic stew that has no meaning but is sung to a systemic rhythm.

What "TO THE RHYTHM" can mean is expanded and enriched if the phrase is parsed as an example of the globalization of gay English, for in that case the words take on myriad meanings and mimetic manipulations that Standard English cannot (and wishes not to) support. There is the obvious rhythm of the dance and the less obvious rhythm of the sexual search and the sexual act, performed mimetically on the dance floor, less publicly in the venue's bathroom or surrounding bushes, or more privately in a rented, borrowed, or owned room. This rhythm is the fundamental reason for using gay English globally in the first place: to meet and greet fellow sex travelers along a shared trajectory of nominally transgressive desire.

Having introduced her transgressive theme among the simplistic syllables, Dana International cuts to the chase and asks, "DO YOU HAVE A RESERVATION?" Although the question seems to come out of the blue, it is grounded in her personal history. After all, she began her divadom with an eponymous song that self-created Dana International as a flight attendant on flight "SIX O SEX TO MONACO" from "SAUDI ARABIAN AIRPORT."[8] The next line makes an abrupt shift to the first, expounding on why it is important for the audience to be introduced to "MY HOUSE": There is a party there. What kind of party? The words are simple and direct: "I SERVE BANANAS." Why bananas? Perhaps because the banana is an international graphic symbol for the penis, something that, in her official biography, Dana International states she lost at a London clinic several years ago. In case anyone misses the meaning, the word is repeated three more times. The video clip shows her riding on a monstrous banana in maniacal fashion, a mythical siren gone berserk when she finally gets what she wants. And if this repetition, so critical to Butler's analysis of performativity, is not sufficient, Dana International adds "potatos [sic] and some coc [sic]." The last syllable may be a misspelling of the English word *cock* or the French word for rooster—or it may be meant as a wink to the term used in Hebrew and French to denote a transgendered male-to-female person.

In a frenzy, Dana International repeats her syllabic stew with some additions, including the title word morphed into "MARAQUITA—CHIQUITITA," which is, again, repeated three more times before "LISTEN TO THE RHYTHM" is reprised four times and the word *rhythm* three more to complete the musical phrase. The linguistic potential of the words, fragments left without verbs and syntactical connectors, is left, whether purposefully or by chance, as ambiguous or ironic and self-reflexive as the title itself, which is repeated after yet another rendition of "THIS IS MY HOUSE." The work ends on a repetition of the word in its phonetic-equivalent but meaning-different, male-sex/gendered ending: "CINQUECENTO" (500). The conclusion thus suggests that Dana International may either have had other ideas from the start or has come to a different place at the end. In any case, the whole is at once richer and less complete than the sum of its parts.

The vision of Dana International riding the banana remains engraved in one's mind long after the music fades. It is a visual use of global gay lingo, nominally English but ultimately more visually than verbally articulated, a perhaps unintended consequence of MTV's supremacy in the youth market. And perhaps the most interesting aspect of the globalization of gay English is not its specific words and phrases but its style, look, and feel and the pride of being gay, lesbian, bisexual, or transgendered—the notion that identity can be named and celebrated. As is the case with modern music, which is most easily digested when coupled with modern dance, Dana International's music is best digested on the dance floor in actual experience rather than in academic pursuit of a meaning that may or may not exist beyond the moment. After all, dance lyrics are notoriously silly and leave little beyond their rhythm, beyond the beat, except for perhaps a catchy refrain such as "it's raining men," "YMCA," or, in this case, "ALORA ROLA" or "CINQUEMILLA." Dana International in her early years (she has since become a mainstream pop singer) was as good as it gets, an icon of global gay English rooted in a language bazaar of the East.

Conclusion

This chapter examines the affinity of LGBT Israelis, especially Jews but Arab citizens and Palestinian neighbors as well, for gay English, which they perceive to be a genderless lingo, and the concomitant engagement of Jewish Israelis with the sex/gendered nature of the Hebrew language to bend it to a more fluid expression of their sexual and gender orientations. I also touch briefly on the political ramifications of the Hebrew language's historical and religious enmeshing with issues of identity, nationality, and place. Jewish LGBTs have tried to include Muslim and Christian LGBTs but with little success. Now, however, the Jerusalem Open House actively recruits non-Jewish participants, and the Agudah maintains a support group for Arab youths. It is a far cry from the early 1990s, when I was involved in the coming-out process of a young Bedouin who could not even publish a paid personal advertisement in Israel's largest, most progressive Arabic newspaper. The university-educated Bedouin member of the Knesset from his town declared that homosexuality brings AIDS to Arabs and offered no solace.

It is ironic that while Israel is one of the most liberal nations on earth in terms of LGBT rights, extending them to its Arab citizens as well, it is uniformly denigrated as racist and colonialist by those who turn a blind eye to Islam's uncompromising position on homosexuality and problematic approach to women's issues, whether in fact or in the written Quran (which, alas, condemns homosexuals to whipping and even being stoned to death). Hopefully, the day will soon come when a democratic and secular Palestine (in the West Bank and Gaza) will thrive alongside a more inclusive Israel, and LGBT citizens of both lands will not be marginalized.

David Bell and Jon Binnie (2000) argue that everyone is a "sexual citizen," whether actively transgressive or passively mainstreamed, and that "finding ways to be a sexual citizen" involves choices between "the choice to disidentify—to remain non-citizens" (a defiant act that, they maintain, makes it easier for those in power to disenfranchise the weak and marginalized) and the choice to "secure status as citizens, and look around at the potential rights claims might have on others," for example, those who question the value of the rights being sought (146). Before any choice can be made, however, the ability to participate in a conversation about culture and politics requires access to that ephemeral "common language" dreamed of by poet Adrienne Rich.

L. L. Zamenhof introduced one variant, called Esperanto, in 1887. His idea was to allow people all over the world, whatever their language or ideology, "to communicate, yet at the same time retain their own languages and cultural identities" because, according to the Web-site for the Esperanto League for North America (ELNA), "Esperanto doesn't replace anyone's language but simply serves as a common second language . . . Esperanto is politically unbiased." But Esperanto has grown where it began, in the literate circles of the educationally privileged. Although it has a strong LGBT following and every international conference includes a gay caucus, it has not gained currency as a global second language. English has. But a "common language" may produce uncommon glitches because of sociocultural biases. Karin Dovring introduces the cautionary concept of "Bodysnatched English," a term she uses to refer to some downsides in the use of English (and, we can extrapolate, gay English) as an international vernacular that is disembodied and nonorganic: "Everybody knows what the other fellow is talking about during travels on the International Superhighway," but Internet English "has a semantic life of its own, with political and practical consequences" that must be acknowledged, "the more so as we become aware of the different voices from global and domestic competing ideologies and goals" (1997, xi). The words may be the same, but the meaning may differ. Thus, it is important to analyze gay English usage in non-English-speaking countries, with particular attention to local language(s), culture(s), and linguistic customs.

In the case of Israel, as I have indicated, the fact that Hebrew (like Arabic) is a fully gendered language makes English both attractive and problematic. As more and more young people come of age in the postcloset era—people who have postmodern sensibilities and eschew the body politic to embrace instead the actual body of their desire—language shifts more and more toward gay English and the global consumer consciousness absorbed from MTV and McDonald's. But the perception of English as a universal languaculture is false, and thus the use of gay English in Israel is neither uniformly applauded nor embraced. Although Dana International's milieu is the global dance scene, for example, dance lingo in Israel is almost exclusively spoken by males, who refer to each other exclusively as female. Such playful sex/gender-bending is lost in gender-free gay English, resulting in a push-and-pull situation in the Israeli LGBT community as it decides on a language of its own.

The use of gay English in Israel is not rampant beyond the basics concerning how we name ourselves and with whom we are in intimate contact. It is a defining language that is gender-free and boundaryless, seemingly free of ideology and politics and of borders and local concerns. It is liberating and universalizing, stylish and sophisticated, and different and familiar all at once. Moreover, Hebrew is changing to meet the challenge, showing resilience despite its ancient roots and cumbersome grammar. LGBT poets/writers, singers, and performers celebrate the differences and the possibilities, but for the heteronormative majority the revolution is televised while they sleep. Whether the impact of gay English and gender-bending Hebrew will be felt in everyday life and speech remains an open but intriguing question.

If in the past the movement for the liberation of sex/gender minorities in Israel (and, by extension, the immediate Middle East) has been one of mainstreaming, as Kama (2000) indicates, certainly that phase is over, having achieved its primary goal. Even though I was one of the architects and implementers of that strategy, however, I think the struggle must now move forward in new ways that reflect the fact that a new generation born into greater acceptance, at least in the large secular segment of society, is stepping into leadership positions.

One of the major factors in this new equation is the proliferation of youth groups throughout Israel, many of which are in areas that do not self-identify as mainstream but as economically and politically marginalized. Susan Kirshner and Jerry Levinson formed and jointly ran the Agudah's first youth groups in 1993. The groups had met clandestinely previously, and it was decided that it was important to have them be as transparent as the rest of the coming-out movement. Levinson has since established the Jerusalem Open House and, as of 2002, was the first and only gay member of the Jerusalem Municipal Council. To my mind, the JOH is poised to lead the LGBT community in Israel (and perhaps Palestine) into the coming century because of its refreshing insistence on inclusion and legitimate debate.

Younger, ahistorical activists are reinventing the LGBT community in their own image—global, fun-loving, educated, stylish, and gender-bending. That grass-roots swell of energy may mean the end of the two older associations, the Agudah and CLAF ("Lesbian-Feminist Community" in Hebrew), the lesbian-feminist group that refuses contact with the Agudah because of its purported sexism. CLAF is now self-absorbed and insular, concentrating on issues of lesbian parenting. The Agudah is seen as a stepping-stone for local and national political office. So far, Michal Eden, a lesbian, and Uzi Even, a gay man, are the only openly gay elected officials. She is a member of the Tel Aviv City Council, and for three months in 2002–3 he was a member of the Israeli Knesset. No LGBTs were elected to the new Knesset in February 2003.

The Jewish sages of old declared that "life and death are in the hands of the tongue," a pun in ivreet as well as in English because "tongue" means both a body part and a language. Linguists may not be renowned for saving lives, nor comparatists, but I hope I have demonstrated the possibilities for fruitful engagement and dialogue about ideology, national identity, and sex/gender that a close reading of literary texts and a careful listening to songs and speech can elicit.

Notes

1. These Hebrew words were first used together in *Min Mig'dar Politica* (Sex Gender Politics: Women in Israel) (Izraeli 1999).

2. Nissim Gal, a lecturer in the history of art department at Tel Aviv University, pointed out to me in an e-mail dated July 15, 2002, that the spring 2002 edition of the Hebrew-language quarterly *Teoria ve Bikoret* (Theory and Criticism) included an article by Doron Narkiss, "English in Foreign Eyes," that presents, for women, a contrary approach to English as a substitute for male-dominated Hebrew. The quarterly's editor, Shenhav, notes that Narkiss considers "language as an arena of struggle and focuses on the teaching of English as a hegemonic language in Israeli society because he points out the dual status of the language for Mizrahi and Palestinian women and for new immigrant women, who learn English in the regional colleges. Even though English is the strongest expression of Western hegemony, for these women it is a means to get around their marginal status as well as the oppressive dimensions of Hebrew" (presumably as a fully gendered language in which the male is dominant).

3. I have articulated my (former) ideas on sex and gender elsewhere (Moriel 1998, 1999a, 1999b). Nora Greenberg, a computer specialist who is also facilitator of the Agudah's transgender support group, brought her objections to such an old-fashioned taxonomy to my attention during a workshop at Giv'at Haviva, Israel, in July 2002, and I thank her for doing so. Hardware (and sex/gender) is much more fluid these days, akin to software.

4. In all these cases I have placed the masculine version of the word before the female version because that is the way the words appear in casual conversation in Israel, where the male is privileged over the female socially and culturally as well as linguistically.

5. The term *languaculture* is borrowed from Michael Agar (1994), who uses it to ensure that "culture" never be divorced from "language." Language, he maintains, is always used in the context of culture and is universal: "True, there are still small groups isolated in space. But information and the consequences of political and economic events move through them and divide them and tie them to the world outside" (122).

6. Avraham Even-Shoshan was the Noah Webster of the Hebrew language. It was Eliezer

Ben-Yehuda who revived the language in the late nineteenth century, but it was Even-Shoshan who codified usage in 1952 and, two decades later, produced a complete, single-volume dictionary of the Hebrew language from antiquity to the modern era. In 1978 Even-Shoshan received the prestigious Israel Prize for his work. The dictionary has no entry for "homosexual" but only for "homosexuality," which is defined as "perverse sexual desire of a man or a woman for those of their own kind" (143). There is a benign definition for les'beet: "an appellation for a woman who has sexual relations with her own kind" (325). There is no definition for either bisexual or transgender. The Alcalay (1975) Hebrew-English dictionary, however, does contain a definition for "homosexual," and it is derogatory: "sick sexual desire of one man for another." Following an angry letter to his office, Minister of Commerce Ran Cohen asked the publishers for an explanation, and they promised a neutral definition in the next edition. As Adi Arbel, the distribution coordinator for the publisher, told the minister, "The current definition is indeed antiquated, insulting and wrong."

7. ABBA (Agnetha Faltskog, Bjorn Ulvaeus, Benny Andersson, and Ani-Frid Lyngstad), a Swedish pop quartet that was a singing and style sensation during the 1970s, came to global prominence in 1974 when they won the Eurovision Song Contest with "Waterloo."

8. At the beginning of her career Dana International spelled her name "Danna International," which is how it is rendered on her first four compact discs. She dropped the unnecessary second *n* (à la Barbra Streisand) in 1998 in preparation for participation in the Eurovision Song Contest.

Works Cited

Agar, Michael. 1994. *Language Shock.* New York: William Morrow.

Alcalay, Reuben. 1975. *The Complete Hebrew-English Dictionary.* Jerusalem: Massada.

Aronson, Jacob. 1999. "Homosex in Hanoi? Sex, the Public Sphere, and Public Sex." In *Public Sex/Gay Space,* ed. William L. Leap, 203–21. New York: Columbia University Press.

Bell, David, and Jon Binnie. 2000. *The Sexual Citizen.* Cambridge: Polity.

Ben-Ari, Adital Tirosh. 2001. "Experiences of 'Not Belonging' in Collectivistic Communities: Narratives of Gays in Kibbutzes." *Journal of Homosexuality* 42(2): 101–24.

Butler, Judith. 1990. *Gender Trouble.* New York: Routledge.

Cameron, Deborah, and Jennifer Coates. 1988. "Some Problems in the Sociolinguistic Explanation of Sex Differences." In *Women in Their Speech Communities,* ed. Jennifer Coates and Deborah Cameron, 13–26. London: Longman.

Coates, Jennifer, and Deborah Cameron. 1988. "Preface." In *Women in Their Speech Communities,* ed. Jennifer Coates and Deborah Cameron, vii–viii. London: Longman.

Dana International. 1996. "Cinquemilla." *Maganona* (CD). Helicon.

Donovan, Josephine. 1980. "The Silence Is Broken." In *Women and Language in Literature and Society,* ed. Sally McConnell-Ginet, Ruth Borker, and Nelly Furman, 205–18. New York: Praeger.

Dovring, Karin. 1997. *English as Lingua France: Double Talk in Global Persuasion.* Westport: Praeger.

ELNA. Esperanto League for North America <http://www.esperanto-usa.org/> accessed on Feb. 25, 2003.

Even-Shoshan, Avraham. 1981. *HaMilon HaIvri HaMercuaz* (The abridged Hebrew dictionary). Jerusalem: Kiryat Sefer.

Fink, Amir Sumka'i, and Jacob Press. 1999. *Independence Park: The Lives of Gay Men in Israel*. Stanford: Stanford University Press.

Friedlander, M., ed. 1953. *Tanah: The Hebrew Bible with English Translation*. Jerusalem: Jerusalem Bible Publishing.

Gluzman, Michael, and Gil Nader. 1996. *Mi'lon A'her* (Alternative dictionary). Tel Aviv: Private printing.

Halpern, Orly. 2002. "Isn't That Queer?" *In These Times*, Aug. 16 <http://www.inthesetimes.com/issue/26/21/culture2.shtml> accessed on Feb. 25, 2003.

Izraeli, Dafna N. 1999. *Min Mig'dar Politikah* (Sex gender politics: Women in Israel). Tel Aviv: Hakibbutz Hameuchad.

Kadish, Ruti. 2002. "Israeli Gays and Lesbians Encounter Zionism." In *Queer Jews*, ed. David Shneer and Karyn Aviv, 224–37. New York: Routledge.

Kama, Amit. 2000. "From Terra Incognita to Terra Firma: The Logbook of the Voyage of Gay Men's Community into the Israeli Public Sphere." *Journal of Homosexuality* 38(4): 133–62.

Kulick, Don. 1998. "Anger, Gender, Language Shift, and Politics." In *Language Ideologies: Practice and Theory*, ed. Bambi B. Schieffelin, Kathryn A. Wooland, and Paul V. Kroskrity, 87–102. New York: Oxford University Press.

———. 2000. "Gay and Lesbian Language." *Annual Review of Anthropology* 29: 243–85.

Labov, William. 1994. "The Study of Nonstandard English." In *Language: Introductory Readings*, ed. Virginia P. Clark, Paul A. Eschholz, and Alfred F. Rosa, 555–62. New York: St. Martin's Press.

Leap, William L. 1996. *Word's Out: Gay Men's English*. Minneapolis: University of Minnesota Press.

Livia, Anna, and Kira Hall, eds. 1997. *Queerly Phrased: Language, Gender, and Sexuality*. New York: Oxford University Press.

Lucy, John A. 1992. *Grammatical Categories and Cognition*. New York: Cambridge University Press.

Luz, Dvora, and Sarah Avni. 2000. *Ima, Yesh Li Mashehu LeSaper Lach* (Mom, I've got something to tell you). Tel Aviv: Shufra.

Mermelstein, Zvi. 1998. *Mehazer Al Pitzei Elyonim veTaxtonim* (Serenading at the gates of angels and men). Tel Aviv: Shufra.

Moore, Tracy, ed. 1995. *Lesbiot: Israeli Lesbians Talk about Sexuality, Feminism, Judaism and Their Lives*. London: Cassell.

Moriel, Liora. 1998. "Diva in the Promised Land: A Blue-print for Newspeak?" *World Englishes* 17(2): 225–37.

———. 1999a. "Dana International: A Self-Made Jewish Diva." *Race, Gender and Class* 6(4): 110–24.

———. 1999b. *Yipea laululintu: Dana International ja Eurovision laulukilpailut* (A proud songbird: Dana International and the Eurovision song contest). *Lahikuva* (Finland), no. 2–3.

Peleg, Dana G. 2000. *Te'enim, ahuvati: sipurim* (Figs, my love). Tel Aviv: Shufra.

Roca, I. M. 1989. "The Organization of Grammatical Gender." *Transactions of the Philological Society* 87(1): 1–32.

Shez. 1996. "Elohim (God)." Unpublished poem. Translated from the Hebrew by Liora Moriel.

Solomon, Harris. 2001. "Skirting Around: Towards an Understanding of HIV/AIDS Educational Materials in Modern Israeli Hebrew." In *Language and Sexuality: Contesting Meaning in Theory and Practice,* ed. Kathryn Campbell-Kibler et al., 225–47. Stanford: Center for the Study of Language and Information Publications.

Wallach, Yona. 1985. "Ivreet" (Hebrew). In *Tzurot* (Forms), trans. Liora Moriel, 17–19. Tel Aviv: HaKibutz HaMe'uhad.

Walzer, Lee. 2000. *Between Sodom and Eden: A Gay Man's Journey through Today's Changing Israel.* New York: Columbia University Press.

5. Language, Belonging, and (Homo)sexual Citizenship in Cape Town, South Africa

WILLIAM L. LEAP

Very different from Zimbabwe, Singapore, and other national settings where the state works hard to silence and discredit homosexual presence and practices, the national project in post-Apartheid South Africa has positioned same-sex identities in the foreground of sexual citizenship. The constitution of 1996 guarantees that all South African citizens will enjoy freedom from discrimination based on race, gender, sex, and marital status as well as sexual orientation; other provisions define the term *citizen* in equally inclusive terms.[1] Discussions of homosexuality are equally evident in ongoing debates over sexuality, whether occurring in South African churches (Germond and de Gruchy eds. 1997), university settings, or programs providing medical care and other social services to the townships, rural communities, and long-neglected areas within cities.

This component of South African nation-building reflects, in part, the willingness of political workers engaged in anti-Apartheid struggles to include sexuality and gender in their blueprints for a more progressive society. It speaks to the success of same-sex-identified South Africans in achieving greater visibility within the political arena, both during the Apartheid period and more recently (Gevisser and Cameron eds. 1994) It also coincides with ongoing efforts of same-sex-identified women and men to claim citizenship in other locations worldwide (Adam, Duyvendak, and Krouwel eds. 1999; see also the chapters by Boellstorff, Jackson, Moriel, Murray, and Provencher in this volume).

Prominent in this emerging visibility are new ways of talking about same-sex desires and erotic practices as well as new ways of naming same-sex-related identities and subjectivities. In part, these ways of talking and naming build directly on South African discourses of sexuality and gender and on the linguistic resources (e.g., Xhosa, Afrikaans, and English) through which those discourses are locally maintained. At the same time, they incorporate linguistic features and cultural frames of reference developed elsewhere (frequently in North Atlantic locations) and imported into South African settings through travel and tourism, news and the entertainment media, internet technologies, and other means.

Although this convergence of "local" and "globalized" linguistic/cultural practices has brought new understandings of sexual citizenship into ongoing conversations about post-Apartheid society, these understandings are not entirely segregated from the older, more enduring assumptions about sexuality and civic practice that are still part of the national and local South African terrain. The tensions between new understandings and older assumptions are especially pronounced in instances (black townships, rural Afrikaner communities) where sexual culture tolerates certain forms of homosexuality while vigorously proscribing its other forms and in instances where same-sex desire may be publically embodied but must remain unspoken and unnamed. Under these circumstances, same-sex-identified South Africans who claim sexual citizenship in "national"/constitutional terms risk becoming outcasts or pariahs within the local/community setting, as much because of the visibility now assigned to their sexuality as their pursuit of transgressive desire.

Understandably, same-sex-identified women and men are searching for ways to give voice to these competing understandings of citizenship and sexuality and articulate the position(s) they claim within these contested domains as sexual persons and as citizens. What emerges from this formation is a creative and flexible language of sexual citizenship which, by incorporating material from a variety of linguistic traditions, allows discussions of sexual identities and experiences in an idiom a broader audience will also be able to understand.[2]

Audience reception is especially important in the South African case, given that the constitutional endorsement of (homo)sexual citizenship precedes its acceptance in many local domains. In this sense, the language under construction not only marks a speaker's status as sexual citizen but also proposes the legitimacy of that status in culturally as well as constitutionally appropriate terms.

Background: On Citizenship, Sexuality, and Language

Defining Citizenship

Citizenship is a central theme in the social and linguistic practices of interest to this discussion, but there are several ways to explain what citizenship actually means in this setting. Perhaps the most familiar frames definitions of citizenship and citizen in neo-liberal terms. Citizenship, for example, is accessible to any individual or group hoping to gain access to its benefits and protections and willing to comply with its obligations. Cindy Patton defines citizenship as "the prescriptive and resistant practices that relate body to nation through rights, duties, responsibilities and membership" (1997, xii). Under that definition, citizenship is not just a status within civil society but is also a mode of social action through which individuals and groups establish a subject position as citizen and from that basis assert other claims to "place" within the broader social domain.

Some theorists recognize that these emerging subject positions are not always uniform. Mouffe describes citizenship as "an articulating principle that affects the different subject positions of the social agent, while allowing for a plurality of specific allegiances and for the respect of individual liberties" (1991, 79). But it is not enough to admit that citizenship is (or can be) multiply constructed. Although the emerging diversity may appear to create conditions of social inclusion (another neo-liberal theme), closer inspection shows a much closer alignment between diverse meanings of citizenship and broader structures of economic and social inequality. As Maurer explains, diverse meanings of citizenship are often transformed into more inclusive distinctions between "good citizens" who are "conceptualized as a group of normative 'individuals' who are defined as similar and equals" and "'(b)ad citizens,' different and unequal," who "are cast as unable to stand alone as true individuals and therefore unable to contribute to the public good" (2000, 101). The status of "bad citizen" becomes marked on the body, in residence practice, through linguistic usage and in other ways. Those markings make it even more difficult for persons assigned to that category to reverse their devalued status. Certainly, the voluntary compliance with authority and power proposed in Patton's and and Mouffe's theorizing of citizenship offers little assistance in that regard.

As an alternative to these neo-liberal treatments, some writers prefer to define citizenship in ways that foreground, rather than erase, its connections to inequality. Studies that contrast "good" and "bad" citizenship address this concern directly, as do studies distinguishing "legal" and "cultural" citizenship (Flores and Benmayor 1997; Murray 1997); studies connecting meanings of citizenship with forms and practices of consumption (Evans 1993; Hennessy 1995; Stychin 1998, 15); and studies that trace the pathways of citizenship within mobile as well as stable geographies (Manalansan 2001; Ong 1999). Repeatedly, the studies remind us that citizenship is not an autonomous construction but a status that gains meaning only within the complex geographies of the state, civil society, and the family and within economic and social structures that diversify and stratify everyday life within those domains. How understandings of citizenship intersect with local histories becomes relevant to these discussions, as does how citizenship engages diaspora, globalization, and other transnational flows.

Citizenship and Sexuality

Under these circumstances citizenship becomes a category of diverse or pluralized meanings "regulated by practices favoring flexibility, mobility and repositioning in relation to markets, governments and cultural regimes. These logics and practices are produced within particular structures of meaning about family, gender, nationality, class mobility, and social power" (Ong 1999, 6). Ong's discussions of family and gender in this regard suggest that understandings of sexuality are also included in these structures of meaning. Indeed, as Bell and Binnie (2000, 10) observe, not only are "the foundational tenants of being a citizen . . . inflected by sexualities [but] . . . many of the ways in which citizenship discourses operate can be read as discourses around the 'sexing' of citizens."[3]

Confronted with such discursive practices, would-be citizens may remain silent about their sexuality, allowing those practices to speak for them whenever the sexual dimensions of their citizenship are called into question. But silence will not always disguise a citizen's transgressive sexuality or shield the citizen from retaliation because of it. Under those circumstances, and under less combative conditions as well, speakers need access to an alternative set of discursive practices capable of marking and mediating civic, cultural, and personal differences in less disruptive, less antagonistic ways.

A language of sexual citizenship becomes an appropriate remedy for this problem. Access to such a language will not ensure an uncontested access to citizenship or guarantee an acceptance of such status by others, even when constitutional authority confirms it. But access can help would-be citizens press the legitimacy of their claims by increasing their visibility as sexual persons as well as would-be citizens within national and local domains. And that is exactly what has unfolded since the early 1990s in post-Apartheid South Africa.

Background: Notes on (Homo)sexual Citizenship in the New South Africa

South Africa's political and sexual terrain changed greatly during the 1990s, first with the transition from Nationalist Party rule to Nelson Mandela's government of national reconciliation and then with the ratification of a new constitution confirming civil rights and liberties for all South African citizens, including freedom from discrimination on the basis of sex, gender, or sexual orientation. The constitution did not nullify laws that criminalized homosexual erotic activities, but its wording encouraged efforts nationwide to have those laws declared unconstitutional, and several court cases have responded accordingly since that time.

Before 1996 homosexuality had been regulated carefully, if somewhat unevenly, in South African daily life.[4] As part of its commitment to white privilege, Apartheid governmentality placed high values on heterosexual marriage, reproduction, and family life and established strict racial and social requirements to determine when procreative sexual activity (and its consequences) would be considered legitimate in the eyes of the state. Homosexuality was problematic under that arrangement to the extent that homosexual object choice prevented sexual subjects from meeting their procreative obligations.[5]

As Mark Gevisser observes, "While sodomy and a range of other 'unnatural offenses' was illegal according to the common law, gay men could only commit statutory offences when in public . . . masquerading as women or soliciting in cruising spots" (1994, 31). In other words, the men in question should not have been conducting themselves in such fashion in public settings. They should have been at home—that is, with their wives and families—where responsible adult men ("good citizens") appropriately belong. Male homosexuality was still illegal if practiced in private locations, but such practices were not ordinarily called into question unless the number of men in a private setting was sufficiently large (three or more, said the legislation) to make the gathering "a party" and therefore a public event vulnerable to police raid, arrest, and prosecution.

Private parties in Cape Town were subject to police regulation under the three-men-at-a-party clause, and many men I have interviewed have stories about such events. Police raids were also conducted in gay and gay-friendly bars and clubs in Cape Town's central business district and in the cruising areas along the beach walk at Sea Point, at nearby Graaff's Pool (an enclosed, oceanfront nude swimming and sun-bathing site frequented by orthodox Jewish men and men looking for male sex partners), and at other locations.

Even when the raids were prompted by some form of interracial transgression, police harassment was not sufficiently frequent to discourage participants from returning to those sites and continuing to enjoy the social opportunities available to them there. Interracial homosexual activities were criminalized not because they constituted a sexual crime but because the intimacy transgressed racial boundaries (Leap 2002a). Even so, interracial homosexuality was a visible part of Cape Town's gay scene, including casual erotic exchange in the railway station's "cottages" (rest rooms) and other locations; informal social exchange at several of the city's gay bars and clubs (although not all were willing to admit persons of color, even when licensing laws allowed them to do so); and as white/colored partnered relationships of somewhat longer duration.

It would be incorrect to suggest that white gay life under Apartheid rule in South Africa was entirely free of state oppression. There were police raids, there was harassment, there were criminal trials, and there were consequences. But while the state retained authority to harass and arrest its homosexual subjects, that authority was inconsistently implemented. Those not already rendered vulnerable under other components of the Apartheid system could use discretion, careful planning, and (when other strategies failed) class and racial privilege to protect themselves from anti-gay harassment.

Conditions were much more complex within the black townships located east of the City Centre. With very few exceptions these were the only sites in the Cape Town area where black residence was allowed, and governmental policies of deliberate neglect sharply limited even the most basic conditions of human comfort—adequate housing, clean water, affordable food and medicine, and protection from violence and crime.[6] Male- and female-centered homosexualities have lengthy histories in these settlements, and their details have been shaped by many sources, including the status assigned to same-sex identities and attractions in the sexual cultures of the indigenous people of southern Africa (Kendall 1999); the male-centered, domestic-labor-based, same-sex relationships that emerged in the labor camps at gold and diamond mines and were supported by mining authorities (Elder, in press; Moodie, Ndatshe, and Sibuyi 1988); and the legacies of white-controlled, predatory homosexuality that took form during the colonial period and echo in today's racially driven (homo)sexual tourism.

Isi tabane, the male-bodied, cross-dressing, township-based public identity that obligates (male) participants to take up the economic and social responsibilities of adult women, is one outcome of this history. Another outcome is reflected in the lives of township men and women whose public personae conceal their same-sex attractions but who pursue those interests actively while outside of the public eye and, now, outside township settings altogether. Here, unlike the case for *isi tabane,* an indigenous term for these persons is not attested in current township sexual discourses. Similarly, and again echoing arguments from Kendall's discussion of Lesotho women, indigenous terms for women-centered, same-sex attractions, however publicly or privately constructed, are not reported in township sexual discourses. If direct reference is unavoidable, loanwords from English are employed.

Diverse forms of homosexuality were also part of sexual cultures of the predominately Afrikaner-based, rural communities at greater distance from Cape Town. Although the Afrikaans-derived term *moffie* has become a synonym for male homosexuality in South African public discourse, "moffie" actually commands a somewhat broader meaning in rural settings and could be used to describe any male-bodied adult not conforming to normative expectations related to marriage, procreation, and family life.[7] Hence, the unmarried pastor of the local Dutch Reformed Church could be described as a moffie whether he was effeminate or more masculine in demeanor and whatever his choice of sexual object. Similarly, villagers could use "moffie" to refer to a dutiful son who, instead of creating his own household elsewhere, chooses to remain at home and take care of elderly parents who would otherwise be unable to provide for themselves. Not so accepted, of course, was the village resident whose pursuit of same-sex desire violated expectations of public discretion. That person, too, may have been described as a moffie, but the label assumed more transgressive, and more serious, meanings in that context.

Building a Language of Sexual Citizenship

The South African constitution speaks to all of these same-sex-related (and, at times, gender-transgressive) identities, experiences, practices, and inequalities when promising protection from discrimination on the basis of sexual orientation. By doing so the constitution has called into being a new, unified category of non-normative homosexuality whose place within post-Apartheid South Africa's national sexual culture is officially sanctioned by state practice. In Pierre de Vos's apt phrasing, "The constitution made us queer" (2001, 194). Given the regulated but still ambiguous status assigned to homosexuality when the constitution was first being drafted (1991–94), this is a remarkable turn-around—a point that South Africa's racially, ethnic, and economically diverse homosexual constituencies have not overlooked.

Diverse as these constituencies remain (and to avoid calling into question the authority of the constitutionally sanctioned, inclusive status that now unites them), same-sex-identified women and men are faced with the task of actualizing this "unity" in their everyday lives. Public events with high visibility, such as the Johannesburg-based gay pride weekend that attracts participants from across South Africa and nearby nations, national mobilizations around HIV-related vaccine trials and the equitable distributions of HIV-related medication, and the foregrounding of lesbian/gay presence within the African National Congress (ANC) and other segments of the anti-Apartheid movement, are just a few of the projects that South African same-sex-identified women and men, and their allies, have undertaken to that end.

One consequence of the projects is the emergence of ways of talking about same-sex desires and experiences and naming same-sex identities. Those ways, while attentive to local understandings of sexual sameness, also allow discussions of these themes and make them meaningful to a wider South Africa audience. Under formation is a language of sexual citizenship that corresponds to the new, constitutionally generated category of *homosexual citizen* and helps strengthen its validity. As of the summer of 2002 the language was not as formalized as Indonesia's *bahasa gay* (Boellstorff, this volume), and its primary concern was not the insider-code functions commonly associated with gay men's English in the United States (Leap 1996), *polari* in Great Britain (Lucas 1997), or the text-making of Kano, Nigeria's *'yan daudu* (Gaudio 1997). Linguistic practices in South Africa are of a somewhat different construction and creatively and flexibly draw on a range of linguistic traditions, yielding discussions of homosexuality and homosexual-as-citizen in an idiom meaningful in local speech contexts and beyond.

About My Research

My interest in this South African language of same-sex experience is nested within a larger project exploring the intersections of sexuality, race, and place in the greater Cape Town area. Working with colleagues at the Triangle Project (a Cape Town–based HIV and lesbian/gay rights advocacy group) and in the Theory of Literature Programme at the University of Cape Town, I have collected descriptions of Cape Town's lesbian/gay geographies and life story narratives as well as other commentary from ninety-two Cape Town–area women and men whose backgrounds are richly stratified along lines of sex, gender, sexual orientation, age, race, ethnicity, class, residence, income, and employment status. I lived in Cape Town for extended periods during each research visit and became immersed in various segments of the City Centre and township gay scene. Those experiences have given me additional perspective on the concerns expressed in the interviews and introduced me to other sources of data as well.

Thanks to the assistance of research colleagues, interviews have been conducted in English, Afrikaans, and Xhosa, frequently with discussions becoming framed in two (or all three) of those languages. The translation tasks (I am fluent neither in Xhosa nor Afrikaans) provided my initial encounters with the "new" ways of talking about homosexuality and (homo)sexual citizenship that have emerged in the Cape Town area, and elsewhere in South Africa, since 1995. Newspaper articles, commercial and public advertising, visual media materials, and countless informal conversations on lesbian/gay topics and related themes have provided additional examples of linguistic texts and linguistic practices.

To illustrate the workings of this language-under-construction, I will examine three sets of data: underlying patterns structuring the naming of gay bars and clubs in Cape Town from 1980 to 1998, the linguistic organization of gay men's classified advertisements, and the language diversity framing the life story narratives of black-township, same-sex-identified women and men.

The Semiotics of Language Choice

The language traditions at issue in these data are English, Afrikaans, and Xhosa, each of which commands its own cultural and political associations within everyday discourses in the Cape Town area.[8] English, for example, is a language closely aligned with North Atlantic experience, and for some South Africans it still calls to mind their ties to the ancestral/colonial homeland. English is also a language of mobility, and its mastery is required for anyone planning to explore opportunities beyond the national boundary. Afrikaans, although also a language with North Atlantic connections, is a product of in-situ colonial process and ensuring efforts to maintain Afrikaner uniqueness in the face of British colonial rule and its aftermath. In that sense, Afrikaans is a language of resistance and a source of Afrikaner pride. At the same time, Afrikaans is the language closely associated with Apartheid rule and with the proponents of Apartheid-based policies of racial segregation and white privilege, then and today. It remains the primary language used by the South African military, police, and administrative bureaucracy that supports their authority.[9]

In contrast to English and Afrikaans, Xhosa has much deeper roots in the South African cultural soil. Its closest linguistic relatives are Zulu, Swati, and Ndebele, the members of the Nguni cluster within the Bantu language family. Other Bantu languages spoken in southern Africa, including northern and southern Sotho, Tswana, Tsonga, and Venda, are also related to Xhosa, if more distantly (Mesthre 1995, xv). For its speakers, Xhosa affirms spatial as well as cultural continuities and is prized all the more because it remains a viable means of communication in spite of the linguistic encroachment of the colonial period and Apartheid. Moreover, and also unlike English and Afrikaans, Xhosa is not a language that non-black South Africans are likely to understand. Conversations in Xhosa can be secret conversations, whether from an outsider or insider perspective.

Example 1: Changes in Names and Naming Practices of Cape Town–Area Gay Bars

Assigning a name to a gay bar or dance club in any location is a strategic linguistic act. The name needs to be noticeable and suggest that the site is appropriately located within some component of the gay culture relevant to the locale. The name needs to attract the attention of those unfamiliar with the local gay terrain, but the references cannot be overly explicit in that regard. In some settings, names cannot be too explicit in these references or else they risk inviting police harassment or the intrusions of others who take issue with the site's accommodation of sexual diversity.

One set of questions included in my interviews with Cape Town–area gay men encouraged them to talk about local bars and clubs that have been important to their gender careers. Many of these sites were also been included in the maps of "Cape Town as a gay city" that respondents drew during the opening minutes of each interview. Because respondents do not always identify the same sites in these discussions, exploring their reasons for inclusion (or omission) of particular sites became an important theme in my analysis of interview materials.

A productive line of inquiry in that regard has been to position bar names along a timeline sequence as determined by when the bar first opened and, presumably, when it was first assigned its name. For example, maps and discussions that focus on Cape Town's gay geography during the years of transition from Apartheid rule and into national reconciliation (1991–94) regularly reference sites listed in Table 5.1a. All of these sites were located within the City Centre, an area proclaimed as a white domain under Apartheid spatiality.

What respondents had the most to say about Cape Town's gay geography during this period was consistent with this history. Gay men of coloured backgrounds talked about Tot's, Club Swing, and Moulin Rouge but had little to say about other City Centre sites. Some respondents indicated that there were gay and gay-friendly sites in the suburbs and in the coloured and black townships on the nearby Cape Flats. These sites were rarely identified by name, however, and never marked on gay city maps focusing on this period, not even when the maps were drawn by coloured or black respondents.[10]

Table 5.1. Cape Town–Area Gay Bars and Clubs, by Time Period, as Identified during Respondent Interviewing

5.1a. Respondent-identified gay bars and clubs, 1991–94
  Henry's
  The Fireman's Arms
  Tot's
  Club Swing
  Moulin Rouge
  Club Eyes
  Straubs
  Brunswick

5.1b. Respondent-identified gay bars and clubs, 1994–96
  Angels
  The Bronx
  Detour
  Castro's
  Moulin Rouge
  Brunswick
  Odyssey

5.1c. Respondent-identified gay bars and clubs, 1999–2001
  Angels
  The Bronx
  Detour
  Company Bar/Bar Code[1]
  Off-Broadway
  De Waterkant Café
  Moulin Rouge
  Beehive
  Blah Bar[2]
  Brunswick
  Manhattan's

1. Company Bar closed in the summer of 1999 and re-opened the following fall, under new management, as Bar Code. Its leather/Levi's focus was maintained.
2. The Blah Bar was bombed by unidentified assailants in the spring of 1999.

Along with those sites, respondents also mentioned a broad range of coffee bars, restaurants, and all-night cafes, most of which were not gay-identified locations so much as places where gay men were one component of a larger, more diverse clientele. Some also mentioned Club Welgelen, the one self-identified gay steam bath in the Cape Town area during this period. But, as they noted, the club was located in one of the southern suburbs and not in an area connected to the City Centre.

Maps and discussions focusing on Cape Town's gay geography during the years when the constitution was being developed and debated (1994–96) regularly reference sites listed in Table 5.1b. Only two sites identified during the earlier time period are listed, Brunswick and Moulin Rouge, both of which were popular with gay men of coloured as well as white backgrounds. The changes in the inventory reflect, in part, a shift in the primary location of City Centre gay bars away the central business district (Long and Bree streets) and into an area bounded by the old waterfront (De Waterkant), the Cape Malay neighborhood of BoKap, and the open parkland and beachfront areas along Green Point/Mouille Point. That area, particularly Somerset Road, continues to be the focal point for City Centre commercial gay life. It is important to note that dance clubs are the prominent type of site that appeared during this time. The clientele includes persons of diverse racial, ethnic, and class backgrounds as mediated only by the costs of cover change/admission, price of refreshments, and the (at times arbitrary) decisions by doorkeepers to deny admission to persons who did not appear to be suitable additions to the on-site clientele.

There is also a sharp decline in the frequency of references to restaurants, cafes, and coffee bars, locations that were not explicitly gay in ambience but were sites where, in earlier years, same-sex-identified gay men could meet and socialize with friends without fear of reprisal. The protections guaranteed in the constitution made possible a openness of sexual presence that had not been part of Cape Town's collective gay culture in previous years. Because sites catering explicitly to a gay clientele no longer needed to conceal their clientele's sexual preferences, the security promised by mainstream-based, gay-friendly locations was no longer in such great demand.

Consistent with this change, maps and discussion from this period identify two additional bath houses: the Steam Zone and the Long Street Baths, both located within the central business district rather than near the new bars and clubs emerging along Somerset Road corridor in Green Point. Still, their downtown location added to the gay presence emerging in the City Centre and enhanced the visibility of gay presence formerly marked by public advertising for drag shows.

Finally, and extending the explicitness that Cape Town's urban gay presence was now claiming, maps and descriptions given by gay men familiar with Cape Flats geographies also mention the Odyssey, a gay-friendly dance club in the historically coloured township of Athelone. In almost every instance the respondents who mentioned the Odyssey were gay men of coloured background. Black respondents, and some coloured, also mentioned several gay-friendly shebeens in Langa, Guguletu, and Khayelitsha.[11] No one mentioned these sites as alternatives to City Centre gay resources or to the prominence of those resources within the local gay terrain.

Maps and discussions focusing on Cape Town–area gay geography from 1999 to 2001 regularly referenced the bars and clubs identified in Table 5.1c. An increase in the number of explicitly gay bars and clubs identified in the respondents' commentaries is noticeable, as well as the number of sites located in the Waterkant–Green Point area (Blah Bar, Off-Broadway, and De Waterkant Café). Moulin Rouge was the only City Centre bar primarily associated with gay men of colour. White and coloured respondents rarely mentioned Odyssey and other Cape Flats sites. Black township residents described a range of sites in the townships (primarily gay-friendly shebeens) and in the City Centre (primarily public sites like parks and shopping center concourses rather than gay commercial establishments). Some black gay men mentioned how much they enjoy visiting City Centre dance clubs and how expensive it is for them to do so (Tables 5.4 and 5.5).

Discussion

Much can be said about the social and political messages expressed in the names of gay bars and clubs and in the naming practices that favored these selections. Of immediate interest here is how these names and naming practices reflect, in a compact and tightly focused fashion, issues shaping the language of homosexual citizenship, which was also under formation during this period.

First, think of bar names as claims to gay presence and as markers of an emerging gay presence. As bar and clubs with names like Tot's and Henry's are replaced by bars and clubs with names like Detour and Blah Bar, sites with protected or ambiguously defined public gay identities are replaced by sites whose names have a more explicit connection to gay life, even if a still somewhat coded one. There is, for example, Detour, as in "movement in an unexpected direction and into a new and uncharted terrain"; Blah Bar, as in an "'I've seen it all and it isn't really pretty' attitude"; and Off-Broadway, as in "anything connected to musical comedy has to be fabulously entertaining." Similarly, note the change in the names of gay bath houses from an ambiguously titled Club Welgelen to the more explicitly eroticized messages conveyed by the names *Steamers* and *Hot Zone*.

Also important is the fact that—with the exception of De Waterkant (named for the street and the area of the City Centre where the bar is located), all the new bars and clubs have English names, not Afrikaans. Rather than being British or British colonial in their associated imagery—Brunswick, Henry's, Fireman's Arms, and Straubs—the recently chosen names draw explicit connections between Cape Town gay sites and prominent features of North Atlantic gay culture. Bronx, Manhattan's, and Off-Broadway refer to New York City's status as a North Atlantic gay type-site; Company Bar clones the name of a popular leather/Levi's bar in Brussels, Belgium; and Hot House's name and advertising closely resemble those of a well-known gay bath house in Manchester.

Such connections advise patrons of these sites and also passers-by that the gay presence sanctioned in the constitution is not only claiming greater visibility within the local urban landscape but is also part of a transnational dynamic whose points of reference lie firmly within the same North Atlantic cultures in which other segments of South African tradition are also based. Giving Afrikaans names to the bars and clubs would have referenced entirely different claims to history and an entirely different forms of local authority.

That is exactly the message assigned to the Club Welgelen by its Afrikaans name, especially given that only one other gay site in these discussions (De Waterkant) is also named in Afrikaans. Authority and history are also being referenced but have more to do with the area of the city where the bar is located rather than the bar itself. Besides, and again unlike the case for Welgelen, "De Waterkant" is an Afrikaans phrase likely to be familiar to Cape Townians whatever their language backgrounds. In this sense, and framed within gay discursive geography, "De Waterkant" is not an Afrikaans term at all.

Example 2: Linguistic Divisions of Labor in a South African National Gay Newspaper

One of the primary channels through which South African lesbians and gay men were able to communicate points of view about homosexual experience during the Apartheid years was *The Exit,* which now (and deservedly) self-identifies as South Africa's lesbian and gay newspaper. Other, nationally focused lesbian/gay publications have emerged in South Africa since 1995, but all have a magazine/journal format, and their articles often make assumptions of affluence (and, often, affluent whiteness) that are not supported by the lived experiences of the majority of South Africa's lesbians and gay men.

The Exit, in contrast, is very much involved with conditions of everyday life. The newspaper appears monthly and is distributed for a modest price at gay bars, bookstores, community centers, and similar locations. Each issue is filled with news reports addressing lesbian and gay life across South Africa as well as in other parts of southern Africa, the North Atlantic, and beyond; editorials and essays by columnists addressing matters of current interest; articles giving advice on a range of personal topics (love life, safe sex, healthy relationships, and spiritual development); gossip column commentaries, often accompanied by appropriately chosen photographs of individuals under discussion; advertising for hotels, restaurants, clothing stores, sex clubs and other lesbian-gay-related businesses; and, of course, a rich inventory of personal advertisements.

The Exit is also multilingual. The primary languages in each issue are English and Afrikaans, and the division of labor is striking. English is the language used for reporting local, national, and international gay news—even when the event itself involved Afrikaans contexts and concerns. Much of the editorial commentary and some of the gossip columns are also written in English. Afrikaans appears in the English-language writing when a descriptive word or phrase is referentially appropriate to the topic, although such instances are not frequent. More typically, any remarks relevant to the story made by Afrikaner-speakers are presented in English regardless of the language of original statement. The same is true for remarks made by speakers of Zulu, Xhosa, or other non-European-based South African languages. Advice columns, some of the editorial commentary, and many gossip columns are regularly written in Afrikaans. English words and phrases rarely appear in these texts. Even when remarks made by English-speakers are being quoted, they are typically translated into Afrikaans.

Statements in South African indigenous languages are never included in any of these English or Afrikaans texts, by my reading, nor are news reports in those languages. But point-of-view essays and other commentaries are written in Zulu and usually address issues of interest to black South African lesbians and gay men, regardless of ethnic/political background.[12] The text in Table 5.2 is a typical example in that regard. It is an excerpt from a columns written by a Zulu author and published under the title *Umthondo Wesizwe*. *The Exit*'s staff assures me that the primary language in this column is (and is intended to be) Zulu. Still, words and phrases from other languages also occupy a prominent place in the written text, even when the discussion speaks directly to matters specific to Zulu cultural tradition (line 004).

Table 5.2. Language Pluralism in *Umthondo Wesizwe*

001	Girls! girls! girls! uGianni Versace ufile. What am I gonna do? What am I gonna wear?
002	MaRegiesm, maNgobeni kanti kwenzekani? I already got my after tears party invitation
003	from maVersace, but I can't RSVP as a I have a new gay shebeen to review in Soweto.
004	Will you attend in my honour? I need a professional mourner! I'm sure kumama factories
005	ayi few azovala eBangkok as a result of this tragedy. Didn't I warn everyone about the
006	dangers involved in picking up omarhosha (that's rita, dears) in the last issue?

Source: The Exit, Aug. 1997, 13.

The written "Zulu" text contains materials from four languages: Zulu, English, Italian, and Gayle (sometimes, Gala), a heavily coded and distinctively southern African linguistic system that assigns gay-specific meanings to a long inventory of women's names and related references, positioning these items as nouns or verbs in sentences whose remaining details are fleshed out in English (or Afrikaans).[13] Later in the column (in material not cited in Table 5.2), the writer includes additional commentary in Afrikaans, adding a fifth language to the linguistic inventory of the text.

One way to interpret the language pluralism evidenced here is to note the close association between choice of language and topic. The social events and obligations stemming from Versace's death are described in English, while the writer's reflections on these events are expressed in Zulu. Undermining that claim is the discussion of "rough trade" in line 006, which is a statement of the speaker's reflection ("Didn't I warn everybody about the danger involved in picking up omarhosha . . . in the last issue?"). But it is written in English and uses a Zulu term (*omarhosha*) and then a Gayle translation (*rita*) to specify the focus of the intended warning.

The point could be to suggest connections between rough trade and Zulu or coloured/Gayle background. A more likely reading is to note how the writer's language choice, here and elsewhere in the text, guarantees that the audience, regardless of language background, will be able to make sense of the messages of caution and self-restraint expressed in the column's first paragraph and reproduced here. Even without knowing any Zulu or Gayle, a reader fluent only in English could still render a reasonable approximation of the column's message. Enabling such a multilingual literacy act is especially important, given that all readers of the column, whatever their linguistic backgrounds, are likely to be targets of anti-gay violence at some point in their gender careers. In that sense, spreading communicative functions across language traditions incorporates the real-life conditions under discussion as much as it reminds a broad-based audience, collectively, of these facts.

This simultaneously constructed multilingual referencing is presented in a newspaper column entitled *Umthondo Wesizwe*. The column's heading is decorated with an image of an erect penis, positioned like an upright spear, adorned with a pennant, and positioned next to a zebra-striped valentine heart. The images anticipate the sexual and political references presented in the title. *Umthondo,* a Zulu term for "penis" (or, in some usage, "male genitalia" inclusively), gives additional expression to the male-centered, same-sex meanings already displayed in the imagery. *Wesizwe* (the nation) is a Zulu term that members of the inKatha Freedom Party used repeatedly during the struggle against Apartheid to make a coded reference to a united Zulu peo-

ple liberated from European postcolonial rule. The word is likely to be recognized by South African people, whatever their linguistic background. It was
often combined in inkatha political usage with the Zulu term for "spear" to
suggest a readiness for combat and willingness to fight, as a Zulu man or
woman, for the good of the nation. *Umthondo wesizwe* invites analogy to that
more familiar political usage while also indicating the flexible, if still ambiguous, claim to citizenship that a gay Zulu man would express as a co-partic-
ipant in the struggle to build an Apartheid-free Zulu political unity. (Table
5.3b indicates how one Zulu man has tried to establish the legitimacy of his
political and sexual citizenship.)

Personal Advertisements

Items published as part of *The Exit*'s monthly inventory of gay personal advertisements reflect a linguistic division of labor structured somewhat differently than in news report columns and editorials. Advertisements that appear
to be written in Afrikaans (i.e., those having an Afrikaans title and in which
the majority of words and phrases are in Afrikaans) regularly incorporate
material from English. Those written in English are less likely to include material from Afrikaans or other languages and tend to be consistently monolingual. In the few instances where advertisements are written in Zulu or some
other non-European South African language, some segment of the commentary will also be framed in English or, much less frequently, in Afrikaans.

The texts in Table 5.3 illustrate the different forms of language pluralism.
Judging by its title, Table 5.3a is written in Afrikaans, but it also incorporates
English-language references in a provocative and text-message-affirming

Table 5.3. Language Pluralism in South African Gay Personal Ads

5.3a.	IS JY REDELIK SPORTIEF?
001	IS JY REDELIK SPORTIEF?
002	Wanted: young GWM lover for fun life together.
003	JY: Selfgeldend, onafhanklik, on-gebonde, redelik sportief.
004	EK: GWM, vroee 30s, fiks avintuurlustig, hardwerkend, gemaklike lewensuitkyk
005	US: Hopefully long-term committed relationship, if I find my match.
006	[reply number]
5.3b.	Ngifuna indooda
001	Ngifuna indooda
002	Black gay 40/164/70 WLTM a disciplined man, medium cock for suck, sex, romance.
003	Non-smoker who speaks Zulu or Portuguese. My cake likes your banana.
004	Ngilindele indooda ezonguza umfazi wayo ozongonza ukhosikazi sinhlole sobabihi
005	ngiyoku hlonipha nje ngendoda yami. 19–50 welcome.
006	[reply number]

fashion. In Table 5.3b, which is written in Zulu, English again contributes significantly, but rather differently, to the textual message.

I examine multilingual composition of Afrikaans gay personal advertisements elsewhere (Leap 2003) and need only touch briefly on that theme here. It is important to mention the juxtaposition of Afrikaans and English in Table 5.3a. The title (line 001) is in Afrikaans: "IS JY REDELIK SPORTIEF?" (Are you-_{fam} reasonably sportsmanlike—for example, level-headed, honest, willing to play by the rules?). Line 002 is in English: "Wanted, young GWM lover for fun life together" (that is, if *jy* are *redelik sportief* we may be able to have a fun life together).

The writer's expectations and requirements in this regard are then detailed. *Jy*, the ideal partner who is the target for this outreach, is self-motivated, independent, unencumbered, but willing to play by the rules (line 003). *Ek*, the person searching for the ideal mate, am a GWM, early thirties, strong, adventurous, hard-working, and in an easy-going period of my life (line 004). The writer describes himself as a "gay white male" by using an abbreviation (GWM) that circulates widely in gay print media and is likely to be recognized by many gay men whatever their linguistic background. The remainder of both descriptions is presented entirely in Afrikaans, a language choice that suggests the writer himself is of Afrikaner background and that his ideal partner should be the same, or at least be familiar enough with Afrikaans language and culture to be able to understand the ideological position being proposed.

The relationship that results when jy and ek get together is described in English, not Afrikaans, which suggests that the relationship will be grounded in a somewhat different cultural and ideological position. The shift to English could encode the Afrikaner disdain for culturally transgressive (that is, not moffie-based) homosexuality, which could certainly be the case for the male-centered, long-term, same-sex relationship under discussion. Or the shift could merely suggest that entering into such a long-term commitment would mark the beginning of a new period (*lewesuitkyk*, repeating a term from the writer's self-description in line 004) in both men's lives and thus require them to engage in a different sort of social and linguistic discourse, whether with each other or with the world.

Either way, the outcome the writer hopes to obtain is substantially different from his current condition, and his shift in language of reference underscores that difference. As the linguistic construction of the text makes clear, even if their relationship is not deemed legitimate within an Afrikaner setting the two men may be able to maintain Afrikaner ties while seeking validation for enacting their sexual preferences from other South African and transnational (English) sources. In that sense Table 5.3a becomes a statement about the position the writer hopes he and his (hoped-for) partner may claim, as citizens as well as sexual persons, within the new South African state.

In Table 5.3b the writer's use of Zulu versus English expresses a very different set of sexual and cultural meanings. English complements, rather than establishes, contrast, and the writer's point of view is expressed through his primary language. The title of the advertisement, "Ngifuna indooda" (looking for the [a particular] man), speaks directly to that point of view (line 001). In English, he describes the man in question as someone who is of reasonable physique and enjoys sexual activity as well as romance, is a non-smoker, and is also fluent in one or more of the additional languages relevant to the southern African scene (lines 002–003). A short statement at the end of line 003, also presented in English, brings a wealth of gay-male-centered imagery to the discussion: "My cake likes your banana." The statement implies the writer's willingness to be the recipient of the indooda's sexual assertiveness and also paves the way to the remarkable promises of commitment presented in the remaining two lines of the advertisement:

Ngilindele (I am waiting waiting for)	indooda (the man)	ezonguza (who can make me)	umfazi wayo (woman his)
ozongonza ([If] you make me)	ukhosikazi (a respectable woman, e.g., we get married)	sinhlole sobabihi (we will stay together, the two of us)	
ngiyoku hlonipha (and I will "show you respect")	nje ngendoda yami. (as my man.)		

What the writer is proposing is that he and the ideal indooda marry, which, according to Zulu tradition, would mean that the indooda made the writer "a respectable woman." The writer, in turn, promises to be a good, faithful, and dutiful wife, including "showing respect" to him and his lineage by avoiding any direct or indirect linguistic references to any of the indooda's deceased relatives (Finlayson 1982; Herbert 1995).

As suggested here, by observing *hlonipha* (the Nguni term for this language-based avoidance practice) a wife shows that she accepts the responsibilities and obligations expected of her by her husband's kinfolk. In this case, the "wife" is male and the marriage is unlikely to be sanctioned by Zulu tradition or recognized by the "husband's" kin and lineage authority. At the same time, by proposing to practice hlonipha on the indooda's behalf the writer suggests a powerful strategy for asserting the legitimacy of their relationship within Zulu tradition.

In other words, Table 5.3b is not only a statement of desired partnership but also a claim of sexual citizenship within the Zulu nation, thereby matching the status of citizenship constitutionally promised to the writer. Understandably, the segment of the advertisement that articulates these claims is presented in Zulu. But lines 004 and 005 make sense only if read in terms of the particulars of desire detailed in lines 002 and 003, that is, the remarks that describe the indooda as a sexual person, not as a member of the Zulu nation. And, appropriate to the argument, the remarks are presented in English.

Example 4: Language Diversity in Life Story Narratives

Life story narratives are forms of storytelling in which speakers revisit particular moments of personal experience and draw connections between those experiences and the larger concerns which, from their point of view, give meaning and coherence to their lives (Linde 1993; Plummer 1995). Life stories figure prominently in the interview data my colleagues and I have collected in Cape Town, and a close reading of these texts shows how the speakers see the intersections of race, ethnicity, class, sexuality, and history affecting who and where they are in post-Apartheid South Africa.[14]

Julie (Table 5.4) is a twenty-five-year-old, black South African woman who describes herself as a lesbian in English and Xhosa conversations. She discusses her favorite lesbian/gay dance clubs in the City Centre and some of the reasons she enjoys visiting the clubs. Julie lives in Guguletu, a black township on the Cape Flats. Because Guguletu is located at some distance (approximately ten miles) from the City Centre, her visits to the clubs (or to any City Centre location) depend on access to some form of transportation. Minibus taxis and regional train service operate regularly between townships and City Centre locations during daytime hours. After sundown, however, travel depends on finding a friend (or a friend of a friend) who has an automobile. Townships residents otherwise travel to the City Centre on the last train or taxi, spend the evening at the clubs or similar locations in town, and the next morning take the first train or taxi back to their homes.

Additional considerations mediate township residents' access to clubs: the cover charge required for admission, the cost of drinks and snacks, and issues of appropriate attire as well as occasional questions about the suitability of a township presence within an upscale, City Centre setting. Whatever the concerns stemming from race and class differences, however, dance clubs are relatively free of anti-gay harassment and violence, outcomes that arise

Table 5.4. Township Perspective on a City Centre Nightclub

001 iAngles ise town iAngles Cape Town.
002 Angles ok yi nightclub ye ne gays ne lesbians.
003 Ziyangena but inightclub yabantu abastraight,
004 so iAngles ne Bronze zimelene.
005 So xo indilapha Bronze ndiyakwazi ukunyuka isteps noliye eAngles.
006 Na xa ndilapha eAngles ndiyakawzi ukuryaka isteps noliye eBronze.
007 So ke yayizindawo ok umuntu was wakwazi ke ngoko ugaphambi ukonwaba
008 phayana, but ngoku itho eyenzekayo ngoku xa uya eAngle okavefee eBronze into
     abayibuzayo iphiID akho.
009 Unanga phi ininyaka yakho, nd ke negoku ufumanise ke noba siyaya kwezindawo
     kufumaniseke ukuthi itransport esibibanayo yokubuya.
0010 Kufuueka uhlale iwhole nights ulinde ezatrain zokuqala,
0011 nakwe za train zokuqola ziwrong,
0012 cause asantu bayarobbery batheni bathemo Babulawe.
0013 So ke ngoku ndayeke ukuzihamba exi ezindawo ezi andafelisha comfortable.

English translation:
001 Angels is in town; Angels is in Cape Town.
002 Angels is a nightclub for gays and lesbians.
003 Lesbians go there but also straight people go to the nightclub.
004 So Angels and Bronx are close to each other.
005 So if I am there at Bronx, I can go up the stairs to Angels.
006 So when I am also in Angels, I can go up the stairs to Bronx.
007 So Bronx and Angels they are two of the places where people are able to enjoy our-
     theirselves, back then.
008 So what is happening now when I go to Angels or to Bronx what they ask you where is your
     i.d. document in those years before.
009 Even though we go to Angels and to Bronx, we found out that sometimes we don't have
     transport to go back home.
0010 And then you stay the whole night in the night club or you wait for those early hours train.
0011 Even in those early hours trains, it is very wrong.
0012 Because people get robbed, they get killed, etc etc.
0013 So I end up not going to those places anymore because I don't feel much comfortable
     with it.

Note: Julie prepared the transcription of her narrative during a follow-up session with the interviewer and me. She also translated each segment of her Xhosa narrative into English, and her translation follows the Xhosa text. The line numbering in the English translation corresponds to the line numbering in the original Xhosa text.

more frequently each time Julie and her friends visit any of the shebeens near her home. At the same time, shebeens do not charge entrance fees and have more affordable drinks and snacks and less rigid dress codes than dance clubs, and a Xhosa background does not present a convenient excuse for on-site discrimination.

What results is a difficult trade-off for same-sex-identified township residents. The convenience of a shebeen, along with the attendant dangers there, are balanced against obstacles limiting access to the City Centre's gay bars and clubs as well as their safety and freedom. Moreover, as comments in many of these township residents' life stories make clear, neither option is entirely satisfactory. Simon, a twenty-six-year-old resident of Khayelitsha, spoke to this issue quite powerfully (Table 5.5). He leaves the township, hoping to find "a safer space for myself in Cape Town" (line 003), where he sees many gay people enjoying opportunities not available in the townships. However, "I go there, and I refused to be entered" (lines 004–005). There is no transportation back to Khayelitsha until the morning, therefore, he asks, "So what am I going to do?" (line 007).

My interview with Simon was conducted entirely in English, yet his remarks closely parallel the reflections on township and City Centre contrasts presented in the life story narratives given in Xhosa. As Julie's remarks suggest, these Xhosa-based narratives also contain English words and phrases. English materials are not included arbitrarily or randomly, however. Narrators use English along with Xhosa to frame their remarks about the importance of City Centre gay nightclubs, the dangers associated with travel between township and City Centre sites, and the barriers to admission that limit their access to these sites (Table 5.6). Narrators also use English and Xhosa to provide evaluations of City Centre experiences.

There is also one instance in these texts where narrators use English

Table 5.5. Catching the Last Train from Khayelitsha

Speaker: Simon
001 Just imagine me, catching the last train from Khayelitsha, at 10 past nine, telling myself
002 that I am getting away from this situation here of humiliation and harassment and all
003 that stuff, trying to get a safer space for myself in Cape Town where I see many gay
004 people being free and wandering about nicely and having good time. I go there, and I
005 refused to be entered. There's no train going back home. The next train going back home
006 will be only at six in the morning. So tell me where do I have to stay for the whole night?
007 And what am I going to do?

Table 5.6. Categories of English Words Occurring in Julie's Narrative

Category	Textual Example
City Centre context	Town
Names of City Centre night clubs	Angels, Bronze (Bronx)
Marking relative location	Close to each other, steps
Sexual identities	Gay, lesbian, straight
Memories of Apartheid control	ID
Travel	Transport, train
Transportation-related crime	Robbery
Narrative timeframe	Whole nights
Evaluations of these conditions	Wrong, [don't feel] comfortable

uniquely—to specify their own sexual orientation and those of co-participants—township- and City Centre-based—in their narratives. Given the
contrasts between township and City Centre experiences that are being addressed in these remarks, and the associations with Apartheid racial hierarchy and discrimination invoked by those contrasts, the absence of Xhosa
reference in these discussions of personal identity may seem peculiar. Two
interrelated considerations apply.

First, township residents regularly make use of Xhosa sexual discourse to
discuss same-sexual identities when township-based institutions, practices,
and ideologies provide the context for discussion. In the narratives in question, sexual identities under discussion are situated within City Centre–based
institutions, practices, and ideologies. These contexts have close associations
with English-based sexual discourse and (again, given the City Centre location) with English-defined, English-labeled sexual geographies. To use Xhosa
sexual discourse in these discussions might draw attention to relevant township–City Centre tensions, but it would also imply that township-based sexual meanings extend unproblematically outside township boundaries, the
very point Julie's and Simon's remarks call into question.

Second, it is not clear how frequently Xhosa sexual discourse actually
names same-sex identities. One instance where naming does occur is *isi tabane,* the male-boded status that imposes gender-transgressive economic,
social, and sexual obligations on those who identify themselves in terms of
its claims. Otherwise, same-sex-based preferences and practices may be acknowledged in various ways but are not always labeled as such in public conversation. Not using Xhosa in discussions of township residents' experiences
in City Centre sexual geographies is consistent with that discursive position.

Competing understandings of sexual citizenship are the central theme in
all of these reference choices. In township settings, whatever rights to citizenship that a homosexual subject may have are defined in terms of Xhosa
sexual traditions and township political cultures (themselves responses to
Apartheid-era policies of enforced displacement and benign neglect) as much
as in response to the constitution. Locally accepted labeling and descriptions
of sexuality provide the appropriate framework for negotiating these rights
because such linguistic practices are already embedded in this setting and
used to negotiate township-based claims to citizenship under other (e.g.,
non-sexual) circumstances. If the outcome of that negotiation requires a si-
lencing of homosexual referencing, then silence would figure prominently
within the ensuing linguistic practice.[15]

Entirely different considerations defined the homosexual subject's rights
to citizenship, and discussions of those rights, within City Centre domains.

Judging by like story narratives, newspaper articles, and other data, particulars of same-sex desire are regularly subordinated to broader considerations of race and class in City Centre locations, and same-sex subjectivities are diversified and stratified accordingly. As Julie noted, "What is happening now when I go to Angels or Bronx what they ask you where is your i.d. document in those years before" (Table 5.4, line 008).[16] Simon stated, more directly, "I go there, and I refused to be entered" (Table 5.5, lines 004–005).

Clearly, under these circumstances alignments with whiteness will not guarantee that a subject will be able to enjoy the protections defined by the constitution, but such alignments will help subjects press their own demands to that end and encourage others to respond accordingly. Given Xhosa's centrality to township experience and Afrikaans' lingering associations with the narrowly defined white governmentality under Apartheid, English is the appropriate linguistic modality for pressing those claims. That is precisely the point expressed through the linguistic practices informing Julie's and Simon's City Centre–related text-making.

Conclusion: On the Emergence of a Language of Sexual Citizenship

Ways of talking about homosexuality—as well as ways of not talking about it or about any other feature of sexual identity or experience—are in no sense atypical features of South African sexual cultures. I do not argue that the language of sexual citizenship examined in this essay is without cultural or historical precedent. But it is my position that this language is promoting radically new forms of public sexual discourse as it gains broader circulation in post-Apartheid South Africa. It is also providing radically new understandings of sexual identity. Existing ways of talking about homosexuality, for example, provide insider-code strategies to conceal the messages from outsiders, submerging categories of sexual preference within more inclusive discourses of effeminacy or celibacy or invoking alliances between local sexualities and transnationally defined sexual identity.

The language of homosexual citizenship at issue here allows speakers to address similar communicative tasks in individual speech settings and also, as needed, within the same textual moment. It allows discussions of homosexuality in English, Afrikaans, Xhosa, Zulu, and other South African languages and in settings where a single language tradition or a combination of several such traditions is appropriate. The language is adaptable enough to enable the naming of bars, articulate tensions between racial and sexual identities, and bring coherence to life story narratives. Although some of its features call to mind facets of North Atlantic, post-Stonewall gay cultures, the distinctively gay English text-making that resonates so vividly in North Atlantic domains is not as prominent in South Africa as are text-making practices aligned more closely with localized sexual politics.

In some cases, as suggested by Julie's remarks (Table 5.4), by the English and Afrikaans "intrusions" in the "Zulu" language column in the gay newspaper (Table 5.2), and by other gay men's personal advertisements I have reviewed (Leap 2003), the results of this synthesis could be described as code-switching. The texts reflect "the use of two or more languages in the same conversation, usually within the same conversational turn, or even within the same sentence of that turn" (Myers-Scotten 1993, vii). But such a description disregards how closely these examples of text-making parallel the conditions of citizenship and the location of the would-be citizens these linguistic practices seek to describe. In other words, and guided by the linguistic and political conditions presented in the examples, this language of homosexual citizenship is "regulated by practices favoring flexibility, mobility and repositioning in relation to [among other considerations] markets, governments and cultural regimes" (Ong 1999, 6).

That it is a flexible language (Leap 2003) and constructed through a convergence of linguistic and cultural traditions rather than in terms of a single such option ensures that same-sex-identified persons of differing racial, ethnic, and class backgrounds are able to "speak" the same sexual language and in the same conversation underscore particulars of sexual and other experiences of individual concern. If, as de Vos has suggested, "the constitution made us queer," it is the flexible language of (homo)sexual citizenship that allows that ambiguous unity to be reproduced in everyday life.

Notes

My thanks to the many Cape Town–area women and men interviewed for this project and to the Triangle Project (Salt River, South Africa) for sponsoring this research. The discussion of belonging and citizenship builds on helpful conversations with Tom Boellstorff, Roger Lancaster, Denis Provencher, and Alan Hersker. Thanks also to Florence Babb for her careful and supportive reading of this chapter in an earlier draft and to Wolfram Hartmann, Glen Elder, and John Noyes for encouragement and helpful suggestions throughout this research.

1. Article 9(3) of the South African constitution states: "The state shall not unfairly discriminate directly or indirectly against any one or more grounds, including: race, gender, sex, pregnancy, marital status, ethnic or social origin, colour, sexual orientation, age, disability, religion, conscience, belief, culture, language, and birth" (de Vos 2001, 198).

2. I use the term *language* deliberately in this context to draw attention to the linguis-

tic and cultural knowledge (grammar) and the cultural and sociolinguistic practices (discourse) on which such situated conversations (text-making) about sexual citizenship unavoidably depend. I provide a more detailed discussion of this argument elsewhere (Leap 2002b).

3. Examples of the sexual dimensions of citizenship include the pervasive referencing of "the family" as an appropriate formation for living together and caring for each other in contemporary society (Bell and Binnie 2000, 10–11; see also Brown 1997, 24–26) as well as efforts to claim "rights to privacy" and promote distinctions between "public" and "private" locations within local geographies (Bok 1982; Leap 1999, 8–12). To the extent that late capitalsim treats consumption and accumulation of credit and debt as acts of responsible citizenship (Evans 1993; Gluckman and Reed 1997), sexual dimensions of citizenship surface in efforts to commodify (sexual) object choices and practices and evaluate the authenticity of individual sexual identity in terms of the standards and ideal reflected in those commodities (Bordo 1999, 168–225).

4. The remarks in this section attempt a synthesis of arguments presented in Elder (1995), Gevisser (1994), Gevisser and Cameron, eds. (1994), and de Vos (2001) framed against the recurring themes presented in the life story narratives and other recollections I have collected from Cape Town–area, same-sex-identified women and men.

5. Consistent with that point (and suggesting the patriarchal bias that underlies it), homosexual activity between women was never criminalized as such under South African law.

6. This is not the place to review how sexuality generally, and homosexuality in particular, were implicated in the formations of township geography and governmentality. Important work on this theme can be found in Elder (in press) and in several essays in Gevisser and Cameron, eds. (1994).

7. Ironically, the Afrikaans term for a female-identified, female-bodied adult, *man-vrou* (lit. man-woman), implies that the subject has assumed a head-of-household-like, masculinist status within the sexual relationship. Other rural Afrikaner terms for female-identified women are not discussed in the research literature or were not referenced by the women I interviewed.

8. These three languages, along with Sipedi, Sesotho, Setswaana, siSwati, Tshivenda, Xitonga, isiNdebele, and isiZulu, are identified as "official languages" by the South African constitution.

9. Many of the gay white men interviewed for this project told me that they developed proficiency in Afrikaans while completing their mandatory term of military service.

10. Similarly, the listings of gay bars and clubs in *The Exit,* the South African national lesbian and gay newspaper, began identifying township-based, lesbian/gay friendly locations in 1998.

11. A shebeen is a black township bar based in the owner's home rather than in a separate commercial facility. Food is often available at a shebeen, as are jukebox music, pool tables, and other recreational materials.

12. Xhosa-speaking colleagues tell me that someone literate in Xhosa can, with only minimal discomfort, make sense of a written Zulu text. (How literate a Xhosa must be, to this end, and how many Xhosa-speakers have acquired such skills are unclear, howev-

er.) It is unlikely that this option is so readily available to black South Africans who do not speak the Nguni languages.

13. Gayle is commonly reported to have close associations with urban coloured/moffie culture, and references to those themes figure prominently in Gayle usage, whatever the background of the speaker (Kleinbooi 1995; Olivier 1994).

14. Life story narratives are subjective statements and do not necessarily present a literal, empirical accounting of events and experiences they describe. The point of life story research is to use the textual reflections of subjectivity as an entry point for understanding a speaker's point of view on these themes and the attendant ideologies with which that point of view is associated (Leap 1996, 138–39).

15. Consistent with that point, same-sex-identified township residents explain that their most effective response to verbal and physical harassment within a shebeen is to leave the site and find another shebeen where the environment is more accommodating. Leaving the township and searching for such a setting within the City Centre is another expression of the same strategy. Simon spoke to that point (Table 5.5, lines 003–004).

16. During the Apartheid years, all South African citizens were required to carry government-issued identification documents ("passbooks" in township parlance) indicating, among other details, their name, address, and racial classification.

Works Cited

Adam, Barry D., Jan Willem Duyvendak, and Andre Krouwel, eds. 1999. *The Global Emergence of Gay and Lesbian Politics: National Imprints of a Worldwide Movement.* Philadelphia: Temple University Press.

Bell, David, and Jon Binnie. 2000. *The Sexual Citizen: Queer Politics and Beyond.* London: Polity Press.

Bok, Cecilia. 1982. *Secrets: On the Ethics of Concealment and Revelation.* New York: Pantheon Books.

Bordo, Susan. 1999. *The Male Body: A New Look at Men in Public and Private.* New York: Farrar, Strauss and Giroux.

Brown, Michael. 1997. *RePlacing Citizenship: AIDS Activism and Radical Democracy.* New York: Guilford Press.

de Vos, Pierre. 2001. "The Constitution Made Is Queer: The Sexual Orientation Clause in the South African Constitution and the Emergence of Gay and Lesbian Identity." In *Law and Sexuality: The Global Arena,* ed. Carl Stychin and Didi Herman, 194–206. Minneapolis: University of Minnesota Press.

Elder, Glen. 1995. "Of Moffies, Kaffirs and Perverts: Male Homosexuality and the Discourse of Moral Order in the Apartheid State." In *Mapping Desire,* ed. David Bell and Gill Valentine, 56–65. London: Routledge.

———. in press. *Malevolent Geographies: Sex, Space and the Apartheid Legacy.* Columbus: Ohio State University Press.

Evans, David. 1993. *Sexual Citizenship: The Material Construction of Sexualities.* London: Routledge.

Finlayson, Rebecca. 1982. "Hlonipha: The Women's Language of Avoidance among the Xhosa." *South African Journal of African Languauges* (supplement), 35–60.

Flores, William V., and Rina Benmayor. 1997. *Latino Cultural Citizenship: Claiming Identity, Space and Rights.* Boston: Beacon Press.

Gaudio, Rudolf P. 1997. "Not Talking Straight in Hausa." In *Queerly Phrased: Language, Gender, and Sexuality,* ed. Anna Livia and Kira Hall, 416–29. New York: Oxford University Press.

Germond, Paul, and Steve de Gruchy, eds. 1997. *Aliens in the Household of God: Homosexuality and Christian Faith in South Africa.* Cape Town: David Philip.

Gevisser, Mark. 1994. "A Different Fight for Freedom." In *Defiant Desire: Gay and Lesbian Lives in South Africa,* ed. Mark Gevisser and Edwin Cameron, 14–88. Johannesburg: Ravan Press.

Gevisser, Mark, and Edwin Cameron, eds. 1994. *Defiant Desire: Gay and Lesbian Lives in South Africa.* Johannesburg: Ravan Press.

Gluckman, Amy, and Betsy Reed. 1997. "Introduction." In *Homo Economics,* ed. Amy Gluckman and Betsy Reed, xi–xxxi. New York: Routledge.

Hennessy, Rosemary. 1995. "Queer Visibility in Commodity Culture." In *Social Postmodernism,* ed. Linda Nicholson and Steve Seidman, 142–84. New York: Cambridge University Press.

Herbert, Robert K. 1995. "The Sociohistory of Clicks in Southern Bantu." In *Language and Social History: Studies in South African Sociolinguistics,* ed. Rajend Mesthre, 51–67. Cape Town: David Phillip.

Kendall. 1999. "Women in Lesotho and the (Western) Construction of Homophobia." In *Same-Sex Relations and Female Desires: Transgender Practices across Cultures,* ed. Evelyn Blackwood and Saskia E. Wieringa, 157–78. New York: Columbia University Press.

Kleinbooi, Hein. 1995. "A Zelda on My Stoep." *Bua* 9(4): 26–29.

Leap, William L. 1996. *Word's Out: Gay Men's English.* Minneapolis: University of Minnesota Press.

———. 1999. "Introduction." In *Public Sex/Gay Space,* ed. William L. Leap, 1–21. New York: Columbia University Press.

———. 2002a "'Strangers on a Train': Sexual Citizenship and the Politics of Public Transportation in Apartheid Cape Town." In *Queer Globalizations: Citizenship and the Afterlife of Colonialism,* ed. Arnaldo Cruz-Malave and Martin Manalansan IV, 219–35. New York: New York University Press.

———. 2002b "Studying Lesbian and Gay Languages: Vocabulary, Text-making and Beyond." In *Out in Theory: The Emergence of Lesbian and Gay Anthropology,* ed. Ellen Lewin and William L. Leap, 128–54. Urbana: University of Illinois Press.

———. 2003. "Language and Gendered Modernity." In *Blackwells Handbook on Language and Gender,* ed. Janet Holmes and Miriam Meyerhoff, 401–22. London: Basil Blackwell.

Linde, Charlotte. 1993. *Life Stories: The Creation of Coherence.* New York: Oxford University Press.

Lucas, Ian. 1997. "The Color of His Eyes: Polari and the Sisters of Perpetual Indulgence." In *Queerly Phrased: Language, Gender, and Sexuality,* ed. Anna Livia and Kira Hall, 85–94. New York: Oxford University Press.

Manalansan, Martin F. 2001 *Remapping Frontiers: The Lives of Filipino Gay Men in New York.* Durham: Duke University Press.

Maurer, Bill. 2000. *Recharting the Caribbean: Land, Law and Citizenship in the British Virgin Islands*. Ann Arbor: University of Michigan Press.

Mesthre, Rajend. 1995. "Introduction." In *Language and Social History: Studies in South African Sociolinguistics*, ed. Rajend Mesthre, xv–xx. Cape Town: David Phillip.

Moodie, T. Dunbar, Vivienne Ndatshe, and British [Mpande Wa] Sibuyi. 1988. "Migrancy and Male Sexuality in the South African Gold Mines." *Journal of South African Studies* 14(2): 228–56.

Mouffe, Chantal. 1991. "Citizenship and Political Community." In *Community at Loose Ends*, ed. the Miami Theory Collective, 70–82. Minneapolis: University of Minnesota Press.

Murray, David. 1997. "The Cultural Citizen: Negations of Race and Language in the Make-up of Martiniquais." *Anthropoligical Quarterly* 70: 79–91.

Myers-Scotton, Carol. 1993 *Social Motivations for Codeswitching: Evidence from Africa*. New York: Oxford University Press.

Olivier, Gerret. 1994. "From Ada to Zelda: Notes on Gays and Language in South Africa." In *Defiant Desire: Gay and Lesbian Lives in South Africa*, ed. Mark Gevisser and Edwin Cameron, 219–24. Johannesburg: Ravan Press.

Ong, Aihwa. 1999. *Flexible Citizenship: The Cultural Logics of Transnationality*. Durham: Duke University Press.

Patton, Cindy. 1997. "Foreword." In Michael Brown, *RePlacing Citizenship: AIDS Activism and Radical Democracy*, ix–xx. New York: Guilford Press.

Plummer, Ken. 1995 *Telling Sexual Stories: Power, Change and Social Worlds*. London: Routledge.

Stychin, Carl F. 1998. *A Nation by Rights: National Cultures, Sexual Identity Politics, and the Discourse of Rights*. Philadelphia: Temple University Press.

6. *Takatāpui,* Gay, or Just HO-MO-SEXUAL, Darling? Māori Language, Sexual Terminology, and Identity in Aotearoa/New Zealand

DAVID A. B. MURRAY

Ka ngaro te reo, ka ngaro taua, pera i te ngaro o te moa.
(If the language be lost, man will be lost, as dead as the moa.)

—Māori proverb presented at the Waitangi Tribunal on the
  te Reo Māori Claim

Roimata said, "Don was Māori, he had mana and, from what I've
heard, he wasn't called Long Dong Silver for nothing. He was
totally suitable but what did you do? You rejected him and became
a—a potato queen."

"Look" I answered. "I like white boys. When I put my brown
hands on them it makes me feel so dirty."

Roimata knew I was joking. Even so, she couldn't resist pushing
home the point.

"I only wish, Michael dear, that you would see that you've been
colonised twice over. First by the Pakeha [New Zealander of Anglo-
European settler descent]. Second by the gay Pakeha . . . don't you
understand, Michael? The issues of identity and space—of
sovereignty, of tino rangatiratanga—that our people have been
fighting for within Pakeha society are the same issues for gay Māori
within Pakeha gay society today!"

—Witi Ihimaera

In Aotearoa/New Zealand the dominant language of everyday life for the
majority of the country's population is English.[1] It is also a society in which
"gay" is the most commonly used term for "homosexual identity" in public
institutions such as the government and media as well as in more informal
day-to-day conversations. New Zealand, however, is also home to an indig-

enous population known as Māori that consists of approximately 15 percent
of the national population (Te Puni Kōkiri 2000, 13). Before colonization, the
Māori spoke a language now referred to as *te Reo Māori* (the Māori language,
or sometimes *te Reo*). In contemporary Aotearoa, however, it is estimated that
only between 4 and 8 percent of the Māori population are fluent in that language. According to most reports, despite a major language revitalization
movement spanning more than twenty years, te Reo Māori remains in danger of disappearing or being reduced to a language of ritual only.

In discussions with self-identified homosexual Māori men since 1995, I
have noted an increase in the use of a te Reo Māori term—*takatāpui*—as a
way of identifying oneself as homosexual and Māori.[2] The increasing presence of the term raises a number of questions about the centrality of language
in relation to sexual and other identities. How does language figure in the
negotiation of same-sex desires and identities among indigenous people who
live as a minority in an Anglo-European colonized society? How central is
language to these negotiations? Are there forms of same-sex talking and text-
making among a group whose primary language is that of the colonizer and
whose native language is only spoken fluently by a minority? Is language the
primary boundary marker for sexual and ethnic identifications? With what
other sociopolitical boundaries does language interact (or transgress) in iden-
tity-making projects?

This chapter is an introductory investigation into questions that address
the complex relations among sexuality, language, and identity in Aotearoa. I
am particularly interested in teasing out the sociopolitical implications of
language and linguistic practices in identity discourses and analyzing the
multiple interpretative possibilities that occur when a subaltern or minority language (or specific terms derived from that language) is used in relation
to sexual identification in a postcolonial settler society.[3] The development of
minority-language terms to replace English sexual terminologies and the
insertion of those terms into predominantly English-language contexts are
empowering for some, but there may be others who do not agree with or feel
comfortable using the terminology for a variety of reasons. The varying reactions to just one minority-language term for sexual identity that are presented here indicate the complex relations that individuals of a minority
group have with issues of identity and sexuality in a society created through
colonization.

This chapter therefore underlines a foundational observation in sociolinguistic inquiry—language is a key domain of struggle over difference and
inequality and a means of conducting that struggle (Heller 2001)—and demonstrates the "intersectional character of sexuality" (Boellstorff and Leap, this

volume) through analyzing how sexual subjectivities are linked to language. Put slightly differently, we will see how articulations about sexual self/identity are structured through debates about language, how articulations about language (*"la langue"*) are structured through debates about self/identity, and how this dialectical relationship is embedded in the cultural particularities of a contemporary Anglo-Western settler society.

I will also stress the contextual connection among language, identity, and authenticity when takatāpui is articulated. In some discussions, fluency in te Reo Māori may operate as an index of one's ability to be "fully Māori," such that even the insertion of a single term like "takatāpui" into an English conversational context carries politicized symbolic value through invoking an association with an authentic cultural identity. Although this value is not shared by all Māori by any means, it highlights how language and identity may be conceptualized as essential, mutually constitutive domains reflecting a dominant Western cultural logic that places colonized populations identified as indigenous into highly restricted representational regimes. In other conversational contexts, however, a range of English terms like "poofter," "gay," or "queen" are used alongside "takatāpui" with no apparent different intentionality, reference, or meaning, indicating synonymy across the linguistic divide and, by inference, uncoupling the politicized value of linguistic competence from an authentic ethnic identification.

The preliminary observations I offer about issues of non-heterosexuality, language, and linguistic practice in contemporary Māori society should not be assumed to be discoveries in any sense of the word. As I will outline in more detail, since the 1980s there has been a proliferation of writing and research on "alternative sexualities" in Māoridom by professionals in New Zealand's sexual and reproductive health sectors, such as the New Zealand AIDS Foundation (NZAF), researchers and lecturers in Māori studies departments in New Zealand universities, and in Māori literature, both in te Reo Māori and English. In the social sciences, and in most Anglo-European–dominated media and institutions, there continues to be very little information on or theorizing about this topic. This chapter is dedicated to providing a bridge between what is already being identified and analyzed in some institutional and informal domains and the segments of academia and society that remain relatively unaware of these developments.

I begin with a brief overview of anthropological research on alternative sexualities among indigenous groups in Anglo-American settler societies.[4] Sexuality has been analyzed through relatively few theoretical and thematic lenses. The most prolific discussion in this area has been the debate over terminology and categorization of the Native American "berdache," a phenomenon some anthropologists claim to be an example of "third gender." The debate provides limited insights into questions of sexuality among contemporary North American indigenous societies and provides comparisons to developments in contemporary Aotearoa. Following a brief summary of anthropological research on language and sexuality in Māori society, I present a more detailed analysis of the recent history of the term *takatāpui*, noting the convergences of three sociopolitical movements in the late 1970s and 1980s that influenced its emergence and fluorescence. I conclude with comments from a few Māori men that begin to convey the interpretative and contextual complexity of minority-language sexual terminologies in daily discourse and practice.

Anthropology, Language, and Sexual Terminologies in Indigenous Societies

Since the 1980s there has been a steady increase in anthropological research focusing on sexuality. As Kath Weston (1993, 1998) has pointed out, however, much of the ethnographic material produced during the 1970s and 1980s was problematic. Its emphasis on culturally discrete and different sexual practices in non-Western societies risked perpetuating orientalist stereotypes and further reinforced the implicitly primitive "them" versus modern "us" binary. This critique also applies to research on "indigenous" societies that has been constructed, until recently, through the idea of modernity. "Indigenes" are located in societies where the colonizing population (us) is said to manifest a modern, cosmopolitan identity and the colonized population (them) is said to have a "traditional indigenous" identity represented through a totalizing, static, pre-European contact culture concept, revealing "indigenous" to be a very modern term and thus complicating the borders of the us/them binary.[5]

Furthermore, anthropologists (as well as others) investigating gay and lesbian communities in North America, Britain, and other Anglo-American societies have been uncovering the social diversity within them, rendering the concept of "a" gay or "a" lesbian identity or community problematic.[6] The new ethnographies have situated sexuality in relation to numerous other sociological categories, such as class, race, ethnicity, age, or political orientation, rendering it much more complex in its definition and application. What is true "at home" is most likely true for "out there" as well, but that complexity is only now being recognized.

When it comes to indigenous sexualities in postcolonial Anglo-American settler societies, anthropology's track record continues to be spotty at best.

In her bibliography on gender and sexuality in Native American societies, Woodsum (1995) notes that scholarship on native women has slowly increased since the 1970s, but scholarship on native sexuality and gender variance has been relatively sparse. Nevertheless, anthropologists have studied one aspect of sexuality in Native American societies in great depth, that popularly known as the "berdache," which some claim to be a third gender category. This is a hugely debated issue, and my brief summary will do it injustice. It is important to mention it, however, if only because it represents a sustained (bordering on fetishistic) discussion among anthropologists on issues of sexuality, language, and terminology among a population colonized by Anglo-Americans and thus addresses some issues pertinent to the Māori context.

It appears that many societies throughout pre-contact native North America (at least sixty-five according to Will Roscoe [1998]) had an institutionalized role for men who dressed as women and/or specialized in women's work (or for women who dressed as men and/or did men's work). Although there was great variance in terms of roles and occupations, men who wore women's clothes and did women's work often became artists, ambassadors, and religious leaders; women who dressed as men and did men's work often became warriors hunters and chiefs (Jacobs, Thomas, and Lang, eds. 1997; Roscoe 1998, 4). But who exactly were "they"? Were they the Native American version of homosexuals? Were they transsexuals? Transvestites? Another gender altogether?

The debate that has ensued in anthropology is not one of terminology, for what lies at the foundation of these terms are cultural understandings of language, sex, and gender and the relationship among them, a relationship connected to a wider debate about the utility of emic versus etic categorizations in anthropological analysis. As Roscoe and others have pointed out, it is very difficult to find an appropriate label in the English language for this category of person, because all the terms carry their own historical, political, and social baggage.

Although much of this material is illuminating for its ability to show gendered and sexual diversity within Native American societies historically, precious little anthropological material focuses on contemporary issues of language and sexuality. Roscoe (1998, 109) has published material on contemporary "Gay American Indians," noting the adaptation of the term *two-spirit,* which is seen as an alternative to both "berdache" and "gay" (see also Roscoe 1988; and Williams 1986). He outlines how, since the 1980s, a cultural revival movement has centered on recovery of berdache practices, although many lesbian and gay-identified Native Americans are not comfortable with the term *berdache,* which is an adaptation of a Persian word used by Europeans who recorded their observations of these individuals.

At the same time, these Native Americans have not been comfortable with the labels *gay, lesbian,* or *bisexual* because they are from the colonizer's culture and a language that does not properly represent who they are (Roscoe 1998, 111). Roscoe argues that part of the popularity of "two-spirit" is due to the fact that it manages to encompass both sexual and ethnic identities and is inclusive of men and women. Roscoe notes, however, that adaptation of the term *two-spirit* is not universal. In some reservations outside urban centers, one finds a combination of terms that may include local-language words for multiple-gender individuals alongside more Western terms, such as "gay" or "homosexual" (1998, 112–13).

The crafting of new sexual subjectivities among native North Americans and the role and significance of language(s) in relation to these subjectivities—linked to other identifications, which, in turn, raise issues of authenticity and tradition—have numerous parallels with the Māori situation and begin to illustrate the complex terrain through which indigenous sexual identifications are formed in a postcolonial setting.

Anthropology, Sexuality, and Language in Contemporary Māori Society

When we turn to issues of alter-sexualities in contemporary Māori society, we get next to nothing from anthropology. Although I have by no means searched every possible library or archive, I have so far only found one article published by two anthropologists (Arboleda and Murray 1985) that speaks directly to questions of homosexuality in Māori society. They were reacting to a 1974 article published in the *Australian and New Zealand Journal of Psychiatry,* which concluded that homosexuality did not exist among the Māori before European contact because there is no mention of it in historical records. Murray and Arboleda noted a number of reasons why that reasoning is faulty. First, the absence of any mention of homosexuality in early documentation of Māori society has more to do with the morals and values of the authors, that is, nineteenth-century Europeans (130). Second, if there were no words for homosexuality in te Reo Māori, that may indicate the possible absence of an institutionalized homosexual role but not the absence of homosexual behavior per se (131). And, third, a number of neighboring Polynesian societies have well-documented traditions of "gender-defined" homosexual roles (Besnier 1994), increasing the likelihood that a similar role may have existed among the pre-contact Māori.[7]

In contrast to this lone and rather tentative anthropological statement about Māori sexualities in relation to linguistic evidence, there has been a fluorescence of material from other professions and disciplines. In literature, there have been a number of novels, biographies, and autobiographical pieces on growing up and experiencing being homosexual and Māori (for example, this chapter's epigraph by Witi Ihimaera). "Sexuality" is also a key topic in some Māori studies departments in New Zealand universities.[8] In the area of health research, important work has been generated through the HIV/AIDS crisis and the critical need for better understanding of the ways in which sociocultural and economic factors are related to prevention and treatment of the virus. One of the most important publications in this sector has come from the New Zealand AIDS Foundation: *Male Call* (Waea Mai, Tāne Mā) (Aspin et al. 1997a, 1997b). It consists of twelve reports, with one focusing on Māori men who have sex with men, and provides rich data based on a nationwide telephone survey of 1,852 respondents, 170 of whom identified as Māori.

In one section of the report that focuses on sexual identity, respondents were allowed to choose as many labels as they felt appropriate. On average, Māori respondents chose 2.6 identities, with just over ⅔ choosing the term *gay.* The second most popular was "homosexual," at 58.8 percent (Aspin et al. 1997a, 1997b, 7). The report also notes, however, that proportionately fewer Māori than non-Māori chose "gay" or "homosexual," indicating that these terms are not appropriate to all Māori by any means. The third and fourth most popular identity terms among Māori respondents were "bisexual" and "queer," respectively, followed by takatāpui, which was chosen by 31.1 percent (1997, 8).

Although it is fifth in terms of self-descriptive popularity among respondents, I will focus on the emergence of the term *takatāpui;* discussions about it are important in demonstrating how language constitutes and is constituted through sexual and cultural identity labels but that no clear-cut alignment between categories of language, cultural identity, and sexuality emerges. The *Male Call* report notes, "Historically, the term *takatāpui* was used to describe an intimate companion of the same sex. The word features in Williams Dictionary which was first published in 1844. However, in contemporary Aotearoa society the term is understood to describe same-sex attraction, and it embraces men, women and transgender people" (Aspin et al. 1997a, 1997b, 25 [quotation]).[9]

In researching the usage of the term in Māori dictionaries and among Māori informants, I have found that the distinction between past and present meanings is not quite so clear-cut. When I looked up the words *homosexual* and *gay* in the English-Māori section of *Te Matatiki* (a dictionary of words produced or adapted by Te Taura Whiri i te Reo Māori [the Māori Language Commission, or MLC]), there were two terms: *tāne takāpui* and *tāne mate tāne,* the latter of which roughly translates as "men who desire men" (Māori Language Commission 1992).[10] In the Māori-English section, takatāpui was translated as "intimate companion of the same sex." In other contemporary references, for example, the *English-Maori Dictionary* (Ngata 1993), the word is also translated as "close companion" or "intimate friend of the same sex," a definition that does not by any means clearly communicate a sexual desire or preference for someone of the same gender.

I called the MLC's office in Wellington to ask why takatāpui was not translated as "homosexual" or "gay" in their dictionary, because it was clearly being used in that way by a substantial number of Māori, according to the *Male Call* report and my conversations. A MLC researcher informed me that this was a good example of an ongoing debate within the commission over the importance of retaining "traditional" meanings of words as opposed to the need to adopt, change, or extend older words to fit new concepts or objects. Some MLC members preferred a "purist" approach, trying to maintain the connection between words and their original meanings. They would argue that takatāpui represents a unique concept for which there is no direct English equivalent; to attach an aspect of sexual relations to it would be to redefine it completely. Other members favored a more pragmatic approach. If, they argued, a Māori word comes to take on new meaning(s) and is widely diffused and recognized throughout Māoridom, then the MLC should accept it. "Takāpui" as a Māori word for "gay" was developed by MLC "purists" in the early 1990s as an adaptation of "takatāpui" that would allow the latter term to retain its original meaning. Both the researcher and I agreed, however, that the wider Māori community had not adopted it into everyday usage.

The conversation revealed the influence of a discourse of "authentic" indigeneity created through a "pure" language produced by a faction within a powerful Māori institution responsible for regulating te Reo Māori (which, in turn, reveals the influence of a discourse of modern nationalism and its desire for exclusive linguistic purity attached to exclusive cultural purity). It also revealed the difficulties of popularizing a marginal language in which very few among the general population are fluent.

As a number of Māori (both homo- and heterosexual) explained, their understanding of the word *takatāpui* up until the 1980s was similar to the definition in Ngata's dictionary, but they were now aware of the additional, sexualized meaning.[11] Although most expressed no opinion about this (which I took to mean acceptance or tolerance), a few did say that they preferred the "original" definition of "intimate friendship" and thought another word should be developed for "gay" because they liked a specific, non-sexualized term for "close friend of the same sex" and preferred to be able to use it without any assumption of a sexual relationship.

Almost all Māori men with whom I spoke who use the term *takatāpui* as a term of self-ascription are aware of its original, "non-sexual" definition. In fact, a number identified the person they believed to have created its more recent connotative transformation, indicating keen awareness of developments in the Māori language and willingness to incorporate innovative usages of it for purposes of self-representation. This ability to pinpoint quite precisely the moment at which a word transforms in meaning allows us to examine not only the wider political and social milieu that contributed toward the development of new sexual terminologies and their (various) meanings but also how subaltern languages are related to sociopolitical transformations at local, national, and transnational levels.

The emergence and increasing popularity of the word *takatāpui* during the 1980s and 1990s can be linked to the combined influence of at least three sociopolitical influences that occurred throughout Aotearoa just before that time: gay and lesbian activism, HIV/AIDS, and a Māori political and cultural renaissance. The three factors are mutual. No single influence, that is, necessarily "produced" the word and the sociolinguistic debates around it, which demonstrates the historical contingency, politics of, and connectivity between linguistic and cultural production.

The first influence, gay and lesbian activism throughout New Zealand (although particularly in urban centers), began to gather momentum during the late 1970s and early 1980s. The movement was dedicated to overturning New Zealand's discriminatory laws against homosexuals, and their primary focus became a national campaign for homosexual law reform (the Homosexual Law Reform Bill was passed in 1986). The gay media at that time did not indicate any significant presence of Māori within the leadership of the various activist groups, but several Māori men with whom I spoke remembered participating in rallies and protests supporting the passage of the Homosexual Law Reform Bill.[12] One transgender individual, however, maintained that she and her Māori friends were too busy "trying to get by" and had no time or resources to become very involved, even though they supported the objectives of the movement in principle. Another self-identified takatāpui man told me that he had not felt particularly strongly about the movement because he was more interested in dedicating his time to social justice issues for all Māori people. Thus although lesbian and gay activism for homosexual law reform was influential in bringing issues of sexuality to the foreground of public culture in New Zealand, it cannot be identified as the only factor to bring about a transformation in Māori sexual terminologies.

The second influence was the rise of HIV/AIDS in Aotearoa throughout the 1980s. HIV/AIDS was rapidly recognized as a threat to Māori people, who at the time were contracting the virus at a disproportionately higher rate than other ethnic groups. The AIDS crisis galvanized the gay community and forced into circulation what had heretofore been taboo topics for public discussion. Soon after the establishment of the New Zealand AIDS Foundation in the mid-1980s, a parallel Māori organization, Te Rōpu Tautoko Trust, was established. Because of limited funding, however, its efforts were supplemented by regional initiatives that had origins in gay urban Māori communities (Aspin 1996, 48–49). These regional groups specified takatāpui as their key target clientele, reflecting the term's newfound presence and legitimacy, at least among certain segments of Māori society. Thus by the mid- to late 1980s sexual terminologies, practices, and identities were increasingly circulated among such public institutions as the government and the mainstream media and at the same time were being received and processed with recognition of ethnic differentiation, which, in turn, was highlighted (at least in part) through language differentiation.

The third influence came from the increasingly powerful voices of Māori activist groups that were changing the political and cultural landscape within Māori society and at a national level. Throughout the 1970s and 1980s, profound and unsettling changes continued in Māori sociocultural life. One of the most significant, begun during the 1950s, was the continuation of a massive population shift from rural to urban centers. Whereas 10 percent of the Māori population lived in urban centers in 1936, the percentage had shifted to 76 percent in 1976 and 86 percent in 1996 (Spoonly 1993, 13; Te Puni Kōkiri 2000). For many, however, socioeconomic improvement did not follow. Many disparities between Māori and non-Māori in the areas of income, unemployment, health, and education have increased since the 1980s (Te Puni Kōkiri 2000, 7).

During this rural to urban shift there was also a noticeable decline in te Reo–speakers. Current statistics on those fluent in te Reo range from 4.45 percent to 8 percent (Te Puni Kōkiri n.d.). The decline has been noticed and acted upon by Māori leaders since the 1970s. Hauraki Greenland (1991, 92) argues that this generation of leaders, influenced by black power in the United States, women's liberation, and "alternative culture" movements, therefore produced new strategies in which politics and culture dovetailed (see also Rata 1996; Sissons 1993, 1998; and Walker 1996).[13]

A key aspect of cultural revitalization strategy was language, and numerous efforts were initiated throughout Māoridom to revitalize the status and usage of te Reo. One of the first efforts was an adult education program (Te Atārangi), followed in the 1980s by the establishment of *Kōhanga Reo* ("language nests," i.e., Māori-language preschools) in which more than 14,032 children were registered by 1996 (Te Puni Kōkiri 1998, 22). Māori-language broadcasting also began in the 1970s, and its presence increased in both radio and television throughout the 1980s. In 1987 the Māori Language Act was passed, making te Reo Māori an "official" language of New Zealand and establishing the Māori Language Commission to protect and promote its use and development as a living language (Te Puni Kōkiri 1998, 5, 13). The Language Act also conferred the right to speak Māori in court and at tribunals, coroners courts, and commissions of inquiry (Te Puni Kōkiri 1998, 13). By 1998, government spending on Māori-language issues amounted to $50,200,000.[14]

Thus te Reo Māori has occupied center stage in much public discourse around the "revitalization" or "renaissance" of Māori culture and identity at the same time as "homosexual" culture and identity have been increasingly circulated in public discourses. That confluence has resulted in some segments of Māori society developing new sexual terminologies from te Reo Māori. It should be kept in mind, however, that despite the increased recognition and funding of Māori-language education, those who are fluent in it continue to remain a minority. Given that reality, what may emerge is a variety of terminological patterns that depend on an individual's exposure to te Reo, immersion in Māori-identified groups and activities, and other context-specific criteria.

The combination of these sociopolitical influences has meant that indigenous language, identity, and practice—and sexual language, identity, and practice—have been combined and diffused through highly visible and politicized public discourses at national levels as well as in more Māori-specific (but equally politicized) venues like the *marae* (meeting house) and other urban Māori community networks that together have created a context ripe for the development of new terminologies and meanings. This discursive production of a term demonstrates its historical contingency and results in outcomes that are not straightforward in terms of alignments among language, sexuality, and identity.

Takatāpui in Context

Most takatāpui-identified speakers with whom I spoke indicated that they now use the term in addition to or instead of the label *gay* for reasons similar to those put forward by Native American two-spirit individuals as outlined by Roscoe. The term *takatāpui* incorporates a sense of indigenous identity and communicates sexual orientation. It is different from two-spirit in that it is not English and thus operationalizes a code that highlights difference when inserted into an English sociolinguistic context (and is given much of its meaning through this contrast). Thus it creates a political impact every time it is used in an English conversation. Some Māori men were supportive of the non-gendered specificity it encapsulates because, they said, all Māori of non-heterosexual orientation could find solidarity through common identification as takatāpui. Others, however, preferred to make a distinction among *takatāpui tāne* (men), *takatāpui wāhine* (women), and *whakawāhine* or *whakatāne* (transgendered individuals), indicating that a powerful model of gendered difference undergirds or bisects any construction based upon a uniform "alter" sexual identity. To complicate things still further, one sexual health worker told me that it was important to distinguish between takatāpui and *tāne moe tāne* (men who sleep with men) because many Māori men have sexual relations with other men but do not think of themselves as having a homosexual orientation because they also sleep with women.

Furthermore, not all homosexual-identified Māori men use the term *takatāpui* as their only label of self-identification, a situation similar to Roscoe's observations of the sexuality terms that Native Americans "on the reservation" use when away from urban centers. I noticed that many men, when outside the office or official interview, would use additional terms to describe themselves or others. Conversations while having a smoke outside a marae or after dinner at someone's home could contain a variety of English identity terms, such as "gay," "queen," "poof," "poofter" or "gay Māori," in addition to takatāpui. If an unfamiliar name was mentioned, people would often ask whether that person was "a poof" or "gay." One day at a pub in Wellington I asked Matthew, who works in a Māori organization and is active in Māori social and political activities, whether he identified as takatāpui. "Takatāpui, poofter, fag," he replied. "They all mean the same thing: we're homosexual, darling, HO-MO-SEXUAL!" Another man, who describes himself having a "mixed" heritage of Māori and Pakeha, claimed he did not feel comfortable using the term for himself because he had not been greatly involved in Māori affairs for much of his life. A third individual who works for a sexual health agency told me that he used the term carefully and strategically because he was aware of its potential to create solidarity and to alienate, depending on who was being addressed. He said that he would use "takatāpui" freely among Māori who are comfortable and confident with te Reo, claim a homosexual identification, and feel they have strong attachments to other

Māori. But when speaking to Māori he thought were not necessarily "homo-sexually" identified, did not feel confident with te Reo, and/or were not very connected to a Māori community, he would be much more cautious in us-ing the word. They might, he felt, think he was trying to be superior through his use of Māori linguistic terms.

That comment indicates the complex political value of a minority language associated with an indigenous identity spoken only by a few living in an English-dominated, postcolonial society. For some Māori, fluency in te Reo is seen as a marker of Māori-"ness," that is, a sense that one is knowledgable of Māori cultural concepts and therefore secure in one's identity as a Māori. Others feel that if they are not fluent they will be judged to be less knowl-edgable of Māori cultural concepts and therefore viewed as more alienated from their Māori identity. The speaker had thus recognized how, in various contexts, the use of one word had different potential outcomes related to sensitive issues about indigenous identity and the language associated with it. The term *takatāpui* had the potential to unify or fracture an identification built around alternative sexual and ethnic identification.

The comments also highlight the performativity of linguistic practice whereby meaning (or successful communication of meaning) cannot be deduced only through the intentionality of a speaker or the perception of a listener. Rather, meaning emerges through a more complex and dense ana-lytic terrain that factors differentiating individual experiences, specific spa-tial and temporal contexts, and wider linguistic sociocultural and political tropes framing the particular linguistic exchange. Thus failure, misinterpre-tation, and/or ambivalence are allowed to be as structurally integral to the exchange as mutual comprehension (Kulick 2000, 268–69; see also Livia and Hall eds. 1997, 12–13).

The social and political consequences of these terminological twists and turns should not be assumed to be relevant only in the realm of Māori lan-guage and identity. There is great debate about the connections between "gay," "lesbian" and the English language and whether gay/lesbian languages exist. In the situation I am examining, however, the issue is not whether a gay Māori language exists but rather how a minority sexual subjectivity and language are positioned in relation to a dominant language and cultural discourse in a postcolonial society. To put it briefly, Māori language and gay/takatāpui Māori men as a group do not currently occupy the same sociopolitical sta-tus as the English language and white European gays and lesbians. Te Reo Māori is a minority language in New Zealand, and despite great changes since the 1980s it faces a daily battle for survival and legitimacy in a wider social spectrum that is benignly uncaring or aggressively hostile to accommodat-

ing its presence on an equal footing with English. That applies to social relations as well. Many takatāpui/gay Māori have had negative experiences within
Anglo-European gay communities. Some have faced rejection from their own
families so that their relationships with other takatāpui/gay Māori men become critically important as a primary support network. A great deal is at
stake because the debates over language use, identity, and sexuality may have
profound consequences for these people's health and well-being.

Conclusion

"Takatāpui" is a term that communicates more than just sexual identity and
indigeneity. It is also/always a political statement when it occurs in public
(English) discourse because it conveys information about the current status
and import of te Reo Māori in Aotearoa in relation to English, which simultaneously conveys a political message about Māori cultural identity in relation to Anglo/Pakeha cultural identity. It also reveals a great deal about the
more recent history of the constructions of gendered and sexual identifications in Māori and non-Māori communities in New Zealand and changes
that have occurred to both. Finally, it reflects desire for the expression of a
"silenced" sexual subjectivity, but the articulation is problematic because it
reveals its origin in and engagement with already circulating discourses of
"authentic indigeneity" and authentic "gay" identity, both of which have been
produced in a modernizing, colonial context.

   We cannot forget that almost two-thirds of the respondents to the NZAF
survey did not choose the term *takatāpui* or chose other English-language
terms in addition to it and that "gay/homosexual" are still the most prevalent terms of self-identification. That may be due to the genesis of the sexualized definition of takatāpui; the numbers may change, certainly among
the urban Māori with whom I spoke. The majority are comfortable with describing themselves as takatāpui, albeit in addition to other identification
labels. Perhaps the situation in Aotearoa is similar to Roscoe's observations
about the two-spirit term in relation to urban/rural divisions and multiple
labeling. The NZAF report suggests that "takatāpui" may be more popular
among urban Māori than rural (Aspin et al. 1997a, 1997b, 26).[15] Moreover,
my research has indicated that "takatāpui" often co-exists with other English terms. Clearly, there is still some ambiguity surrounding the term. The
fact that many Māori use multiple identity labels indicates both the influence
and a critical rethinking of English gender and sexuality terminologies and
how such terms are not sufficient for the identities they index (Boellstorff,
in this volume).

This discussion of the etymology of sexuality terms and their relationship to language, linguistic practice, and cultural identity by no means fully reveals the diversity and complexity of the daily life of those who use them, nor should we assume that any simple generalizations about character or personality can be made on the basis of knowing the sociopolitical genesis of a single identity label. The need for further ethnographic research is critical in order to flesh out and represent the diversity of these gay or takatāpui lives as they are currently lived, to better understand the relationship between English and te Reo Māori in everyday conversations, and to better understand the ways in which these are connected to wider social and political forces. A number of linguists, for example, have identified "Māori Vernacular English," which is more a "style of English than an actual separate dialect" (Gordon and Deverson 1998, 144). This style has a number of distinctive phonological, prosodic, and syntactical features, one of which is regular code-switching and lexico-semantic borrowing from Māori (Stubbe and Holmes 2000). The epigraph from Witi Ihimaera's novel and the insertion of "takatāpui" into primarily English discourse may be examples of this style.

At the same time, I would suggest that while there may be other "subdialects" within Māori society, one of which could be oriented around the practices of some homosexually-identified Māori individuals, they cannot and should not be taken as proof of a singular, autonomous sociocultural or sexual identity. To do so would oversimplify and reify the dense, layered, and inter-related contexts of linguistic and cultural production and their varied outcomes. This is the challenge for anthropology, which has too long ignored sexuality as a valid domain of research and only recently recognized the cultural and political complexity of language and linguistic practices in relation to sexual minorities, indigenous people, and their ongoing battles for social justice and respect.

Notes

Research for this essay was conducted with funding assistance from the Australian Research Council and Adelaide University. The Stout Research Centre at Victoria University provided generous support during the writing phase. I would also like to thank Te Ripowai Higgins, Lee Smith, Mereana Hond, and the rest of the staff of Te Kawa a Māui (the School of Māori Studies) at Victoria University, Wellington, New Zealand. Without their support, comments, and criticisms this work could never have been written. Thanks also to Tom Boellstorff and Bill Leap for their insightful comments and criticisms. Many other individuals throughout Aotearoa/New Zealand generously took the time to answer my questions and patiently correct my mistaken assumptions in interviews and conversations about sexuality and indigeneity. My deepest gratitude to them. I have done my best to accurately represent their opinions and positions, but the full complexity and brilliance of their lives can never be completely presented in a such a brief exercise. I dedicate this essay to Pat Uttiera—thank you for sharing.

1. Aotearoa is the Māori word for the nation of New Zealand. I will use these terms interchangeably throughout this essay.

2. The majority of informants mentioned in this chapter are men who claim an exclusively homosexual orientation in their sexual and romantic practices. It is important to keep in mind that there are Māori men who have sex with men but do not necessarily view themselves as having a homosexual "identity" (Aspin et al. 1997a, 1997b).

3. The difference between "language" and "linguistic practice" is discussed in the introduction to this volume.

4. Although I recognize that the term *indigenous* is problematic in terms of referencing and defining a social group because it cloaks the process of colonial relations that have, through modernity, created the category of "indigenous" (as opposed to "settlers" or "immigrants"), I will continue to identify Māori as indigenous throughout this discussion because it is a popular term of self-reference and other terms ("ethnic" or "racial") would be equally problematic if not more so. I will attend to the sociolinguistic implications of this colonialist binary terminology.

5. Thanks to Tom Boellstorff for this point.

6. See for example, Murray (1996) and Newton (1993).

7. There is a debate, however, regarding the appropriateness of labeling this role "homosexual" when it may in fact have more to do with gender malleability than sexual proclivity.

8. Victoria University of Wellington's School of Māori Studies, for example, offers an undergraduate course on Māori sexuality entitled "Te Huinga Takatāpui."

9. Lee Smith, a linguist in the Department of Māori Studies at Victoria University, indicated to me that the term is not present in *Nga Moteatea* (a collection of nineteenth-century Māori songs, geneologies, and mythological stories).

10. Thanks to Lee Smith for this translation.

11. Others told me that they had never heard of this word until the 1990s, but these individuals tend to be primarily monolingual (English) with little experience/education in te Reo.

12. There are hardly any references to ethnic subdivisions within gay and lesbian communities in gay media of the time.

13. "Culture" is not clearly defined in this text but appears to support an exclusivist, autochthonous application.

14. Only a small portion, however, went to the commission. The majority was spent on Māori television broadcasting (Te Puni Kōkiri 1998, 25).

15. Researchers conducted a "logistic regression" in order to investigate the effect of demographic and social milieu variables on the likelihood of Māori men identifying as takatāpui and and found that those who lived in cities were significantly more likely to so identify, as were those attached to the gay community (defined in relation to membership in gay organizations, reading gay newspapers/magazines, and the respondent's own set of criteria through which he decided that he is part of the community) (Aspin et al. 1997a, 1997b, 26).

Works Cited

Arboleda, Manuel, and Stephen O. Murray. 1985. "The Dangers of Lexical Inference with Special Reference to Māori Sexuality." *Journal of Homosexuality* 12(1): 129–34.

Aspin, Clive. 1996. "Gay Community Development in New Zealand in the 1970s and Implications for the Health of Gay Māori Men in the 1990s." *Social Policy Journal of New Zealand,* no. 7, 42–51.

———et al. 1997a. *Male Call* (Waea Mai Tāne Mā). Report 3: *Māori Men Who Have Sex with Men.* Aukland: New Zealand AIDS Foundation.

———et al. 1997b. *Male Call* (Waea Mai Tāne Mā). Report 5: *Sexual Identity.* Aukland: New Zealand AIDS Foundation.

Besnier, Niko. 1994. "Polynesian Gender Liminality through Time and Space." In *Third Sex/Third Gender: Beyond Sexual Dimorphism in Culture and History,* ed. Gilbert Herdt, 285–328. New York: Zed Books.

Gordon, Elizabeth, and Tony Deverson. 1998. *New Zealand English and English in New Zealand.* Auckland: New House Publishers.

Greenland, Hauraki. 1991. "Māori Ethnicity as Ideology." In *Nga Take: Ethnic Relations and Racism in Aotearoa/New Zealand,* ed. Paul Spoonly, David Pearson, and Cluny Macpherson. Palmerston North: Dunmore Press.

Heller, Monica. 2001. "Critique and Sociolinguistic Analysis of Discourse." *Critique of Anthropology* 21(2): 117–41.

Ihimaera, Witi. 2000. *The Uncle's Story.* Auckland: Penguin Books.

Jacobs, Sue-Ellen, Wesley Thomas, and Sabine Lang, eds. 1997. *Two-Spirit People: Native American Gender Identity, Sexuality, and Spirituality.* Urbana: University of Illinois Press.

Kulick, Don. 2000. "Gay and Lesbian Language." *Annual Review of Anthropology* 29: 243–85.

Livia, Anna, and Kira Hall, eds. 1997. *Queerly Phrased: Language, Gender and Sexuality.* New York: Oxford University Press.

Māori Language Commission (Te Taura Whiri i te Reo Māori). 1992. *Te Matatiki.* Wellington: Māori Language Commission (Te Taura Whiri i te Reo Māori).

Murray, Stephen O. 1996. *American Gay.* Chicago: University of Chicago Press.

Newton, Esther. 1993. *Cherry Grove, Fire Island.* Boston: Beacon Press.

Ngata, H. M. 1993. *English-Maori Dictionary.* Wellington: Learning Media.

Rata, Elizabeth. 1996. "*Whanau* Revival and Retribalisation: Establishing the Context of Tribal-Capitalism." *Sites,* no. 32, 1–22.

Roscoe, Will. 1998. *Changing Ones: Third and Fourth Genders in Native North America.* New York: St. Martin's Press.

Roscoe, Will, ed. 1988. *Living the Spirit: A Gay American Indian Anthology.* New York: St. Martin's Press.

Sissons, Jeffrey. 1993. "The Systematisation of Tradition: Māori Culture as a Strategic Resource." *Oceania* 64(2): 97–117.

———. 1998. "The Traditionalisation of the Māori Meeting House." *Oceania* 69(1): 36–57.

Spoonly, Paul. 1993. *Racism and Ethnicity.* New York: Oxford University Press.

Stubbe, Maria, and Janet Holmes. 2000. "Talking Māori or Pakeha in English: Signalling

Identity in Discourse." In *New Zealand English,* ed. Allan Bell and K. Kuiper. Wellington: Victoria University Press.

Te Puni Kōkiri (Ministry of Māori Development). 1998. *Review of Te Taura Whiri I te Reo Māori.* Wellington: Te Puni Kōkiri.

———. 1999. *Te Tāoma: The Māori Language: The Steps That Have Been Taken.* Wellington: Te Puni Kōkiri.

———. 2000. *Progress towards Closing Social and Economic Gaps between Māori and Non-Māori.* Wellington: Te Puni Kōkiri.

———. n.d. *Summary Report of National Māori Language Survey.* Wellington: Te Puni Kōkiri.

Walker, Ranginui. 1996. *Nga Pepa a Ranginui* (The Walker papers). Auckland: Penguin.

Weston, Kath. 1993. "Lesbian/Gay Studies in the House of Anthropology." *Annual Review of Anthropology* 22: 339–67.

———. 1998. *Long Slow Burn: Sexuality and Social Science.* Chicago: University of Chicago Press.

Williams, Walter L. 1986. *The Spirit and the Flesh: Sexual Diversity in American Indian Culture.* Boston: Beacon Press.

Woodsum, Jo Ann. 1995. "Gender and Sexuality in Native American Societies: A Bibliography." *American Indian Quarterly* 19(4): 527–55.

7. "Authentic, of Course!": *Gay* Language in Indonesia and Cultures of Belonging

TOM BOELLSTORFF

Imagine that you, the reader, spoke Indonesian and boarded a minibus with me one night to visit *gay* Indonesian men in the city of Surabaya in East Java.[1] Arriving at the Joyoboyo bus station, we leave the crowded terminal—an open space filled with more than a hundred minibuses—and walk down a narrow street that runs alongside the Brantas River, a still sweep of inky, fetid water winding to the sea on the north edge of town. Under blue tarps, sellers in stalls lit with harsh fluorescent light watch over shoes, shirts, and music cassettes. The bus station at a safe remove, we see about thirty men in small groups extending down the street for a hundred yards or so. As we approach, one man calls out "Welcome to *Texas*" (*selamat datang di Texas*)![2] I introduce you to these men, who call themselves *gay*. Even though you know Indonesian, however, you have trouble understanding their speech. One man says something like "I've been Hungarian for two hours; let's go get some fried rice!" His friend responds, "Eyesore donut wonton" (which you later learn means "I don't want"). As the men joke with each other, you keep hearing one particular response: "*Asli lho!*" (Authentic, of course!).[3]

Several questions might come to mind. Why do these men speak in this manner? How have they come to call themselves *gay?* What does their way of speaking tell us about them and about contemporary Indonesian culture more generally? Why do they joke about authenticity?

Indeed, what does it mean to say that something is "authentic"? That is an important question for lesbian, gay, bisexual, transgendered, intersexed, and otherwise queer persons (whom I will refer to as "LGBT persons").

Around the world it has been common for LGBT persons to be termed strangers to our own cultures, including languages—leading in some cases to the search for "another mother tongue," in Judy Grahn's memorable phrase (Grahn 1984). Sexual and gender minorities seem to be treated as authentic only when it can be shown that "traditionally" we were valued as shamans or healers. The paradox is that in such cases the claim to a modern sexual selfhood (like "gay") is interpreted as abandoning such traditions for the temptations of globalization or consumerism. Authenticity, it seems, lies in the distant past for LGBT persons, always receding beyond our grasp.

Authenticity has additional meaning for persons living in postcolonial nation-states. Most such states take their boundaries from the colonizing power, and those boundaries do not correspond to historical lines of ethnic and religious difference or physical geography (thus, for instance, the straight borders of many African nation-states). Yet postcolonial states claim a kind of direct or organic link to their citizens that the colonizer as an "outsider" did not possess. Great energy is expended on defining and policing the definition of who will count as a "real" member of a nation-state and what kinds of people will count as the ideal of what authentic citizens should look like, think, and do. In postcolonial societies, then, discussions about authenticity typically carry implications concerning belonging. For LGBT persons in post-colonial societies, the burden of authenticity is doubly heavy because the heterosexual nuclear family is so often held up as microcosm of, and foundation for, the nation-state.

This chapter differs from the others in this volume in that it does not look at the use of gay English outside Euro-American centers of power. Instead, it investigates questions of authenticity and belonging through examining a unique linguistic phenomenon called *bahasa gay* (*gay* language). Roughly speaking, this is slang, but I will refer to it as "*gay* language" rather than "*gay* slang," not only because that is how it is described in Indonesia but also because the regularity of its derivational patternings make it more complex than the kinds of languages usually described by the English term *slang*. Bahasa *gay* is spoken in Indonesia by men who term themselves *gay* and also by the male-to-female transgenders known since the late 1970s as *waria,* an amalgamation of *wanita* (woman) and *pria* (man).[4]

Following an introduction to *gay* lives in Indonesia, I discuss the structure of bahasa *gay*. I then turn to its patterns of use; in particular, I show that bahasa *gay* acts not as a "secret language" (as LGBT languages are so often assumed to do) but as a language of belonging. When *gay* Indonesians speak bahasa *gay,* they "voice" a sense of belonging to a *gay* community that stands apart from the larger national society yet is part of that society. The increasing appropriation of bahasa *gay* by Indonesian popular culture further illustrates this interplay of belonging and alienation and shows how, for *gay* Indonesians, authenticity is not static but actively shaped and open to interpretation.

In focusing on questions of authenticity and belonging, I deliberately pass over many dimensions of bahasa *gay,* some of which I will address elsewhere. These include details of bahasa *gay* grammar and the relationship between local variations and national-level bahasa *gay.* In addition, although I touch upon the relationship between bahasa *gay* and national discourse in this chapter I will not go into a detailed discussion of that relationship. My task here is to show how bahasa *gay* acts not to hide *gay* conversations from outsiders but to mark a conversation as *gay* in the first place—and how in so doing it represents a commentary on national belonging. Bahasa *gay* reveals how marginalized persons think through questions of belonging on a transpersonal level—at the level of cultural and linguistic norms—even when such questions are not the explicit topic of discussion.

Indonesia and *Gay* Indonesians

Readers may find it interesting to compare this chapter with Peter Jackson's insightful chapter on Thailand (chapter 9). Indonesia is Thailand's neighbor in Southeast Asia and boasts a long history of trade and cultural interaction with Thailand, yet it differs from Thailand in many respects. These differences will have implications for the character of *gay* language in Indonesia. Thailand, with sixty-three million inhabitants, is hardly a small country, but it is dwarfed by Indonesia, the world's fourth most populous nation. Because nearly 90 percent of Indonesians are Muslim, Indonesia is home to more Muslims than any other country, although Islam is not the sole official religion. Its 6 million citizens are spread out over more than 230 thousand islands and speak, by some accounts, nearly seven hundred "local" languages alongside the national language of Indonesian (I will return to this notion of a "national language"). Like Indonesian itself, most of these languages belong to the Austronesian linguistic family. That family has the largest historical geographic spread of any language family in the world, stretching from Madagascar in the west to Hawaii and Easter Island in the east and from highland Taiwan in the north to the Indonesian archipelago in the south.

Indonesia differs from Thailand in more than size and diversity, however; their encounters with colonialism diverge quite radically. As Jackson notes, Thailand was the only Southeast Asian nation never to be directly colonized, although the pressures of the colonial world surrounding it forced Thais, who

historically had a range of royal and tribal polities, to reconceive these relationships in Western terms of nationhood (Winichakul 1994). In contrast,
the islands now called Indonesia, stretching from Sumatra in the west to half
of the island of New Guinea in the east (a distance almost a thousand miles
greater than that from California to New York), and from two-thirds of
Borneo in the north to Java and Bali in the south, shared little before the
advent of colonialism. Powerful polities existed historically in the archipelago, notably the Buddhist Srivijaya kingdom centered in Sumatra and the
Majapahit kingdom centered in Java, but neither had the scope or intensity
of European colonialism. And that colonialism had a particular character.
Although the Portuguese, British, and Japanese had short periods of rule in
the region, it was Dutch colonialism over a period of almost 350 years that
forged the entity known as the "Netherlands Indies" or "Dutch East Indies."
It was that entity, not the Srivijaya or Majapahit empires or any other kind
of polity, that became Indonesia during the 1940s.

For purposes of my discussion, the most significant feature of this history is that the Dutch, in contrast to colonial powers like France or Britain—
which worked actively to change the cultures of those they ruled—tended
to treat the inhabitants of the Indies as a source of cheap labor. So long as
that labor supply was uninterrupted, the beliefs and practices of the colonial
subjects were not a high priority. This does not mean that the impact of
Dutch colonialism was not extensive. It means that the intermingling of
cultural norms from the colonial power with those of the colony was secondary to a system of indirect rule that drew from—and reified—conceptions
of local culture and tradition.

One important implication of this policy is that the Dutch, unlike most
other colonial powers, did not encourage the propagation of their language,
which they preferred to keep as a language for themselves and their domestic and civil servants. As a result, at the time of independence fewer than 2
percent of Indonesians spoke Dutch (Groeneboer 1998, 1), a figure that has
dropped to nearly zero now. In place of a European language as lingua franca for this vast archipelago, the Dutch seized upon Malay, an Austronesian
language employed for centuries as a trade language in island Southeast Asia,
using it for communicating with their colonial subjects and encouraging its
use as a means of inter-ethnic communication as well. By the 1920s an emerging nationalist movement in the Indies had renamed this language "Indonesian" and made its use a key symbol of nationalist consciousness. It was
further disseminated during the brief but intense period of Japanese rule
during World War II. In contemporary Indonesia almost all Indonesian citizens are competent in the Indonesian language, and a rapidly increasing

number speak it as their sole mother tongue or learn it alongside one or more local languages from childhood. I will return to the important place of this language later in this chapter. First, however, I will turn to *gay* men and their ways of speaking.

Gay Men and Bahasa *Gay*

Since 1992 (as an HIV/AIDS and gay activist) and 1995 (as an anthropologist) I have worked with *gay* men in Indonesia as a researcher, advocate, and ally.[5] (When I speak of "*gay* men," I refer to Indonesian men who call themselves *gay*, in other words, not based on my own determination of who is *gay*.) Although there is a persistent stereotype that people in the "third world" who use transformed versions of the terms *gay* and *lesbian* are highly educated or wealthy, most *gay* Indonesian men are poor (like most Indonesians), have never traveled outside Indonesia, and can be found in rural as well as urban areas (although the largest concentrations are in cities). They also rarely speak English. Because Indonesia was a Dutch colony, English was rare in the archipelago before independence. Indonesians are aware of English's status as the de facto international language of commerce and popular culture, but few learn more than a few rudimentary phrases, whether from courses or from imported movies and television programs.[6]

The idea of *gay* subjectivity, then, did not "globalize" to Indonesia (as that term is usually understood) in terms of a dominating discourse that presented a complete picture of homosexual selfhood. It came into being as Indonesians actively pieced together, and thus reconfigured, fragmented concepts of homosexuality gleaned through the mass media (Boellstorff 2003). Due to state law, these mass media are almost entirely in Indonesian, the national language, not local languages such as Javanese or Balinese. There are no pride parades in Indonesia and little in the way of rainbow flags and pink triangles, nor do most *gay* Indonesians know what those symbols and activities mean elsewhere.

Despite these differences, however, it is clear from the narratives of *gay* men with whom I have worked over the years, as well as from the informally published magazines that *gay* men have produced (Boellstorff 2003b) that *gay* men tend to feel a sense of connection to LGBT communities outside Indonesia, even if they are unsure exactly how those communities work. They do not feel that the concept *gay* is an outside imposition. After all, Indonesians have been taking in concepts from the outside (and transforming them) for centuries, from religions like Islam, Buddhism, Christianity, and Hinduism to nationalism and capitalism. While aware of global inequality, when it comes to homosexuality the dominant assumption is one of lateral linkage. This possibility of a nonthreatening and nonantagonistic relationship to processes of cultural globalization is almost completely absent in the LGBT literature on globalization. *Gay* men in Indonesia, then, have built conceptions of homosexual selfhood that are unique to Indonesia even while assuming a kind of connection to LGBT people outside Indonesia. The connection is mostly an imagined one, because few *gay* men meet gay or lesbian persons from elsewhere (unless they live in areas that attract tourists and they speak English), read Western LGBT mass media, or travel outside Indonesia themselves.

Within Indonesia, *gay* men assume there are distinctive features to what they term the *"gay* world" (*dunia gay*): informal networks of friendship, sex, and romance; places like parks, shopping malls, and rented rooms; and correspondence with *gay* people in other parts of Indonesia and travel to meet them. After all, without some distinguishing features it would be impossible to know when one is in the *gay* world in the first place. One of the most salient such features is a way of speaking that is often called "bahasa *gay*" and also *bahasa hémong* (*hémong* is a bahasa *gay* variant of *homo*, an Indonesian term usually used to refer to male homosexuality). This way of speaking is also called *bahasa waria, banci,* or *béncong.* These are all terms for male-to-female transvestites. Those persons also speak bahasa *gay,* and many Indonesians still confuse such persons with *gay* men. This chapter focuses on bahasa *gay* as spoken by *gay* men.

For an outside observer—and certainly in the context of the other chapters in this volume—one of the most striking features of bahasa *gay* is that there is no gay English in it. Indeed, the term *gay* is one of only a handful of English-derived terms that appear in bahasa *gay.* Another striking feature of bahasa *gay* is that it is always based on Indonesian, the national language, and never (to my knowledge or the knowledge of interlocutors) on a "local" language like Javanese. That is probably due to at least three factors: first, the sense of incompatibility between "local tradition" and the self-consciously modern *gay* subject position (which appears to have come into being in the 1970s); second, the fact that the mass media are almost exclusively in Indonesian; and, third, that in most urban centers the mixing of persons from various ethnic groups means that Indonesian is the dominant language of daily interaction.

But if bahasa *gay* is not based on gay English, how does it work? I learned it the way I saw *gay* men learn it, acquiring terms one by one and then patterns, sometimes through explicit instruction and sometimes through imitation. I say "patterns" because bahasa *gay* is not just a set of lexical items. It is a series of derivations that speakers can use to coin new terms on the spur of the moment, some of which become widely known and others of which die out.[7] Based on fieldwork in a number of Indonesian cities, primarily Surabaya (on the island of Java), Makassar (on the island of Sulawesi or Celebes), and Kuta/Denpasar (on the island of Bali), I pieced together the various ways of creating bahasa *gay* and was then excited to find in the late 1990s that a colleague, Dédé Oetomo, had independently come up with an almost identical list (Oetomo 2001).

How to Make Bahasa *Gay*

Making terms of bahasa *gay* usually involves taking a word of Indonesian (less often, a word from a local language, a word from English (not gay English), a brand name, or the name of a celebrity), keeping the first syllable relatively unchanged; and then modifying the ending.[8] Most bahasa *gay* terms thus "comment" on standard language and in that sense "resist" dominant norms, although such resistance is not always overt (Oetomo 2001, 67–71). Particularly since the mid-1990s (according to Oetomo), and certainly in my experience, the most popular derivational process is what I call "syllabic substitution." This is when a term (usually from standard Indonesian) replaces a word with the same first syllable. *Cap cai* in standard Indonesian means a "mixed vegetable dish," but in bahasa *gay* it means "fast," replacing *cepat* (fast). *Kelinci* means "rabbit" in standard Indonesian but "small" in bahasa *gay* due to the first syllable it shares with standard Indonesian *kecil* (small). *Tinta* ("tint" in standard Indonesian) replaces *tidak* (no, not); *mawar* ("rose" in standard Indonesian) replaces *mau* (want); and *sutra* ("silk" in standard Indonesian) replaces *sudah* (already). Occasionally, these terms are limited to certain cities or even friendship networks (particularly if they are recent coinages), but it appears that terms that survive over time eventually become part of the national bahasa *gay;* they are understood by *gay*-speakers in many different parts of the nation.

 Next to syllabic substitution, the second important derivational process in bahasa *gay* is what I term "suffixation and vowel shift." To make bahasa *gay* words using this process, a suffix—most often *-ong*, but also *-es* and *-i*, which is a less productive variant that arose in the 1990s (Oetomo 2001)—is added to the first syllable of a word. The vowel of this first syllable shifts to *é*. *Banci* (in standard Indonesian) becomes *béncong* or *bénces; puluh* ("tens" in standard Indonesian, as in *tiga puluh* "thirty") becomes *pélong; ke mana* ("where to?" in standard Indonesian) becomes *keménong;* and *homo* becomes *hémong* or *hémes*. Although it is very easy for speakers of bahasa *gay* to coin new terms using suffixation and vowel shift, formed in this way can (like other kinds of bahasa *gay* terms) remain in use for decades, as indicated by the earlier mention of terms like *hémong* and *keménong* (Budiman 1979; Chambert-Loir 1984).

Beyond these two means for creating bahasa *gay* words, there are a series of less frequent derivational patterns. These include "si- prefixing," where the first syllable of a term is retained and prefixed with *si-* and a consonant added at the end if the syllable ends in a vowel. *Si* is a Javanese and Indonesian particle indicating categories of persons; as a prefix in bahasa *gay*, it usually refers to persons as well. Examples include *silan* (from Javanese *lanang*, or "man"); *sihom* (from "homo"); *siban* (from "banci" [waria]); and *siG/siL* for *gay/lesbi* (the letter *g* is pronounced "gay" in Indonesian, and *l* is pronounced "él"). With "-in- infixing" the infix *-in-* is "inserted between the consonant and vowel of every syllable, usually with a shortening of the product so that it becomes two syllables long" (Oetomo 1999, 28, my translation). "Banci" becomes *binancini* which becomes *binan*. *Linak*, a bahasa *gay* term for "man," is another example of this process (*laki* > *linakini* > *linak*), as is *lines* for "lesbian" (*lesbi* > *linesbini* > *lines*). Oetomo (2001) notes that the process appears to have begun in Jakarta and Bandung but has spread across Indonesia; it is, for instance, well known in Makassar.

In "-se' suffixing" ("se" with a glottal stop), the first syllable of a word (and the first consonant of the following syllable if the first syllable ends in a vowel) is retained and suffixed with *-se'*: *homo* > *hom* > *homse'*, or *Cina* (Chinese) > *Cin* > *Cinse'*. Yet another means of forming gay language terms that appears to originate in the city of Bandung in West Java (and is likely spreading) is the reinterpretation of standard Indonesian terms as acronyms. For example, *kopi susu* (coffee with milk) can mean *(ko)ntol (p)anjang (i)tu (s)angatk(u) (su)ka* (I really like that big cock) (Boy and Yasiano 1999).[8] A final source for bahasa *gay* terms is outright neologism, for example, *akika* ("I") shares a first syllable with the standard Indonesian *aku* ("I"). Only a handful of bahasa *gay* terms originate in this manner, however; it is primarily a language of transformation.

Beyond Lexicon: Bahasa *Gay* in Use

As has been noted for some time, studies of LGBT speech typically equate language with lexicon (Leap 1995, ix); that is, they focus on words seen as unique to LGBT-speakers. To the extent that scholars of LGBT language focus on lexicon in this manner, they reflect a broader phenomenon noted by linguists from Benjamin Lee Whorf to Michael Silverstein: Certain aspects of language tend to be more present to speakers' (and scholars') consciousness than others. In particular, elements of language that can be broken into discrete units (e.g., words) are more salient to speakers than elements that do not break into such units (e.g., grammatical gender). Pragmatics (or rules of use for language, under which I include "rules for rules for use" or what are sometimes called "metapragmatic" phenomena) are also less salient to speaker consciousness, but that does not mean they are not important to language. By turning to the pragmatics of bahasa *gay,* I will show how that way of speaking is linked to questions of authenticity and belonging in contemporary Indonesia.

When, over the years, I have asked *gay* men about how *gay* men talk, the only element they proffer other than lexicon is intonation: They assert that *gay* men often speak in an effeminate manner, in particular with a rising pitch. But when *gay* men discuss why bahasa *gay* exists at all (either because of my questioning or because the topic comes up in conversation), two consistent justifications appear. Bahasa *gay,* it is said, is a secret language (*bahasa rahasia*) and/or it is a language of association and interaction (*bahasa gaul*).

One of the clearest expressions of the belief that bahasa *gay* acts as a secret language in my fieldwork came not from a *gay* man but from Rita, a masculine lesbi woman, who, like many such women, had learned bahasa *gay* through socializing with *gay* men in hair salons, shopping malls, and parks. While visiting a mystic pilgrimage site in eastern Java with Rita, she and I stayed in the house of Dadang, an innkeeper who knew nothing of our sexualities. One morning Rita and I saw an effeminate man on the neighbor's porch, cutting someone's hair. "That's my younger brother," Dadang said. "He moved to the city a few months ago and works in a salon there." I wondered if the younger brother might be *gay* but thought no further until about half an hour later, when Rita made a joke and Dadang added *péres,* a bahasa *gay* term meaning "gotcha!" derived from *pura-pura* (pretend). We hid our surprise as Dadang related how his younger brother had "learned a new language at the salon in town." On the ride back to Surabaya that afternoon, Rita was incensed. "Dadang's younger brother isn't very professional [*kurang profesional*] to tell everyone about bahasa *gay.* That's for our group alone, so we can talk without other people understanding."

I do not think Rita or the *gay* men who say that bahasa *gay* can be a secret language are lying. Rather, it appears that the use of bahasa *gay* for secrecy is subordinate to uses linked to belonging that are not always apparent to bahasa *gay*'s speakers. Although "the theme of secrecy is a familiar one in what we might call 'folk anti-linguistics' . . . it is unlikely to be the major cause of [its] existence" (Halliday 1976, 572; see also Bolton and Hutton 1995; and Goyvaerts 1996). By moving "beyond lavender lexicon" to my ethnographic work with *gay* men as they speak bahasa *gay,* it can be shown that bahasa *gay* rarely acts as a secret language.[9] It is through its non-secretive character that we can gain some insight into the questions of authenticity and belonging that prove such enduring themes in *gay* lives.

The first indication that the view of bahasa *gay* as a secret language fails to tell the whole story is that not all *gay* men know bahasa *gay;* they are not all privy to the "secret." *Gay* men who avoid *gay* places (and, for example, interact only with a small circle of friends) may have little or no knowledge of it. It is neither a necessary nor sufficient condition for *gay* subjectivity. Persons who do not know a word of bahasa *gay* can identify as *gay,* and non-*gay* Indonesians who spend time in *gay* places (e.g., waria, lesbi women like Rita, female sex workers, pedicab drivers, and hair salon workers) can become proficient.

The second reason bahasa *gay* is not primarily a "cryptolect" (Aceto 1995) is that whole clauses of bahasa *gay* are rare. Occasionally, every word of an utterance will be in bahasa *gay* (examples 1 and 2). In example 1, standard Indonesian "I don't want" is replaced by "*Akika tinta mawar*" (I [neologism] tint rose). The effect is roughly like what an English-speaker would hear if "I don't want" were replaced with "Eyesore donut wonton," or if "that boy is cute" were replaced with "that Boeing is Q-Tip." In example 2, (*Lékes cékes, méses ngéses?*), each lexical item is replaced by a suffixed bahasa *gay* variant. The effect is somewhat like an English-speaker substituting for "cute boy, you'd like to suck him?" the pig-Latinesque phrase "Cutong boyong, wantong sukong?" (Cute boy, want suck?).

Example 1:

Standard Indonesian:	Aku tidak mau. (I don't want.)
Can be replaced by bahasa *gay:*	Akika tinta mawar. ([neologism] tint rose.)
Roughly analogous English rendition:	Eyesore donut wonton. [which sounds like "I don't want"]

Example 2:

Standard Indonesian:	Lelaki cakep, [kamu] mau ngésong [fellate]? (Boy cute, [you] want fellate?)
Can be replaced by bahasa *gay:*	Lékes cékes, méses ngéses?
Roughly analogous English rendition:	Cutong boyong, wantong sukong?

Such linguistic strings, however, are atypical. The language game of bahasa *gay* is usually played by altering only a single foregrounded word in the utterance, as with "hungry" in example 3, which is replaced with the Indonesian term for "open field." The result is somewhat like an English-speaker saying "I've been Hungarian for two hours." But this makes bahasa *gay* rather easy for outsiders to decipher: The meaning of "I've been Hungarian for two hours" soon becomes clear. The fact that only one or two lexemes per utterance are typically changed into bahasa *gay* makes the argument that it is a secret register doubtful.

Example 3:

Standard Indonesian:	Saya sudah lapar dua jam. (I already hungry two hours.)
Can be replaced by bahasa *gay:*	Saya sudah lapangan dua jam. (I already open field two hours.)
Roughly analogous English rendition:	I've been Hungarian for two hours.

A precedent exists for such pragmatics; many languages in Indonesia (but not Indonesian itself) have honorific language levels. The best-known example is Javanese, commonly described as having an overall distinction between "high" (Jv. *krama*) and "low" (Jv. *ngoko*), although the strata of distinctions is more complex (Errington 1985). This is like the *tu/vous* or *du/Sie* distinctions in French and German except that the distinction affects many parts of speech in addition to pronouns and verb conjugation. The relationship between Indonesian and bahasa *gay* parallels that between High and Low Javanese. For instance, given that High Javanese has a vocabulary of only about a thousand words (Anderson 1990, 208), entire utterances in High Javanese are infrequent. Many common terms have no High Javanese equivalent: "The word for table is *meja* no matter to whom one is speaking" (Geertz 1960, 249). Substituting a single High Javanese lexeme in an otherwise Low Javanese utterance, however, marks that entire utterance as High Javanese. Similarly, one or two bahasa *gay* lexemes turn an Indonesian utterance into bahasa *gay,* inaugurating a *gay* conversation.

To utter only a few words of bahasa *gay,* then, shapes a larger cultural context. Like High Javanese, bahasa *gay* marks and structures social relationships: "The Javanese speaker . . . has to find out where the hearer fits in society, and then speak as though the words were attached to the status, part of the nature of the world. . . . To speak High Javanese, then, is constantly to uncover the unchanging nature of the social world" (Siegel 1986, 19). One motivation for the choice of Indonesian as a national language was the absence of such registers. The registers reappear, however, with bahasa *gay.* It thereby serves not the cause of secrecy but reveals and sustains the interlocutor's inclusion in the *gay* world within the terms of the nation-state's hegemony.

A third reason why bahasa *gay* does not appear to be a "secret language" is that it is usually spoken in the *gay* world and when outsiders are not immediately present—in a deserted corner of a park, for example, or in an apartment or on benches at a shopping mall. Bahasa *gay* is rarely spoken in mixed company as a social screen. When that happens (I have heard it used on a bus to comment on an attractive man, for instance), it may temporarily mask the content of what is being said. Yet utterances like "I've been Hungarian for two hours" attract rather than deflect attention by their oddity. Rita's anger over the disclosure of the "secret" was pragmatic and not semantic; it was in regard to inappropriate use and not revealed content.[10]

A fourth indication that bahasa *gay* does not act as a secret language—that it is increasingly appropriated by Indonesian popular culture—seems to run counter to my point concerning its typical use between persons sure of each other's *gay* status. In fact, however, the patterns of bahasa *gay*'s appropriation illustrate its position as a language of interaction—of national interaction. That interaction further reveals how state hegemony shapes bahasa *gay*.

As indicated by Rita's story, when it is safe to do so *gay* men interact as *gay* men with many other kinds of people, including *lesbi* women, *waria*, and co-workers in certain environments, particularly hair salons. Through such persons, not just terms but entire derivational patterns of bahasa *gay* continually enter vernacular Indonesian. They thereby become part of a national "slang." Bahasa *gay* thereby becomes a "language of interaction," a *bahasa gaul*. In what *gay* Indonesians call the "*normal* world" (using the Indonesian term *normal*), switching a word or two in an utterance to bahasa *gay*/gaul appears to invoke an Indonesian public culture of freedom from official stricture.

This process of appropriation probably dates to the beginnings of bahasa *gay*, but its pace has dramatically increased. Above all, this rapid growth in appropriation is fed by the entry of bahasa *gay* terms into the mass media.[11] By the mid-1990s, during the twilight years of the New Order, as President Soeharto's thirty-year dictatorial reign is known, *gay* men commented on how talk show hosts and celebrity guests on television shows like *Abad 21* (Twenty-first century) or *Portret* (Portrait), on the Indosiar and SCTV stations, respectively, would sprinkle their patter with such bahasa *gay* terms as "*tinta*" and "*sutra*." The appropriation of bahasa *gay* has increased since controls on the mass media loosened after Soeharto's fall in May 1998. In 1999 *GAYa Nusantara*, the largest of several informally published *gay* zines, ran "Bahasa Gay Becomes Bahasa Gaul" (Ibhoed 1999). The article noted the rapid increase of bahasa *gay*'s presence in the mass media during the late 1990s (bahasa *gay* being equated with lexicon):

Words of the homo "nation" [*kebangsaan kaum hémong*] . . . frequently slide
with ease from the lips of Indra Safera or Eko Patrio [stars of the television
program *KISS*]. . . . Their guests like Anjasmara, Inneke Koesherawati, Hedy
Yunus, Cut Tari and others don't fail to speak similar words. . . . It could be said
that the program "Lenong Rumpi" on station RCTI was the one to begin introducing *hémong* language . . . it's even said that Jakarta youth that can't use
this language are said to be socially inept and behind the times. (Ibhoed 1999,
29–30)

Bahasa *gay* took an even greater leap into the Indonesian public eye with
the publication of *Kamus* (Dictionary) *Bahasa Gaul* by a television personality, Debby Sahertian (1999). It is, once again, a dictionary of terms rather
than a grammar of derivational patterns. An instant hit when first published
in 1999 and in its eleventh edition by early 2002, the text openly acknowledges
that much of bahasa gaul comes from bahasa *gay*.[12]

Mass media coverage of bahasa *gay* is increasing, both locally and internationally. When a *gay* man appeared on a local talk show in Surabaya, the
Jawa Post, a newspaper covering the event, noted on September 25, 2000, that
"when answering questions, he often used terms that are frequently used by
the *gay* community in Surabaya; for instance, '*Texas*' for a meeting place and
'*endang*' for the word '*enak*' [good]." On January 12, 2002, the *Australian
Financial Review* ran an article on bahasa *gay,* which it called "bahasa gaul"
(Dodd 2002). The article stated correctly that bahasa gaul is based on Indonesian, the national language, and also identified its origins in waria and *gay*
communities. A number of examples of bahasa gaul were included, most of
which I have not encountered, perhaps because they are from Jakarta, not a
major fieldsite in my research, and bahasa *gay,* like many "slangs," changes
quickly. All of the novel terms of bahasa gaul in the article, however, are cases
of syllabic substitution—the best-known derivational process for creating bahasa *gay* lexemes. Examples include *Kentucky* for *kentut* (to fart); *bye-bye love*
for *baik-baik* (fine); *Imelda Marcos* for "e-mail"; and *Brad Pitt* for *berapa* (how
much). The author consciously selected examples where an English term sub-
stitutes for an Indonesian one but noted that, for the most part, Indonesian
terms substitute for other Indonesian terms.[13]

Authenticity and the Nation

The "secret" of bahasa *gay,* then, was never in the bag. From its beginnings
it has been a language of interaction, knitting together the *gay* world. Because
bahasa *gay* is based on the national language and is, despite local variations,
distributed across the archipelago, it also shapes a sense that *gay* men are part

of a national community. The overlap between bahasa *gay* and national discourse explains how bahasa *gay* can be so amenable to cooptation by Indonesian popular culture. An additional motivation for its appropriation may be that LGBT languages and cultures, to the extent they represent communities understood not to originate in tradition, are amenable to cooptation by popular cultures that constitute themselves as modern. This raises comparative questions of LGBT culture and appropriation for future research.

There is, however, an apparent paradox: Indonesian popular culture has appropriated bahasa *gay* without a correspondingly greater social acceptance for *gay* men. Indonesia's civil code (based on the colonial-era Dutch civil code, based in turn on the Napoleonic Code) has little in the way of antisodomy laws. (In its neighbor Malaysia, by contrast, antisodomy sections 377A and B originate in the common law that Malaysia inherited from its former colonial power, Britain.) Virtually no antihomosexual arrests or prosecutions have ever occurred in Indonesia, making this nation a vexing problem for human rights advocates who work from traditional legal conceptions of harm. Religious or other authorities make occasional condemnations of homosexuality in Indonesia, but their attention is primarily directed at ostensibly deviant heterosexuality (adultery, female sex work, and the like). In other words, although the lives of *gay* men can be difficult in contemporary Indonesia, they are not so much directly oppressed as ignored by the larger society. In fact, bahasa *gay* is not only called "bahasa béncong" because waria also speak it but because most Indonesians still confuse *gay* men with waria.

In contemporary Indonesia, *gay* men consider themselves authentically national. They do not see their sexualities as originating in local tradition and consider themselves part of a national community, as reflected in bahasa *gay*. Yet that sense of belonging to the nation is not acknowledged by the national culture in a positive sense (as a valued element of Indonesia's diversity) or a negative sense (as a threat to the nation). The lack of even negative recognition is significant. As Foucault has shown, subjectivities can take form through a "reverse discourse" that rejects yet is foundationally influenced by a discriminatory conception of a kind of person. That appears to have happened in the case of many LGBT subjectivities in the West in relation to psychiatric and sexological conceptions of "the homosexual" (Foucault 1978, 101).

The apparent fact that *gay* subjectivities (and bahasa *gay*) have not come into being as reverse discourses illustrates a key way in which *gay* subjectivity is not merely an import or a globalized version of Western gay sexuality. As Jackson finds in the case of Thailand, Foucauldian theories of sexuality in Indonesia do not seem to fit the evidence. That would come as no surprise to Foucault, of course, whose analyses were carefully limited to the primarily European sources with which he worked. However, this state of affairs does suggest the need for a different theoretical approach to the relationship between bahasa *gay,* authenticity, and belonging.

The search for theoretical frameworks is an activist one. It is not merely academic hand-waving but the means by which we lift our heads from the minutiae of daily experience and seek the patterns and processes that shape possibilities for social justice. To fail to theorize—to lock in analyses at the level of description—does not make academic or activist work more reflective of the "real world" but less. It induces myopia toward the trans-situational dynamics in which all social relations are embedded. In the case of bahasa *gay,* a theoretical concept that seems to hold promise (while remaining, of course, a conceptual toehold rather than an all-encompassing principle) is that of hegemony. In the modern era, the concept of hegemony was developed most persuasively by the Italian social critic and activist Antonio Gramsci. Although some uses of the concept have strayed from his original formulation (Kurtz 1996), anthropologically informed transformations of his thought are helpful because they emphasize how power structures shape (but do not completely determine) common sense.

When a hegemony (that is, intellectual and moral leadership held by a "historic bloc," a coalition of ruling groups and economic interests) becomes established, it secures social control not by requiring that everyone think and act in a certain way but by establishing boundaries for recognizable—authentic—ways of being. In developing these conceptions of hegemony, social theories react to a double dissatisfaction. On one hand, there is rejection of concepts of ideology that presume those in power dictate how everyone thinks. On the other hand, however, there is rejection of voluntarist theories of liberation or resistance that paint oppressed people as endlessly creative, omniscient communities able to break clean with dominant views of the world. In place of this binarism, theories of hegemony describe a state of affairs in which "ruling or dominant conceptions of the world [may] not directly prescribe the mental content of . . . the heads of the dominated classes. But the circle of dominant ideas . . . becomes the horizon of the taken for granted: what the world is and how it works, for all practical purposes. Ruling ideas may dominate other conceptions of the social world by setting the limit to what will appear as rational, reasonable, credible, indeed sayable or thinkable, within the given vocabularies of motive and action available to us" (Hall 1988, 44). That way of thinking fits well with the ways in which bahasa *gay* (and *gay* subjectivities in general) transform a national discourse in ways the nation-state never intended yet remain profoundly shaped by the "horizon" of nationalist thinking.

An item of bahasa *gay* that appeared in the very first paragraph of this chapter neatly captures these struggles over authenticity and belonging: the phrase *asli lho!* (authentic, of course!). Like so many terms in bahasa *gay,* the phrase is linked to popular culture and appeared during the 1990s in an advertisement for a kind of pastry.[14] In 2002 I saw it again on a television advertisement for a health tonic. Indonesians (like people around the world) often like to mimic phrases from television commercials, but when used in the *gay* world (I have heard the phrase used most often in Surabaya), *asli lho!* gains a unique set of implications.

Asli can be translated as "authentic," but it is a complex term. One dictionary gives its meaning as "original, genuine, authentic, indigenous, native, autochthonous, aboriginal, primitive, innate, inborn" (Echols and Shadily 1997, 32). In my own ethnographic work, I have heard someone term a person who is "from" a place, rather than an immigrant, as "asli Bali," "asli Indonesia, or "asli Amerika." I have also heard someone speak of a lake or well as "asli" water (in comparison to piped water) or complain that the coldness from air-conditioning can make your arthritis hurt whereas the asli cold found in a mountain village is pleasant. An adopted child can sometimes be distinguished from an asli child.

In contemporary Indonesia, the notion of *asli* exists in concert with the false or inauthentic (*palsu*) (Siegel 1998, 52–65). Indonesians—like postcolonial subjects in many parts of the globe—struggle with the knowledge that their national boundaries (and thus national imaginaries) are taken in toto from the colonial regime, yet postcolonial consciousness pivots around recuperating (or forging for the first time) a sense of belonging separate from the colonial encounter. Postcolonial societies are by definition a "derivative discourse" (palsu) striving for a sense of authenticity (asli). That dynamic is key to the postcolonial condition—indeed, perhaps its only common element (Chatterjee 1986).

Lho, the second item of this phrase, is also difficult to parse in English. Found in both Javanese and Indonesian, in clause-final position it is what Errington (following Matisoff 1979) terms a "psychoostensive." Indonesian has many such psychoostensives, "extensive repertoires of discourse particles which index their users' subjective states . . . endowed with functions which can be called . . . broadly conative (i.e., other-oriented) and emotive (i.e, self-expressive). They are thus integrally bound up with interactional self/other relations, and the interactional dynamics in which they are situated" (1998, 100). Errington observes that *lho* is one of the most important psychoostensives and indexes "the speaker's concern for the addressee's stance to a state of affairs spoken of . . . that the addressee be aware of the significance . . . of what has been said" (101). *Lho* therefore marks "the salience of what has just been conveyed for an addressee, and indexes the speaker's concern that s/he take heed" (102). If asked, for example, "Can we send this letter by express mail?" an Indonesian-speaker might reply, "That would cost too much money *lho*" (that would cost too much money—and you as a member of our discursive community should already be aware of that important fact).

Asli lho! thus means "authentic—and you should already be aware of that important fact!" or "authentic, of course!" Significantly, *gay* men primarily use the term in jest. A man will approach a friend in *Texas* and jokingly gesture toward the friend's chest: "What a beautiful bosom you have!" "*Asli lho!*" will be the smiling response. A man will comment that someone has a nice pair of jeans, and the addressee's response of "*asli lho!*" means "they're not imitation but a real brand label, and don't you think I would ever own anything but the best." Someone will remark on the effeminate walk of a *gay* friend, to which the friend will reply, "*asli lho!*" (this is my real walk, not an affected walk, this is who I really am and you should know that). The pattern is clear. *Asli lho!* is a *gay* psychoostensive and "integrally bound up with interactional self/other relations." As used in the *gay* world, it disarmingly refutes the imputation that the *gay* self is inauthentic. Its use reveals a dynamic of self/other relations in which sexual/gendered authenticity is in question. The term jokingly embodies a claim that it is possible to transform a sexual subjectivity from the outside, and thus it complicates the distinction between inside and outside.

To understand the relationship between language and subjectivity it is necessary to "consider each language as integrally bound up with a distinct mode or strategy of territoriality" (Errington 1998, 6). Like the Indonesian on which it is based, bahasa *gay* is bound up with a national "strategy of territoriality." Keane maintains that if in Indonesia "to discover that one speaks a 'local language' may affirm that one does indeed have a 'place'" (1997, 53); to discover that as a *gay* man one speaks a translocal language affirms that one's "place" is the nation. With reference to Sumba, an island in eastern Indonesia, he adds, "It is as if speakers could discover in Indonesian a transcendent metalanguage into which local referents can be translated. This would mean that the authority of Indonesian is not simply due to its association with national identity or institutional power, nor is it a direct result of any purposeful state policy" (1997, 52). That statement, applicable to *gay* Indonesians, reflects how speakers' senses of selfhood can result from "no purposeful state policy" yet remain shaped by state hegemony.

Wittgenstein emphasized that "to imagine a language means to imagine a form of life" (1953, 9). Through bahasa *gay, gay* Indonesians imagine a form of life in which they are authentic members of the nation. Bahasa *gay* shows how structures of power claim metaphysical status when they create life-worlds for those dominated by them. It also shows that such life-worlds are never complete and always vulnerable to unexpected reconfiguration.

Notes

Research in Indonesia has been funded by the Social Science Research Council, the National Science Foundation, the Morrison Institute for Population Studies at Stanford University, and the Department of Cultural and Social Anthropology of Stanford University. Parts of this chapter were developed while I was a postdoctoral fellow in Southeast Asian Studies in the Department of Anthropology, Research School of Pacific and Asian Studies, the Australian National University, and a visiting assistant professor in the Department of Cultural Anthropology at Duke University. I thank these institutions for their support. Valuable comments were provided by Joseph Errington, Miyako Inoue, Don Kulick, William Leap, Johan Lindquist, Bill Maurer, Dédé Oetomo, Richard W. Perry, Beth Povinelli, and Michael Silverstein. I, of course, remain responsible for the arguments of this essay. All names are pseudonyms.

1. As in all my work, I italicize the term *gay* not only because it is part of the contemporary Indonesian language but also to underscore how *gay* subjectivity in Indonesia transforms what was once an ostensibly Western term into something "authentically" Indonesian. In other words, *gay* is more than just "gay" with an Indonesian accent.

2. Throughout this chapter standard Indonesian terms are italicized at their first use and bahasa *gay* terms are underlined and italicized, following standard Indonesian orthography except that I write the front, unrounded vowel /é/ (spelled *e* in Indonesian, along with the schwa) as *é*.

3. This rough translation retains the sense in which *gay* men use the phrase. It could also be rendered "Authentic, duh!" or, "It's genuine, really!"

4. The everyday term for *waria, banci* ("male-to-female-transvestite" in standard Indonesian) is derogatory, and I will not use it here.

5. I also work with *lesbi* women and waria but do not discuss these communities in this essay.

6. The period of British rule under Thomas Stamford Raffles (1811–24) was too short to have a lasting effect on English's presence in the archipelago.

7. Such wordplay is quite common in Indonesia, as can be seen in *prokem,* an urban language based on Indonesian (Chambert-Loir 1984; Dreyfuss 1983; Rahardja and Chambert-Loir 1990; Saleh 1988).

8. To my knowledge, bahasa *gay* terms are never formed from Arabic or Sanskrit loanwords, despite their frequency in contemporary Indonesian. This likely reflects the close relationship between *gay* subjectivities and the mass media rather than Islam or the historical links between Indonesia and India.

9. In prokem and other Indonesian slangs, such reinterpretations are a long-standing form of wordplay (Chambert-Loir 1984, 107). I have often heard examples in everyday vernacular Indonesian.

10. I am far from alone in encountering this view of bahasa *gay* as a secret language. Budiman, for example, refers to bahasa *gay* as *"bahasa rahasia"* (1979, 103). Howard, in his study of *gay* men in Jakarta, notes that "individuals explained to me that they use gay slang because they could speak freely about their homosexual desires and experiences without worrying that other people could understand what they were saying." Howard adds perceptively that "the use of gay slang also functions to foster a sense of belonging to a community" (1996, 9; see also Oetomo 2001, 67). Gay men in the Philippines also explicitly justify "gayspeak" or "swardspeak" in terms of "communicating with each other in a way in which the outside . . . world is unable to make sense of it" (Manalansan 1995, 202).

11. A similar pattern of use can be found in the "street language" of bahasa prokem: "While *bahasa prokem* is sometimes used as a secret language by criminals and street children, university students "do *not* use it in public or at home with the intention of not being understood by others. . . . They use *bahasa prokem* . . . among themselves" (Chambert-Loir 1984, 116, emphasis in the original).

12. Elements of Philippine swardspeak have also entered Philippine popular culture (Manalansan 1995, 203).

13. I have heard *gay* and lesbi Indonesians express frustration at Sahertian for "revealing our secrets," and it is said that she once apologized for popularizing bahasa *gay*.

14. I thank Sharyn Graham for bringing this article to my attention.

15. Dédé Oetomo, personal communication, July 27, 2002.

Works Cited

Aceto, Michael. 1995. "Variation in a Secret Creole Language of Panama." *Language in Society* 24: 537–60.

Anderson, Benedict. 1990. "Sembah-Sumpah: The Politics of Language and Javanese Culture." In Benedict Anderson, *Language and Power: Exploring Political Cultures in Indonesia,* 194–240. Ithaca: Cornell University Press.

Boellstorff, Tom. 2003a. "Dubbing Culture: Indonesian *Gay* and *Lesbi* Subjectivities and Ethnography in an Already Globalized World." *American Ethnologist* 30(2): 225–42.

———. 2003b. "Zines and Zones of Desire: Mass-Mediated Love, National Romance, and Sexual Citizenship in Gay Indonesia." *Journal of Asian Studies,* in press.

Bolton, Kingsley, and Christopher Hutton. 1995. "Bad and Banned Language: Triad Secret Societies, the Censorship of the Cantonese Vernacular, and Colonial Language Policy in Hong Kong." *Language in Society* 24: 159–86.

Boy and Yasiano. 1999. "Bahasa Hemong di Bandung" (Gay language in Bandung). *GAYa Nusantara* 64: 41–43.

Budiman, Amen. 1979. *Lelaki Perindu Lelaki: Sebuah Tinjauan Sejarah dan Psikologi Tentang Homoseks dan Masyarakat Homoseks di Indonesia* (Men who desire men: A historical and psychological perspective on homosexuality and homosexual community in Indonesia). Semarang: Tanjung Sari.

Chambert-Loir, Henri. 1984. "Those Who Speak Prokem." *Indonesia* 37: 105–17.

Chatterjee, Partha. 1986. *Nationalist Thought and the Colonial World: A Derivative Discourse.* Minneapolis: University of Minnesota Press.

Dodd, Tim. 2002. "Indonesia's New Lingo Is Talk of the Street." *Australian Financial Review,* Jan. 12.

Dreyfuss, Jeff. 1983. "The Backwards Language of Jakarta Youth (JYBL), a Bird of Many Language Feathers." In *Studies in Malay Dialects,* ed. James Collins, 52–56. Jakarta: Badan Penyelenggara Seri NUSA, Universitas Atma Jaya.

Echols, John, and Hassan Shadily. 1997. *Kamus Indonesia Inggris: An Indonesian-English Dictionary.* Jakarta: Gramedia Pustaka Utama.

Errington, J. Joseph. 1985. "On the Nature of the Sociolinguistic Sign: Describing the Javanese Speech Levels." In *Semiotic Mediation: Sociocultural and Psychological Perspectives,* ed. Elizabeth Mertz and Richard J. Parmentier, 287–310. Orlando: Academic Press.

———. 1998. *Shifting Languages: Interaction and Identity in Javanese Indonesia.* New York: Cambridge University Press.

Foucault, Michel. 1978. *The History of Sexuality,* vol. 1: *An Introduction.* New York: Vintage Books.

Geertz, Clifford. 1960. *The Religion of Java.* Glencoe: Free Press of Glencoe.

Goyvaerts, Didier L. 1996. "Kibalele: Form and Function of a Secret Language in Bukavu (Zaire)." *Journal of Pragmatics* 25: 123–43.

Grahn, Judy. 1984. *Another Mother Tongue: Gay Words, Gay Worlds.* Boston: Beacon Press.

Groeneboer, Kees. 1998. *Gateway to the West: The Dutch Language in Colonial Indonesia, 1600–1950: A History of Language Policy.* Amsterdam: Amsterdam University Press.

Hall, Stuart. 1988. "The Toad in the Garden: Thatcherism among the Theorists." In *Marxism and the Interpretation of Culture,* ed. Cary Nelson and Lawrence Grossberg, 35–57. Urbana: University of Illinois Press.

Halliday, M. A. K., 1976. "Anti-languages." *American Anthropologist* 78(3): 570–84.

Howard, Richard. 1996. "Falling into the Gay World: Manhood, Marriage, and Family in Indonesia." Ph.D. diss., University of Illinois at Urbana-Champaign.

Ibhoed. 1999. "Bahasa Gay Menjadi Bahasa Gaul" (Bahasa gay becomes a slang). *GAYa Nusantara* 60: 29–30.

Keane, Webb. 1997. "Knowing One's Place: National Language and the Idea of the Local in Eastern Indonesia." *Cultural Anthropology* 12(1): 37–63.

Kurtz, Donald V. 1996. "Hegemony and Anthropology: Gramsci, Exegeses, Reinterpretations." *Critique of Anthropology* 16(2): 103–35.

Leap, William L. 1995. *Beyond the Lavender Lexicon: Authenticity, Imagination, and Appropriation in Lesbian and Gay Languages.* Newark: Gordon and Breach.

Manalansan, Martin. 1995. "Speaking of AIDS: Language and the Filipino 'Gay' Experience in America." In *Discrepant Histories: Translocal Essays on Filipino Cultures,* ed. Vincente L. Rafael, 193–220. Philadelphia: Temple University Press.

Matisoff, James. 1979. *Blessings, Curses, Hopes, and Fears: Psycho-ostensive Expressions in Yiddish.* Philadelphia: Institute for the Study of Human Issues.

Oetomo, Dédé. 1999. "Introduction" to *Dictionary of Bahasa Gay. GAYa Nusantara* 62:28.

———. 2001. "Embrong! Bahasa Binan: Main-Main Yang Melawan" (Indeed! Binan language: A game of resistance). In Dédé Oetomo, *Memberi Suara Pada Yang Bisu* (Giving voice to those who cannot speak), 61–71. Yogyakarta: Galang Press.

Rahardja, Prathama, and Henri Chambert-Loir. 1990. *Kamus Bahasa Prokem* (Dictionary of prokem). Jakarta: Pustaka Utama Grafiti.

Sahertian, Debby. 1999. *Kamus Bahasa Gaul* (Dictionary of slang). Jakarta: Pustaka Sinar Harapan.

Saleh, Budiman. 1988. "Prokemkah 'Argot' Itu?" (Is prokem an argot?). In *Nuansa-Nuansa Pelangi Budaya* (Nuances of the rainbow of culture), ed. Kusman Mahmud, Kusnaka Adimihardja, and Wiwi Martalogawa, 11–18. Bandung: Pustaka Karsa Sunda.

Siegel, James T. 1986. *Solo in the New Order: Language and Hierarchy in an Indonesian City.* Princeton: Princeton University Press.

———. 1998. *A New Criminal Type in Jakarta: Counter-Revolution Today.* Durham: Duke University Press.

Winichakul, Thongchai. 1994. *Siam Mapped: A History of the Geo-body of a Nation.* Honolulu: University of Hawaii Press.

Wittgenstein, Ludwig. 1953. *Philosophical Investigations.* New York: Basil Blackwell.

8. *Gay* Adaptation, *Tom-Dee* Resistance, and *Kathoey* Indifference: Thailand's Gender/Sex Minorities and the Episodic Allure of Queer English

PETER A. JACKSON

Since the 1990s, numerous authors (Altman 1995, 1996; Miller 1992; Sullivan and Leong 1995) have described the global proliferation of gay and lesbian identities and cultures. Altman describes the emergence of "the global gay" as "part of the rapid globalisation of lifestyle and identity politics" (1996, 33). More recent work on the topic has resisted the idea that the globalization of homosexualities represents a trend toward homogeneity among the planet's same-sex and transgender cultures. Altman has emphasised the global/local tensions in the emergence of "gay" as an internationally recognized label (2000). Patton and Sánchez-Eppeler describe the "extraordinarily complex picture of the frictional relation between geopolitics and embodied desires" (2000, 3) reflected in new, non-Western, same-sex cultures, and Drucker uses the expression "combined and uneven social construction" (2000, 15) to describe the fact that gender/sex cultures around the planet are changing but not always in the same ways or at the same rate.

In this chapter I reflect on the diverse ways that Thailand's gay, lesbian, and transgender cultures relate to English in order to develop Drucker's idea of "combined and uneven social construction" as the distinguishing feature of globalizing influences in the domains of gender and eroticism. In tracing the histories of contemporary Thai terminologies for male and female same-sex and transgender identities and mapping their disparate relationships to queer English, I question some of the universalist assumptions that dominated early

discussions of "global queering." The labeling of Thai male homosexual identities as *gay* has involved a high degree of appropriation from English.[1] Thai
homosexual women, however, have a much more ambiguous relationship to
English categories, actively resisting the label *lesbian* while adapting other
English terms in coining the paired expression *tom-dee* (from "tomboy" and
the second syllable of la*dy*) to refer to butch-femme relationships. In contrast to both cases, terms for male-to-female transgenders, such as *kathoey*
(male-to-female transgenders) and *phu-ying praphet sorng* (second type of
woman), largely ignore English and continue to reflect long-established Thai
terminologies for same-sex eroticism.[2]

I contextualize the influence of queer English in Thailand by outlining the
continuing dominance of gender in the imagining and constitution of all
Thai erotic categories. New identities such as *gay, tom,* and *dee* have emerged
since World War II without the concomitant borrowing of a Western discourse of sexuality. Gender and sexuality remain an integral discursive domain in Thailand, both being understood in terms of the overarching local
notion of *phet* (eroticized gender).[3] Foucault's genealogy of sexuality in *The
History of Sexuality* (1980) cannot be used as a model for understanding the
historical proliferation of Thai erotic identities.

My analysis diverges from Morris's (1994, 1997) attempts to account for
Thailand's new transgender and same-sex cultures in Foucauldian terms. The
different historical relationships of each of Thailand's same-sex and transgender cultures to queer English, as well as the absence of a Foucauldian
discourse of sexuality (Foucault 1980), force a rethinking of the meaning of
global queering. To consider the full range of Thailand's same-sex and transgender minorities and not limit the focus to gay cultures alone reveals the
influence of Western sexual cultures to be highly uneven.

About Queer Thailand

Although the term *queer* is a convenient way to refer collectively to all minority genders and sexualities, it is not used in Thailand; to date, Western queer
theory has had only a minor impact in that country. Altman's general comments are also accurate for Thailand: "American 'queer theory' remains as
relentlessly Atlantic-centric in its view of the world as the main-stream [West-
ern] culture it critiques. Equally interesting is the apparent lack of interest in
'queer' theory in most of the non-Western world, and the continued usage by
emerging movements of the terminology 'lesbian' and 'gay'" (2000, 138).

Thailand (called Siam until 1939) is the only Southeast Asian country never
colonized directly by a Western power. It retained political independence and

a high degree of cultural and linguistic autonomy throughout the period of Euro-American imperialism and into the contemporary era. Since the 1850s, however, successive generations of Thai political elites have actively appropriated Western models of scientific education, public administration, and government in locally controled efforts at market-based modernization and dramatically transformed the Buddhist kingdom's physical and cultural landscapes. Like Japan, Thailand is one of the few Asian societies to initiate cultural engagement with the West largely on its own terms, although in the Thai case that engagement was inflected in terms of acquiring the technological and economic power to preserve political autonomy in the face of British and French imperialism.

One consequence of Thailand's century and a half of integration into international trade and communications networks has been the emergence of the nation's capital and largest city, Bangkok, as the "gay capital" of Southeast Asia. Home to one-sixth of the Thai population of sixty-three million, Bangkok is also the site of the largest and most visible transgender and male and female same-sex cultures in the region. The size, visibility, and growing cultural and economic impact of Thailand's multiple sexual cultures, in addition to the rare combination of unbroken political autonomy and a long historical engagement with globalizing political and economic forces, are important in understanding the international proliferation of forms of gendered and sexual diversity during the twentieth century.

It is also important to note that the issue of new homosexual and transgender identities in Thailand is not so new. Visible gay and transgender subcultures emerged in Bangkok during the early 1960s, and the word *gay* was used as a self-identificatory label by masculine-dressing homosexual men in that city some years before the Stonewall uprising in New York City in June 1969 saw the establishment of the modern gay liberation movement in the West. Bangkok's commercial gay scene is contemporaneous with those in such Western countries as Australia, New Zealand, and Canada. In studying Thailand, the issue is not to consider how these homoerotic cultures appeared after they did in the West but rather how they emerged at much the same time as they did in many parts of the West. It is necessary to revise accounts that imagine the West, in particular the United States, as the sole originary site of contemporary gay identities and see multiple, and parallel, forms of gayness emerging in diverse locales.

Method

This analysis is a historical study of discursive shifts and also draws on ethnographic research on the lives of homosexually active men and women. It is based on extensive readings of accounts of gender/sex difference in the Thai press and Thai academic studies of same-sex eroticism and transgenderism (Jackson 1995a, 1995b, 1996, 1997a, 1997b, 1997c, 1999a, 1999b, 1999c, 1999d, 2000). My reading of Thai-language sources has been informed by several periods of extended research in Thailand since the 1980s, including interviews with men and women from the country's same-sex and transgender cultures. In interpreting documentary sources I have also drawn on a growing body of ethnographic research on Thailand's same-sex and transgender cultures (Borthwick 1999; de Lind van Wijngaarden 1999; McCamish 1999; Sinnott 1999, 2000; Storer 1999a, 1999b; ten Brummelhuis 1999).

The expression *gender/sex* used here inverts the order of terms in Gayle Rubin's (1984) much-cited notion of "sex/gender system" and marks the continuing priority of gender over eroticism in Thai identities. The inversion of Rubin's term also signals my disagreement with most queer theorists' contention that gender and sexuality can be considered separate constructs that require distinctive theories and modes of inquiry (Jackson 2000). I translate the largely interchangeable Thai terms *chai* and *phu-chai* variously as "man" or "male" and the synonyms *ying* and *phu-ying* as either "woman" or "female," using inverted commas to mark the distinctive local meanings of these terms. I follow Thai usage in referring to "gay men" as *gays*. Thai does not mark the plural of nouns or pronouns, with grammatical number being inferred from context. In order to accord with English grammar and avoid ambiguity, however, I add an *s* to transliterated Thai expressions when a plural is denoted (e.g., *gays, kathoeys*).

About the Thai Language

Together with close cognates such as Lao (the national language of Laos), Shan (northern Myanmar), and Dai (Yunnan Province of China), Thai belongs to a distinctive family of mainland Southeast Asian tonal languages variously called Tai or Tai-Kadai. Modern Thai has an extremely rich vocabulary based on centuries of borrowings from many sources. The ancient Indian languages of Sanskrit and Pali, the religious languages of Hinduism and Theravada Buddhism, respectively, provide the source of most religious and contemporary technical and scientific terms. After the Siamese conquered the medieval Cambodian capital of Angkor in the fifteenth century C.E., the language of the Cambodian court was borrowed extensively. Large-scale Chinese immigration since the nineteenth century has led to hundreds of terms from the southern Chao Zhou (also called Theo Chiu) dialect entering modern Thai, and the global dominance of English has seen a considerable, and still growing, number of borrowings from that language.

Thailand has little history of cultural angst about issues of linguistic "puri-ty," and hybrid Thai-Sanskrit, Thai-Chinese, and Thai-English expressions are very common in the coining of new expressions for same-sex and transgen-der behaviors. Terms for new ideas, or new expressions for old ideas, often combine an element from an exotic language with a familiar term or idiom. For example, a common expression for a bisexual man is *seua bai* (literally, "bi-tiger"). During the middle decades of the twentieth century local gangsters were often called *seua* (tiger) because they often sported tiger tattoos, magical sym-bols believed to protect the wearer from attack. "Bai" is a Thai nickname. Seua Bai was a famous gangster or *seua* of the 1950s whose name was popularized in a much-read, eponymous novel about his Robin Hood–like exploits. For-tuitously, "bai" is widely used as an abbreviation for the borrowed term *bisex-ual* (Thai: *bai-sek-chuan*). The contemporary expression for a masculine bi-sexual man, *seua bai,* thus has several overlapping nuances.

Another term that draws on multiple Thai and English resonances is *tut* (short vowel, high tone), a derogatory synonym for gays and male-to-female transgenders. The term appears to be derived from the long-established use of *tut-tu* as a synonym for *kathoey. Tut,* however, became a tremendously popular "hit word" (*kham hit*) after advertisers used the syllable in translat-ing the title of *Tootsie,* the Dustin Hoffman film of the 1980s, as *tut-si. Tootsie* was a smash hit in Thailand, and subsequently the common first syllable of the old term joined the first syllable of the film title to become a widely used derogatory expression for all homosexual men. Thai *gays* and *kathoeys* de-test the term, perhaps because its derogatory connotations derive from pop-ular associations with anal sex. The colloquial Thai term for "backside" is *tut* (long vowel, low tone).

Although often tolerated, homosexuality and transgenderism have never been considered acceptable behavior in Thailand. The press as well as local ac-ademic studies draw upon a rich condemnatory vocabulary that was expand-ed during the twentieth century by the coining of a range of calques from pathol-ogized English terminologies (e.g., *biang-ben,* "to deviate" or "to be deviate").

Phet: The Frame for Thai Gender/Sex Discourses

Phet is the conceptual frame within which sex, gender, and sexuality are all imagined in Thailand. During the twentieth century, it became the central term in expressions for sexual desire (*khwam-torng-kan thang-phet,* "sexual wants"); for sexual acts (*ruam phet,* "to have sex," *phet samphan,* "sexual relations"); and for describing masculinity/maleness (*phet-chai*) and femi-ninity/femaleness (*phet-ying*). In current usage, *phet* denotes a distinctive type of gendered existence that has its own characteristic form of eroticism or sexual desire. "Eroticised gender" is a reasonable translation. In its present form, *phet* appears to be a twentieth-century construct but draws on a considerable history in Thai Buddhist thought. The Thai term (perhaps borrowed via Khmer) derives from the Sanskrit *vesha* and the Pali *vesa*, which both originally meant "dress" or "apparel" but also came to mean "to impersonate or assume a disguise."

In the nineteenth century, the Christian missionary and Thai lexicographer D. B. Bradley ([1873] 1971) recorded the word being used to denote the distinguishing forms and visual characteristics of three sets of beings. Cosmologically, *phet* denoted the differences among humans, animals, and divine beings; in the human realm, it denoted the gender/sex difference between men and women as well as the religious/erotic distinction between ordained Buddhist monks, who renounce sexuality, and laypeople. That is, at that time *phet* denoted systematic difference in a range of domains, including cosmology (human versus nonhuman), gender/sex (masculine/male versus feminine/female), and religious/erotic status (lay/sexual versus clerical/celibate).

The word is no longer used in a cosmological sense to denote the differences among humans, animals, and divine beings. It is still widely used, however, to mark the celibate status of Buddhist monks. The expressions *samana-phet* and *phet-banphachit,* for example, both denote a religious renunciate's asexual *phet* status. These expressions are contrasted with *phet kharawat,* the *phet* of being a layperson who inhabits the worldly domain of eroticism. In these usages notions of sacred versus profane intersect with understandings of asexual versus sexual. That intersection survives in the uncommon term *lakkaphet* (literally, "to steal [somebody else's] *phet* [by impersonation]"). Although most commonly used to describe cross-dressing by either males or females, the word also describes the impersonation of a monk by a layman who illicitly shaves his head and dons clerical robes in order to deceive others about his sanctity. The word also denotes a wilful and illicit transgression of the boundaries which, within Thai understandings of Buddhist teaching, structure the cosmological order, namely, the male/female divide and the ritual separation of the sacred from the profane.

A focus on gender/sex difference as the main sense of *phet* is a twentieth-century development. Echoes of the older religious and cosmological associations, however, persist with contemporary *phet* categories and, most important, the opposition of masculine/male and feminine/female, widely being seen as a "natural" (*thammada, thammachat*) distinction that reflects the cosmic order described in Buddhist teachings and adhered to through righteous behavior. Modern Thai terms for "nature" and "natural" are derived from the central Buddhist concept of *thamma* (Pali: *dhamma*), which denotes both the ordering principle of the cosmos, by which the law of karma operates, as well as ethical behavior.

The precise ways in which Western understandings of sex and gender, and Thai contact with Western gendered performances and forms of erotic desire, have influenced the development of contemporary ideas of *phet* are not clear. Efforts of Thai academics, physicians, psychologists, and others to translate such English terms as "sex," "gender," and "sexuality," however, have undoubtedly influenced the term's development. The semantic reduction of *phet* to a primary sense of gender/sex difference may have resulted from the effort to construct Thai translations of these English terms. Although *phet* is used to translate "sex," "gender," and "sexuality," no clear distinction among those notions is made in popular understandings.

In the contemporary Thai discourse of *phet,* the essentialist and biologistic senses of "sex" are not distinguished from the cultural constructionist sense of "gender" in contemporary English. This is reflected in the fact that the single term *chai* (and its synonym *phu-chai,* "a person who is *chai*") variously denotes "male," "man," and "masculine." The single term *ying* (and its synonym *phu-ying,* "a person who is *ying*") denotes "female," "woman," and "feminine." Notions of masculine or feminine gender identity are not clearly differentiated from sexuality in the contemporary English sense of an identity based on erotic preference for partners of either the same sex or the opposite sex.

Some Western-educated Thai academics have sought to "educate" the Thai public on the difference between the Western understanding of transgenderism as a gender status and the sexual condition of "homosexuality," a term represented by the neologism *rak-ruam-phet* ("to love the same *phet,* or "same-*phet* love"). A parallel but rarely used technical neologism has been coined to translate "heterosexual": *rak-tang-phet* ("to love a different *phet,*" or "other-*phet* love").[4] However, the academic attempt to introduce Western understandings of homosexuality as something different from transgenderism/transsexualism in order to differentiate a new category, *gay,* from an established identity, *kathoey,* has largely failed. The invocation of the notion of *phet* to render "homosexuality" into Thai has meant that it has generally been appropriated to preexisting dominant notions of gender rather than to create the intended categorical distinction. *Rak-ruam-phet* and *rak-tang-phet* have come to mark variations within the singular gender/sex domain of *phet* rather than a categorical separation between gender and sexuality. Non-cross-dressing, *gay*-identified Thai men do see themselves as different from cross-dressing, male-to-female transgenders and transsexuals, and they often trenchantly resist the transgender label of *kathoey*. To the chagrin of large numbers of these *gay*-identified men, however, dominant understandings outside Thailand's minority sexual cultures still do not consistently distinguish *gay* from *kathoey*. In general usage, the borrowed term *gay* is most often seen as a new synonym for the old transgender term *kathoey*. Even Thailand's English-language press regularly fails to distinguish between the two.

Western discourses of sexuality are not completely absent in Thailand. The impact of Western sexual and gender knowledges upon Thai discourses of *phet* is undeniable. Attempts to introduce Western ideas of sexuality, however, have been appropriated to local, gendered understandings. The persistence of *phet* as the frame within which both gender and sexuality are understood is reflected in the fact that even in Thai academic discourses only one expression exists to translate "sexual identity" and "gender identity": *attalak thang-phet*. In using that expression, some more careful academics do state whether they are referring to an identity based on erotic preference or to a person's sense of masculinity or femininity. In Thai, however, it is extremely difficult to be consistent in sustaining the notion of desire for a particularly sexed body (whether male or female) and hence of sexual identity from the idea of a preference for enacting a particular gender performance (whether masculine or feminine) and hence of gender identity. The difficulty does not reflect a temporary inadequacy in the technical vocabulary available to those who speak Thai. It indicates that gender and sexual identity, within Thai cultural understandings, including in technical and academic discourses, are a unitary category. The single expression *attalak thang-phet* ("gender identity" and/or "sexual identity") reflects the prevalent form of subjectivity in Thailand in which personal identity is simultaneously gendered and erotic.

Understandings that most closely approximate a Western discourse of sexuality and notions of sexual identity are found only among a relatively small number of men and women, who are often Western-educated, and as a counterdiscourse or self-conscious resistance to dominant, gendered understandings of *phet*. The counterdiscourse is found among two groups: overseas-educated academics and health professionals seeking to reproduce Western understandings and some (by no means all) masculine-identified *gays* who resist being feminized by having their gender/sex difference conflated with that of the cross-dressing *kathoey*. Neither resistance has been successful in challenging the gender/sex hegemony of *phet*, however, and has had only minor impact in the wider homosexual/transgender community.

It is, of course, possible that the integral discourse of *phet* might fissure into distinct domains of sex, gender, and sexuality, as in the contemporary

West. Indeed, the discourse does exhibit contradictory tendencies and is a site of considerable contestation, just as discourses of gender and sexuality are in the West. Those Thais who have sought to establish a discrete discourse of sexuality have faced the hurdle of a hegemonic set of understandings, which, despite a century and a half of intensifying engagement with Western societies, have had no need to establish a marked distinction between eroticism and gender performance. Within these understandings, all attempts to talk of sexual desire are appropriated to notions of gender.

Premodern *Phet* Categories

Historically, three main forms of *phet* were recognized in public discourses: normatively masculine men (*chai, phu-chai*), normatively feminine women (*ying, phu-ying*), and an intermediate category, *kathoey*. Buddhist monks were also recognized as a distinctive fourth, asexual *phet,* but the other three categories were grouped together as characterizing laypersons living in the worldly domain of eroticism. Before the dramatic changes in sexual culture and language use in the twentieth century, early modern Thai already possessed a vocabulary to refer to homoerotic and transgender behaviors. *Len pheuan* (to play [with] a friend) denoted either male or female homosexual activity and was sometimes specified as *len pheuan ying* (to play [with] a female friend) or *len pheuan chai* (to play [with] a male friend). *Len sawat* (love play) referred specifically to male homosexual sex, often connoting anal sex, whereas *ti ching* (a clash of cymbals) described sex between women. The term *lakkaphet* denoted cross-dressing by either men or women. All these expressions, however, referred to behaviors rather than identities. The only premodern Thai term for a non-normative gender/sex identity was *kathoey* and its technical Buddhist synonyms, such as *bandor* (Pali: *pandaka*) and *napungsaka.*

The term *kathoey* variously denoted a person, whether male or female, who exhibited hermaphroditic or intersex features or expressed behavior considered inappropriate for their gender. The term has long been called the "third *phet*" (*phet thi-sam*) within both popular and academic discourses, a notion similar to nineteenth-century Western ideas about homosexuals constituting a "third sex." It is possible that these ideas reached Thailand. Ideas of three original *phet,* and of all humans as blending genders in varying degrees, can also be traced to the influence of ancient Indian and Buddhist teachings adopted in Thailand. If the ideas of Western authors who wrote about the "third sex" did reach Thailand, they would no doubt have received a warm reception because they matched local understandings so closely.

On the premodern system of *phet* categories, Rosalind Morris observes that it is "unlikely that there ever existed a period in accord with the completely triadic vision [of "man," *kathoey*, "woman"]. . . . However, what texts we do have suggest a tradition of sexual and gendered identities incompatible with Western binarism [of homosexual versus heterosexual]" (1994, 22). An idealized intersex *kathoey* category, apparently derived syncretically from Thai creation myths as well as Hindu-Buddhist mythology, functions as the symbolic fulcrum of the historical and contemporary system of *phet* identities. The mythical *kathoey* represented an equal blending of maleness/masculinity and femaleness/femininity and continues to have an iconic place in Thai imaginings of gender and eroticism. The masculine/feminine opposition underlies all forms of erotic expression in Thailand, but the notion that the two domains intersect to varying degrees within the body and desire of all individuals is also central to understandings of gender/sex difference. A proliferation of new phet categories have emerged from a refinement of the premodern notion of gender/sex intersection, and unequal blendings of masculinity and femininity are seen as producing new categories that are neither "truly men" (*chai thae*), "truly women" (*ying thae*), nor "truly kathoey" (*kathoey thae*).

An Explosion of Thai Identities, 1960–85

In analyzing Thai discourses, a startling phenomenon has become apparent. Over the quarter century from 1960 to 1985 the number of *phet* categories for labeling distinctive types of gendered/sexed beings almost tripled in number and then stabilized at the new, higher level. Using sources such as the Thai press, popular magazines, and academic publications, it is possible to date the emergence of the new categories into public discourse. In the mid-1960s, perhaps earlier, the *kathoey* category began to split into a number of masculine, feminine, transvestite, and intersex variants:

- *kathoey thae:* A true hermaphrodite (*thae*, "true, genuine").
- *kathoey thiam:* Variously, a pseudo-hermaphrodite or a cross-dressing man (*thiam*, "false, artificial").
- *kathoey sao:* A cross-dressing young woman (*sao*, "a young woman"). Other 1960s' expressions for masculine women were *sao lakkaphet* (a cross-dressing young woman) and *ying plorm pen chai* (literally, "a woman who impersonates a man").
- *krathiam:* A humorous term that literally means "garlic" and combines the first syllable of the old spelling of *kathoey* (*krathoey*) with the term for "false" or "artificial" (*thiam*). *Krathiam* meant "a false *kathoey*," or a man sexually

PETER A. JACKSON

attracted to other men but who did not cross-dress or act effeminately like a
stereotypical *kathoey.*

- *kathoey num:* A masculine young homosexual man (*num,* "a young man").
- *kathoey phu-chai:* A masculine adult homosexual man (*phu-chai,* "man").
- *kathoey praphet sorng:* "A second type of *kathoey,*" that is, a man who prefers
  males but does not cross-dress or act effeminately.

Newspaper headlines from the 1960s reflect how the terms circulated widely
at that time. In 1961 a jealousy-inspired shootout between teenaged youths who
fought over the affections of another teenaged boy was reported as "Teenage
Youths Fight over Kathoey, Shoot Each Other Dead on the Spot." In the same
year, a cross-dressing young woman who murdered a male rival in a fight over
a woman was reported as "Young Female Kathoey [*kathoey* sao] Viciously
Murders Rival." Several years later, another female homosexual crime of pas-
sion was reported as "Female Transvestite [*ying lakkaphet*] Shoots Female
Lover Dead," and the tragic end to two women's failed attempt to elope was
reported as "Young Transvestite Woman [*sao lakkaphet*] Climbs Building to
Meet with Millionaire's Daughter; Slips, Falls and Crushes Her Skull."[5]

The various expressions for masculine types of male *kathoey*—*kathoey
num, kathoey phu-chai, kathoey praphet sorng,* and *krathiam*—were short-
lived and became obsolete in the late 1960s, all being replaced by *gay. Gay,*
the first English-derived label for a *phet* category, entered the language around
1965 and originally denoted masculine male prostitutes and their clients
(Jackson 1999a). By the early 1970s, the new category had split into *gay king*
(sexually insertive) and *gay queen* (sexually receptive) subtypes. Within the
Thai gender/sex system, in which gender oppositions are central to all erotic
relationships, the single English term *gay* was found inadequate to represent
the masculine-feminine dynamic that *gay*-identified men saw as a defining
feature of their relationships. The Thai category *gay* split into paired *gay king*
and *gay queen* variants almost as soon as it became established as the recog-
nised term for non-cross-dressing, homosexually active men. Although a *gay
king* is often considered to be butch and a *gay queen* to be effeminate, in some
cases the terms refer only to the preferred sexual role (i.e., top or bottom,
respectively) rather than to a publicly enacted gender role. Furthermore, although the Thai borrowing of "queen" reflects long-standing English associations of that term with effeminacy, the idiomatic pairing of *gay king* and
gay queen appears to be a distinctively Thai coinage. *Gay king* does not occur in the gay argot of any English-speaking country.

At times, gay kings are equated with bisexual male *seau bais* (masculine
males who prefer *kathoey* partners). At other times, a *gay king* is understood
as the partner of a performatively masculine and sexually receptive *gay queen.*

The commonality across these shifting meanings is that such a man is understood as a masculine male who relates with one or more persons perceived as expressing femininity, whether those people are *gay queens, kathoeys,* or "real women" (*ying thae*).

By the early 1970s, masculine homosexual women were being relabeled with the English-derived terms *lesbian* and *dai* (from "dyke"). The final consonant of "dyke" was written in Thai but not pronounced, being marked by a silent (*k*). Other expressions for masculine homosexual women used in the press in the 1970s were the Thai-English compounds *sao dai* (a young woman who is a dyke) and *sao lesbian* (a young woman who is a [butch] lesbian). From that period, only males were called *kathoey.*

Sex change operations were also first performed in Thailand in the early 1970s, and the category of male-to-female transsexual (*plaeng phet,* "to change one's *phet*") first emerged during that decade. For example, on November 10, 1972, *Thai Rath* reported, "Transsexual Kathoey [*kathoey plaeng-phet*] Seeks Right to Compete for Miss Thailand [contest]" (1). Although male-to-female transsexuals are called *kathoey* or, more fully, *kathoey plaeng phet,* no colloquial expression has been coined for female-to-male transsexuals other than the descriptive phrase *ying plaeng phet pen chai* (a woman who changes *phet* to a man). Female-to-male transsexuals do not exist as a marked *phet* category distinct from cross-dressing masculine women, with whom they are often subsumed.

As *kathoey* came increasingly to mean only transgender and transsexual males during the 1970s, intersexed people began to be re-labeled as "two-sexed people" (*khon sorng phet*) rather than *kathoey,* although the expression *true kathoey* (*kathoey thae*) is at times used in academic literature to describe intersex conditions.

Differentiation of new types of *phet* continued into the late 1970s and early 1980s. Masculine homosexual women were yet again relabeled during the second half of the 1970s, this time with the borrowed expression *tom boy,* which in the 1980s was shortened to *tom. Tom* has replaced and rendered obsolete all previous expressions for masculine homosexual women, such as *kathoey sao, ying lakkaphet, lesbian,* and *dai.* Masculine homosexual women in some other East and Southeast Asian societies such as Taiwan and the Philippines are also called "Tom Boy" or "T" (Chao 2001), suggesting a history of intra-Asian contact in the emergence of the category rather than a unidirectional borrowing from the West.

A male bisexual category, the *seua bai,* emerged in the early 1980s, as did a new feminine female homosexual category, the *dee* (abbreviated from "lady") as a label for the feminine partner of a masculine tom. The compound expression *tom-dee* (a butch-femme female homosexual couple) is often used in the press. In 1987, for example, the public engagement of two women was reported as "Tom-dee Engaged, Flying Off to Celebrate in Switzerland," and in 1995 the marriage of two women received page one billing under the banner "Sensational Reception Party: Dee Marries Tom!"[6]

The term *lady* had been used in Thai before being given its current sense of a femme homosexual woman. It was not appropriated, however, in its general sense of "woman" but in the specific sense of "gentlewoman." In calling themselves first *lady* and then *dee,* Thai femme female homosexuals aligned themselves with notions of high-class, socially respectable, forms of femininity. The use of the term represented an effort to establish the legitimacy of female homoeroticism and distance it from the whorish connotations that often attach to Thai understandings of *lesbian.*

The term *lesbian* is still occasionally used within popular discourses to describe female homoeroticism, but it is strongly resisted by homosexually active women and not used as a self-identificatory label within Thailand's female homosexual cultures because the term entered the language to describe female homosexual visual pornography produced for a heterosexual male audience. Thai homosexual women perceive the term as representing woman-centred relationships in overly sexualized terms, and many prefer to imagine their relationships as emotional rather than explicitly erotic.[7] Anjaree, a Thai social and activist group for homosexual women, eschews use of "lesbian," preferring instead the generic expression "women who love women" (*ying rak ying*). Reinfelder notes that the term is avoided or actively resisted by women loving women in many non-Western countries: "The Western connotation or the danger the term [lesbian] can bring with itself often leads to the use of the term 'women-loving-women' or the euphemistic 'independent women,' 'single [*sic*] women' and 'women who are not attached to men'" (1996, 2).

Toms' and *dees'* resistance to the hypersexualized meanings that attach to Thai understandings of "lesbian" was made clear in July 1984 in a *Bangkok Review* interview with a self-identified *tom-dee* couple, Alice (Alissa?) Christian and Yortsoi Komanchun, "Two young female actors who admit that they are tom and dee" and "live together like husband and wife" (5–8). The interview was published only a couple of years after the paired expression *tom-dee* had begun to become popular, and the *Bangkok Review* boasted that "no newspaper has ever before interviewed young women who truly live as a tom-dee couple." Alice and Yortsoi had agreed to go public about their relationship in a lifestyle magazine in order to counter the senationalist *Thai Rath*'s accusations that the rapidly increasingly numbers of tom-dee couples congregating on Bangkok's streets and in the capital's shopping malls were "social trash" (*khaya sangkhom*). "Society now acknowledges men who are gay," the couple retorted indignantly. "Then why can't people accept toms and dees? Men dress as women. Why can't women dress as men? Social attitudes don't add up." In response to the question, "Are tom-dee different from lesbians?" the women differentiated the sexualized meaning of the word *lesbian* in Thai from the gendered senses of *tom* and *dee:* "They're not the same. 'Lesbian' means women who dress as women and make love [*len rak kan*]. A tom is a woman who dresses as a man. A dee is a tom's partner."

The Proliferation of *Phet* Categories

After a period of rapid transformation from the early 1960s to the mid-1980s, the system of *phet* categories stabilized. Something approaching a new discursive equilibrium has been established. No new varieties of *phet* have been formed since the 1980s apart from the periodic emergence and disappearance of terms recognized as synonyms for existing categories. The new terms *tut* and *pratheuang*, for example, are understood as synonyms for *kathoey* or *gay* but not as distinct categories. This striking phenomenon of the proliferation of culturally recognized forms of *phet* and the emergence of distinctive erotic cultures based on identification with the new categories suggest that Thai gender/sex discourses suffered a major disruptive influence during the 1950s or early 1960s. The disruption led to a two-decade period of instability, during which a range of new categories emerged and older identities of "man," *kathoey,* and "woman" were redefined.

There is no general agreement in Thailand on how many types of *phet* exist in that country. Some people think that men (*phu-chai*) and male bisexuals (*seua bai*) are members of a single *phet.* Others, however, distinguish them as different types of *phet.* Some regard transvestite and transsexual *kathoeys* as varieties of the same *kathoey* category, whereas others consider them distinctive—*kathoey lakkaphet* and *kathoey plaeng phet,* respectively. What is universally agreed upon, however, is that within living memory only three *phet* were found in Thailand and that now many more varieties exist. Most commentators appear to count at least seven contemporary types of *phet:* "man," *gay king, gay queen, kathoey, tom, dee,* and "woman."

Significantly, awareness of this proliferation is not localized in Bangkok or within minority erotic cultures. Through the national media almost every adult in the country is familiar with the labels for these seven types of people, and individuals claiming each identity can be found in remote agricultural villages as well as in large industrial cities. Many appear to migrate to the more liberal and anonymous environment of Bangkok, although it is common to find them in small towns across the country. The distinctive erotic cultures that focus around each label exist as national phenomena.

Since the middle of the 1960s, four distinctive sexual communities have come into existence in Thailand, all based on identification with one or another erotically paired *phet* category: "man"/"woman," *gay king/gay queen, tom/dee,* and *kathoey/*"man"*/seua bai/gay king.* There is no clear identity category for either bisexual men or for the partners of transvestite or transsexual *kathoeys.* Bisexual men are called *seua bai,* and the masculine partners of *kathoeys* are variously called "men," *seua bais,* or even *gay kings.* Yet despite the existence of these labels, and widespread recognition of a type of male who relates sexually with more than one type of feminine person, there is no self-identifying *seua bai* community. Ethnographic work suggests (Storer 1999a, 1999b) that bisexual males and partners of *kathoeys* are more likely to identify as normative "men" than as *seua bais* or *gay kings.*

From a linguistic standpoint, the major, but not the only, epicenter of the explosion of new gender/sex categories was the old *kathoey* identity. Historically, it had included all forms of gender/sex variation, from normative forms of maleness/masculinity (*chai*) and femaleness/femininity (*ying*). During the 1960s, however, the category fractured into an array of *kathoey* varieties that labeled specific forms of difference in the domains of gender (cross-dressing and transsexualism) and eroticism (homoeroticism). Many had only a brief existence in public discourses and were quickly relabeled, establishing a differentiation from categories that continued to be labeled as types of *kathoey.* In succession, *gays,* intersexed people and then butch and femme women who love women were relabeled and differentiated from *kathoeys.* The linguistic and conceptual shift has been so great that younger Thais are no longer aware that a woman who dressed like a man during the 1960s was called a type of *kathoey.* By the 1970s, the word had come to mean only a person who is born male but subsequently enacts a feminine role (*kathoey lakkaphet*) or undergoes a sex change operation (*kathoey plaeng phet*).

Although the *gay* and *tom* identities as well as the male transgender and transsexual identities labeled *kathoey* all appear to have developed from the old, undifferentiated *kathoey,* the *dee* and *seua bai* seem to have a different origin. The femme *dee* and male bisexual *seua bai,* respectively, appear to have split from the old normative female and male categories.

The explosion of types of *kathoey* did not leave normative constructions of femininity and masculinity untouched, leading to a somewhat delayed fracturing of the two poles of the gender continuum. Before the 1980s, femme partners of *toms* were usually not distinguished from the female partners of "men." Women now called *dee* used to be called "women" (*ying, phu-ying*), even when they related with someone labeled as *lesbian, dai,* or *tom.* This femme identity appears to have been hived off from the normative female identity, *phu-ying.* Similarly, *seua bai* appears to be a subdivision of the normative masculine category of "man" (*phu-chai*) rather than being considered a variant of *gay.* The distinction between *seua bai* and "man" is still not universally understood, although it is generally understood that a "man" is probably a more masculine type of person than a *seua bai* or *gay king.*

The complex genealogies of the new *phet* categories is further suggested by distinctive processes of renormativization within contemporary discourses by which the gender/sex difference of each new category is reduced to one or other of the three historical categories of "man," *kathoey,* or "woman." Within popular discourses circulating in the Thai press and electronic media (e.g., television sitcoms and chat shows) *gay queens* are sometimes conflated with *kathoeys, dees* are regularly conflated with normative "women," and *seua bais* and even *gay kings* may be conflated with normative "men." It is sometimes claimed that *gay queens* are "really *kathoeys,*" that *dees* are "really women," and that *seua bais* and *gay kings* are "really men." "Uncle Go," the pen name of an advice columnist for *gays, kathoeys,* and *dees,* reflects these views in his fortnightly sections of the long-running popular magazine *Plaek* (Jackson 1995a).

Such renormativizing accounts imply that these types of people are only pretending to be different, or that they are wayward types of *kathoeys,* "women," and "men," respectively, who would conform to one of the old ternary set of gender/sex norms if only they stopped being so "modern" (*than-sa-mai*) and "rebelliously stubborn" (*deu*). In addition to providing clues to the different origins of the various new categories, the existence of conservative renormativizing discourses also reflects the high degree of contestation over the legitimacy of new varieties of *phet.* Conservative Thai psychologists, social workers, and educators have made unsuccessful efforts to stem the proliferation of gender/sex difference and return to the "good old days" when there were only three types of gendered persons in Thailand: "men," *kathoeys,* and "women" (Jackson 1997c).

Combined but Uneven Development: *Gay* Adaptation, *Tom-dee* Resistance, and *Kathoey* Nonchalance

While English-derived terms came to mark some new identities (*gay, tom, dee*), in some cases the words merely replaced preexisting Thai expressions. Their introduction did not mark the emergence of a new phenomenon but rather a relexification. Recognition of masculine men sexually attracted to other masculine men, for example, pre-dated use of the label *gay*, with *krathi-am, kathoey num, kathoey phu-chai*, and the other expressions used for these men in the early 1960s. Nevertheless, terms derived from English, but modified to fit Thai gender expectations, mark all categories that do not match the premodern ternary models of "complete maleness," "complete femaleness," or "complete *kathoey*." That is, members of those Thai gender/ sex minorities who feel they do not conform to any of the patterns available in the old model of "man"-*kathoey*-"woman" have turned to English to label their identities and cultures. These minorities, however, have also found English homosexual vocabularies inadequate to represent the specificity of local forms of gender/sex difference and have shown a high degree of agency in adapting English terms, often coining new ones. This innovative linguistic playfulness is especially noteworthy given that Thailand was never colonized and competence in English is generally poorer than in former colonies such as Malaysia, Singapore, and the Philippines.

Perhaps the most curious aspect of the transitions in the discourse of *phet* in the second half of the twentieth century was the rapid and complete expulsion of females from the domain of the *kathoey* and the restriction of that category to males. This, it seems likely, reflects the cultural privileging of maleness/masculinity over femaleness/femininity because another notable feature of the expanded set of *phet* categories concerns the more culturally recognized categories for types of males ("man," *seua bai, gay king, gay queen, kathoey*) than for types of females ("woman," *dee, tom*) in the reformulated gender/sex system. The old ternary model of "man"-*kathoey*-"woman" (in which the ideal *kathoey* was an equal blend of male and female) had an appearance of gender balance. In the period immediately before the explosion in the number of *phet* categories, however, that discursive image of gender balance masked the fact that *kathoey* was more commonly associated with males than with females. The image of gender balance, however, has now been shattered. In the new gender/sex system, the domain of maleness is much more finely differentiated (in terms of varying degrees of ascribed masculinity) than that of femaleness (in terms of degrees of ascribed femininity).

The categories still labeled *kathoey* are those that most closely match the mythical equal blending of maleness/masculinity and femaleness/femininity (or a male who balances masculinity and femininity within himself) that lay at the core of the older meanings of the term. The linguistic persistence of the term *kathoey* means that popular English terms for transsexuality and transgenderism (e.g., "drag queen" or "tranny") are all but unknown in Thailand except among those who have traveled to the West. The expression "lady boy" is sometimes used by Thai-speakers to denote *kathoey,* but only in contexts where English is used to communicate with those who do not speak Thai.[8]

It is also noteworthy that Thai typically relies on terms from its own vocabulary, not English, to refer to the effeminacy of the *kathoey.* The verbal adjectives *kratung-krating* and *tung-ting* (to be ostentatiously effeminate) are the most common derogatory terms for an effeminate man or a cross-dressing *kathoey.* Thai has, however, borrowed the English term *man* to expand the range of descriptors for masculinity. Historically, the adjectival descriptor *khem* (to be intense or dark) was used to denote a dark, brooding, and powerful form of masculinity. That term, however, has been supplemented with *man;* the Thai-English hybrid *mat man* denotes a butch, masculine attitude. *Man* is commonly used to describe males who match Thai imaginings of Caucasian masculinity, that is, muscular, hairy, unshaven, and often sullen and unsmiling. Since the proliferation and reconstruction of *phet* categories, Thai terms for masculine males, *chai* and *phu-chai,* have tended to be restricted to denoting a male who only relates sexually with women. Although *seua bais, gay kings,* and even some *gay queens* may look, talk, and act no differently from men labeled *phu-chai,* they are generally excluded from this most masculine of the *phet* categories. The only available Thai terms to denote masculinity, *chai* and *phu-chai,* denote heterosexual preference. "Man" has been borrowed to denote butch masculine gender performance, regardless of heterosexual (*phu-chai*), bisexual (*seua bai*), or homosexual (*gay king/gay queen*) preference. Within Thai *gay* culture the English-derived compounds *man-queen* and *man-king* are used to emphasize the masculinity of homosexual men who prefer receptive and insertive anal sex, respectively.

Thus the Thai borrowing of English terms for new types of gender/sex difference has been highly selective and involves a high degree of playful innovation. Male same-sex cultures have enthusiastically appropriated the now-dominant English label for male homoeroticism, "gay." They have also, however, reflected the persistent gendering of male homoeroticism through the uniquely Thai opposition of *gay king* and *gay queen.* In contrast, female same-sex cultures have resisted the dominant English label for female homoeroticism, "lesbian," instead appropriating and adapting the terms "tom boy" (to *tom*) and "lady" (to *dee*) to reflect the gendering of female same-sex relations.

From a linguistic standpoint, Thailand's transgender and transsexual subcultures are largely uninfluenced by English borrowings and continue to use the long-established term *kathoey.* New synonyms such as *pratheuang* are more likely to draw on Thai than English. The complexity of these histories—involving a combination of enthusiastic appropriation, resistance, playful adaptation to local patterns, and disinterest—suggests that an unmediated process of borrowing from the West is an unlikely sole source of the explosion of *phet* categories. Even when English terms have been borrowed to label or relabel Thai categories, they have been remodulated in distinctive ways to reflect the persistent dominance of gender oppositions (e.g., *gay king* versus *gay queen* and *tom* versus *dee*) in all Thai erotic identities.

When the Thai press refers to Western transgenders and homosexual men and women it labels them in distinctive ways that reflect the complex histories of the new *phet* identitites. Western gay men are typically labeled *gay,* the same term used for masculine homosexual men in Thailand. Western homosexual women are commonly called "lesbian," a term Thai homosexual women resist and from which they differentiate themselves. Western transgenders, however, are either labeled *kathoey* or one of that term's several synonyms. This pattern of labeling reflects the distinctive way in which the relationship of each of Thailand's gender/sex minorities to their parallel Western sexual culture is imagined. As Dennis Altman has pointed out, Thai and Western homosexual men are imagined to be common members of a single new transnational category: gay. In contrast to Altman's claims, however, Western and Thai homosexual women tend to be seen as members of distinctive but perhaps intersecting foreign (lesbian) and local (*tom-dee*) categories. The situation for Western transgenders is different yet again. They are appropriated to the indigenous category of *kathoey.* The possibility that Western transgenders and transsexuals may express a culturally distinctive form of gender/sex difference is not acknowledged because it is believed that they conform to Thai transgender norms.

Popular usage reflects the fact that Thai gays and Western gay men, on the one hand, and Thai and Western transgenders, on the other, are imagined to be common members of the transnational categories gay and *kathoey,* respectively. The imagined "international" nature of gay, however, is quite different from that of the *kathoey.* The term *gay* is linked with ideas of modernization and Thai self-modification and self-adaptation in order to acquire the skills to be able to participate as an autonomous agent in a Western-dominated world. *Gay* is also linked with imaginings of transforming Thailand to match "international" (*sakon*) or Western norms and standards.

In contrast, the fact that Western transgenders are called *kathoey* reflects a quite different type of imagined internationalization, the perception that foreign forms of transgenderism conform to local Thai patterns. When Rebecca Wilson, a twenty-five-year-old Australian male-to-female transsexual traveled from Sydney to compete for the Diamond Crown of the Miss Siam "second type of woman" beauty contest in 1972, for example, the *Thai Rath* daily ran the page one headline, "Foreign Kathoey Competes, Hundreds

Apply for Miss Second Type," on December 21. It also referred to Rebecca as "yort kathoey Rebecca," *yort kathoey* being a dated expression for an especially beautiful male-to-female transsexual, a *"kathoey* diva." On March 11, 1999, more than a quarter century later, the same newspaper ran a front page item reporting that Thailand had become a global center for male-to-female sex change operations: "Foreign Pratheuang Come Shrieking in Droves to Thailand" *Pratheuang* is a late-1990s' synonym for *kathoey.*

The imagined relationship between Thai and Western homosexual women is different yet again from that of *gays* and *kathoeys.* Because Thai female homosexuals—*toms* and *dees*—are differentiated from Western lesbians, and because many *tom-dees* imagine lesbians to be a different type of person from themselves, a sense of disjuncture and difference is created between Thai and Western female homosexualities. That disjuncture does not prevent Thai and Western homosexual women from establishing relationships or working together in same-sex activism. Nevertheless, *tom-dees* are more likely to remark that Western lesbians are "not like us" than Thai *gays* are to state that Western gay men are different from themselves.

More than linguistic factors contribute to local perceptions about Thai *gays* and Western gay men being essentially the same, whereas Thai *tom-dees* are different from Western lesbians. The *gay king–gay queen* opposition is established primarily by private sexual preferences rather than by any publicly recognizable differences in dress, speech, or mannerism between *gay* partners. Even Thai *gay* men often need to ask a prospective sexual partner if he is *king* or *queen* when negotiating sex. The different gender/sex discursive world that Thai *gays* inhabit is not marked visibly. In contrast, *tom* and *dee* roles are visibly differentiated in public. *Toms* typically cross-dress in masculine-style clothing, eschew makeup, have short hair (cut above the shoulders), and swagger; *dees* dress as feminine women and have long hair. The persistence of butch-femme role-play (the English terms "butch" and "femme" are not used in Thailand's *tom-dee* culture) in almost all Thai female homosexual relationships creates a sense of distinctiveness from Western lesbian cultures that have downplayed or critiqued gender role-playing.

Whence the Explosion of Thai Identities?

I have had two primary objectives in this chapter: to describe the empirical phenomenon of the explosion in the number of Thai gender/sex identities between 1960 and 1985 and to argue that the novel varieties of *gay, tom, dee,* and *kathoey* varieties of *phet* that emerged during this period each has a distinctive relationship to queer English. The latter point suggests that Thailand's diverse same-sex and transgender cultures have distinctive histories and relationships with Western sexual cultures.

Rather than a singular "history of Thai homosexuality," it is necessary to think in terms of multiple histories of diverse Thai homosexualities. My ongoing research focuses on what each distinctive historical narrative looks like and which processes led to the explosion of Thai *phet* identities from the 1960s to the 1980s. More work needs to be done before definitive answers emerge, but preliminary research suggests that three broad processes converged after World War II to fracture earlier Thai understandings of eroticism and gender identity.

First, statist culture interventions to restructure Thai gender norms along "civilized" Western lines appear to have had significant consequences in the domain of erotic desire. During the late nineteenth and early twentieth centuries, the Siamese state's efforts at "self civilization"—a response to imperialist Franco-British critiques of "Siamese barbarism"—led to a range of interventions in everyday life. From the 1890s, a new regime of biopower (Foucault 1980) emanated from a range of state instrumentalities with the objective of "civilizing" the entire populace of Siam. The new regime included autocratic interventions in the public performance of masculinity and femininity, which, among other measures, legally enforced the re-gendering of men's and women's dress codes, speech forms, and personal names. The state program of forced re-gendering was most intense, and reached into even the remotest Thai villages, under the World War II–period, fascist-aligned government of Field Marshal Phibun Songkhram, who styled himself as "The Leader" (*phu-nam*) on the model of Mussolini and Hitler.

The *kathoey* category began to fractionate just a few years after Phibun's "civilized" norms of masculinity and femininity had become institutionally entrenched in Thai law, bureaucratic structures, and medical discourses and practices. Significant for the arguments in this chapter, the Thai state's "civilizing" interventions in everyday life were much more intense in the domain of gender (forcibly reconstructing norms of masculinity and femininity) than in the field of sexuality. Indeed, same-sex behaviors almost completely escaped the attention of state authorities during the decades-long period of "self-civilization."

Greater emphasis on gender identity and the relative insignificance of sexual identity for all contemporary Thai *phet* identities may well proceed from this distinctive history of state interventions in gender in the name of "civilization." That history also appears to confirm Judith Butler's (1993) insistence on the fundamental importance of gender in all patterns of sexuality. Thailand's new, gender-focused *phet* identities would seem to have emerged from an unintended disruption of older patterns of erotic desire that accompanied the state-enforced restructuring of cultural norms of masculinity and femininity, even in the absence of state intervention in same-sex behaviors, in the first half of the twentieth century.

A second major influence leading to the explosion of identity categories in the years after 1960 has undoubtedly been the rapid marketization of the Thai labor force and urbanization of the population since that decade. After almost a half-century of economic stagnation, the 1960s marked the beginning of several decades of rapid growth in Thailand as internal migration transformed Bangkok into a mega-city of more than ten million inhabitants in less than three decades. John D'Emilio's (1993) analyses of the role of nineteenth- and early-twentieth-century capitalism in the rise of American homosexual cultures provide a starting point for thinking about the impact of mid-twentieth-century economic changes in Thailand on that country's gender/sex cultures. State interventions in gender culture in the first half of the twentieth century may have shifted the discursive ground of understandings of *phet,* but in the second half of that century capitalism and urbanization may have provided material opportunities for Thai men, women, and transgenders to build new forms of collective existence, that is, new gender/sex cultures, around novel *phet* identities.

Finally, representations of Western gender/sex cultures communicated via cinema, radio, television, and the Internet, together with greater international travel, have contributed to the imagining of new forms of eroticized being. While they are part of the narrative of the explosion of the Thai identities, however, globalizing media and other Western cultural influences cannot explain all features of contemporary Thai gender/sex cultures. In particular, globalization studies cannot explain processes of cultural selectivity. Why, for example, are some aspects of Western homosexual cultures imitated enthusiastically in Thailand whereas others are rejected or ignored? Why has "gay" been borrowed into Thai but not "queer"? Why do many Thais love imitating Western drag queens such as seen on satellite transmissions of Sydney's Gay and Lesbian Mardi Gras parade, but there is no Thai S/M or gay fetish scene despite decades of exposure to these prominent aspects of Western queer cultures? I suspect that the legacy of state gender interventions and the particular forms of Thai capitalism and urbanization (i.e., the nation's peripheral location in global flows of capital and information) provide a distinctive set of conditions that significantly influences patterns of receptivity toward or rejection of forms of Western queer cultures. The precise articulations of multiple factors of state power, capitalism, urbanization, globalizing media, and international travel in inciting the rise of Thailand's diverse gender/sex cultures requires detailed future study.

Gay Identity without "Sexuality"

Even when an English term such as "gay" has been borrowed phonetically unchanged, its location within the context of Thai erotic culture means that it does not have precisely the same sense as in Western sexual cultures. Patton and Sánchez-Eppeler have commented on the complex renegotiation of meaning that takes place when terms such as "homosexual," "gay," and "lesbian" are used in other language-culture contexts: "There is both a surplus and a lack to the external label. In this mismatch there is a negotiation of meaning in which the local practice may stretch to meet the [originally foreign] label, and the label gets infused with the particularity of the local practice" (2000, 10).

All Thai gender/sex categories continue to be understood in terms of the indigenous conception of *phet,* which incorporates sexual difference (male versus female), gender difference (masculine versus feminine), and sexuality (heterosexual versus homosexual) within a single formation. Within this local discourse, *gay* and *kathoey* are not distinguished as a sexuality and a gender, respectively. Rather, these terms— together with "man," "woman," *tom,* and *dee*—are collectively labeled as different varieties of *phet.*

The historical system of three *phet* ("man," *kathoey,* and "woman") has been the productive source of all the new categories by a mathematical refinement of the gender continuum. In interviewing both *gay* and non-*gay* men, I have found that categories such as *gay queen* and *gay king* tend to be imagined first in terms of their position on a scale of relative masculinity and femininity and only secondarily in terms of homoerotic partnering. The "sexuality" of some new *phet* categories such as *seua bai* and even *gay king* is often obscure.

What is much clearer about all *phet* categories, however, is the imagined relative balance of femininity and masculinity that constitutes their reflexive sense of identity and is believed to mark the character of their erotic desire. *Suea bais* and *gay kings* may not be able to be defined as either homosexual or heterosexual, but they are most certainly masculine-identified males who desire partners who express femininity, whether in public gender performances or private sexual acts labeled as feminine.

Thai *gays* often describe themselves and other *gays* in terms of quantitative metaphors, "60–40," "70–30," and so on. The reference to blending imagined percentages of *king* (masculine and sexually insertive) and *queen* (feminine and sexually receptive) reflects increasing recognition, at least in Bangkok, that large numbers of homosexually active men engage in a wide range of sexual behaviors that do not always reflect stereotypical understandings of *king* and *queen.*

A percentile imagining of gender-blending among gays reflects general understandings of eroticism. A common Thai expression for a "real man" is *phu-chai roi persen* (100 percent man), which denotes both butch masculinity and heterosexual preference. Common percentage metaphors reflect the fact that all categories within the contemporary schema of *phet* are imagined as proportional blendings of masculinity and femininity. A "real man" is assigned a score of "100 percent masculinity." An ideal *kathoey* is thought of as blending masculinity and femininity in equal measure. A *gay queen* is imagined as more masculine than a *kathoey*, a *gay king* is thought of as being yet more masculine than a *gay queen*, and a *seua bai* is considered more masculine yet again but perhaps not quite "100 percent man."

In this system, the sexual versatility of a *gay* who is "60–40," "70–30," or some other percentage combination is seen as emerging from a masculine/feminine blending believed to exist in a relatively constant proportion during an individual's lifetime. That is, in the gender/sex system of *phet,* an individual's masculine-feminine gender balance is the fixed and determining pivot around which sexuality orbits as a potentially shifting and subordinate variable. It is a person's location on the multipositional gender scale of *phet*—from "100 percent man" at one end, to "100 percent woman" at the other, and a large number of proportional combinations between—that is imagined as determining his or her erotic preference.

Within the *phet* gender hierarchy, it is more important to know how masculine or feminine one is than the types of sexed bodies and gendered performances one finds erotically interesting. Erotic desire is conceived of as flowing as a "natural" consequence of gender status. As Halperin (2000, 91) observes, the most distinctive feature of the contemporary Western model of homosexuality and Western gay and lesbian identities is that they privilege sexuality over gender. In contrast, premodern Western, and also many contemporary non-Western, cultures privilege gender over sexuality.

It is not that eroticism is absent from Thai conceptions of phet or that gender is not a part of popular understandings of gay and lesbian sexualities in the contemporary West. Rather, eroticism and gender are articulated in markedly different ways in the two cultures' discourses and identities. In the Thai system, the intensity of a man's homosexual preference is believed to flow from the extent to which his "body/self" (*tua*) or "heart/mind" (*jit-jai*) is marked by feminine characteristics, whether visibly expressed or only present within the mind. Within the discourse of *phet,* that is, a male is "homosexualized" by his femininity. In contrast, the opposite relation exists within the Western discourse of sexuality, which, as Halperin observes, emphasizes the determinative power of sexual object choice. In Western societies, a male is feminized by his homosexuality.

Conclusion: Global Sexual Citizenship?

Dennis Altman (1997, 433) observes that the idea of sexual citizenship based on shared rights that transcend cultural and national boundaries presumes the existence of a universal homosexual or transgender subject who claims such a citizenship and possesses such rights. The diverse ways in which Thailand's different gender/sex minorities imagine their respective relationships to apparently similar minorities in other societies forces the presumed universality of homosexual or transgender identities (and hence the possibility of global sexual citizenship as currently imagined) to be questioned. The lack of a transnational homosexual or transgender identity appears to underpin another distinctive feature of Thailand's queer cultures: development of a complex series of *gay, tom-dee,* and *kathoey* cultures and commercial scenes in the relative absence of a homosexual rights movement.

Since the mid-1990s the Anjaree group of women has been outspoken in calling for the rights of all gender/sex minorities in Thailand. Although Anjaree has achieved a degree of national media prominence, it emerged long after the new gender/sex cultures and related commercial scenes became well established. The organization's role has been to seek to extend Thailand's significant gender/sex cultural achievements of the past decades. Furthermore, while championing the constitutional and legal rights of *gays, toms, dees,* and *kathoeys,* Anjaree remains a relatively small group and is staffed exclusively by women. There is no parallel political organization of Thai *gays* or *kathoeys* despite the much greater cultural and commercial presence of those two groups compared to women who love women. No united homosexual rights movement has ever existed in Thailand. The emergence of one of the world's largest, most diverse series of queer cultures during the decades leading up to the 1990s in the absence of a political movement, reflected in the historical absence of Thai queer delegates in international homosexual rights forums such as the International Lesbian and Gay Association (ILGA), raises questions about how central political issues and activisms are to the emergence of modern gay, lesbian, and transgender identities and cultures.

Altman acknowledges that "the Thai case suggests that a political movement may be the least likely part of Western concepts of homosexual identity to be adopted in many parts of the world, even as some enthusiastically embrace the mores and imagery of Western queerdom" (2000, 153). Such contrasts have led Altman to question the assumption of global queer homogenization, upon which contemporary homosexual rights and sexual citizenship discussions tend to be based:

> If we abandon the idea that the model for the rest of the world—whether political, cultural, or intellectual—need be New York or Paris, and if we recognize

the emerging possibilities for such models in Bangkok and Harare, we may indeed be able to speak of a "queer planet." We may even recognize the need to question whether Anglo-American queer theorists are saying much of relevance to the majority of people in the world who are developing a politics out of their shared sexuality in far more difficult conditions than those within which western lesbian and gay movements arose. (1997, 433)

The presence of Western discourses of gender and sexuality in Thailand has had an impact on older Thai understandings, but the outcome of such foreign contact has not been the emergence of a discourse of sexuality, as Foucault proposed occurred in Western societies in the nineteenth century. The interaction of Western discourses with other cultures/discourses does not necessarily reproduce the gender/sexuality split widely represented as being hegemonic in the West. Rather, the proliferation of Thai categories and identities should be understood as the result of an initial destabilization of the originally ternary discourse of *phet* followed by the institution of a new, more complex, multivalent form of that distinctive Southeast Asian formation—and not in terms of the unmediated reproduction of a Western-modeled discursive regime.

Simplistic accounts of global queering as being equivalent to "Westernization" or "Americanization" mistakenly assume that Western discourses, because of the West's technological, economic, and political dominance, are equally robust on the global stage and will eventually overwhelm and dominate local understandings. Such discourses, however, are nowhere near as powerful as Western economies or military technologies; local discourses often prove remarkably resilient. When members of Thailand's diverse gender/sex cultures have engaged Western discourses, they have appropriated foreign categories to local understandings rather than abandoning their society's dominant gender-based view of human eroticism.

The complex genealogies of contemporary Thai vocabularies for gender/sex difference suggest that a complex range of influences—East-West borrowing and adaptation, intra-Asian contact, and local evolution—have been at work in instigating the dramatic proliferation of culturally recognized forms of gendered and erotic being since the 1960s. The mix of creative adaptation, active resistance, and nonchalant indifference that the country's *gay, tom-dee,* and *kathoey* cultures, respectively, show to queer English indicate a highly uneven mix of forces in the explanation for global queering. Although the impact of the West is part of this many-chaptered story, the view that it is the sole source of all novel forms of homosexual and transgendered identity across the planet is mistaken. Future explorations of the manifold processes of global queering must move beyond a narrow analytical focus on the history of individual gender/sex identities and develop overlapping compar-

ative narratives in which the histories of lesbians, transgenders, and gay men
as well as "normative" men and woman all play significant roles.

Notes

1. Where English words such as *gay, lesbian,* or *Man* have been borrowed into Thai, I
use italics to mark their inscription within Thai discourse. *Gay,* in other words, is a foreign Thai word when italicized.

2. The final diphthong of *kathoey* is not found in English, although the sound represented
in French by *oeil* is quite similar. A French transcription of "kathoey" would be *gatoeil.*

3. To Australian and British ears, *phet* (falling tone) sounds somewhat like "pairt!"
North Americans are inclined to hear the word as similar to the way that they pronounce
"pate!"

4. The Thai expression for the word "homosexuality" seems to be older than the word
"heterosexuality." The contemporary word *rak-ruam-phet* is an abbreviation of *rak ruam
phet diao-kan,* which combines intersecting expressions for "same-*phet* love" (*rak phet diao-
kan*) and the formal Thai expression for "sexual intercourse" (*ruam phet*). Once *rak-ruam-
phet* had become an accepted academic and medical term for "homosexuality," the term
for "heterosexuality" (*rak-tang-phet*) was coined as a variant expression by replacing the
middle term of *rak-ruam-phet* with *tang* ("to be other or different," or "hetero-").

5. The stories appeared in *Thai Rath,* April 28, 1961, 1, 8; *Nangseu-phim Siang Ang
Thorng,* Oct. 17, 1961, 1, 16; *Thai Rath,* July 4, 1969, 1, 2, and Dec. 29 1969, 1, 16.

6. See *Thai Rath,* Jan. 15, 1987, 1, 20, and Dec. 4, 1995, 1, 18.

7. Personal communication with Anjana Suvarnananda, (1996). Suvarnananda is co-
founder of the Bangkok-based group Anjaree.

8. The fact that many native English-speakers find it difficult to pronounce *kathoey*
correctly, often mispronouncing it as "kathoi," may explain why the term *lady boy* is used
when Thais speak English with foreigners.

Works Cited

Altman, Dennis. 1995. "The New World of 'Gay' Asia." In *Asian and Pacific Inscriptions:
    Identities, Ethnicities, Nationalities,* ed. Suvendrini Perera, 121–38. Melbourne: Meridi-
    en Books.
———. 1996. "Rupture or Continuity? The Internationalisation of Gay Identities." *So-
    cial Text* 14(3): 77–94.
———. 1997. "Global Gaze/Global Gays." *GLQ: A Journal of Gay and Lesbian Studies* 3(4):
    417–36.
———. 2000. "The Emergence of Gay Identities in Southeast Asia." In *Different Rain-
    bows,* ed. Peter Drucker, 137–56. London: Gay Men's Press.
Borthwick, Prudence. 1999. "HIV/AIDS Projects with and for Gay Men in Northern Thai-
    land." In *Lady Boys, Tom Boys, Rent Boys: Male and Female Homosexualities in Con-
    temporary Thailand,* ed. Peter A. Jackson and Gerard Sullivan, 61–79. New York:
    Haworth Press.
Bradley, D. B. [1873] 1971. *Dictionary of the Siamese Language.* Bangkok: No publisher.

Butler, Judith. 1993. *Bodies That Matter: On the Discursive Limits of Sex.* New York: Simon and Schuster.

Chao, Antonia. 2001. "Drink, Stories, Penis and Breasts: Lesbian Tomboys in Taiwan from 1960s to 1990s." In *Gay and Lesbian Asia: Culture, Identity, Community,* ed. Gerard Sullivan and Peter A. Jackson, 185–209. New York: Haworth Press.

D'Emilio, John. 1993. "Capitalism and Gay Identity." In *The Lesbian and Gay Studies Reader,* ed. Henry Abelove, Michèle Aina Barale, David M. Halperin, 467–76. New York: Routledge.

de Lind van Wijngaarden, Jan Willem. 1999. "Between Money, Morality and Masculinity: The Dynamics of Bar-based Male Sex Work in Chiang Mai, Northern Thailand." In *Lady Boys, Tom Boys, Rent Boys: Male and Female Homosexualities in Contemporary Thailand,* ed. Peter A. Jackson and Gerard Sullivan, 193–218. New York: Haworth Press.

Drucker, Peter. 2000. "Introduction: Remapping Sexualities." In *Different Rainbows,* ed. Peter Drucker, 9–42. London: Gay Men's Press.

Foucault, M. 1980. *The History of Sexuality,* vol. 1: *An Introduction,* trans. Robert Hurley. New York: Vintage Books.

Halperin, David. 2000. "How to Do the History of Male Homosexuality." *GLQ: A Journal of Gay and Lesbian Studies* 6(1): 87–124.

Jackson, Peter A. 1995a. *Dear Uncle Go: Male Homosexuality in Thailand.* Bangkok: Bua Luang Books.

———. 1995b. "Thai Buddhist Accounts of Homosexuality and AIDS." *Australian Journal of Anthropology (TAJA)* 6(3): 140–53.

———. 1996. "The Persistence of Gender: From Ancient Indian *Pandakas* to Modern Thai *Gay Quings.*" *Meanjin* (University of Melbourne) 55(1): 110–20.

———. 1997a. "*Kathoey* > Gay > Man: The Historical Emergence of Gay Male Identity in Thailand." In *Sites of Desire, Economies of Pleasure: Sexualities in Asia and the Pacific,* ed. Lenoire Manderson and Margaret Jolly, 166–90. Chicago: University of Chicago Press.

———. 1997b. "From *Kamma* to Unnatural Vice: Male Homosexuality and Transgenderism in the Thai Buddhist Tradition." In *Queer Dharma: A Buddhist Gay Anthology,* ed. Winston Leyland, 55–89. San Francisco: Gay Sunshine Press.

———. 1997c. "Thai Research on Male Homosexuality and Transgenderism and the Cultural Limits of Foucaultian Analysis." *Journal of the History of Sexuality* 8(1): 52–85.

———. 1999a. "An American Death in Bangkok: The Murder of Darrell Berrigan and the Hybrid Origins of Gay Identity in 1960s Bangkok." *GLQ: A Journal of Lesbian and Gay Studies* 5(3): 361–411.

———. 1999b. "Tolerant but Unaccepting: Correcting Misperceptions of a Thai 'Gay Paradise.'" In *Genders and Sexualities in Modern Thailand,* ed. Peter A. Jackson and Nerida M. Cook, 226–42. Chiang Mai: Silkworm Books.

———. 1999c. "Same-Sex Sexual Experience in Thailand." In *Lady Boys, Tom Boys, Rent Boys: Male and Female Homosexualities in Contemporary Thailand,* ed. Peter A. Jackson and Gerard Sullivan, 29–60. New York: Haworth Press.

———. 1999d. "Spurning Alphonso Lingis's Thai 'Lust': The Perils of a Philosopher at

Large." *Intersections: Gender, History and Culture in the Asian Context,* 2, at <wwwsshe.murdoch.edu.au/intersections/issue2/jackson.html> accessed on March 3, 2003.

———. 2000. "An Explosion of Thai Identities: Global Queering and Reimagining Queer Theory." *Culture, Health and Sexuality* 2(4): 405–24.

McCamish, Malcolm. 1999. "The Friends Thou Hast: Support Systems for Male Commercial Sex Workers in Pattaya, Thailand." In *Lady Boys, Tom Boys, Rent Boys: Male and Female Homosexualities in Contemporary Thailand,* ed. Peter A. Jackson and Gerard Sullivan, 161–91. New York: Haworth Press.

Miller, Neil. 1992. *Out in the World: Gay and Lesbian Life from Buenos Aires to Bangkok.* New York: Random House.

Morris, Rosalind. 1994. "Three Sexes and Four Sexualities: Redressing the Discourses on Gender and Sexuality in Contemporary Thailand." *Positions* 2(1): 15–43.

———. 1997. "Educating Desire: Thailand, Transnationalism, and Transgression." *Social Text* 15(3–4): 53–79.

Patton, Cindy, and Benigno Sánchez-Eppeler. 2000. "Introduction: With a Passport Out of Eden." In *Queer Diasporas,* ed. Cindy Patton and Benigno Sánchez-Eppeler, 1–14. Durham: Duke University Press.

Reinfelder, Monika. 1996. "Introduction: Weaving International Webs." In *Amazon to Zami: Towards a Global Lesbian Feminism,* ed. Monika Reinfelder, 1–10. New York: Cassell.

Rubin, Gayle. 1984. "Thinking Sex: Notes for a Radical Theory of the Politics of Sexuality." In *Pleasure and Danger: Exploring Female Sexuality,* ed. Carole S. Vance, 267–319. London: Routledge and Kegan Paul.

Sinnott, Megan. 1999. "Masculinity and Tom Identity in Thailand." In *Lady Boys, Tom Boys, Rent Boys: Male and Female Homosexualities in Contemporary Thailand,* ed. Peter A. Jackson and Gerard Sullivan, 97–119. New York: Haworth Press.

———. 2000. "The Semiotics of Transgendered Sexual Identity in the Thai Print Media: Imagery and Discourse of the Sexual Other." *Culture, Health and Sexuality* 2(4): 425–40.

Storer, Graeme. 1999a. "Rehearsing Gender and Sexuality in Modern Thailand: Masculinity and Male-Male Sex Behaviours." In *Lady Boys, Tom Boys, Rent Boys: Male and Female Homosexualities in Contemporary Thailand,* ed. Peter A. Jackson and Gerard Sullivan, 141–59. New York: Haworth Press.

———. 1999b. "Performing Sexual Identity: Naming and Resisting 'Gayness' in Modern Thailand." *Intersections: Gender, History and Culture in the Asian Context,* 2, at <http://wwwsshe.murdoch.edu.au/intersections/issue2/storer.html> accessed on March 3, 2003.

Sullivan, Gerard, and Laurence Wai-Teng Leong, eds. 1995. *Gays and Lesbians in Asia and the Pacific: Social and Human Services.* New York: Harrington Park Press.

ten Brummelhuis, Han. 1999. "Transformations of Transgender: The Case of the Thai Kathoey." In *Lady Boys, Tom Boys, Rent Boys: Male and Female Homosexualities in Contemporary Thailand,* ed. Peter A. Jackson and Gerard Sullivan, 121–39. New York: Haworth Press.

9. *Pájaration* and Transculturation: Language and Meaning in Miami's Cuban American Gay Worlds

SUSANA PEÑA

As a hub of globalized labor, cultural projects, information, and capital, Miami, Florida, is the site of bilingual gay cultures, with a predominant Cuban American influence, historically linked to U.S. urban gay life and Latin America. Although Dennis Altman (1997) has focused attention on the "globalization of gay culture" (i.e., the influence of "Western" Anglo gay culture in predominantly urban locations in developing nations), my focus is on a different side of these globalization processes and how migration from throughout Latin America to the United States through entry cities like Miami has an impact on gay culture and gay languages. I will explore how gay men of Cuban descent living in Miami draw from U.S.- and Cuban-based cultural and linguistic histories and use Cuban Spanish, English, and "Spanglish" to construct communities and transnational identities.[1] I will also analyze how urban Anglo U.S.-based gay culture and language are incorporated, used, rejected, or rearticulated in a multilingual U.S. city increasingly defined by immigrants from Latin America and the Caribbean.

Although the influence of U.S.-based ways of organizing and naming homosexuality is irrefutable, transculturation better approximates the linguistic practices observed in Miami. These practices can be placed within a cultural matrix that includes complex interrelationships among lived experiences, self-identifications, social institutions, produced texts, and the more ephemeral form of cohesion that Raymond Williams (1977) called a "structure of feeling." Transculturation provides the best theoretical mechanism for understanding the linguistic and cultural transformations in which gay men of Cuban descent participate.

I draw on semi-structured interviews with homosexual men of Cuban descent as well as on observations of Miami-area gay clubs and drag venues in 1998 and 1999. I conducted seventeen confidential interviews with men of Cuban descent who identified as gay or homosexual. Within the category "men of Cuban descent" I include both first- and second-generation immigrants. First-generation Cuban Americans were born in Cuba and immigrated to the United States; second-generation Cuban Americans were born in the United States to Cuban-born parents. I conducted the interviews in English or Spanish, depending on the preference of the interviewee. In this chapter, I analyze how language is used to construct gay and ethnic communities.

Language Autonomy: Spanish in a U.S. Context

The use of Spanish in the United States is a highly politicized issue; the struggle for language autonomy has been a primary battleground for Latino communities. English Only legislation, antibilingual education initiatives, and informal stigmatization of Spanish-language use have been used throughout the country to thinly veil anti-immigrant attitudes. What is at stake is an attempt to limit the incorporation of Latino immigrants as citizens and their impact on what is termed "eroding American culture." New immigrants struggle to become fluent in a second language and are often humiliated and ignored if they speak accented or non-Standard English. Consequently, pan-ethnic Latino communities have mobilized to support bilingual education, oppose English Only legislation, and win the right to speak Spanish in the workplace and in schools.

Political battles around language have been central to both narrow and wide definitions of citizenship for Spanish-speaking Latinos in the United States. In the narrowest sense, political conservatives have tried to make English-language proficiency a requirement for being naturalized as a U.S. citizen. In terms of the broader definition of cultural citizenship (Benyamor and Flores 1997), Latinos have struggled for language rights in order to claim public space, defend the rights of people of diverse language backgrounds to make claims on the state, and limit the extent to which imposed English useage circumscribes daily practices.

During the 1980s, Miami became a battleground around issues of immigration and language autonomy. Between April and September of that year, nearly 125,000 Cubans arrived in the United States via the highly publicized Mariel boatlift.[2] The U.S. media assessed the arrivals and cited high levels of so-called criminals, prostitutes, mental patients, and homosexuals among them.[3] Also in 1980, and perhaps not surprisingly given that year's mass migration of predominantly non-English-speaking immigrants, voters in

Dade County, which includes the Miami metropolitan area, overwhelmingly supported an English Only initiative placed on the ballot by the Citizens of Dade United (Portes and Stepick 1993, 161).[4] Passed in November 1980, the initiative "made it unlawful to use county funds 'for the purpose of utilizing any language other than English, or promoting any culture other than that of the United States'" (García 1996, 74, quoting Tasker 1980, 1A). The success of the election and campaign in Dade County was a sign that non-Latino, non-immigrant, U.S. voters had reached the limits of their tolerance. In 1988 that sentiment was reinforced statewide when an English Only amendment to the Florida state constitution was passed by 84 percent of the state's voters (Portes and Stepick 1993, 161).

English Only became the battle around which Dade County and Florida residents who considered themselves rightful citizens (as the name "Citizens of Dade United" suggests) asserted what they believed to be their legitimate claim to political rights, social services, and government funding. Perhaps more profoundly, though, the "natives" asserted their claim to the heart and soul of the city through the English Only battle. Because some area residents feared the loss of "their" South Florida, the political mobilization in favor of English Only was an attempt to ensure that the city's language (and ethnicity) would continue to be English- and Anglo-dominant.

Although Miami's English Only proponents won several battles during the 1980s, by the year 2000 it was clear that the language war had been lost. In May 1993 the Dade County Commission overturned the 1980 English Only initiative. Signs at government buildings are posted not only in English and Spanish but also in Haitian Creole. The worst fears of the English Only proponents have been met. In vast areas of Greater Miami it is possible to conduct bank transactions, buy groceries, make travel arrangements, find out about government services, and see a doctor without ever speaking English.

Several factors contribute to the prevalence of Spanish use throughout Miami, among them the unique history of the reception of Cuban Americans compared with other Latino groups. Large numbers of Cuban immigrants to the city in the first wave during the early 1960s generally had high levels of education and previously high socioeconomic backgrounds. The U.S. government relatively welcomed those who arrived before 1980 because they represented the failure of communist governments during the cold war. As a result, the U.S. government facilitated immigrant legalization and provided assistance through the Cuban Refugee Program. The immigrants from Cuba and the rest of Latin America who continued to arrive in Miami entered a city with established Latino businesses, enclaves, and social communities. This facilitated the entry of Spanish-speaking immigrants into varied economic strata.

The continued entry of immigrants from Latin America and the Caribbean coupled with decreasing white non-Hispanic and black non-Hispanic
populations have also intensified the hispanicization of the city. Business
interests from throughout Latin America continue to house parts of their
operations in Miami (leading to the city to be called the "gateway to the
Americas"), and Spanish has become more and more entrenched as a language of social interaction as well as business.

I place my discussion of the globalization of gay culture within the context of battles over language autonomy, the ethnic makeup of a city, and the
rights of immigrants to shape local culture. Spanish is not only a language
with great currency in heterosexist settings but also one that is widely used
in Miami's gay worlds. In gay social settings catering specifically to Latino
audiences, Spanish is both the language of social interaction and the language
of performance. In "mainstream gay clubs" (those that do not cater specifically to Latinos and most of whose clientele is a mix of Anglos and Latinos)
it is common to hear patrons and occasionally drag performers use Spanish. During the 1990s two Spanish-language gay magazines were published
in the area. Bilingualism and language autonomy are a fact of life in gay circles as well as heterosexual ones in Miami.

Sexual Systems, Language, and Culture

In the context of a city and local gay scene deeply influenced by pan-Latino
culture and Spanish language, Cuban gay transculturation is an important
factor in the social construction of sexuality. The lived practices of gay men,
including language, challenge both conventional notions of Latino sex/gen-
der systems and what I call "mainstream gay culture."

Discussion of Latino and Latin American sexual systems has often focused
on the misuse of U.S. linguistic categories to understand Latino/Latin American sexual systems. Anthropologists working throughout Latin America have
documented similar sex/gender systems across national boundaries.[5] Tomás
Almaguer (1991) has published a useful and influential overview of the varied literature on Latin American sex systems that suggests the application of
this knowledge for understanding Latinos in the United States. The general
premise of the literature is that sex and gender systems are historically and
geographically specific. Moreover, because sex and gender are organized differently in Latin America than in the United States, U.S. English language
categories cannot be simply translated to understand Latin American cultural categories and lived experience.

Using Almaguer's terms, sexual object choice is the primary determinant of

sexual identity in the United States. A man who chooses to have sex with another man is gay or homosexual, whereas a man who desires to have sex with
a woman is straight. In contrast, in the Latin American sex system, sexual aim
is the primary determinant of identity. "Sexual aim" refers to the act that is
desired. The desire to penetrate, be it a woman or another man, is deemed to
fall into the boundaries of masculine behavior. In the Latin American system,
a man who penetrates another man, sometimes referred to as a *bugarrón* or
activo, is barely stigmatized, if at all, according to this literature. The desire to
be penetrated "like a woman," however, marks one as a *joto,* the sexually deviant category. The *joto* (or *pasivo, maricón, cochón,* or *loca,* according to a country's labeling) is highly stigmatized. According to this typology, pasivos will not
desire each other sexually, nor will activos. Rather, the "feminine" will search
out the "man" and vice versa. These sexual roles are assumed to correspond
to socially visible gendered manifestations. Therefore, effeminate men are assumed to be jotos or pasivos, but it is unlikely that a masculine-appearing man
would be seriously accused of being a joto. In the Latin American system, out-
ward gender markers, sexual roles, and social power are highly conflated.

In summary, according to this research it would be incorrect to assume
that being a joto in Mexico or a maricón in Cuba is the same thing as being
gay in the United States. Jotos or maricones are more likely to identify as
feminine and understand this gendered identity to be related to sexual preference of men. Moreover, it is more likely that jotos and maricones will understand specific sexual acts to be gendered (i.e., anal penetration as masculine for penetrator or feminine for penetrated).

My description admittedly oversimplifies the nuanced ethnographic data
collected by anthropologists who have contributed to an understanding of
the Latin American sex system. Studies note that globalization's effects have
made it difficult to discuss the Latin American sexual system and the U.S.
sexual system as completely distinct and independent. In fact, researchers in
Latin American countries have noted the extent to which middle-class Latin American men in urban centers such as Mexico City are increasingly identifying as gay and understanding sexuality in terms of sexual object choice
instead of sexual aim (Almaguer 1991; Carrier 1989; Parker 1999). That is due
in part to increased personal and cultural contact between Latin America and
the United States. Processes of gay globalization make it more likely for Anglo
gay men from the United States to vacation in Havana, Mexico City, and Rio
de Janeiro and for men in Cuba, Mexico, and Brazil to watch films, read articles, and have information about U.S. gay urban cultures. Likewise, through
its attempts to replicate successful U.S. programs to reduce male-to-male
sexual transmission of HIV in Latin America the globalized AIDS industry

has reinforced U.S. gay categories in the region. Therefore, information about U.S. gay cultures, with the attached international economic power and social influence of the United States, is increasingly influential throughout Latin America, especially in urban centers.

Transculturation

A Cuban-born man who has sex with men and has been raised primarily understanding himself in terms of the Latin American sex system does not bring a static system of meanings, pleasures, desires, and languages when he immigrates to the United States. Rather, these systems of meanings are transformed by new experiences during that man's life. What about a second-generation Cuban American gay man raised by parents who transmit the values of a Latin American sex/gender system, is educated in U.S. schools, has unrestrained access to U.S. mass media, and explores U.S. gay clubs, films, and culture as he comes to understand his sexual identity? What languages might he use to make sense of his desires and identifications?

The experiences of these men can best be understood through the theoretical mechanism of transculturation. In *Cuban Counterpoint*, Cuban anthropologist Fernando Ortiz ([1940] 1995, 97–103) introduced the concept of transculturation. The term *transculturation* was meant to supplant the use of "acculturation," a term gaining prominence among U.S. sociologists who analyzed white immigrant experience in urban settings. For Ortiz, the term *acculturation* emphasized the acquisition of the dominant culture. That acquisition necessarily implied the loss of the culture of the home country, which he labeled "deculturation." The concept of transculturation involves acculturation and deculturation as well as "neoculturation," the creation of a new culture that maintains elements of the two meeting cultures but is in the end quite different from both.

When applying the concept of transculturation to gay culture, Ortiz's theory suggests that immigrants do not assimilate into a static U.S. gay culture and adopt its language, symbols, and sexual systems. Rather, U.S. gay culture is itself changed by extensive contact with immigrant, non-English-speaking homosexual men and women.[6] The theory of transculturation also points to the importance of the culture of Cuban male homosexuals, which, in Miami, is reconstructed through memories, nostalgia, and contact with Cubans from the island. Because of the racial, economic, and political power that Cuban Americans hold in Miami relative to other minority groups, multiple spaces exist for the development of Cuban cultural projects if they do not contradict a general anti-Castro agenda. Allowed at least a marginal space for development, a hybrid that draws on the experiences of first- and second-generation Cuban American gay male men (a Cuban American gay neoculture) has flourished. This neoculture holds traces of both Cuban and U.S. histories but is a new formation made possible by a specific historic conjuncture.

These processes of gay transculturation are evident in the language and meaning systems of Cuban American gay men. I will discuss three linguistic practices I observed that illustrate the processes of gay transculturation:

1. Men of Cuban descent use the term *gay* in both Spanish- and English-language accounts to describe their sexuality and communities. Although the adoption of this terminology sometimes implies an adoption of a U.S.-based sex/gender system, the gay linguistic marker can also coincide with a gendered sexual identity associated with Latin American sexual structures. Linguistic and cultural markers that suggest reliance on U.S.-based gay culture (such as the use of "gay" as a self-identifier) are invested with divergent meanings by Cuban-descent gay men and must be interpreted within a bicultural framework in order to understand their significance.

2. Men of Cuban descent use Cuban Spanish gay argot in Miami's predominantly Latino gay club settings and occasionally in more ethnically mixed gay settings. Use of expressions like *perra* and *loca* reflect both the maintenance of Cuban male same-sex cultures and the learning and incorporation of these linguistic traditions by young, second-generation Cuban American gay men.

3. Men of Cuban descent invent linguistic innovations that involve a mixture of Spanish and English. These linguistic innovations reflect and create an ethnic, bilingual, and bicultural gay culture. *"Pájaration"* is but one humorous linguistic invention that joins Cuban Spanish and U.S. English and marks a bilingual listener as an insider to Cuban American gay male hybrid culture.[7]

Linguistic Practice 1: Redefining What "Gay" Means

Homosexual men of Cuban descent often use the term *gay* pronounced in English and in Spanish (*gai*) within the contexts of both English- and Spanish-language conversations. I found that men used the word *gay* to identify themselves, communities around them, and even same-sex practices in Cuba. In Spanish-language accounts, the word was used both as an adjective—as in *"el mundo gay* (gay world)," *"la vida gay* (gay life)," and *"un lugar gay* (a gay place)"—and as a noun, *"los gay* (gay people)" and *"un gay cubano* (a gay Cuban man)."* In these accounts "gay" was sometimes used interchangeably with *homosexual.*

Because the term *gay* is sometimes associated with a U.S.-based sex/gender system that can be contrasted with a Latin American sex/gender system, it might be assumed that the use of the term coincides with an adoption of the U.S. sex/gender system.[8] In other words, perhaps the men who use the term *gay* in Spanish-language accounts are referring to all men who have sex with men and have a nongendered notion of male homosexuality. That is not necessarily the case. Although the adoption of this terminology sometimes implies adoption of a U.S.-based sex/gender system, the "gay" linguistic marker can also coincide with a gendered sexual identity associated with Latin American sexual structures.

Two examples illustrate how men of Cuban descent invest the term *gay* with different meanings. Miguel is forty-seven and came to the United States in 1980 as part of the Mariel boatlift. Using a heavy mix of English and Spanish throughout the interview, he employed the term *gay* within the context of English and Spanish phrases and sentences. His definition of the term closely coincides with a U.S.-based system of meaning. I asked about whom he includes in his category of "gay":

SP: ¿Por ejemplo, un hombre que tiene sexo con hombres pero que no se identifica como gay, [qué] es?

M: Para mí ese es un *closet case.*

SP: ¿Entonces sí es gay?

M: Ese es un *closet case, but he's still gay.*

SP: OK

M: Pero hay muchos, como te decía, *old gay or the old school* que tienen que tener un hombre, un hombre que inclusive esté casado y tenga hijos. Que yo siempre he dicho, bueno si el hombre está casado y tiene hijos pero se acuesta con otro hombre, *there's something weird there.* Pero a la misma vez, es esa cosa latina; yo me imagino que tu habrás encontrado eso mucho. Que hay ciertos hombres que están casados, tienen hijos, se acuestan con gays, pero ellos son hombres y tú no. Y entonces pues eso es lo que a mí me molesta. El hecho de imaginarme que yo estoy teniendo una relación sexual con un hombre que

SP: For example, a man who has sex with men but doesn't identify as gay is?

M: To me he's a closet case.

SP: Then he is gay?

M: He's a closet case, but he's still gay.

SP: OK

M: But there's a lot, like I was telling you, old gay or the old school who have to have a man, even a man who's married and has kids. And I always said, if he's married and has kids but he sleeps with another man, there's something weird there, but at the same time, it's a Latin thing. I imagine you've come across that a lot. That there's certain men who are married, have kids, they sleep with gay men, but they are men and you are not. Well that bothers me. Imagining that I'm having sex with a man who thinks that he is a man but I'm not. I'm a man too, a man who likes men, but I am a man, I'm not a woman, and

piensa que es un hombre y yo no. Yo soy un hombre también, un hombre a quien le gustan los hombres pero soy un hombre, no soy una mujer, ni soy menos que tú, ni soy ninguna otra cosa. . . . Ese es el tipo de relación que a mí no me, nunca me ha convencido. . . . Como te decía, en los tiempos antiguos, *and this is a bad word, I'm sorry I have to use it,* bugarrones. Ese tipo de relación yo no la entiendo, nunca la he entendido, nunca la he tenido, no me interesa.

I'm not less than you, or anything else. . . . I've never been convinced by that type of relationship. . . . As I was saying, in the old times, and this is a bad word, I'm sorry I have to use it, *bugarrones.* I've never understood, never had, and never been interested in that kind of relationship.

Miguel used the term *gay* to refer to all men who have sex with men, regardless of gender identity and preferred sexual role. This is the meaning of "gay" as used in the U.S. sexual system, and Miguel superimposed that definition, with which he identified, onto men who identify according to the Latin American sex system as activos or *bugarrones.* He described the U.S. sex system, in which all men who desire men are equally gay, as more egalitarian than a Latin American sex/gender system that would define him as "not a man" and therefore inferior to a "real man" and unequivocally distanced himself from that system.

Juan, a fifty-one-year-old Cuban who left Cuba in the 1970s, also used the term *gay.* During the interview he spoke almost exclusively in Spanish and used the term often, even to refer to life in Cuba. His definition of "gay," however, was quite different than Miguel's:

A mí no me gusta la gente gay en el sentido que me gustan los hombres, que es el tipo de gente que tú, que yo encontraba en Cuba, y que yo disfrutaba en Cuba. . . . Entonces, es muy difícil para una gente como yo porque la gente gay no me, no me llama la atención.

I don't like gay people in the sense that I like men. That's the type of person I used to find and that I enjoyed in Cuba. . . . So, it's very hard for someone like me because I'm not attracted to gay people.

Although Juan used the term *gay* within his Spanish-language account, as did Miguel, he clearly meant something quite different than Miguel. He seemed to use the word as almost an equivalent to "maricón," the passive category in the Latin American sex system, in the sense that "gay" refers to nonmasculine men who have sex with men in contrast to "real men" who have sex with men. Because the terms *maricón, pájaro,* and *joto* are all highly stigmatized in Latin American countries, the term *gay* has the advantage of not carrying with it that history. Therefore, when used in this account, "gay" refers to a category in the Latin American sex/gender system yet does not embody the same extent of stigma as maricón.

One must use a bicultural and bilingual framework to interpret narratives that use the same term ("gay") in the context of Spanish-language accounts to refer to different categories of people. I discuss the use of the term as a metaphor for the varied incorporation of U.S. gay culture and gay English by U.S. residents who are not predominantly English-speakers. My analysis suggests that non-Anglo and non-English-speaking homosexual men in the United States do not simply adopt U.S. meaning structures. Rather, they sometimes redefine gay English and U.S. gay culture or infuse them with other ways of understanding and organizing same-sex desires.

Linguistic Practice 2: Using Cuban Gay Slang

> Perra es . . . en nuestro español caribeño, una palabra de exaltación para todo aquello que sea fabuloso o extravagante. Puede ser Perra alguien, una voz, un vestido, un peinado, una canción, un show, un logro, una frase.
>
> (Perra is . . . in our Caribbean Spanish, an exclamation of praise for all that is fabulous and extravagant. Somebody, a voice, a dress, a hairstyle, a song, a show, an achievement, and a phrase can be *Perra*.)
> —*Perra! La Revista*

The use of Spanish is common throughout Miami. The use of Cuban Spanish gay slang, the second linguistic practice I identify, is a more specific practice that marks a speaker as not only Spanish-speaking but also particularly Cuban or Caribbean and gay.

One of the most widely used Cuban gay expressions is *perra*, which, literally translated, means "female dog." Within the Cuban gay context, however, it is used as a term of praise and has a similar meaning to the word *fierce* in African American gay male communities.[9] Exclamations of "perra" are used to applaud a particularly decadent drag queen or even a female singer identified as a gay icon. The term was defined in May 1995 in the first issue of a Spanish-language gay zine published in Miami and marketed to Latino gay men. The use of the exclamation as the zine's title implied the language of its content, the sexuality of its readers, and the predominantly Cuban slant of its material.

"Perra" is used widely in predominantly Latino gay settings, but I have also heard Latino men use it in predominantly Anglo gay settings and predominantly heterosexual Latino settings. The exclamation marks a speaker as gay or at least as having a gay sensibility. In addition, perra is a particularly Caribbean expression grounded in Cuban "gay" kitsch, requiring evaluative skills that draw on a knowledge of Cuban gay icons and gay expression. The term is a pervasively used and easily observed Cuban gay expression in Miami, yet it is but one small example of Cuban gay language that is maintained and transmitted there.

In some cases the men I interviewed thought that expressions grounded in Cuban gay language and culture more closely captured their experience than English-language expressions. Juan, the fifty-one-year-old Cuban, provided an example. When I asked about his coming-out experiences, he rejected the concept of coming out as "strange":

Cuando una persona es mariquita es mariquita. Tu sabes, no necesita *coming out, coming out* es algo muy raro. Yo, por ejemplo, lo sé desde que tengo siete, o tres, cuatro años. Yo sabía que ese era mi destino, que yo tenía que enfrentarme a eso en algún momento. O sea, yo podría decir que salí del closet a los trece años, porque acepté que me iba a acostar con un hombre y fui a buscarlo. Pero yo eso ya lo sabía.[10]

When somebody is a *mariquita,* they're a *mariquita.* You know, they don't need to come out. Coming out is a really strange thing. For example, I knew since I was seven or three, four years old. I knew that that was my destiny, that I had to face up to that sometime. So, I could say that I came out of the closet when I was thirteen years old, because I accepted that I was going to sleep with a man and I was going to look for it. But I already knew that.

"Mariquita" is used to refer to effeminate gay men. It is related to the term *maricón* but has a diminutive and feminine-gendered suffix. According to Juan, the concept of "coming out" is "strange" because queerness is undeniable from a young age. In this account, male homosexuality is naturalized to the extent that it is seen as inborn trait that is obvious to others. That makes "coming out" an undramatic moment because it is assumed that those around you can see that you are a mariquita.

Instead of the concept of coming out of the closet, Juan proposed talking about "cantar 'La Bayamesa,'" an insider expression not necessarily recognized by nonhomosexuals. "La Bayamesa" refers to Cuba's national anthem. The expression, which can be translated as "singing the national anthem," thus plays off themes of patriotism and valiant masculinity but queers them by using the feminine "La Bayamesa."

[El] canta "La Bayamesa." Significa aceptarse. . . . En Cuba, cantar "La Bayamesa" era un individuo que se acostaba con alguien y que no se escondía.	[He] sings "The Bayamesa." It means to accept oneself. . . . In Cuba, someone who sang "La Bayamesa" was someone who slept with someone and didn't hide.

Whereas the concept of coming out emphasizes the declaration of sexual preference to others, "cantar 'La Bayamesa,'" as defined by Juan, primarily emphasizes self-acceptance and not hiding one's sexual preference. Likewise, Juan emphasized when he came to terms with his preference for male sexual partners rather than any kind of declaration or statement about that sexual preference to others. The objective difference between the terms *coming out* and *cantar "La Bayamesa"* is not the key issue. We might argue that Juan's explanation of "cantar 'La Bayamesa'" strongly overlaps with some understandings of "coming out of the closet." For Juan, however, the two expressions, one in English drawing on U.S. metaphors and one in Spanish drawing on Cuban metaphors, are distinct. One makes more sense to him and has more relevance to what he identifies as the critical moments of his development as a homosexual man.

The use of Cuban gay expressions and slang is also common among second-generation Cuban American gay men who predominantly speak English. They are among those who yell "perra!" at drag shows and will sometimes greet friends at gay clubs with a smattering of Cuban gay slang remarks. Learning and using Cuban gay slang among Cuban American gay men who primarily speak English marks a transmission of Cuban gay sensibility from one generation to the next. It connects young, second-generation Cuban American gay men with a strand of Cuban culture that celebrates male homosexual expression. For example, Manuel, a Miami-born Cuban American in his late twenties, described the significance of his relationship with two older Cuban gay men as "a door to a cultural awakening." When he described what he learned from them, he focused primarily on language and gay icons: "There was a whole language . . . I think in most gay cultures there's a, you know, languages that are, if not specific to them at least typical of them at the time, and I enjoyed listening to the gay, the older gay Cuban language 'cause it was new to me at the time."

Manuel eagerly listened to the two older men. He described being intrigued by the content of their conversations: gay life in Cuba, the iconography of female artists in Cuban gay culture, drag history, and the webs of gossip weaved about the sexuality of celebrities. Manuel also described being intrigued by the language itself ("the older gay Cuban language"). The slang, expressions, intonation, and pacing of their words provided a sense of how the Spanish language was used in the context of a gay culture and, in a sense, how to be gay in Spanish.

Manuel spoke about his relationship with the two older Cuban gay men on another occasion. Did he have to struggle, I asked, to be both gay and Cuban?

> M: No because I've been exposed to a long history of culture that's both.
> SP: Through your friends?
> M: Through older gay Cuban friends. I've been aware that there's been a culture there that existed, that has existed forever. The two things to me aren't mutually exclusive. I think, maybe it's not, while not all the things that are gay about Cuban culture can be easily pinpointed as specifically gay, but maybe there's common trends in things that gay people talked about, people gay people admire. . . . I guess there's traditionally been a gay sensibility that people have, that exists, not that necessarily everybody shares in but, through things like theater and literature and the arts that makes up, like, a gay culture.[11]

The transmission of Cuban gay culture is an important element of second-generation Cuban American gay men's ethnic identity. Elsewhere, I have discussed how second-generation Cuban American gay men who exclusively identified Cuban culture with their parent's homophobia were likely to reject a strong self-identification as Cuban or Cuban American (Peña 1997). Yet second-generation Cuban American gay men who had a notion that Cuban culture was their own and something they could manipulate and change were able to express much more affinity to their ethnicity. Learning Cuban gay slang and tapping into a rich history of Cuban gay sensibility and icons provide a view of Cuban culture that celebrates male homosexuality and facilitates the creation of integrated Cuban and gay identities.

Linguistic Practice 3: Bilingual Linguistic Innovations

Linguistic innovations that involve a mixture of Spanish and English, the final linguistic practice I discuss, reflect and create an ethnic and bilingual gay culture. Drag performances illustrate this hybrid language, but these linguistic innovations emerge from a lived context of life in a multilingual city where English-dominant and Spanish-dominant Latino gay men communicate with one another, have sex with one another, and create communities separately and together. Many consciously bilingual innovations as well as "mistakes" occur in these interactions and can be sources of embarrassment and humor. They can also become the dominant mode of expression. Often they can capture Miami's multicultural reality in an utterance. That is true for hetero and homosexual speakers, but in the case of Cuban American gay men linguistic innovations can create a particular insider standpoint—that of a biculturally gay man.

The creation of an insider position is most obvious and easily observed in drag settings, and exchanges that occur there, particularly those between drag queens and audiences, are important sites for creating and reinventing Cuban gay culture.[12] Drag performances in predominantly gay settings provide a good place to observe both the linguistic innovations of Cuban American drag queens and the audience reception of and reaction to these innovations. Drag queens use linguistic "mistakes" as the basis of stand-up routines and drag humor, and audience members who "get the joke" are privileged as insiders.

The title of this article is drawn from one such drag performance. "Pája-ration" is a linguistic innovation used by Mariloly, a *trasvesti* performer. Mariloly, a Cuban drag queen popular in Latino gay clubs, does a series of stand-up routines that play off of her "Cuban, just off the boat, can't speak English" character. As master of ceremonies and in her performance she works predominantly in Spanish, but she incorporates bilingual elements in ways that highlight the humor of the new immigrant experience.

In a typical routine, Mariloly speaks to the audience in Spanish and then tries to speak in English to a monolingual club manager who is imagined to be offstage. As she fumbles through her translation for the manager, she tries to come up with a word that describes the characteristics of the audience to the imagined English-speaker. She says, "Here, here" (pronounced in a thick Cuban accent), pointing to the audience around her. Not finding the right word, she asks more to herself (as many Spanish-speakers have done many times when not being able to come up with an appropriate word in English), "Ay, ¿cómo se dice?" (Oh, how do you say that? What's the word?). Again, as many Latinos have done before her, she proceeds to make up a word, using a Spanish-language base word and an English-language suffix: "Here, *mu-cho pájaration.* You understand?"

"Pájaration" is pronounced in a thick Cuban accent (pa-ha-ray-shon). The linguistic innovation is a play off the Spanish-language derogatory slang for gay men, *pájaros,* which literally translates as "birds." "Pájaro" is used to refer to a homosexual man, most likely an effeminate gay man.[13] The term *pájara-tion* joins the derogatory *pájaro* with an English-language ending, *ation.*

I saw the skit performed several times, and every time the crowd erupted with laughter when Mariloly said "pájaration." The joke and its instant crowd response mark bicultural audience members as insiders. To "get" the joke it is necessary to know the term *pájaro* and the English-language conjugation *ation* and also recognize the incongruence of the two.

Mariloly's stand-up routine also allows a Latino audience to laugh at the mistakes of an un-Americanized immigrant. Because the joking occurs in the context of a Spanish-language routine, however, the assumed listener is more likely to be a person who himself has been in similar situations.[14] Within that context what is devalued most is the monolingual English-speaker who would not be able to understand the majority of Mariloly's routine and most likely not get the joke about pájaration. Given this, and the fact the performance occurred in a club catering to Latino gay men, I interpret this poking fun as an "in joke" understood best by those who have either been through the immigrant experience themselves or have seen close relatives in similar situations.

The use of linguistic innovation in this example points to common experiences that characterize Cuban American life in Miami and emerges from an intersection between Cuban gay Spanish and English. In terms of my larger ethnographic study of Cuban American gay male culture, "pájaration" is a linguistic innovation that stands for all the times men throw together seemingly incongruous elements to create a fusion culture in daily life.

Conclusions

In the daily use of languages people infuse known words with new meanings, make up new words, and heavily use particular expressions while ignoring others within their vocabulary. In this chapter I have examined how language can create a bridge between older and younger Cuban American gay men and invoke cultural signifiers that are necessarily transformed in their journey. I have explored the way Cuban American gay men try to categorize and systematize desires and identities with language and how assumed linguistic categories do not necessarily correspond with people's complex systems of meaning. New expressions emerge in a particular multicultural urban setting that reflect a bicultural gay reality; Cuban gay culture and U.S.-based gay culture transform each other. The form that transculturation takes is partially determined by Cuban Americans' dominant minority position in Miami, where they hold a significant amount of economic, political, and social power.

Each linguistic practice discussed in this chapter provides insight into the linguistic practice of transculturation. Men of Cuban descent invest the use of "gay" (and of other cultural symbols of the U.S. gay movement, such as freedom rings and pink triangles) with a range of meanings. We cannot assume that when a Cuban American man says he is gay he means quite the same thing as an Anglo man in the United States would. Analyses of the effects of U.S. gay culture on cultures of same-sex activity throughout the globe have to account for this process of meaning-investment. Although we cannot ignore the cultural imperialism and economic power of U.S. values, we also cannot assume that the rest of the world passively accepts that power without resistance and transformation. In Miami, a process of transculturation is occurring that has changed the meanings of identification terms such as "gay."

Young, second-generation Cuban American gay men who might have no direct contact with gay life in Cuba draw on Cuban gay expressions as a form of cultural exchange. Although the education process might be transformative for the young gay men I interviewed, expressions like "perra" are also transformed by new uses. When someone screams "perra" in a South Beach club to a leather-wrapped drag queen lip-synching to Grace Jones, it has a slightly different meaning than when "perra" is directed toward Cuban trasvestis who have applied their eyelashes with shoe glue and are lip-synching to a Sarita Montiel song in a Cuban housing project.[15] The change in meaning reflects a change in gay sensibilities and material realities that have expanded to include Latin American songstresses and North American gay icons. Although Cuban gay slang such as "perra" is much more dominant in clubs that cater to a majority Latino population, it has also seeped into Miami's mainstream gay club and drag activities. This is especially true of mainstream drag events that attract a strong Latino contingent. The presence of Spanish-language elements in "mainstream" gay locales may make these settings less alienating to Latino gay men, especially those who speak Spanish.

And then there's pájaration. Cuban American character-oriented drag queens like Mariloly are extremely important social commentators. They have built a following precisely because they are able to document Cuban and Latino gay experiences. They draw from bicultural experiences and through humor are able to touch nerves of connection between different generations of Cuban American gay men. The culture that is both reflected in and created through their performance and audience reception illustrates gay transculturation.

It is important to look at languages other than English to understand gay cultures. We must be careful not to equate English (gay or otherwise) and U.S. gay cultures with liberation, egalitarianism, or freedom without also questioning about how these languages and cultures are experienced by non-English-speaking, non-Anglo homosexual men. The struggles over language autonomy are reminders that English-language use, in the context of the United States, is imposed through a series of social, legal, and political methods complexly intertwined with racism and anti-immigrant attitudes. In that context, the use and maintenance of Spanish and the development of Spanglish also embody elements of resistance, liberation, and freedom. The languages of gay expression and pleasure are increasingly plural and shifting.

Language categories and ethnic/racial categories do not fully correspond. Many Cuban Americans are not most comfortable when speaking Spanish, just as many Spanish-speakers in Miami are not of Cuban descent. All second-generation Cuban Americans with whom I spoke were fluent in English and felt comfortable speaking it in most contexts. That is likely true of most second-generation Cuban Americans in Miami. Yet Spanish language and, more narrowly, Cuban gay language continue to develop in the context of Miami's multilingual world. That limited development and the use of this language through greetings, exclamations, and iconography are a significant cross-generational cultural exchange.

Although Miami is a unique U.S. city in many ways, it also has much in common with other urban centers. Like Miami, most U.S. cities that have recognized areas of gay concentration (i.e., San Francisco, New York City, and Los Angeles) also have some of the most racially, ethnically, and linguistically diverse populations in the country. Lily-white gay ghettoes filled with middle- to upper-class men, if they ever existed in the way they were represented, do not exist now. Studies that have explored the multilingual and multicultural realties of those urban gay worlds indicate that gay life in these cities is far from homogenously white and English-speaking (Cáceres and Cortiñas 1996; Cantú 2000; Guzmán 1997; Manlansan 1994, 1995). Therefore, applying the theory of transculturation can enable productive discussions of diverse gay communities. Rather than ask whether gay men are crossing national/linguistic borders and using gay English, we should ask (if they are doing so) how they are investing the language with meaning. Moreover, in what ways are they transforming gay English cultural/linguistic practices; are elements of other languages and other cultural systems gaining importance within U.S. boundaries; and in what ways are the migrations of Latin American, Caribbean, and Asian men transforming gay culture in the United States?

Notes

Research for this chapter was assisted by a fellowship from the Sexuality Research Fellowship Program of the Social Science Research Council with funds provided by the Ford Foundation and the University of California's President's Fellowship. All translations are by the author, and all respondents' names are pseudonyms.

1. "Spanglish" is a term used to describe a mix of Spanish and English. It can refer to constant code switching between English and Spanish or to specific terms that incorporate English and Spanish language elements.

2. Haitians were also arriving to South Florida in large numbers during this time. Throughout the late 1970s and early 1980s, peaking in 1980, sixty thousand Haitians fled their island nation in boats.

3. Elsewhere (Peña 2002, 28–59) I discuss how the issue of homosexuality was dealt with in the context of the 1980 Mariel boatlift and the ways Cuban gay men who arrived in the United States through the boatlift were both highly visible and silenced.

4. The English Only legislation repealed a county ordinance passed in 1973 by the county board, the Bilingual-Bicultural ordinance, which "designated Spanish as the county's second official language and called for the establishment of a Department of Bilingual and Bicultural Affairs, the translation of county documents into Spanish, and increased efforts to recruit Latinos to county jobs" (García 1996, 114).

5. For more on Latin American sexual systems, see Lancaster's (1992, 1998) discussion of Nicaragua; Taylor (1978) and Carrier's (1989, 1995) descriptions of Mexico; Parker's (1991, 1999) work on Brazil; and Young (1981), Leiner (1994), and Lumsden's (1996) descriptions of Cuba.

6. The effects of non-Anglos on U.S.-based gay culture may be seen in exoticizing discourses of desire. That is evident in the eroticization of Latino masculinity in gay circles, seen in most exaggerated form in gay pornography such as that marketed by the Latino Fan Club. Transculturation does not guarantee liberatory results.

7. For other analyses of linguistic innovations involving humor in Latino communities, see Limón (1997) and Reyna and Herrera-Sobek (1998).

8. See Murray and Arboleda ([1987] 1995) for a discussion of the use of the term *gay* in Latin America during the 1970s and 1980s.

9. This was the English-language translation provided by the editor of *Perra!* magazine, Eduardo Aparicio (personal interview, June 27, 1999, Miami).

10. During interviews conducted in Spanish, I tried to use a variety of English and Spanish versions of the concept of "coming out." In this interview, I specifically asked, "¿Que significa la expresión 'coming out' para ti? ¿O 'salir del closet', [o] 'declararse'?"

11. Research on gay and lesbian people of color who live in the United States has been based on an identity-conflict model (Espín 1987; Morales 1990; Peterson 1992; Sears 1990). Identity-conflict models assume that gay and lesbian people of color must balance competing demands from ethnic/racial and sexual communities and that, therefore, their ethnic/racial and sexual identities are experienced as split or in conflict. In some cases scholars have asked respondents to rank their sexual and racial/ethnic identities (Espín 1987; Sears 1990). I chose to take a step back and ask whether they felt their identity was in conflict ("Do you feel you have to struggle to be both gay and Cuban?").

12. In this section, I refer to a particular brand of drag that has three characteristics: (1) drag queens who primarily host or MC functions, as opposed to those who primarily compete in drag pageants; (2) drag queens who primarily use Spanish or Spanglish in performances; and (3) drag queens who have developed a character that emphasizes Cuban ethnic elements and a bicultural shtick. Although the discussion here is of Mariloly, the local drag queens Adora and Julie Mastrozzimone are also in this category.

13. I found some evidence of the reclamation of derogatory terms such as *maricón* and *pájaro* by Cuban American gay men, which could be a fourth linguistic practice. "Pája-ration" can be seen as divesting *pájaro* of its negative power through humor. In a gay Latino club, with Mariloly saying it, the stigma-laden history of "pájaro" makes it funni-er and inspires the crowd to further heckle Mariloly. This, however, is a partial process, and the positive investment in stigma-laden terms works only in particular settings.

14. I have purposely chosen to use the male "himself." The club where this performance was observed catered almost exclusively to men, and typically audiences were more than 90 percent male.

15. I draw the South Beach example from personal observation and the Cuban exam-ple from *Mariposas en el Andamio* (Butterflies on the scaffold) (1995), a documentary about drag expressions in Cuba.

Works Cited

Almaguer, Tomás. 1991. "Chicano Men: A Cartography of Homosexual Identity and Be-havior." *Differences* 3(2): 75–98.

Altman, Dennis. 1997. "Global Gaze/Global Gays." *GLQ: A Journal of Gay and Lesbian Studies* 3(4): 417–36.

Benmayor, Rina, and William V. Flores. 1997. *Latino Cultural Citizenship: Claiming Iden-tity, Space, and Rights.* Boston: Beacon Press.

Cáceres, Carlos F., and Jorge I. Cortiñas. 1996. "Fantasy Island: An Ethnography of Alco-hol and Gender Roles in a Latino Gay Bar." *Journal of Drug Issues* 26(1): 245–60.

Cantú, Lionel. 2000. "Entre Hombres/Between Men: Latino Masculinities and Homosex-ualities." In *Gay Masculinities,* ed. Peter M. Nardi, 224–46. Thousand Oaks: Sage Pub-lications.

Carrier, Joseph. 1989. "Gay Liberation and Coming Out in Mexico." In *Gay and Lesbian Youth,* ed. Gilbert Herdt, 225–253. New York: Haworth Press.

———. 1995. *De Los Otros: Intimacy and Homosexuality among Mexican Men.* New York: Columbia University Press.

Espín, Oliva M. 1987. "Issues of Identity in the Psychology of Latina Lesbians." In *Lesbi-an Psychologies: Explorations and Challenges,* ed. Boston Lesbian Psychologies Collec-tive, 35–55. Urbana: University of Illinois Press.

García, María C. 1996. *Havana U.S.A.* Berkeley: University of California Press.

Guzmán, Manuel. 1997. "'Pa' La Escuelita con Mucho Cuida'o y por la Orillita': A Jour-ney through the Contested Terrains of the Nation and Sexual Orientation." In *Puerto Rican Jam: Essays on Culture and Politics,* ed. Frances Negrón-Muntaner and Ramón Grosfoguel, 209–28. Minneapolis: University of Minnesota Press.

Lancaster, Roger N. 1992. *Life Is Hard: Machismo, Danger, and the Intimacy of Power in Nicaragua.* Berkeley: University of California Press.

———. 1998. "Transgenderism in Latin America: Some Critical Introductory Remarks on Identities and Practices." *Sexualities* 1(3): 261–74.

Leiner, Marvin. 1994. *Sexual Politics in Cuba: Machismo, Homosexuality, and AIDS.* Boul-der: Westview Press.

Limón, Jose. 1997. "Carne, Carnales, and the Carnivalesque: Baktinian, Batos, Disorder, and Narrative Discourses." In *Situated Lives: Gender and Culture in Everyday Life,* ed. Louise Lamphere, Helena Ragoné, and Patricia Zavella, 62–84. New York: Routledge.

Lumsden, Ian. 1996. *Machos, Maricones, and Gays: Cuba and Homosexuality.* Philadephia: Temple University Press.

Manalansan, Martin F. IV. 1994. "Searching for Community: Filipino Gay Men in New York City." *Amerasia Journal* 20: 59–73.

———. 1995. "Speaking of AIDS: Language and the Filipino 'Gay' Experience in America." In *Discrepant Histories: Translocal Essays on Filipino Culture,* ed. V. L. Rafael, 193–220. Philadelphia: Temple University Press.

Mariposas en el Andamio (Butterflies on the scaffold). 1995. Produced by Margaret Gilpin and Kangaroo Productions. Directed by Margaret Gilpin and Luis F. Bernaza.

Morales, Edward S. 1990. "HIV Infection and Hispanic Gay and Bisexual Men." *Hispanic Journal of Behavioral Sciences* 12(2): 212–22.

Murray, Stephen O., and Manuel G. Arboleda. [1987] 1995. "Stigma Relexification: 'Gay' in Latin America." In *Latin American Male Homosexualities,* ed. Stephen O. Murray, 138–44. Albuquerque: University of New Mexico Press.

Ortiz, Fernando. [1940] 1995. *Cuban Counterpoint: Tobacco and Sugar,* trans. Harriet de Onís. Durham: Duke University Press.

Parker, Richard. 1991. *Bodies, Pleasures, and Passions: Sexual Culture in Contemporary Brazil.* Boston: Beacon Press.

———. 1999. *Beneath the Equator: Cultures of Desire, Male Homosexuality, and Emerging Gay Communities in Brazil.* New York: Routledge.

Peña, Susana. 1997. "'Oye Loca': Cuban American Gay Male Identities and Culture." Master's thesis, University of California at Santa Barbara.

———. 2002. "Visibility and Silence: Cuban American Gay Male Culture in Miami." Ph.D. diss., University of California at Santa Barbara.

Peterson, John L. 1992. "Black Men and Their Same-Sex Desires and Behaviors." In *Gay Culture in America: Essays from the Field,* ed. Gilbert Herdt, 147–64. Boston: Beacon Press.

Portes, Alejandro, and Alex Stepick. 1993. *City on the Edge: The Transformation of Miami.* Berkeley: University of California Press.

Reyna, Jose R., and Maria Herrera-Sobek. 1998. "Jokelore, Cultural Differences, and Linguistic Dexterity: The Construction of Mexican Immigrant Chicano Humor." In *Culture across Borders: Mexican Immigration and Popular Culture,* ed. David R. Maciel and Maria Herrera-Sobek, 203–26. Tuscon: University of Arizona Press.

Sears, James T. 1990. "Black or Gay in a Southern Community: Jacob and the Bus Boycott." In *Growing Up Gay in the South: Race, Gender and the Journeys of the Spirit,* ed. James T. Sears, 117–43. New York: Haworth Press.

Tasker, Frederic. 1980. "Anti-Bilingualism Approved in Dade County." *Miami Herald,* Nov. 5, 1A.

Taylor, Clark L. 1978. "El Ambiente: Male Homosexual Social Life in Mexico City." Ph.D. diss., University of California at Berkeley.

Williams, Raymond. 1977. *Marxism and Literature.* New York: Oxford University Press.

Young, Allen. 1981. *Gays under the Cuban Revolution.* San Francisco: Grey Fox.

10. Mother Knows Best: Black Gay Vernacular and Transgressive Domestic Space

E. PATRICK JOHNSON

Negro Faggotry is the rage. Black gay men are not.
—Marlon Riggs

The imperialism of heteronormativity is ubiquitous. From television, billboard, and magazine advertising to sitcoms and Hollywood films and public displays of affection by heterosexual couples, the representation of heterosexuality reiterates and performs the cultural logic of the American Dream. Insofar as the American Dream (or nightmare, depending on one's orientation) embodies a white, heterosexual, middle-class male utopian vision of "nationhood," heteronormative images implicitly secure a sense of belonging—indeed, of American "citizenship." In reality, however, the homogenous melting pot of heteronormativity not only leaks but also boils over when the spices of race, class, and sexuality cannot be absorbed into the discursive roux. Rather than signify a site of productive identity contestation, the melting pot metaphor paradoxically highlights the impossibility of the monolithic "American" and calls attention to the ways in which the erasure, or "melting," of difference signals the hegemony of white supremacist patriarchy.

Accordingly, black gay men have constantly developed technologies of self-assertion to create a space to legitimize black gay subjectivity. Drawing upon strategies similar to those blacks use in the struggle for equality, black gay men employ heterosexual tropes of domesticity to resist homophobia and heterosexism in black communities, racism and classism in white gay communities, and multiple forms of oppression in white supremacist society. Insofar as heterosexual formulations of "home" and "family" are intimately sutured to notions of nationhood and citizenship, reappropriating such terms in black gay communities suggests a transgressive deployment that recasts the domestic space in a queer manner.

Black gay men's appropriation of domestic discourse also offers a rework-
ing of "gay English." In a seminal study, William L. Leap (1996) distinguishes gay English from other forms of spoken English by delineating the specific
features of English used by gay men: cooperative discourse, exaggeration,
turn-taking, pauses, and terminals. Most if not all these features are found
in the English spoken by black gay men, but there are still differences peculiar to black gay culture. Although black gay men's speech may share general linguistic features recognizable in gay English, black gay men's discourse
draws mostly from black vernacular traditions that black gay men then deploy in black gay contexts. Leap suggests, for example, that gay English derives from both a "gay-specific knowledge of language" and "from sources
external to linguistic knowledge—personal identity, speech context, content
or topic of discussion—and gay language is a specialized vocabulary" (4–5).

In both instances, race distinguishes black gay men's usage of English from
that of others because they draw from gay knowledge of language that circulates in black gay culture and from their identity as black men. An exchange
between two black gay men at a dinner party I attended in Atlanta is representative of the uniqueness of black gay language without gay English:

> M1: [Rising to leave.] Well, girls, I need to head out. I have company coming
> tomorrow, so I need to get home and clean my dirty house.
> M2: [The host.] Can't you stay just a little bit longer? You know your house ain't
> *that* dirty. I worked all week and still had time to cook and clean my house
> before y'all came over tonight.
> M1: Oh Miss Ann, puhlease. You know Consuela came over here and beat this
> place into shape—don't even go there. But I ain't mad at 'cha. If I was makin'
> your coins, Consuela would be up in my house too. (field notes, June 12 1998)

In this exchange M2, the host, tries to persuade M1 not to leave by placat-
ing him, suggesting to him that cleaning his home will take no longer than
it took the host to clean his home in spite of having "worked" all week. M1
could let the statement escape without comment but knows that M2 is being facetious. All in attendance know he has a housekeeper. Thus, M1 takes
the comment as an opportunity to "read" M2 about having reached middle-
class status.[1]

What makes the exchange different from typical gay English or ritual gay
insult (the latter of which is derivative of black verbal dueling, or "playing
the dozens") is the use of "Miss Ann," a derogatory term for any white woman
or a black woman who is considered "uppity" or "acts white" (Smitherman
1994, 48). Black women who work as domestics in white homes also use the
term (Childress 1986). By referring to the host as "Miss Ann," M1 draws si-

multaneously on a black cultural reference meant to undermine racial oppression and the general gay vernacular practice of referring to each other as the other gender. In many black gay settings, gay-specific knowledge is conjoined with race-specific knowledge that distinguishes it from gay English used by white gay men and black vernacular used by black heterosexuals. Moreover, some black gay men disavow certain idiomatic words and phrases that the larger (white) gay community embraces. The gay community has reappropriated the once derogatory "queer," for instance, which is not a term that enjoys wide circulation in black gay communities because of its association with (white) sexuality to the exclusion of other attendant issues such as race and class (Cohen 1997; Johnson 2001).

Ultimately, black gay language or black gay vernacular is a hybrid discourse that relies solely on neither gay English nor black vernacular but draws from each and functions in relation to its users' specific contexts, needs, desires, and social and political purposes. As "outsiders within," black gay men incorporate their experiences as blacks in a racist society and gays in a homophobic society in order to create a "dark purple" ("blurble" in black vernacular) lexicon, as opposed to a "lavender" one, that speaks specifically to their subject positions.[2]

The research for this study draws from interviews of self-identified black gay men between twenty-five and forty-five who reside in the United States, including Atlanta, Greenville, South Carolina, Durham, North Carolina, Washington, D.C., New York City, Springfield, Massachusetts, Chicago, and San Francisco. Pseudonyms are used to protect the identity of each informant.[3] A good portion of the data stems from participant observation and personal experience in such black gay settings as informal dinner parties, nightclubs, and church services. Finally, the essay draws on films such as *Paris Is Burning* and *Living with Pride: Ruth C. Ellis @ 100,* both of which feature some form of black gay vernacular in the ways I will articulate. The analysis of these texts provides space to examine in more detail the ways in which black gay men appropriate the heteronormative discourse of domesticity. In doing so, they disrupt the idealization of the nuclear family and the cultural logic of sexual citizenship as lodged in "normative" sexuality. In other words, the emergence of black gay vernacular into popular discourse challenges the naturalization of heterosexual sex as representative of normal sexual citizenship. Through vernacular appropriations of heterosexual domestic tropes, black gay men ultimately resist monolithic notions of blackness and gayness and provide space for community-building and sexual agency.

"A House Is Not a Home": Deconstructing the American "House"

In his 1981 hit single "A House Is Not a Home" written by Hal David, Luther Vandross sensually croons over a full orchestra the words to a song that so-lidifies the notion of "home" as opposed to "house" as the epitome of the heterosexual American Dream: "A chair is still a chair even when there's no one sitting there / But a chair is not a house / And a house is not a home when there's no one there to hold you tight."

Following the logic of the song, an empty chair is still physically as well as symbolically a chair. A home, on the other hand, is a mere house unless in-habited physically by two loving (heterosexual?) people. It could be argued that the song applies to homosexuals as well as heterosexuals who desire to "nest," yet the lyrics' subtext undergirds the pervasive heteronormative log-ic that "home-making" is the ultimate sign of wholeness. Single persons, for example, who do not wish to live with another, who prefer polygamy over monogamy, or who are not heterosexual may only inhabit "houses" because a "house is not a home" if "there's no one there you can kiss goodnight." I take "there" in this instance to mean the door to the "house" at the top of the stair that can become a home if and only if the speaker's significant oth-er is waiting behind the door to declare her (his?) love.[4]

The lyrics emphasize the depth of the discourse on heteronormativity in the fabric of American popular culture. This investment in heteronormativity has everything to do with maintaining the image of the American Dream: the stereotypic portrait of a (white) father, mother, two kids, and a dog out-side their home, which has a white picket fence. This image is back in circu-lation despite the fact it (and other images, songs, and discourses) has long since been diminished by the economic realities of late capitalism, the chang-ing face of America, and the end of the cold war.[5] Although most Americans are living in "houses," the imperialism of patriarchy dictates that the happy image of the home be maintained.

Having been denied access to the dream or reality of home (at least in the Norman Rockwell sense), black gay men have reconfigured the discourse of "home" as "house." One place where this transgression has occurred is within the space of black gay nightclubs. The clubs, like many sites of counter-cul-tural performance, provide a space where black gay subjectivity is celebrat-ed and affirmed (Johnson 1998). That celebration and affirmation occurs through "house" music. Disavowing the heterosexual mask of songs such as "A House Is Not a Home," house music is unapologetically gay and unmis-takably black. The roots of house, according to Anthony Thomas (1990), a former Chicago DJ, are in the Chicago black gay club scene: "Like the blues and gospel, house is very Chicago. Like rap out of New York and go-go out of D.C., house is evidence of the regionalization of black American music. Like its predecessors, disco and club, house is a scene as well as a music, black as well as gay" (438).

Although Thomas locates Chicago as the scene of origin for house, it enjoys a wider circulation in black gay nightclubs around the country. Indeed, house music is one of the most integral aspects of black gay subculture. It has become so because it is a musical genre that emerged within the context of the black gay dance clubs, "the only popular institutions of the gay black community that are separate and distinct from the institutions of the straight black majority" (Thomas 1990, 438), as well as white institutions, straight or gay. Therefore, "Gay black dance clubs . . . have staked out a social space where gay black men don't have to deal with the racist door policies at predominately white gay clubs or the homophobia of black straight clubs. Over the past twenty years the soundtrack to this dancing revolution has been provided by disco, club, and now—house music" (438).

Predating the emergence of house music is the concept of the "house party." In Yvonne Welbon's documentary *Living with Pride* (1999), for example, a hundred-year-old black lesbian, Ruth Ellis, tells the story of how she and her partner, Ceceline "Babe" Franklin, bought a house in Detroit that became a safe haven for black gay, lesbian, bisexual, and transgendered people. Between 1941 and 1971, Ruth and Babe's house was the "gay spot" for black homosexuals denied admission to the city's white gay bars. It was also a shelter for those who had been dispossessed by their families and needed a place to stay until they "got on their feet." Ellis recalls that most people who frequented their house were black gay men. She and Franklin even helped many of them attend college:

> We paid for it [the house] in seven years. It didn't cost but five thousand dollars. And that's the house where we had all the lesbians and gay people to gather on the weekend. There weren't very many places to go when I first came to Detroit, unless it'd be somebody's home. And then after we bought our home we just opened our home to gay people. Everybody knew where Babe and Ruth were because we had a gay couple who lived down stairs . . . so if we had a party, we'd open up the whole house. Now most of them were college students going to college trying to finish college. Every Saturday we'd have a little get together, play the piano and they would sing. And some of them would play cards and some of them would just sit and talk. And that's the way we'd spend the evenings. It was sort of a haven for the young people who didn't have no place to go. Mostly, it would be men or boys [who] would come in. And we'd let them

stay until they'd get on their feet. Sometimes we'd try to help them through school. We tried. It wasn't much because we didn't have much back in then.

The sense of compassion and community-building explicit in Ellis's description captures the ways in which the term *house* has evolved in the black gay community. In general, the notion of "house party" derives from black people's practice of creating their own spaces to socialize because white racism often blocked entrance to public spaces. House parties were not only agents of solidarity against racism but also communal sites where black homosexuals could love and support one another. Similarly, those ostracized by their heterosexual brothers and sisters came to escape homophobia and build a sense of community.

In Jennie Livingston's documentary *Paris Is Burning* (1990), black and Latino men who participate in the drag/vogue balls of Harlem also belong to "houses."[6] In the film, "legendary" drag/vogue ball performer Dorien Corey says that a house is a family: "They're families, for a lot of people don't have families. But this is a new meaning of family. The hippies had families and no one thought nothing about it. It wasn't a question of a man and a woman and children, which we grew up knowing as family. It's a question of a group of human beings in a mutual bond."[7]

That definition of "house" dovetails with Ruth Ellis's insofar as ball houses serve as places where black gay men who may be homeless or in need of shelter can go. Banned from both the public spaces of the heterosexual black "home" and white gay clubs, black gay men and women create private spaces (the nightclub, another gay person's house, or a ball house) to create community. Indeed, "private spaces . . . may be the only spaces where [black gay men] feel comfortable expressing their sexuality or adopting dress codes that signify their membership as members of particular sexual communities" (Hubbard 2001, 57). Black gays' appropriation of the popular and very public meaning of "house," however, signals a transgression of heteronormative configurations of sexual and American citizenship in two important ways. First, it subverts "dominant notions of sexual [and American] citizenship [as being] based on the normalization (and encouragement) of the idealized nuclear family" (Hubbard 2001, 57). Second, it counters the assumption that houses are only occupied by these same heterosexual nuclear families.

For drag/vogue ball performers, membership in a house also means being loyal to your "family." Many of the performers in the film, for instance, speak with great pride when narrating how they became members of their particular houses, how their house is the grandest, and how other houses do not compare. That sense of loyalty belies the myth of the treacherous, racially disloyal sissy and highlights the paradoxes of representing the "healthy," stable, morally superior heterosexual household. That 50 percent of heterosexual marriages end in divorce and most children are not raised in two-parent households is testament to the dissolution of the American heterosexual idealization of family. That some house members are the dispossessed offspring of heterosexual homes is even more ironic given that they exhibit more love and support toward each other than they were shown in their biological families' homes.

In this way, a "house" as configured in drag/vogue communities becomes a place where members "make themselves from scratch," to borrow Joseph Beam's poignant phrase. They are places where people "make do" with leftovers from a world that has disowned and abused them. Houses become a polyglot space of celebration and affirmation as well as an image of a dream deferred. Essex Hemphill has captured ball houses well:

> In a country where "membership" and "privileges" translate into white, male heterosexuality . . . *Paris Is Burning* comes to the screen with a dressing room full of articulate butch/femme queens who collectively say, "I am" and are so, so real.
>
> Transsexuals, drag queens, gays and sexual transgressives, gender benders, legendary children, up and coming legendary children, mothers, fathers, elders; surrogate families are constructed from this to replace the ones that may no longer exist as a resource, or that may be too dysfunctional to offer any sense of safety support, or love. Houses of silk and gabardine are built. Houses of dream and fantasy. Houses that bear the names of their legendary founders or that bear the names of fashion designers such as Chanel or Saint Laurent parade and pose at the balls. Houses rise and fall. Legends come and go. To pose is to reach for power while simultaneously holding real powerlessness at bay. (1992, 126)

Hemphill's description of houses as opposed to homes suggests that houses are much more than a venue where those who share a sexual identity can come together. They are also sites of creativity, imagination, performance, and liminality where identity simultaneously is affirmed and in process. The dialectic of identity creation is an example of what Victor Turner calls "communitas." According to Turner, communitas is not "a structural reversal, a mirror-imaging of 'profane' workaday socioeconomic structure, or a fantasy-rejection of structural 'necessities.'" Rather, it is "the liberation of human capacities of cognition, affect, volition, creativity, etc., from the normative constraints incumbent upon occupying a sequence of social statuses, enacting a multiplicity of social roles, and being acutely conscious of membership in some corporate group such as a family, lineage, clan, tribe, nation, etc., or of affiliation with some pervasive social category such as a class, caste, sex or age division" (1982, 44).

The "liberation" from "normative constraints" is what is at the center of the houses. Rather than a rejection of the structural norms of heterosexual "home" or of black cultural rituals, black gay men engage in what José Muñoz (1999) calls "disidentification" by working on and against oppressive forces while at the same time remaining inside that system. In other words, black gay house-dwellers create communitas by maintaining the heteronormative structural concept of "house" while subverting the hegemonic limitations on the term by appropriating its heteronormative familial and domestic connotations in relation to "homes."

We Are Family: I Got All My "Sisters" with Me

As revealed in *Paris Is Burning*, the term *family* is used to name the "mutual bond" that black gay men feel toward one another. For members of ball houses and black gay men in general, the concept of family is less about biological relationships and more about kinships formed through a sense of communitas. Again, that conception had roots in the black community at large in that black communities have always valued the notion of extended family whereby nonbiological kin are considered as part of one's kinship circle. Growing up in a small town in western North Carolina, for instance, I had several "aunts," "uncles," and "cousins" who were unrelated to my family by blood but either lived in my neighborhood or were long-time close friends of my biological family. Residential proximity and personal history contributed to this sense of extended family. In most cases, my "aunts" and "uncles" were also surrogate "mothers" and "fathers" because they were allowed to punish their peers' children if they caught them misbehaving. In almost formulaic ways, many a black person who grew up in this kind of environment will testify that a whipping from your "aunt" was just a precursor to the whipping you would get when you got home.

As "bi"-cultural workers, black gay men incorporate and expand this notion of family within gay circles. Thus, "family" has come to signify anyone who is gay, whether or not they are out. Rather than ask directly whether a person is gay, one might ask if he is family. In that context, the term is coded in the presence of heterosexuals and also part of ordinary vernacular in all-gay contexts. One informant, Rob, a native North Carolinian, explained in 2000 why "family" is used in both contexts:

> You might use "family" in front of straight people, but only say it to another gay person in the room. You know how straight folks take everything so literally anyway [laughter]. Case in point: I remember going home with one of my friends to his family reunion. He introduced me to one of his uncles who was

fine as hell. And I was getting this little tingle ling from my gaydar when he shook my hand. So, I asked my friend if his uncle was family, and his mama turned around and said, "Yes, he's family. That's Roger's uncle." Me and Roger just fell out because we both knew what I meant! So we use "family" as a code, but we also use "family" when it's just gay people. I don't know why, because it's not a code in that context because we don't have to hide, but I guess it's just a way of including someone into the fold. It's like you enjoy the fact that somebody else may be like you.

Homosexual use of the term *family* in heterosexual company purposely disguises its gay vernacular meaning. One reason heterosexuals are unable to read the double meaning of the term, in addition to "taking everything so literally," is that many of them view the world from a heteronormative perspective. African Americans, in general, may practice a more inclusive definition of the term *family,* but that practice does not necessarily include sexual dissidents. Thus, in Rob's anecdote, Roger's mother's misreading of the term's meaning may have had as much to do with the ways her heterosexuality limited possibilities of what the term could mean as it did her ignorance of gay vernacular.

The example also calls attention to how black gay vernacular differs from what might be called a "universal" gay English or discourse. The function of "family" among black gay men draws on black discursive and social practices and incorporates them in ways that simultaneously maintain and subvert their meaning. In other words, black gay culture practices "family" in the same ways black heterosexuals do, apart from using the term to include other gays. The bi-culturality of black gays allows for a dual function of certain social practices that discursively manifest in black gay idiom. From that perspective, Rob's comment about using family to "include someone into the fold" dovetails with the way "family" functions in black communities in general. That should not be surprising, Anthony Thomas (1990, 438) observes, because "unlike their white counterparts, gay black Americans, for the most part, have not redefined themselves—politically or culturally—apart from their majority community. . . . Lesbian and gay Afro-Americans still attend black churches, join black fraternities and sororities, and belong to the NAACP." At the same time, the use of "family" by black gays is more nuanced and malleable than that of black heterosexuals:

> Rob: If I ask somebody if another person is family, I want to know if the other person is gay or not. To me, it just means another person who is like me or gay, and so they're "family." Most of the time if I'm asking the question, it means that I suspect that the other person is gay, but I can't tell for sure—my gaydar may be on the outs. [Laughter.] So if I'm asking it means I'm not

sure, but if I *know* the person's gay but trying to perpetrate I'll just say, "Oh Chile, he's family."

EPJ: So "family" is sort of a generic term for someone who's gay? Why would you refer to someone as family if they are trying to pass as straight? Why would you want someone in your "family" who doesn't want to be included?

Rob: Because they're included whether they want to be or not. It's like black people who try to act white. No matter how much they try to get away from who they are they still black. And most black folk will still claim them even if they don't claim their blackness. Black is black like gay is gay. And family is family. We just have to love all of our disillusioned brothers and sisters.

Although his response borders on an essentialistic view of identity ("black is black like gay is gay"), Rob's point is clear: Those who share a common signifier of difference in relation to majority culture are family whether or not they claim to be. Thus "disillusioned" (i.e., closeted or self-hating) gays or blacks must be loved and cared for in spite of themselves. This is a more ecumenical practice than that among heterosexual black families in that homosexuality often places an individual outside the bounds of "blackness," "home," and "family."

Members of the "Family"

No family is complete without "members." In a traditional family, the father is the head of the household and thus responsible for taking care of "his" family. Although in a white, heterosexist, patriarchal, phallocentric society the mother may do all the actual care-giving that involves children and supervise the family's daily activities, deference is always given to the "Law of the Father."[8]

Historically, black families have not been afforded the "privilege" of being headed by males. As White (1985, 145) notes, "Slave traders frequently perceived the slave family as a woman and her children. Thus, when sale destroyed a slave family, wives lost husbands but husbands very often lost wives and children." The conditions of slavery to a larger extent defined the parameters of black family life, including the roles each member could play in it. To the extent that black men were denied agency over their lives, for good or naught, they were unable to participate in white forms of masculinity, whether protecting their wives' honor, keeping their families together, or being allowed to support them in material ways. The limited access to the role of provider and protector became the source of a very complicated trajectory for black families. Black men may have felt emasculated by black women, who themselves had no more power than their male counterparts but could, because of racism, obtain work as domestic workers. In that sense, black women became the de facto heads of households, which further pathologized them as emasculators, particularly after the infamous Moynihan Report of 1965.[9] Thus, the black family emerged as a nontraditional site in relation to white families, as did the roles men and women played within them.

For the purpose of this study, I wish to focus on how black gay men in particular have appropriated particular roles of the heteronormative family to create their own sense of family. Given the historical backdrop of the black family in the United States, it is not surprising that the term *father* is not an integral part of black gay vernacular. On the one hand, the fact that many black households were and are headed by single mothers may explain why the father figure is not a prevalent trope in black gay vernacular. On the other hand, some of the reasons for the absence may also be due to the fact that black heterosexual men are often as sexist and homophobic as their white counterparts. Indeed, historically, black male leaders, especially those who were part of more militant organizations such as the Black Panthers, have been some of the most outspoken opponents of homosexuality. Homosexuality, these leaders have suggested, is not only anathema to the survival of black peoples, but also an instance of black self-hatred (Cleaver 1968).

Given the general machismo found in the black communities, femininity in black men is frowned upon, and homosexuality is considered an affront to black masculinity. Consequently, when a son comes into his homosexuality it is likely that his father will react most negatively; in the eyes of many heterosexual men, homosexuality and masculinity are incongruous. In "The Father, Son and Unholy Ghosts," Essex Hemphill has captured the deadly silence and tension that strangles black father–gay son relationships:

> A black hole, gaseous,
> blisters around its edge,
> swallows our estranged years. . . .
> I want to be free, daddy,
> of the black hole between us.
> The typical black hole.
> If we let it be
> it will widen enough
> to swallow us. (1987, 51–52)

The "black hole" that stands between the speaker and his father is a metaphor for what the father has reduced his son's (homo)sexuality to—"a black hole, gaseous/blisters around its edge." The father's answer to Leo Bersani's disturbingly profound question—"Is the rectum a grave?" (1998, 197)—is a resounding yes. Consequently, homosexual sex announces the death knell of the father's desire for (biological) grandchildren and wish to pass along the family (i.e., his) name. It means the loss of his son because of the ways in which AIDS is thought of as a gay disease. In some cases, it also signals the death of the black community because homosexuals are not "real" men and therefore cannot possibly lead their people.[10]

Other possible explanations for why black gay men adopt more tropes of black femininity are just as complex.[11] One might be a general connection to black women as another oppressed minority (e.g., Carby 1998). Because black gay men and black women have been at opposing ends of racial, gender, and sexual oppression, their creative responses to such oppression overlap in some ways. Origins of particular vernacular terms, phrases, and gestures, for example, are often disputed between the two groups because they are performed in both (Johnson 1995). Another possible reason may stem from black gay male misogyny. The fact that black gay men choose tropes of black femininity to perform may suggest that black masculinity (or masculinity in general) is a stable, fixed construct and therefore not susceptible to appropriation. I have witnessed a general misogyny among black gay men that manifests itself in references to women as "fish" or "cunts" and repulsion at the sight or mention of female genitalia.

Gil, a native of California's Bay Area, now lives in New York City. He explained black gay men's simultaneous admiration and rejection of black women after being asked why very few tropes of black masculinity exist in black gay culture:

EPJ: Why don't you think there is a counterexpression, "father" or whatever?
Gil: Well, I think part of that is that there has been, perhaps, a cultural convention among many black gay men to do a gender switch in talking about themselves and each other. And I think there are a whole bunch of reasons why that happens. Some of them have to do with . . . some of them come from different directions. Sometimes they come from polar opposite directions. So I think the reasons why black gay men will identify themselves and others as women stem, on the one hand from a recognition of women as a less powerful and oftentimes a group, who, like gay men, are . . . targets of violence, of powerlessness—those kind of realities. But at the same time, it also stems from, in some respects, a certain abiding misogyny that exists among black gay men. That often happens, I think . . . when men talk about each other in a way that really signifies of the most stereotypically "least desirable" attributes of women: the cattiness and the simplistic sort of image consciousness, even in some cases the sort of libidinousness that's assumed to exist within black women. Those are some often very negatively understood traits, and that's partly what's being treated.

Gil's candidness is compelling on a number of different levels. That the same group could hold another in high regard while at the same time hold them in such ill-repute should come as no surprise given the history of American race relations. The fact that whites held black people in bondage for more than three hundred years yet appropriated next to all of their art forms as well as other aspects of their culture is testament to this paradox. Nonetheless, my intention is to unravel some of these paradoxes as they pertain to black gay men's performance of femininity within the domestic space.

Mother's Pearls

As opposed to "father," the mother figure is perhaps the most prevalent familial trope in black gay vernacular and culture. To be hailed as "mother" is to be held in high esteem and regarded with great respect. According to Pepper LeBeija, mother of the House of the LeBeija in *Paris Is Burning,* "When someone has rejection from their mother and father, their family, when they get out in the world they search. They search for someone to fill that void. I know this from experience because I've had kids come to me and latch hold to me like I'm their mother or like I'm their father. They can talk to me and I'm gay and they're gay and that's where a lot of that ball mother business comes in. Because their real parents give them such a hard way to go, they look up to me to fill that void." Willie Ninja, the mother of the House of Ninja narrates a similar story: "You have to have something to offer in order to lead. The mother usually becomes the mother because she's usually the best one of the group. To be mother of the house you have to have a lot of power. Take a real family, it's the mother that's the hardest worker and the mother gets the most respect."

Both Pepper LeBeija and Willie Ninja became "mothers" because they were seen as leaders and "elders" who not only had compassion for those who became their "children" but also were wise about "the life" and what it takes to live on the margins of society. Men in these houses "latch hold" to the mothers as if they were their biological children, seeking advice, support, and nurturing. Because they "have something to offer," the mothers in turn take care of their flock in the same ways a female mother would take care of her children.

The term *mother* has currency outside the context of the ball/vogue houses of Harlem, however. As the interviewees in this study attest, "mother" is used in black gay communities around the country and as a general way to address the "elders" of the black gay community:

EPJ: "Mother." For you what does that signify? What does that term mean for you?

Gil: Well, basically it means a nurturing, loving kind of person. Now, I have a friend, Clarence, who was introduced to me as mother. I understood from the mutual friend who introduced us that he was often referred to as mother, and he, in fact, will refer to himself as mother. And in a sense it has a lot to do with his place as a somewhat older gay man. It's a sort of acknowledgment that his experience is something more profoundly varied perhaps, or more extensive obviously than mine because he's older. And because the moment that we live in there [has had] so many profound changes from year to year in the experiences and the rights of gay people—gay black people— it serves as an acknowledgment of someone who has been, if you will, through the storm and has perhaps survived a lot.

The important thing in Gil's commentary is that the position of mother does not necessarily come with chronological age. Indeed, designating someone "mother" stems from the perception that the person so-called is a mentor, leader, or nurturer. North and South Carolinians Kirby and Vancouver provided similar definitions:

Kirby: Mother is a wise, gay man, a gay man who's number one, very comfortable in being gay and who has been there, done that, has seen the ups and downs, and is the force of stability and reason for gay males who are not necessarily younger, but who are in the infancy of their coming-out process. And mothers are funny, they make you laugh and they're venerated, I mean, you've got to love them.

Vancouver: Usually it's somebody, like myself, who generally gives advice, who generally is, in situations of friendship—close friendship—is the nurturing one, the one who generally is in the middle. You know, if there's a dispute between friends, they're generally . . . they understand this friend, they understand the other friend, they try to make situations better. They're the nurturing type. I think that in terms of the gay community, that's what that term closely aligns itself with.

EPJ: And how is one bestowed that title?

Vancouver: Through friendships.

EPJ: Any friendship? Age is probably a factor, right?

Vancouver: I don't think age has anything to with it as much as, you know, one's disposition. I've met people of all age ranges—young and old—and some have a disposition that . . . I've seen the old people that just don't have no concept, just go out and do stuff, don't even think about it. And then I know some young people who, you know, think of all the consequences, who have similar "mother" type instincts, but have not reached or gained the title of

"mother" yet. . . . It's a respect factor and it's generally an unspoken agreement among a group of folk.

In keeping with Vancouver's definition, and to my surprise, two friends
who live in North Carolina (both younger than I but relatively close to my
age) revealed that they referred to me as "mother." When I asked why, and
why they had never called me that to my face, they said, initially, it was something they did in jest because I was always advising them about their love lives.
After a while, however, they began to call me mother because they realized
that they admire how I led my life as an openly gay man. Because they are
still somewhat closeted, they aspired to being as comfortable as I am in my
sexuality. Now, whenever they call or send e-mail, the first thing they say is,
"Hey, Mother, it's the children."

In each of these instances, the use of the term *mother* is an appropriation
of the word as signified in heteronormative discourse. Beyond the obvious
discursive cross-gender performative of dislodging "mother" as ontologically
cemented to the female gender, the transubstantiation of it as "black gay man"
sutures the familial rupture that those abandoned by their biological mothers experience. This kind of role-playing is more than an instance of gender
performativity, then, because the black gay male performance of "mother"
is a resistive act against hegemonic heterosexuality and homophobia as well
as an agent of community-building and communitas.

The term *mother* also enjoys a usage that is beyond the stereotypical reference to someone who is nurturing. In black gay discourse, a speaker may
refer to another black gay man as "mother" whom he believes to be a diva
who deserves respect, or he may refer to himself as "mother" in the third
person. In these contexts the term calls attention to the admiration of black
mothers in the black community. Seen as a kind of "every woman," black
women who mother are admired because of the sheer stamina necessary to
care for a family (in most cases alone), work full time, make sacrifices for the
good of the children, and do all that with grace. In addition, the black mother
is often depicted as being a stern disciplinarian whose mythic status as such
is a mainstay in stand-up comedy acts, television shows, and films.[12] Common formulaic stories circulate among black folk about mothers who need
only to give you a look to stop you from misbehaving, who are known to
administer corporal punishment with the closest available inanimate object,
and who have no patience for back talk. In general, a black mother is "fierce"
in that she does not suffer fools lightly, works hard but makes doing so look
easy, and is the epitome of grace, style, and flair.

These attributes are appropriated and celebrated in black gay discourse.

The following exchange between Kyle, a friend from Atlanta, and me is an example of this usage. I was visiting Kyle for the weekend but had decided not to go with him and other friends to see a drag show. We talked when he returned that evening:

> EPJ: Y'all must have had a good time because it's way past your bedtime. Wasn't the show over at 2?
>
> Kyle: No, Chile. You should have come with us. This was one of the best shows I've seen this year. Those girls WORKED! Oh my God, they were just *too* fierce!
>
> EPJ: Really? What was so great about it?
>
> Kyle: They were just very, very good. But it was this one girl, honey. I think her name was Maxi Cummings or something like that. She gave you DRAMA! Mother came out in this form-fitting, red dress with a scoop neck and these stiletto pumps. Her face was beat back into her temples. Her wig was tight. She was giving you Whitney Houston drama!
>
> EPJ: What did she perform?
>
> Kyle: "I Will Always Love You." But the remix version! Honey, when Whitney started holding that note, Mother started twirling like those heels weren't but a thang! Mother twirled and twirled for life! (field notes, June 12, 1998)

In this context Kyle's reference to the drag performer as "mother" is complimentary of her "dramatic" dress and, more important, her ability to pull off her performance. When a performer's face is "beat back into her temples," the makeup is applied heavily but effectively to give the illusion of femaleness. A "tight" wig is one that is appropriate for the dress and theme of the occasion. "Twirl" could have been a reference to the performer's walk or to her actual twirling. The point is that she was doing so with skill and grace while in stiletto heels. All of these compliments culminate into the status of "mother" as based on attributes associated with black mothers.

"Mother" is also used in self-reference as if one were a "real" black mother. By drawing on what a black mother might say after a hard day's work, just before a daunting chore or by taking on the black mother persona, black gay men align themselves with the figure of the black mother. As Brett, a Jamaican-born immigrant to Atlanta said, "I feel very comfortable using 'mother.' You might say something like, 'Mother's gonna do so and so. Mother *ain't* gonna do so and so.' Like our mothers used to tell us all the time." William from North Carolina stated similarly that when a person designates himself as mother it "means that they're in charge or they're the boss. Normally your mother has the last say and no matter what you do—especially in black families—when Mom says something, that's it. So, I think they just kind of transpose that . . . when they say that 'I'm the mother' [they are communicating] that my word is. What I say goes." The following exchange between Lee, who lives in Washington, D.C., and myself is an example of this usage.[13] The scene is Lee's apartment; he has just come from work:

> Lee: [Plopping down on the couch.] Whew! I am one tired sister.
> EPJ: Hard day at work?
> Lee: Yes, girl. Mother earned her coins today. She was working so hard at one point she had to sling her pumps off! [Pause.] She almost had to clock one of them bitches in the head with one. They get on my *last* nerve sometimes!
> EPJ: Well, you can take a little nap. I figure we can meet Tom and James for dinner around 8.
> Lee: That's a good idea. Mother does need her rest—cause you know she has to be cute for her future husband, Tom. [Laughter.] (field notes, June 19, 2000)

In this exchange it is clear that Lee has transposed, in the way William suggested, the figure of the black mother onto himself. Not only is his alignment with the black mother a commentary on the hard work a black mother has to do in order to make ends meet (i.e., earning "coins") but also the frustration that black mothers sometimes feel toward their work. The latter is captured in Lee's reference to himself as "mother" in the third person as wanting to hit a co-worker ("bitches") with one of "her" shoes ("pumps"). One of the narratives that circulates in black folklore concerns black mothers' propensity for punishing misbehaving children with inanimate objects. A shoe is perhaps one of the most common. Thus Lee's reference is an appropriation of that trope.

Lee's reference to himself as "mother" in this context is an act of self-aggrandizement and a commentary on black gay men's high regard for black mothers. At the same time, it is also a transgression of the trope of "mother" because of the cross-gender reference and the fact that some biological mothers do not support their sons as gay men. In other words, the fact that these men honor even mothers who have disowned them or are embarrassed by them speaks to the complexity of black gay familial relations, the reconciliation of gayness and blackness, and an unwillingness to prioritize one over the other. Ultimately, when black gay men perform "mother" they are reclaiming heteronormative constructions of the "motherly" and queering them in ways that subvert biological determinism and gender ontology. It also disrobes the sham of the heterosexual family as the morally sanctioned site of nurturing and support. When a black gay man "becomes mother," "she" stakes out a claim to full sexual citizenship.

My exchange with Lee highlights another feature that distinguishes black gay vernacular from general gay English. As Lee's interlocutor, I had to be knowledgeable of gay as well as black cultural discursive codes in order to get the full of effect of his commentary. Given the hyperbolic nature of his discourse, Lee counted on my understanding and deciphering—in one fell swoop—the multiple black and gay cultural idioms and references embedded in our conversation. In another context, perhaps in the presence of white gay men or straight blacks, I daresay either group would comprehend the nuances or polyphony of meanings in Lee's discourse. Specifically, heterosexual black interlocutors would likely misread his self-reference as "mother," and white gays would misread the cultural nuances of what "mother" signifies in the black community. Black gay men's language draws from both black and gay culture, and one must have enough cultural currency to read the codes of both within black gay culture.

Other phrases are also associated with those who refer to themselves as "mother." One of the more common, "clutch the pearls," has a slightly different connotation, depending on the context in which it is spoken. "Clutch the pearls" is often used in combination with the gesture of "clutching" or grabbing at an imaginary pearl necklace. As two informants described some of its uses:

> Gil: If we were walking down the street and we saw a beautiful man, one of us might say, "Oh, Child, clutch the pearls." In that context it would mean you've seen a breathtaking man.
> EPJ: So, what does that action connote? What does that mean?
> Gil: For me, it connotes an older woman who goes to church, wears her pearls and who would never say anything salacious or wanton, but for whom the action, in this particular case, indicates a certain realization or recognition of someone who is really very beautiful and very desirable.
> EPJ: So is it a gesture of shock, surprise . . . ?
> Gil: I guess I would call it in that case a gesture of desire.

> EPJ: What about the "clutch the pearls"? What does it mean?
> CB: That someone was surprised, someone was taken aback.
> EPJ: Where does that come from?
> CB: Probably looking at older women, thinking about situations in which older women have been surprised by some sort of news and have literally clutched their pearls or put their hands to their chests and been aghast at something or another.
> EPJ: Older women of any race?
> CB: Well, I guess I think less about race and more about class at that point because it seems like a very middle-class action. So rather than slapping you, [laughter] they clutch their pearls [grabs his chest and gasps as if surprised], "Oh my" and kind of take a step back.

In both instances, "clutch the pearls" indicates some sense of surprise or shock, and, as Gil suggests, the origin of that shock or surprise may be indicative of desire. Nuances of the phrase in both contexts have reference to "mother" and to black gay discourse as an agent of sexual citizenship and the transgression of the heteronormative domestic paradigm.

In the earlier discussion of "mother" the term was associated with stereotypical notions of motherhood that stem from universal as well as black cultural tropes: nurturer, care-giver, confidant, self-efficient worker, disciplinarian, and no-nonsense parent. In relation to the phrase "clutch the pearls," however, yet another persona seems to emerge: mother as a prim and proper lady. Gil's and CB's examples each suggest that this type of mother persona is a hybrid of a black "church" mother and conservative-minded, upper- and middle-class woman. The black church mother persona is a black woman whose propriety does not necessarily stem from socioeconomic standing but more from Christian values.[14] Thus, she refrains from saying anything "salacious or wanton" because doing so would be sinful. Instead, she signals surprise and dismay (or controls the desire to slap someone) by placing her hand over her chest as if "clutching" her pearls.

The metaphor of pearls as opposed to other jewels such as diamonds is based on the cultural value placed on pearls. Diamonds are associated with the rich but not necessarily with those who are "cultured." Pearls, however, are often described in terms of the way they are cultured. Oysters during the process of enclosing irritating objects "cultivate" pearls. Thus, a pearl, like a "lady," is created, made from something less than what it is now. That is why pearls, particularly in southern culture, are given to young women upon their sixteenth or eighteenth birthday to mark coming out or coming into womanhood. Pearls are understated, whereas diamonds are flashy; pearls are associated with the dignified and chaste, whereas diamonds are associated with women who are garish and "knowing." A string of pearls, then, is an apropos metaphor because of its association with a certain attitude about sexual mores and also because of its association with a particular class standing. Dee, a native of New York City, suggested that the word *pearls* is used in the phrase because pearls are "pure" and refer to "high society":

> I think it's a take on the very cultured, sort of Mrs. Howell from *Gilligan's Island,* the very cultured, aristocratic social white, or definitely, lady. . . . I think pearls are a pure gem, a pure stone that somehow is different from diamonds. . . . If you could find a really rare pearl, I think it's worth more in some way, so I think maybe it has to do with social class and maybe women who are on a higher social class would have more pearls than they would diamonds. So, I think maybe it's referencing a high society lady.

Complimenting Dee's suggestion that pearls are "a pure stone" is Gil's mention of yet another phrase that black gay men use: "casting one's pearls before swine." "Casting your pearls before swine means succumbing to the advances of an unworthy suitor. So, for example, you're giving it up to someone who really shouldn't be getting it [sex] in the first place." In the same way a pearl-wearing "lady" might allow an undeserving man to have his way with her, a black gay "mother" might "cast her pearls before swine" by sleeping with someone she feels undeserving. The association of "pearls" with "lady" is integral to how the phrase "clutch the pearls" emblematizes a critique of heteronormative constructions of sexuality.

Gil makes it clear that in the context of his example the expression connotes a gesture of desire. Given that conventions of "proper" feminine gender performance police or seal off a typical "lady's" desire, the black gay male appropriation of a lady persona ("clutch the pearls") to indicate "salacious" or "wanton" desire highlights the fiction of someone who is sexually pure or chaste. For a "real" lady, Gil says, the gesture could be a sign she is "ultimately human and however much she tries to distance herself from the desires of the flesh and the temptations of the flesh, she's still human and she succumbs to those things like any human would." Following Gil's logic, a black gay man's appropriation of the clutching gesture and use of the phrase call attention to the fact that a lady cannot always mask her sexual desire. The gesture reveals vulnerability to the flesh and human sexual desire.

The phrase and gesture as performed by black gay men serves double duty. In one sense it undermines the cultural logic of the heteronormative constructions of femininity. The notion of the virtuous woman is a construct meant to maintain patriarchy and the constant surveillance and objectification of women's bodies. To the extent that Christianity encourages disavowing the temptations of the flesh and bourgeoisie heterosexuality encourages female chastity, it makes sense that black gay men choose to parody the church lady and the "high society" lady.

The parody is reflected in a double entendre; "clutching pearls" also signifies the sexualized act of grabbing someone's "jewels" (testicles). In that light, the phrase is an ironic comment on the repression of female sexual desire and an expression of black gay male desire, a use undergirded by black gay male misogyny, as Gil noted. At the same time, however, it is also a comment on bourgeois heterosexuality as related to citizenship. If, as Phil Hubbard (2001, 53) argues, citizenship refers to "the political and social recognition that is granted to those whose behaviour accords with the moral values underpinning the construction of the nation-state," then homosexual sex necessarily falls outside the conditions of nationhood.

Anathema to the procreative, monogamous family unit, black gay men are deemed noncitizens. Although a "lady" is a sexist construct that maintains gender inequality, a heterosexual woman who performs as a lady nonetheless enjoys the "privileges" of citizenship in ways black gay men do not.[15] Their vernacular performance of "clutch the pearls" is a polymorphous signifier that simultaneously calls attention to black gay male misogyny, admiration of women, the myth of the chaste "lady," the hegemony of heteronormative sexuality, and the free play of gender roles in American society.

What about the Children?

Children are one of the most predominant signifiers of heterosexuality. They not only signal heterosexual sex but also procreation and continuation of the "name of the father." Indeed, the centrality of the nuclear family as the normal or natural site of sexual citizenship "relies on the perpetuation of the idea that mothering and fathering are the only appropriate modes of sexual activity, with procreation represented as the ultimate (and emotionally fulfilling) product of the sexual relation" (Hubbard 2001, 57). Drag/vogue house mothers Pepper LeBeija, Willie Ninja, and Angie Xtravaganza, featured in *Paris Is Burning,* know not of this conception of children. Their offspring are neither the product of heterosexual sex nor biologically related to them, yet in another transgressive move they take on the "name of the mother." Hemphill notes:

> The houses function as surrogate families for Black and Puerto Rican gay youth who may be homeless, orphaned, or rejected by their families because of their gayness. When joining a house, it is customary for members to adopt the name of the house for their surname to signify that they "belong" to a family.
>
> "Mothers" are usually those who have made legendary names for themselves on the ball circuit. A mother's duties can be numerous, but the primary function is to manage and nurture the illusions of the children, because they are all-important. A mother must ready the children for competition. They have to be fierce enough to snatch trophies and bring prestige and honor to the house. (1992, 133)

In the context of a drag/vogue house, "children" are not the progeny of heterosexual procreation but rather emblems of its rejection. As outcasts from their biological families, they become children of houses that celebrate them and are "produced" by cross-gendered "mothers."

In a broader context, "children" is a common term in black gay communities and, according to the black gay men I interviewed, specific to black gay culture. Moreover, to my knowledge it is not part of white gay vernacular. In each of the following instances, the interviewee notes that "children" is a "black gay" term:

> CB: I love the term *children*. People also substitute "kids" for children. "Oh, well the kids need to. . . ." It's the same thing as using "family." It's probably the same kind of origin, but I think that "children" is even more specific be-cause . . . to me [it] seems to imply people of African descent—"the chil-dren"—because that's the context in which I've heard it. I haven't heard white people say "children."
> EPJ: Well, what does it mean?
> CB: It's talking about gay and lesbian people.
> EPJ: Yeah, but when you say that it has to do more with people of African de-scent what do you mean?
> CB: I think that it's used by black gay and lesbian people to refer to black gay and lesbian people.

> EPJ: What about "children"?
> Brett: Yeah, the children of mother. I mean that goes with the name. There's mother and there's children, its just the children: the gay children, the chil-dren. Mother has her children. It could also be the children of God, too. I mean it *could* be. It could be related to that as well.

> Gil: I think on the one hand, it's a very . . . I don't know any white folks that use the term *children*—none. Well, that's not true. I know a couple of white folks who desire to be black and will use the term *children* or at least when I use it understand it. "Children," I think is a very black phrase and it can re-fer to a bunch of different things. I think most commonly that I use "chil-dren" to talk about two categories. There's a category of just younger gay people . . . it's not just younger gay people generally, it's younger gay people who at least in my estimate are in a space where they're really still forming their sexuality. I think it implies in many cases less political awareness, less experience, less worldliness than one might expect them to have, say five, ten years down the road. I also use "children" to talk about just groups of gay people, and mostly black gay people. And they'll say, "Oh, look at the chil-dren who are out tonight." And particularly if you see like a group of black folks walking you'll go, "Oh here come the children." I'm not sure if I would use that to talk about black gay folks who are older than me. If I saw a group of five or six black gay men or women coming down the street who were well into their forties, I'm not sure I would say, "Oh here come the children." I think it becomes a very age-specific kind of thing.

Several things become clear from these various definitions of "children." The term is black gay–specific in usage, at least from the perspective of black gay men who use it. White gays who use the term are most likely to be those who travel in black gay circles and have been privy to that usage. The term also seems to be associated with black Christianity and the comparison many black people make between the plight of blacks and that of the Hebrew "children." Finally, "children" also seems to connote someone of a specific age group or under the tutelage of a "mother." In other words, those deemed "mother" would never be confused as "children."

The use of the term *children* in the black gay community again undermines a number of assumptions about the status of the familial nation state. Its deployment brings to bear a black, culturally inflected notion of what constitutes a family by extending membership to like-minded souls. It also draws on the deep and long history of the black church vernacular that often accords the plight of oppressed groups in biblical stories to black people. That oppression is often associated with the power of white supremacy, which has denied blacks the status of citizen. In its specific usage in black gay communities the term departs from generic gay English because of its black cultural reference. With regard to heteronormative constructions of the family, the term *children* rejects the normalizing trope of the child as an ontological link to heterosexuality and destabilizes the notion of procreation as the sole model of sexual activity.

There's No Place Like . . .

In his powerful essay "Brother to Brother: Words from the Heart," Joseph Beam (1986) captures well the complicated feelings that black gay men feel about "home." Alienated by their sexuality from biological families, from the white gay community because of their race, and from the white heterosexual world because of both, home is an ambivalent site for black gay men. "When I speak of home," Beam explains, "I mean not only the familial constellation from which I grew, but the entire Black community: the Black press, the Black church, Black academicians, the Black literati, and the Black left. Where is my reflection? I am most often rendered invisible, perceived as a threat to the family, or am tolerated if I am silent and conspicuous. I cannot go home as who I am and that hurts me" (233). Beam's hurt soon turns to anger. Rather than use it destructively, however, he desires to cull it in order to rebuild home as place to which he can return: "Use it [anger] to create Black gay community in which I can build my home surrounded by institutions that reflect and sustain me. Concurrent with that vision is the necessity to repave the road home, widening it, so I can return with all I have created to the home which is my birthright" (233).

One way black gay men have culled that anger into a productive rebuild-ing of home is through black gay vernacular performance. Appropriating and reclaiming presumably heterosexual tropes of nation, citizenship, and fam-ily, they have devised intricate discursive as well as material spaces to pro-claim subjectivity as family members and sexual citizens. Through discourse that draws upon the most innovative vernacular practices of black culture and the campy idioms and codes of gay English, black men have created "houses" that allow them to go home "as who they are"; refigure "mother" as a complex mix of fierce gender-bending love and protection; perform the hyperbolic "lady" who "clutches her pearls" with an iron fist in a velvet glove; and become "children" who commune on the dance floor, in the streets, or together against homophobia.

The work of black gay men in the realm of the vernacular to reclaim their subjectivity appears to be merely symbolic, but the pervasiveness of these terms in mainstream popular culture marks the beginning of queering he-gemonic heterosexuality. Indeed, as black gay use of terms and phrases leaks across racial, class, and gender borders it calls attention to a by-now general acknowledgment: Gender and sexuality are unstable categories. The trans-gression of black gay men into the heteronormalized space of domesticity is reflected in the discursive tactics they employ to claim sexual citizenship in a nation that masquerades as homogenous. For black gay men, a generic gay English is insufficient to make that intervention. Their racial and sexual al-legiance necessitates a discourse that simultaneously celebrates black and gay culture as it critiques and resists the oppression found in both.

"Citizenship" implies loyalty to one's own. Because people inhabit mul-tiple social locations, the labor of allegiance to one over the other becomes an impossible burden. Black gay men's appropriation of domestic tropes is a place to begin destabilizing fixed notions of identity and at the same time provide space for communion and community. Ultimately, black gay vernac-ular may answer Essex Hemphill's question "Does your mother know about me?" (1991, xvii), with "Mother knows best."

Notes

1. To "read" someone is to set them straight or to put someone in their place (Johnson 1995). Obtaining a housekeeper is the ultimate sign of middle-class status among black people, particularly in the South. "Consuela" is not the real name of M2's housekeeper but is rather a generic reference to Mexican immigrant women who become housekeep-ers to earn a living. Although not necessarily derogatory, "Consuela" reflects black resent-ment of immigrants, who are seen as "taking over" black employment opportunities, even in instances where the job is an undesirable one. Given demographic shifts, the influx of

Mexican immigrants to southeastern states, and the upward mobility of black Americans, menial labor is no longer the only available employment opportunity for blacks.

2. The term *outsiders within* is used by Patricia Hill Collins (1991) to describe the peculiar conundrum faced by black women whereby they are positioned as other by white feminists because they are black and by black men because they are women. I employ the term to suggest the alienation that black gay men experience within heterosexual black communities and white gay communities.

3. Although the informants in this study live in various parts of the United States, the majority of them live in the South and Northeast. Therefore, while many of the terms and phrases discussed herein are found in various black gay communities, their usage and function may differ according to region. Finally, because of the limitations of this study, I do not examine the vernacular traditions of black lesbians. I might add, however, that there is both overlap and major divergence in the ways in which black gay men and women deploy language, mostly due to gendered ways of speaking.

4. In the black gay community rumors about Luther Vandross's homosexuality have circulated for years. Indeed, the rumors are so embedded in black gay culture that references to his gayness have been incorporated into plays and cited in scholarly essays. Although Vandross has never publicly outed himself, he has often spoken of his significant other in the third person (e.g., "When I find *that* special someone *they* will have to . . ."). On his CD entitled *Songs,* in which he remade love ballads, he does not change the gender of the song's subject in the remake of Roberta Flack's hit, "Killing Me Softly"(e.g., "*He* was strumming my pain"), which led many to speculate that Vandross is indeed singing to another man. For a queer reading of Luther Vandross as cultural icon, especially his remake of "A House Is Not a Home" see King (2000).

5. Mintz and Kellogg (1988) have observed that by the mid-1980s fewer than 15 percent of American households reflected the traditional family. More women were working and postponing marriage for careers, divorce rates were up, birthrates were down, and single-parent homes were becoming a "normal" concept (202–4). It is no wonder then that a feminist backlash occurred, brought on, Faludi (1991) theorizes, by the Reagan presidency.

6. For a detailed analysis of the function of "house" and "home" in *Paris Is Burning* as those terms relate to heterosexual exclusions of gays, see Reddy (1997).

7. In the film, the term *legendary* refers to someone who has won a number of drag/ vogue ball contests.

8. In psychoanalytic terms, the Law of the Father refers to the symbolic law that governs kinship systems in which one is forbidden sexual access to those a father has named as family. The concept has less to do with biology and more to do with a discursive system that maintains patriarchal control, including social laws (Grosz 1990, 67–74).

9. For a critique of the Moynihan Report as well as a well-theorized history of the role of black women in the black family, see Spillers (1997).

10. I do not wish to paint the black community as necessarily more homophobic than white communities. My discussion is offered to explain the complexity of the origin and varying degrees of black heterosexual homophobia. Insofar as black heterosexual men's homophobia is merely a reflection of that found in the white heterosexual supremacist society, black gay men's disavowal of stereotypical masculine tropes and performances

reflects a general disdain of hegemonic masculinity. Given the oppression enacted in the "Name of the Father," it is unsurprising that the black gay men would be hesitant to emulate the father figure in black gay culture.

11. Just as black gay men embrace tropes of black femininity, black lesbians embrace tropes of black masculinity. As Judith Halberstam (1998, 257) notes, for example, "Whereas a white drag king might parody a macho guy from Brooklyn . . . a black drag king tends to lip-synch to a rap song or perform as a macdaddy or playboy or pimp character . . . not to parody, but to appropriate black masculine style for dyke performance." The disavowal of masculine tropes by black gay men and feminine tropes by black lesbians suggests not only the performativity of gender but also that men and women are, as Eve Sedgwick maintains, simultaneously consumers, producers, and performers of masculinity and femininity (Halberstam 1998, 231–66; Sedgwick 1995).

12. Eddie Murphy's stand-up routine in *Delirious* is an example of this depiction of black mothers.

13. The uses of "mother" may vary from region to region. In a scene in Marlon Riggs's documentary *Tongues Untied* (1989), for example, as two black gay men walk down a street, one relates to the camera the way "houses" function on the vogue ball scene. The other, who apparently lives in Washington, D.C., reveals that he has never heard of such practices. To that the other responds, "Well, that's what they do here in New York. Each state, each gay community does different things. Like your community in D.C. speak 'aga.'"

14. This is not to suggest that an actual black female churchgoer does not have middle-class status or that such status would not contribute to her conservatism. I am suggesting instead that the trope of such a persona registers as someone whose religious convictions and not her class status positions her as pious.

15. I realize that I am treading on thin ice here. I neither want to diminish the prevalence of black gay male misogyny nor the fact of black female oppression. My purpose is to discuss the complexities of how identity formations and subject positions may allow more than one social location to be inhabited. White women, for example, are the objects of gender oppression, but at the same time they enact racial oppression.

Works Cited

Beam, Joseph. 1986. "Brother to Brother: Words from the Heart." In *In the Life: A Black Gay Anthology,* 230–42. Boston: Alyson Press.

Bersani, Leo. 1998. "Is the Rectum a Grave?" In *AIDS: Cultural Analysis, Cultural Criticism,* ed. Douglas Crimp, 197–222. Cambridge: MIT Press.

Brett. 1999. Tape-recorded interview by author, Oct. 7.

Carby, Hazel. 1998. *Race Men.* Cambridge: Harvard University Press.

CB. 1999. Tape-recorded interview by author, San Francisco, Nov. 28.

Childress, Alice. 1986. *Like One of the Family: Conversations from a Domestic's Life.* Boston: Beacon Press.

Cleaver, Eldridge. 1968. *Soul on Ice.* New York: Laurel Books.

Cohen, Cathy. 1997. "Punks, Bulldaggers, and Welfare Queens: The Radical Potential of Queer Politics?" *GLQ: A Journal of Lesbian and Gay Studies* 3(4): 437–65.

Collins, Patricia Hill. 1991. *Black Feminist Thought: Knowledge, Consciousness, and the Politics of Empowerment.* New York: Routledge.

Dee. 1999. Tape-recorded interview by author, Holyoke, Mass., April 11.

Faludi, Susan. 1991. *Backlash: The Undeclared War against American Women.* New York: Crown Publishers.

Gil. 1999. Tape-recorded interview by author, New York, April 4.

Grosz, Elizabeth. 1990. *Jacques Lacan: A Feminist Introduction.* New York: Routledge.

Halberstam, Judith. 1998. *Female Masculinity.* Durham: Duke University Press.

Hemphill, Essex. 1987. "The Father, Son and Unholy Ghosts." In *Tongues Untied: Poems,* ed. Dirg Aaab-Richards et al., 50–52. London: GMP.

———. 1991. "Introduction." In *Brother to Brother: New Writings by Black Gay Men,* ed. Essex Hemphill, xv–xxxi. Boston: Alyson Press.

———. 1992. *Ceremonies.* San Francisco: Cleis Press.

Hubbard, Phil. 2001. "Sex Zones: Intimacy, Citizenship and Public Space." *Sexualities* 4(1): 51–71.

Johnson, E. Patrick. 1995. "SNAP! Culture: A Different Kind of Reading." *Text and Performance Quarterly* 15(2): 122–42.

———. 1998. "Feeling the Spirit in the Dark: Expanding Notions of the Sacred in the African American Gay Community." *Callaloo* 21(1): 399–416.

———. 2001. "'Quare' Studies, or (Almost) Everything I Know about Queer Studies I Learned from My Grandmother." *Text and Performance Quarterly* 21(1): 1–25.

King, Jason. 2000. "Any Love: Silence, Theft, and Rumor in the Work of Luther Vandross." *Callaloo* 23(1): 422–47.

Kirby. 1999. Tape-recorded interview by author, Durham, N.C., Jan. 8.

Leap, William L. 1996. *Word's Out: Gay Men's English.* Minneapolis: University of Minnesota Press.

Mintz, Steven, and Susan Kellogg. 1988. *Domestic Revolutions: A Social History of American Family Life.* New York: Free Press.

Moynihan, Daniel Patrick. 1965. *The Negro Family: The Case for National Action.* Washington: Government Printing Office.

Muñoz, José. 1999. *Disidentifications: Queers of Color and the Performance of Politics.* Minneapolis: University of Minnesota Press.

Paris Is Burning. 1990. Directed by Jennie Livingston. Off-White Productions.

Reddy, Chandan. 1997. "Home, House and Non-Identity: *Paris Is Burning.*" In *Burning Down the House: Recycling Domesticity,* ed. Rosemary George, 365–79. New York: Westview Press.

Riggs, Marlon T. 1991. "Black Macho Revisited: Reflections of a SNAP! Queen." In *Brother to Brother: New Writings by Black Gay Men,* ed. Essex Hemphill, 253–57. Boston: Alyson Press.

Rob. 2000. Tape-recorded interview by author, Durham, N.C., June 20.

Ruth C. Ellis @ 100. 1999. Directed by Yvonne Welbon. Our Film Works Productions.

Sedgwick, Eve. 1995. "Gosh, Boy George, You Must Be Awfully Secure in Your Masculinity!" In *Constructing Masculinity,* ed. Maurice Berger, Brian Wallis, and Simon Watson, 11–20. New York: Routledge.

Smitherman, Geneva. 1994. *Black Talk: Words and Phrases from the Hood to the Amen Corner.* New York: Houghton Mifflin.

Spillers, Hortense. 1987. "Mama's Baby, Papa's Maybe: An American Grammar Book." *Diacritics* 17(2): 61–87.

Thomas, Anthony. 1990. "The House the Kids Built: The Gay Black Imprint on American Dance Music." In *Out in Culture: Gay, Lesbian, and Queer Essays on Popular Culture,* ed. Corey K. Creekmur and Alexander Doty, 437–45. Durham: Duke University Press.

Turner, Victor. 1982. *From Ritual to Theatre: The Human Seriousness of Play.* New York: PAJ Publications.

Vancouver. 2000. Tape-recorded interview by author, Chicago, Oct. 6.

White, Deborah Gray. 1985. *Ar'n't I a Woman?: Female Slaves in the Plantation South.* New York: W. W. Norton.

William. 1999. Tape-recorded interview by author, Durham, N.C., April 20.

Contributors

TOM BOELLSTORFF is an assistant professor in the Department of Anthropology at the University of California, Irvine. He has worked with gay, lesbian, and transgendered Indonesians as a ethnographer and activist since 1992, primarily in the cities of Surabaya (East Java), Makassar (South Sulawesi), and Denpasar (Bali). Much of that work has been in the domain of HIV prevention. He has also worked with the International Gay and Lesbian Human Rights Commission and sits on the board of directors for the Institute for Community Health Outreach, an HIV prevention organization based in San Francisco, where he formerly worked as regional coordinator. In addition, he is national co-chair for the Society of Lesbian and Gay Anthropologists. He has been a postdoctoral fellow in the Research School of Pacific and Asian Studies at the Australian National University and a visiting assistant professor in the Department of Cultural Anthropology at Duke University.

ROSS HIGGINS, an anthropologist and linguist by training, is co-founder and honorary president of the Archives Gaies du Quebec, and teaches a course in interdisciplinary studies in sexuality and anthropology at Concordia University. He is studying the meaning of community in Montreal gay men's histories past and present and has published extensively on that topic.

PETER A. JACKSON is a fellow in Thai history in the Research School of Pacific and Asian Studies at the Australian National University in Canberra. He works on modern Thai cultural history, in particular the history of religion and the history of gender/sex transformations. His book *Male Homosexuality in Thailand* (1989, revised 1995) was the first major study of male

homoeroticism in contemporary Thailand. He has conducted extensive research on gay and lesbian communities in Bangkok and is a co-founder of
the Australia-based AsiaPacifiQueer network of researchers documenting
queer cultures in the Asia-Pacific region. He is writing a history of Bangkok's
same-sex and transgender cultures since the nineteenth century.

E. PATRICK JOHNSON is an assistant professor of performance studies at
Northwestern University. His essays have appeared in *Text and Performance
Quarterly, Callaloo,* and *Obsidian II.* He is the author of *Appropriating Black-
ness: Performance and the Politics of Authenticity* and coeditor (with Mae G.
Henderson) of *Black Queer Studies: A Critical Anthology.*

WILLIAM L. LEAP is a professor in, and chair of, the Department of Anthropology at American University in Washington, D.C., where he teaches courses
in linguistics, gender and sexuality, public anthropology, cultural geography,
and lesbian/gay studies.

HEIDI MINNING completed her dissertation at Syracuse University on the
linguistic negotiation of family membership by same-sex couples in Berlin,
Germany. She and her German partner, Gesa, are active in trying to change
U.S. immigration policy that discriminates against same-sex partners.

LIORA MORIEL is a lecturer in the English department and a doctoral can-
didate in the Comparative Literature Program at the University of Maryland,
College Park. She was chair and spokesperson for the Agudah, Israel's umbrella lesbian, gay, bisexual, and transgender rights organization, during the
early 1990s and took it out of the closet and into the media, street, and living
room, ushering in an era of unprecedented legal and social change in Israel.
During the 1980s, while a reporter for the *Jerusalem Post* and Israel Radio,
Moriel produced the first International Women's Music Festival. Her academic publications include a chapter in the Cambridge film handbooks on
Bonnie and Clyde (a queer reading of the film) and articles on the Israeli
transgender dance star Dana International for *World Englishes* (U.K.), *Lähiku-
va* (Finland), and *Race Gender and Class* (U.S.).

DAVID A. B. MURRAY is an assistant professor of anthropology at York University in Canada. His research focuses on sexuality, identity, and performance in the Caribbean. He is the author of *Opacity: Gender, Sexuality, Race
and the "Problem" of Identity in Martinique.*

SUSANA PEÑA is an instructor in the Department of Ethnic Studies at Bowling Green State University in Ohio. She has been the recipient of a Social Science Research Council's Sexuality Research Dissertation Fellowship and the University of California's President's Fellowship. She continues her studies of Cuban American gay male cultures in Miami.

DENIS M. PROVENCHER is an assistant professor of French at the University of Wisconsin–La Crosse, where he teaches courses in French civilization and cultural studies. He has published on the linguistic representation of gender in Jean Genet's novel *Notre-Dame des fleurs,* Genet's continued impact on contemporary French gay popular culture, and the heteronormative narrative strategies in the NBC sitcom *Will and Grace.* His current research explores the coming-out experience of French gay men, part of a larger project examining sexual citizenship and French authenticity in contemporary French gay culture.

Index

Academy of Language, 106
acculturation, 51, 63, 64. *See also* transculturation
ACT UP Paris, 24, 29
Adam, Barry, 7, 9, 25, 41, 57, 134
Advocate, 24, 58
African American gay men, 4, 18, 125, 251–76; language of, 18, 251–76
African National Congress (ANC), 141
Afrikaans (language), 135, 140–43, 147–51, 157–58, 159nn7,9
Agar, Michael, 130n5. *See also* "languaculture"
AIDS. *See* HIV/AIDS
Almaguer, Tomás, 234–35
Altman, Denis, 28, 30, 35, 202, 203, 220, 226–27, 231
American Dream, 251, 254
"Americanization," 227
Amnesty International, 61
anal sex, 219
Angelotti, Philippe, 29, 42n3. *See also* *Générations Gay*
Aotearoa/New Zealand, 163, 164, 166, 169, 172, 176
Apartheid (South Africa), 134, 137, 138, 139, 142–43, 150, 156
Arabic (language), 109–10; contribution to Israeli "gay language, 118–19, 124, 128; gender marking in, 106–7, 128; spoken by Mizrahi Jews, 115
Arboleda, Manual, 168

Arnal, Frank, 23, 25
Aronson, Jacob, 110
articulations of language, 11, 12, 15
Asad, Talal, 1
Austin, John, 69n4
authenticity: dilemma of, 7; indigenous vs. sexual, 153–57, 170, 176; language, identity and, 23–24, 165, 189; national vs. sexual, 17, 23–24, 181–83, 193–98; western vs. indigenous, 198n1
Avni, Sarah, 108, 123

bahasa gay (Indonesia), 16–17, 141, 181–98
Bakhtin, M. M., 76–78, 96
Beam, Joseph, 257
Baum, Dalit, 119
Beam, Joseph, 274. *See also* "Brother to Brother"
Beck, Volker, 64
Bell, David, 127–28, 137, 159n3. *See also* sexual citizenship
belonging, 98, 182–83, 189, 193–98
Ben-Ari, Adital Tirosh, 107–8
berdache, 90, 101, 165, 167–68
Berliner Sonntags-Club, 52, 53
Bhatia, Tej, 59
Binnie, Jon, 127–28, 137, 159n3. *See also* sexual citizenship
Blackwood, Evelyn, 5
"Bodysnatched English," 128
Bourhis, Richard, 74
"Brother to Brother" (Beam), 273

Brown, Penelope, 51
Buddhism, 184, 185, 204, 207–8
butch, 5, 32, 63, 221
Butler, Judith, 69n5, 113, 222

Cameron, Deborah, 13, 112
Campbell-Kibler, Kathryn, 2, 8
Canada: Francophone gay men in, 72–100
capitalism, 5, 27, 35, 186, 223, 254
Chatterjee, Partha, 7, 196
"children" (as African American gay ver-
    nacular), 271–73
Christianity, 9, 110, 127, 186, 207, 270, 273
Christopher Street Day (CSD), 48–52, 63, 64,
    68
"Cinquemilla," 125. *See also* Dana Interna-
    tional
citizenship: conflicting theories of, 136–38;
    conflicting meanings of, 232, 251, 270, 274;
    in France, 41; in post-apartheid South
    Africa, 134, 150, 153, 156; non-citizens and,
    274; sexuality and, 16, 26, 153, 156, 270. *See
    also* sexual citizenship
Coates, Jennifer, 13, 112
code-mixing, 48, 50, 57–59, 61, 63, 66
code-switching, 16, 49, 51, 57, 59, 61, 63–65,
    74, 82
colonialism, 3–4, 14, 184, 204, 246; postcolo-
    nial society, 196
Coluche (French comedian), 38
communism, 233
"communitas," 258. *See also* Turner, Victor
"coming out" (English term): in gay Ger-
    man code-mixing, 47, 48, 60, 62, 64, 66; in
    Québécois gay French, 93; vs. *cantar "La
    Bayamesa"* (Miami Cuban gay Spanish),
    242
coming out stories, 47, 80, 94, 127
Comité d'Urgence Anti-Répression Homo-
    sexuelle (CUARH), 24
cooperative discourse, 30–32, 34–35, 39–42,
    95, 252
Corey, Donald Webster, 89
creolization, 27–30, 52, 65
Cuba, 233–34, 236, 240, 246–47
Cuban-American gay language, 17–18, 241–
    42, 246, 248
Cuban Counterpoint (Ortiz), 236

Dana International, 110, 113, 124–28, 131n8
Daveluy, Michelle, 74

David, Hal, 244. *See also* "A House Is Not a
    Home"
Decoding Advertising, 58. *See also* William-
    son, Judith
D'Emilio, John, 223
Delaney, Carol, 11
de Vos, Pierre, 140, 158, 159n4
Disease and Representation (Gilman), 38. *See
    also* Gilman, Sander
"disidentification," 258. *See also* Muñoz,
    José
domestic-partner bill, 39
Donovan, Josephine, 111
Doring, Karin, 128. *See also* "Bodysnatched
    English"
drag queens, 37, 39, 67, 119, 218, 223, 246, 257,
    266; communities, 257; drag ball/vogue,
    256, 263, 271, 276n13; drag venues, 232;
    multilingual drag shows, 84, 86, 234, 242,
    243–45
Drucker, Peter, 202
Duhamel, Georges, 39
Duyvendak, Jan Willem, 7, 9, 25, 27, 40, 41,
    43n14, 57, 134
Dynes, Wayne, 89

Eckert, Penelope, 8, 9, 47, 63
English (language): as marker of a global
    (gay) space, 117; as "unambiguously queer
    language," 50, 52, 54, 202–3; as "vague
    English creole," 27–30, 41; gender-neutral
    appeal (Israel), 107, 113–14, 123; in *bahasa
    gay* (Indonesia), 190–91; in lavender Ger-
    man code-mixing, 56, 59–65, 78–80; in
    Lesotho sexual discourse, 140; in Montre-
    al gay French code-switching, 73, 78–80,
    82–83, 92–93, 96; in a South African gay
    newspaper code-switching, 148–53; inter-
    national circulation of, 4, 15–17, 28, 35,
    46–48, 52, 85–87, 119, 128, 135, 163, 205;
    resistance to in Māori sexual discourse,
    163–65, 170, 174–75; transculturation
    through, 237–41; U.S. citizenship and,
    231–34, 251, 274. *See also* gay English
English in Foreign Eyes (Narkiss), 130n2
English Only initiative, 233
Erlich, David, 108
Errington, Joseph J., 196, 197, 198
Esperanto, 128
Even-Zohar, Itamar, 107
Exit (South African gay newspaper), 147–53

family (African American gay vernacular), 258–63

fierce (as word), 240, 265

Figs, My Love (Peleg), 123

Fillieule, Olivier, 25, 27, 40, 43n14, 57

Foucault, Michel, 10, 25, 29, 76, 194–95, 203, 222, 227. *See also History of Sexuality*

France, 3, 14, 23–24, 75; lesbian/gay activism in, 24, 90

French (language), 15, 27, 29, 35–41, 90, 92–94; in Israeli gay Hebrew, 115, 126; tu/vous distinction in, 191; vs. English in Montreal, 72–74, 78–80, 84

Front de Liberation Homosexuel (FLH), 73, 87

Front Homosexuel d'Action Révolutionnaire (FHAR), 24, 40

gai, 17, 29

Gai Pied, 24, 29

Garneau, Brigitte, 90, 91

Gaudio, Rudolph, 50, 141

gay culture(s): as mainstream U.S. construction, 236, 240, 246, 247; as western construction, 23, 27, 32, 35. *See also* sexual cultures

"Gay Destinations," 27. *See also* vacations (gay)

gay English: academic debates over, 3, 4, 7–8; as sexual language, 13–15; global circulation of, 2, 3, 5, 25, 46, 109, 114, 125–27, 164, 182, 203, 231, 234; in African American settings, 3, 18, 252–53, 267, 273–74; in Aotearoa/New Zealand, 173–76; in Cuban-American Miami, 3, 235, 239–41, 246–47; in France, 4, 15, 25–27, 32, 42; in Francophone Canada, 3, 15, 73, 88, 90, 99; in Germany, 15, 47, 57–60; in Indonesia, 182, 185, 187; in Israel, 15–16, 107, 109–18, 120–21, 123–24, 126–29; in South Africa, 4, 141, 143–47, 156–58; in Thailand, 17, 204, 217, 219, 221–23. *See also* cooperative discourse; globalization; sexual language

gay French, 4, 7, 15, 27, 29, 35; cooperative discourse in, 36–40; in France, 23–24; in Montreal, 72–74, 78–80, 82–83, 85–55, 90, 92–94, 191

gay identity: American associations of, 23, 29, 34, 237; circularity in analysis of, 7–9; 114; diverse meanings worldwide, 4–5, 17, 34, 55, 66, 118, 164, 202–4, 211–15, 247; outside imposition of, 164, 185–86, 208–10, 220–21, 237–40, 251. *See also* homosexuality; same-sex identity

gay language(s): acquisition of, 186–89, 191, 227; as expression of sexuality and desire, 13–14; intonation in, 88–89, 189, 221; slang in, 86, 89, 119, 181, 240, 245; unique features and practices, 8–10, 30, 75–76, 79–80, 87–88, 95–98, 100,182, 190, 240–45, 247. *See also* Cuban American gay language; gay English; gay French; lavender languages

gay/lesbian bars and clubs: as sites of transnational lesbian/gay culture, 28, 34, 40, 143, 145–47, 157; racial/ethnic contact in, 139, 153–55, 234, 255–56

"Gay Liberation Front." See Front de Liberation Homosexuel (FLH)

"gay world," 186

Gaza and West Bank, 106, 127; and gay soldiers, 109

gender/sex system, 205–28

gender blending, 225

Générations Gay, 29

Genesee, Fred, 74

Genet, Jean, 39, 73. *See also Notre-Dame des fleurs*

German (language): and "vague English creole," 27; gay language in, 15, 46–47, 50, 54, 56, 59–60; speech levels in, 191

Germany, 11, 14–15, 46, 48, 52, 55, 64; "gay language" in, 24

Gevisser, Mark, 138, 159n4

Gibson-Graham, J. K., 6

Gilman, Sander, 38. *See also* disease and representation

globalization, 5–7, 11, 14, 185, 231, 235

"global queering," 203, 227

Gluzman, Michael, 116

Grahn, Judy, 182

Gramsci, Antonio, 76, 195

Greenland, Hauraki, 172

Green Party, 64

Hagel, Markus, 46, 55

Halberstam, Judith, 5, 276n11

Hall, Kira, 69n4, 109, 175

Hall, Stewart, 11–12

Halperin, David, 225

Harvey, David, 2

Hebrew (language), 115–16, 119–21, 123–39, 273

hegemony, 73, 78, 192, 195, 198, 209, 271

Heller, Monica, 74–75, 164

Hemphill, Essex, 257, 261, 274

Herdt, Gilbert, 1, 3, 10, 12

heteronormativity, discourses of, 5, 17, 18, 94, 114, 265, 270, 271

heterosexual identity, 32–34

Higgins, Ross, 3, 13, 15, 78, 84, 91, 96, 100nn3,4

Hinduism, 186, 205

Hirschfeld, Magnus, 64, 69n5

Histoire de France (Lavisse), 26. *See also* Lavise, Ernest

History of Sexuality (Foucault), 203

HIV/AIDS: as feature of transnational gay culture, 82; focus for gay/lesbian political mobilization, 6, 24, 76, 141, 169, 185; formation of gay language and, 171–72; language and education about, 28–30, 37, 40, 56, 109, 169

Homolexis, 89. *See also* Dynes, Wayne

homosexual identity: and citizenship, 135, 141–42, 254, 256; indigenous terminology and, 116, 168–70, 174, 225; vs. gay identity, 46, 55, 63, 163, 174, 221. *See also* gay identity; same-sex identities

Homosexual Law Reform Bill (New Zealand), 171

"house" (as African American gay vernacular), 255, 256–57, 275n6

"A House Is Not a Home" (David), 255

Hubbard, Phil, 270, 271

human rights, 61, 194

identity labels, 90–92

Ihimaera, Witam, 163, 177

immigration: homosexuality and, 83, 84–85, 108, 254

Indonesia, 3, 13, 15–17, 181–98

Indonesian (language), 181, 184, 187–88, 190, 193, 196–97

International Lesbian and Gay Association (ILGA), 61, 63, 226

Islam, 127, 183, 186, 198n8. *See also* Muslim

Israel, 3, 15, 105–10, 112–13, 115–19, 121, 124, 127–30; "gay" languages in, 15, 16, 105–33

Isreali Arabs, 105, 106, 107, 117, 127

Ivreet (Wallach), 123–24

Jackson, Peter, 5, 10, 15, 134, 183, 194, 205, 212, 217

Japan, 23, 184, 204

Javanese (language), 186, 188, 191, 197

Je bande donc je suis (Remes), 39. *See also* Remes, Erik

Johnson, E. Patrick, 10, 13, 15, 18, 254, 262

Kadish, Ruti, 108–9

Kama, Amit, 107, 129

kathoey, 5, 203, 206, 209–12, 215, 222, 224–26, 253

Keane, Webb, 197

Kendall, 139–40

Kristeva, Julia, 13

Krouwel, Andre, 7, 9, 25, 41, 57, 134

Kuhn, Raymond, 24

Kulick, Don, 2, 7–10, 20, 114–15, 175, 198

Labov, William, 111

Lacan, Jacques, 13

"languaculture," 130n5

Lapointe, Ghislain, 90

lavender language, 47, 48, 52, 53, 56–68, 189; dark purple lexicon, 253. *See also* gay language(s)

Lavendar Languages Conference, 3–4, 42

Lavise, Ernest, 26. *See also Histoire de France*

Lemke, Jay L., 97

Le rose et le noir (Martel), 39. *See also* Martel, Frederic

lesbian identity: erotic language of, 56; linguistic reference to, 17, 50, 66, 116, 188, 219–21, 224; local resistance to referent, 168, 203, 213–15, 217

Lestrade, Didier, 24, 29, 42n5

Levinson, Stephen, 51

Leznoff, Maurice, 89, 94

life story narratives, 141–42, 153–57n14

Livia, Anna, 69n4, 109, 175

Livingston, Jennie, 257. *See also Paris Is Burning*

Living with Pride: Ruth C. Ellis @ 100 (film), 256–57

Loubet, Pascal, 24, 43n11

Lucy, John, 112

Luz, Dvora, 108, 123

Madonna, 34, 36

Mainmise (magazine), 72

Manalansan, Martin, 1, 137, 199nn10,12

Mandela, Nelson, 138

Māori (language), 16, 26, 164–65, 170–71, 173–75

Māori Language Act, 173
Marcus, Sharon, 6
Mariel boatlift, 233, 238, 248n3
Martel, Frederic, 26, 39, 237. *See also Le rose et le noir*
Martin, Biddy, 94
Marxist Theory, 11
mass media: promotion of local gay culture through, 192–93, 216, 243
Maurer, Bill, 136, 198
McConnell-Ginet, Sally, 47, 63
McDonaldization, 26, 35, 128
media: gay-specific print, cooperative discourse in, 36–40; language choices in, 25, 29, 47–153, 158; promotion of local gay culture through, 27, 171, 158, 240–41; promotion of transnational gay culture through, 23, 28, 32, 57, 72, 185, 247. *See also Exit; Têtu*
Mermelstein, Zvi, 110, 119–21, 123
Miller, Daniel, 18
Minella, Alain-Gilles, 29, 42n5. *See also Générations Gay*
Minning, Heidi, 15, 69n2
Mom, I've Got Something to Tell You (Luz and Avni), 123
Moonwomon, Birch, 5
Moriel, Liora, 3, 10, 15, 16, 130n3, 134
Morris, Benny, 108
Morris, Rosalind, 203, 211
Mouffe, Chantal, 136
"mother" (as African American gay vernacular), 263–71
MTV, 124, 126, 128
Muñoz, José, 258
Murray, David A. B., 16, 134, 137
Murray, Stephen O., 168, 178n6, 248n8
Muslim, 110, 183. *See also* Islam
Myers-Scotten, Carol, 158
Myer, Ulf, 60

Nader, Gil, 116
Narkiss, Doron, 130n2. *See also* "English in Foreign Eyes"
nationalism, 17, 130, 170, 186, 193–98, 253
New Zealand, 3, 15, 16, 163, 165, 169, 171, 173, 175–76
New Zealand AIDS Foundation (NZAF), 165, 172
Nigeria, 141
Notre-Dame des fleurs (Genet), 39, 43n13. *See also* Genet, Jean

"October Crisis," 72, 81
Oetomo, Dédé, 187–88, 198, 199n15
Ong, Aihwa, 2, 137, 158
Orthodox Jews, 105, 108; and nude beaches, 138
Ortiz, Fernando, 236. *See also Cuban Counterpoint*
"outing," 29, 36–37, 62; and language, 113. *See also* coming out
Ozouf, Mona, 26

PaCS bill (in France), 40, 41
pájaration, 237, 239, 244, 246
Palestine, 106–7, 117, 127
Paris Is Burning (film), 253, 257–58, 263, 271, 275n6
Parker, Richard, 5, 235, 248n5
Patton, Cindy, 136, 202, 224
Peleg, Dana, 123. *See also Figs, My Love*
Peña, Susana, 17–18
phet, 203–6, 213, 215–17, 218, 220, 222, 224–25
Pink Times, 108, 116, 118–19
Podesva, Robert, 2
Pride Company, 58
Provencher, Denis, 3, 7, 10, 13, 43n13, 134

The Queens' Vernacular, 89. *See also* Rogers, Bruce
queer, 46, 47, 55, 65, 66, 111, 118, 169, 203, 221, 223, 227, 254
queer studies, 118
queer theory, 204, 227

Registered Life Partners Law (Eingetragene Lebenspartner Gesetz), 65
Reinfelder, Monka, 214
Remes, Erik, 39. *See also Je bande donc je suis*
Rich, Adrienne, 107, 128
Riggs, Marlon, 251, 276n13
Ritchie, William, 59
Roberts, Sarah J., 2, 8
Roca, I. M., 111–12
Rodgers, Bruce, 89
Roscoe, Will, 167–68, 174, 176
Ruben, Gayle, 205. *See also* "sex/gender system"

same-sex identity: in Aeotearoa/Māori, 16, 164; in post-apartheid South Africa, 134–35, 138–39, 140–42, 145, 151, 157, 158; in Thailand, 202, 203, 226
Sánchez-Eppeler, Benigno, 202, 224

schema theory, 77. *See also* Swales, John
Schock, Axel, 60
"sex/gender system," 205, 234, 236, 237–40.
    See also Rubin, Gayle
"sexual aim," 235
sexual citizenship: defined, 13, 227; dilem-
    mas surrounding, 26, 127–28, 134–35, 150,
    253, 270; language of, 16, 137, 140–41, 146,
    150, 156–58, 267
sexual cultures, 12–14
sexual language, 12–14, 234–35
Sheinfeld, Llan, 122–23
Shez (poet), 110, 119, 120, 121–22, 123
shreiks and over-enunciation, 88–89, 221
Shufra (Israeli publishing company), 122–23
Siegessäule (magazine), 48, 56
Silverstein, Michael, 188–89, 198
Singapore, 134, 218
Skinner, Jody, 60
Society for the Protection of Personal
    Rights (SPPR), 115
Solomon, Harris, 109, 119
SOS-Racisme (France), 40
South Africa, 3, 13, 23; (homo)sexual citizen-
    ship in, 134–35, 138–41, 147–48, 153, 157–58,
    158; post-apartheid constitution, 158n1;
    sexuality and language choice-making in,
    16, 143–47, 147–53; township sexuality in,
    4, 153–57
Spanish (language), 27, 231–32, 233–34, 237–
    39, 243–45, 248
"Spanglish," 231, 248n1
speech (discourse) communities, 2, 8, 76–78,
    97
speech genres, 76–78, 88, 95; as storytelling,
    95–96
Stanton, Elizabeth Cady, 122. *See also The
    Woman's Bible*
Stonewall, 2, 18, 25, 68, 158, 204
"structure(s) of feeling," 231
Summer Gay Games, 37
Swales, John, 77, 96

Talbot, Mary, 32, 42n9
Tannen, Deborah, 13, 112
takatāpui, 164–66, 169–77
Têtu (magazine), 24, 25, 27–34, 36–39, 42n4,
    43n11
Thailand, 3, 15; compared to Indonesia, 183–
    84; diversity in sexual identities 17, 194,
    202–6, 211–15, 224–26; "gay" vs. "trans-
gender" in, 220–21; "lesbian" vs. "tom-
    dee," 213–15, 220
Thai (language), 205, 208, 209, 212–13, 215,
    219
Thibault, Pierrette, 75
"third gender," 166
Thomas, Anthony, 255–56, 259
"tom-dee," 5, 203, 214–17, 220–21, 224, 226,
    227
transculturation, 17, 231, 236, 236–37, 247
transvestites, 186
Turner, Victor, 25, 75, 83, 85, 257
Tzur, Eran, 120

United States, 61, 115, 118; as source of glo-
    balizing media depictions of gay culture,
    38–39; French media depictions of gay
    culture in, 38–39; gay culture and, 2, 23, 27
    25, 40, 204, 231; media depictions of gay
    culture in, 38–39; sexual and cultural
    diversity in, 9, 17–18, 58, 231, 236, 240,
    246–47. *See also* globalization
urbanization, 223

vacations (gay), 32–34, 37–39. *See also* gay
    destinations
Vandross, Luther, 254, 275

Wallach, Yona, 110, 119–20, 123–24. *See also*
    "Ivreet"
Walzer, Lee, 13
Welbon, Yvonne, 255. *See also Living with
    Pride*
Weston, Kath, 166
White, Deborah Gray, 261
Whorf, Benjamin Lee, 188–89
Williams, Raymond, 231. *See also*
    "structure(s) of feeling"
Williamson, Judith, 58. *See also Decoding
    Advertising*
Wittgenstein, Ludwig, 197
The Woman's Bible (Stanton), 122
Wong, Andrew, 2, 8
Woodsum, Jo Ann, 167

Xhosa (language), 153–58

Yanagisako, Silvia, 11

Zionism, 105, 108, 120
Zulu (language), 142–52, 159nn8,12

The University of Illinois Press
is a founding member of the
Association of American University Presses.

———————————————————————

Composed in 10.5/13 Minion
by Jim Proefrock
at the University of Illinois Press
Manufactured by Thomson-Shore, Inc.

University of Illinois Press
1325 South Oak Street
Champaign, IL 61820-6903
www.press.uillinois.edu